Gender, Cult̶u̶r̶e̶ 0122450 al Change

An engaging c̶o̶ b̶ ̶rned on or before ̶ ̶ ̶ ̶ gender and organizations, ̶ ̶ ̶ ̶ ̶ ̶ *Organi* te below. ̶ ̶ ̶ ̶ *Change* ̶ ̶ ̶ ̶ based inequality ̶ ̶ ̶ ̶ ns. It consid̶ ̶ ̶ ̶ ̶ between wo̶r̶ ̶ ̶ ̶ ̶ ̶ed on sexuality, pow̶er̶ and control shape the cultures, structures ̶ ̶ ̶ ̶ ̶ ̶ organizations and the experiences of men and women working in them. The book is unusual in that it focuses on culture and change and the reciprocal relationship between theory and practice that brings about such change.

Gender, Culture and Organizational Change represents a decade of experience of managing change in public sector organizations during a period of major social, political and economic transition and analyses the progress that has been made. It expands to make wider connections with women and trade unions in Europe and management development for women in the 'developing' countries of Africa and Asia. It will be valuable reading for students and academics in social policy, gender studies, sociology and organizational studies, and to professionals and managers with an interest in bringing about change in the workplace.

The contributors, who are managers, management trainers and consultants, equal opportunities officers and academics, are well known for their innovative theoretical and practical approach to gender and organizations.

Catherine Itzin is an Inspector in the Social Services Inspectorate at the Department of Health writing in a personal capacity as Honorary Research Fellow in the Department of Applied Social Studies at the University of Bradford. **Janet Newman** is a Lecturer in Public Policy and Strategy at the Institute of Local Government Studies (INLOGOV) at the University of Birmingham.

Gender, Culture and Organizational Change

Putting theory into practice

Edited by Catherine Itzin
and Janet Newman

London and New York

First published 1995
by Routledge
11 New Fetter Lane, London EC4P 4EE

Simultaneously published in the USA and Canada
by Routledge
29 West 35th Street, New York, NY 10001

Typeset in Times by Michael Mepham, Frome, Somerset

Printed and bound in Great Britain by
Mackays of Chatham PLC, Chatham, Kent.

British Library Cataloguing in Publication Data
A catalogue record for this book is available from the British
Library

Library of Congress Cataloguing in Publication Data
A catalogue for this book has been requested

ISBN 0–415–11186–2 (hbk)
ISBN 0–415–11187–0 (pbk)

Contents

Illustrations

Editors and contributors

EDITORS

Catherine Itzin is an Inspector in the Social Services Inspectorate at the Department of Health. Previously she worked as a senior manager in local government with responsibility for human resources, organizational development and women's employment. She is writing here in a personal capacity as Honorary Research Fellow in the Violence Abuse and Gender Relations Research Unit in the Department of Applied Social Studies at the University of Bradford. She has a PhD in Sociology, a Diploma in Public Sector Management and an IPM Certificate in Personnel Practice. She is the author and editor of, and contributor to, many books on issues of gender.

Janet Newman works at the Institute for Local Government Studies (INLOGOV), part of the School of Public Policy at the University of Birmingham, engaged in teaching, research and consultancy on change in the public sector. Previously she worked for the Women and Work Programme at the University of Aston. She has written extensively on the managerialization of the public sector, and on gender, management and change. She has a PhD in cultural studies.

CONTRIBUTORS

Cynthia Cockburn is a Research Professor based at the Centre for Research in Gender, Ethnicity and Social Change at the City University, London.

Kate French is a consultant in organizational development and researcher in gender relations in the workplace. She was previously Senior Research Fellow at the City University.

Elizabeth Harlow is a Lecturer in Social Work at the University of Bradford.

Jeff Hearn is Senior University Research Fellow at the University of Manchester and was previously Reader in Sociology and Critical Studies on Men at the University of Bradford.

Jackee Holder is a freelance trainer and consultant in personal and organizational development, counselling skills and mentoring programmes for organizations. She was previously Training Officer in the Women's Unit at the London Borough of Southwark.

Marion Macalpine works as a management trainer and organization consultant in the UK and in 'developing countries'. She was formerly Head of Training and Staff Development for the Inner London Education Authority, and worked as an Equal Opportunities Officer in the GLC.

Sue Maddock is a psychologist working as an equality and organizational development consultant, and teaches for the British Council and for the University of Manchester Business School.

Averil Nottage is a Deputy Chief Inspector in the Social Services Inspectorate at the Department of Health.

Di Parkin is a consultant on equality issues. She was previously Head of the Women's Unit at the London Borough of Ealing.

Wendy Parkin is Senior Lecturer in Sociology and Social Work at the University of Huddersfield.

Chris Phillipson is Professor of Applied Social Studies and Social Gerontology and Head of the Department of Applied Social Studies at the University of Keele.

Munira Thobani is Head of the Equalities Unit at the London Borough of Hounslow.

Judy White works in the Centre for Urban and Regional Studies at the University of Birmingham.

Fiona Williams is Professor of Applied Social Studies, University of Bradford.

Gwendoline Williams is Deputy Dean in the Faculty of Social Sciences and Head of the Department of Management Studies at the University of the West Indies, Trinidad and Tobago.

Acknowledgements

We would like to acknowledge the people who have helped shape this project through their work for change. In particular, Catherine Itzin would like to mention the women and men with whom she has worked and learned about managing organizational change, including contributors to this book: Janet Newman, Kate French, Marion Macalpine, Jackee Holder, Munira Thobani, Averil Nottage, Chris Phillipson and Jeff Hearn, and most recently Paul Brearley at the Department of Health.

Janet Newman would like to acknowledge the insights, perceptions and experience of all the women she has met on workshops and training programmes; and of her colleagues and friends at the Women and Work Programme and at the School of Public Policy at the University of Birmingham.

We would like to thank Janet Edwards for typing many of the manuscripts, and we would like to pay tribute to the very stimulating and creative partnership we have developed in producing this book.

Introduction

Recent years have seen a growing interest in issues of gender, and there have been a number of new titles on women in management (Davidson and Cooper 1992), on sexuality in organizations (Hearn *et al.* 1989), and on gender and organizations (Mills and Tancred 1992; Savage and Witz 1992). All have made important contributions to our understanding of organizations in relation to issues of gender. *Gender, Culture and Organizational Change* is intended as a contribution to this growing body of knowledge and interest.

Where it differs is in its focus on organizational change. The book is concerned with the dynamics of changing organizational cultures, structures and practices within the wider social context in which organizations are situated. It is concerned with both the theory and practice of change: with using practice to inform and develop theory and exploring how theories of gender, of diversity, of culture and of organizations can assist in the processes of bringing about change. This interrelationship between theory and practice is the central organizing theme of the book.

We are concerned mainly with organizations in the public sector: central and local government, health and social services. The book collects together a decade of experience of managing change and looks at what has been learned from that experience. There have been many initiatives during this period to change organizations to improve the situation of women and black and disabled staff (and sometimes lesbians and gay men). This book came into being in part because that work is being done, some progress is being made, and there is much to learn from it.

The material is firmly located in the specific historical context of Britain in the 1980s and early 1990s, and reflects the social, political and economic factors of this period. It is concerned therefore with attempts to bring about change in the social relations within organizations at a time when the whole of the public sector has undergone radical transformation as a result of external pressures. The book also makes wider international connections through chapters on women and trade unions in Europe, and on management development for women from Africa and Asia.

Gender is the central concern and focus of this book. By gender we mean the socially constructed and culturally determined characteristics associated with women and men, the assumptions made about the skills and abilities of women and men based on these characteristics, the conditions in which women and men live and work, the relations that exist between women and men, and how these are represented, communicated, transmitted and maintained. We include sexual and social relations, relations based on sexuality, and relations of power and control based on gender. The book is about how gender (so defined) pervades the cultures, structures and practices of organizations and the experience of women and men who work in them.

The book is about gender differences and how these become gender differentials, forming the basis of discrimination and inequality. Various chapters offer ways of theorizing gender, gender relations and gender-based inequality in organizations. But there is an activist as well as an academic dimension to the book. It describes programmes that have been developed to bring about change in the cultures, structures and practices of organizations to shift the balance of power and control towards greater parity between women and men.

The book is, then, about 'equal opportunities' – for women, and for other groups for whom difference (of race, ethnicity, disability, sexuality) becomes the basis of discrimination and the precondition of disadvantage (poverty, harassment, violence). The book is also concerned with equal opportunities because this has been the major organizational discourse and site in which gender has been articulated in the public sector over the last decade. We have also attempted to consider issues of diversity in relation to gender and within equal opportunities. In considering the situation of women we have addressed the diversity amongst women determined by race and disability and sexuality, and conceptualized this as a set of complex and dynamic relationships. We have tried to reflect this in the structure and content of the book.

The other discourse and site where gender inequality has been articulated and located has been 'women and management'. This book has deliberately taken a broader focus on gender, culture and organizational change because the under-representation of women in senior positions in organizations is only one of many manifestations of institutional inequality.

Part I is concerned with *gendering organizational culture* at the level of theory and analysis, with accounts and explanations of organizational activity and behaviour. Janet Newman (Chapter 1) explores the gender dynamics of organizational culture, the shifts in these dynamics as public sector organizations respond to external change, and some of the tensions in theorizing culture and bringing about cultural change. Catherine Itzin (Chapter 2) describes research carried out in a local authority as part of an initiative to improve the position of women within the organization, and uses the findings to illustrate the many dimensions of gender divisions and to develop a concept of a 'gender culture'. Kate French (Chapter 3) considers the ways in which senior male mangers contribute to the shaping and continuation of an organization's culture, and explores the relationships between organizational culture, the structural arrangements of bureaucracies and the organization of work. Di Parkin and Sue Maddock (Chapter 4) show how organizational cultures can be revealed through the use of 'equality audits', and identify a range of gender characteristics typical of organizational culture.

Catherine Itzin and Chris Phillipson (Chapter 5) describe the combined effects of ageism and sexism on women's conditions of employment and career opportunities and conceptualize 'gendered ageism' as an aspect of organizational culture. Elizabeth Harlow, Jeff Hearn and Wendy Parkin (Chapter 6) explore different facets of gendered power and look at how the 'silence and din' of domination and subordination operate in various groups and organizations. Janet Newman and Fiona Williams (Chapter 7) assess the significance of gender as a social division in the restructuring of social welfare, and in the pattern of change in public sector organizations, conceptualizing the relations between gender and other social divisions and identity.

Part II is concerned with *strategies for organizational change*. It demonstrates how an understanding of the gender dynamics of organizations and the application of strategic change theory can provide a basis for making changes in organizations. In Chapter 8 Catherine Itzin provides a case study of a gender and organizational change initiative carried out in a local authority over a five-year period between 1987 and 1992, and describes a process of 'crafting strategy' to bring about changes in the culture, structure and practices of the organization, aimed at improving the position of women. Munira Thobani (Chapter 9) describes her experience as a black woman working for equality in the London Borough of Hounslow, exploring the role of an equalities unit in influencing change. Jackee Holder (Chapter 10) gives an account of the development and operation of a mentor scheme for black students developed within the BBC as part of its positive action strategy. Averil Nottage (Chapter 11) describes a programme of activities initiated by the Department of Health's Social Services Inspectorate, directed at managers and trainers in social services agencies. Judy White (Chapter 12) evaluates a research project on leadership based on the work of fifteen women chief executives in local government: she provides a critique of traditional approaches to theorizing leadership, and a discussion of emerging models. In Chapter 13 Cynthia Cockburn considers whether women are being enabled to use their skills in the new cross-national activities of trade unions in Europe and to develop working contacts with their counterparts in other EU member states. Gwendoline Williams and Marion Macalpine (Chapter 14) describe the pioneering international management development programme for women from 'developing countries', which uses a technique of looking through a 'gender lens' to make visible the gendered relations of power within the Civil Service as a way to intervene and change both the institution itself and the gendered outcomes of the services it delivers. In Chapter 15 Catherine Itzin develops a materialist analysis of gender, culture and power as it applies to society in general and organizations in particular, and uses this as a basis to consider what change means. In the last chapter (Chapter 16) Janet Newman draws some of the threads of this book together by identifying themes in the gendered dynamics of organizations, and exploring some of the tensions and challenges which have emerged in developing strategies for change.

The authors draw on a diversity of approaches and methodologies, but there are both explicit and implicit connections between chapters. Together they present a complex and multifaceted approach to both theory and practice. Each contribution stands alone and illustrates organizational life at a level of detail that is unusual and often fascinating. Cumulatively they build up an ever larger picture of gender, culture and organizational change.

Linking theory and practice is never easy; but our attempt to do so here has been based on core assumptions about the limits of developing theory (grand or otherwise) in isolation from practice, and about the importance of building theories through and out of lived experience. This does not, however, mean falling back into a preoccupation with pragmatic action with little space for reflection and understanding. To avoid the difficulties associated with 'grand theorizing' on the one hand, and 'pragmatic realism' on the other, we have tried to develop grounded ways of linking theory to practice. The various chapters of this book have different emphases, but each reflects key themes which have arisen in a decade of activism and struggles for change.

The approaches and methodologies of the different chapters constellate around four core themes. The first theme is that of research. Many of the authors have identified ways of using research to surface the ways in which gender operates as a social division within an organization, using both quantitative and qualitative techniques to identify issues both in the structures of gender, race, age and other social divisions within an organization, and in the experience of women workers. Itzin (Chapter 2) describes a five-part methodology using a survey, interviews, group discussions, statistical data and participant observation to explore the culture and practices of the organization and to collect data on the position and experience of women. Parkin and Maddock (Chapter 4) describe a process of 'equality audits' which are based on both quantitative and qualitative data. French (Chapter 3) shows how interviews with members of a male management team were used to identify ways in which the organizational culture was structured and reproduced. Nottage (Chapter 11) describes a programme which began through a series of workshops attended by women managers, and was followed by gathering data on the position of women in social services departments. In each case, the research process was not seen as a pure, academic activity, but had an active relationship with the development of change strategies. It was usually experience that was researched, men's as well as women's, in recognition of men's roles as key change agents who need to be mobilized.

The book shows how the process of collecting data can in itself lead key people in the direction of desired change, and can also provide a strategic point around which links can be built with other interests and groups in the development of change initiatives. As well as providing data which can be used to progress change, research has a value in that it can articulate experience, and create discourses which may (in limited ways) 'speak for' women and permit women to speak. Research has been one of very few organizational sites to which women have had access, where they have been able to exercise some power, control and influence, and where an agenda of gender and organizational change can be 'hidden' behind something (a research methodology) which has professional and institutional credibility.

This leads to the second theme emerging from the approaches and methodologies of the book: that of how research on and with women (and men) can be used to develop ideas and to challenge male-dominated theory. It is a truism to say that most organization and management theory has been developed by men and has been based on research on predominantly male subjects. Although such theory tends to be overtly ungendered in its assumptions and conclusions, it is one of the means through which male-typified patterns of behaviour, values and styles are established as the 'norm' against which women are defined as 'other'. This is not to suggest that research must focus on male and female 'differences': much of the research which attempts this is profoundly unsatisfactory. It is to suggest, however, that some aspects of organization and management theory might usefully be remodelled by drawing on research on women's experience and ideas. For example, many of the chapters in Part I of this volume suggest how new ways of theorizing organizational culture are emerging from work with women in organizations; and White's study of women leaders (Chapter 12) stemmed from a concern to develop new perspectives on leadership by exploring women's approaches and styles in their own right, rather than in comparison with those of men. As White's chapter illustrates, this approach often involves an explicit attempt to build theory *with* women rather than *for* women by working participatively with the women concerned, seeing them as 'partners' in the research process rather than as 'subjects' of research with little or no power, and involving an active relationship between researcher and researched.

The third theme we want to highlight is that of developing ways of conceptualizing the relationships between power, culture and identity. The chapter by Harlow, Hearn and Parkin is concerned with the development of new conceptions of power and how it operates; and some of the issues raised in drawing on 'post-Fordist' and 'postmodern' approaches in reconceptualizing power are referred to in Newman and Williams (Chapter 7). The chapters in Part I examine culture as a key site in which issues of power and identify are enmeshed, and in which male power is reproduced. Newman (Chapter 16) considers gender as experience, and culture as a site of gendered meanings and identities.

The final methodological theme is that of modelling change and crafting strategy. Newman (Chapter 1) considers the limitations of the rigid models of culture found in management texts and suggests a view of organizational culture as fluid, dynamic and fragmented. The implications of this for the management of change are taken up in the chapters in Part II. These suggest that the development of strategy requires a view of change which challenges the rational-linear progress towards a distant goal. Itzin (Chapter 8) talks of 'crafting strategy' rather than designing change, and the various contributions to the book suggest a range of strategies for change. The focus of these differs in important ways, but one of the interesting features of the chapters in Part II is how they tend to draw on a range of approaches in order to develop a multilayered, multifocused strategy, in which the focus of action shifts over time to respond to wider contextual changes (social welfare, the state, the new managerialism). One strand is the need to work at both grassroots and policy levels. Contributors describe a range of 'grassroots' initiatives with women to create pressure from below; but they show that support is needed at the top too. Nottage illustrates how the position of the Social Services Inspectorate gave added legitimacy to the local government change project at a policy level by underpinning it with the authority of central government; and French stresses the symbolic importance of the commitment to change (or lack of it) of elected local authority politicians.

A further strand is that of shifting the focus of action over time. The most productive initiatives seem to have been those which use a range of strategies, shifting the focus depending on the organization's responses to wider contextual changes. Itzin's case study (Chapter 8) illustrates this process. At one point, senior managers became concerned about the recruitment and retention of women, and the original gender and organizational change objectives were recast in a new mould to take advantage of this concern. Later, and partly as a result of this recasting, the gender and organizational change project moved from the margins of equal opportunities to the mainstream of human resources management, thereby acquiring a stronger power base within the organization. Later still we can see the development of a business culture which, together with the impact of the recession, undermined the initiative, especially due to its previous casting in terms of demographic arguments. But it did lead to the possibility of reframing issues in terms of a discourse of marketplace needs. Itzin comments: 'Strategically – and sometimes cynically – employee entitlement was replaced by market forces and management expediency.'

A number of underlying principles have guided the collection and the content of the chapters in this book. One was the belief that academic theory and activism can interact and inform each other. Another is the basis of the book in practice: not only is work described in the chapters, but the theory is practice-based, and many of the contributors are 'practitioners' of organizational change. There is also the commitment to using theory to develop strategy and to shape and direct practice, and in turn the use of practice to 'craft strategy' and to construct theory. Another is the gendering of power relations and the effects of this on attitudes, beliefs, identity and the divisions within socially, politically and organizationally subordinated groups, as well as the divisions between dominant and subordinate groups. Still another was a wish to be grounded in a particular culture and historical period and yet not be wholly Eurocentric.

A further principle was a belief that the commonality of women's experience is an essential basis for action, but also a recognition that the diversity of women's experience is important, and a desire to find a way of theorizing this which reflects the dynamic and fluctuating interaction between these dimensions of experience. It was also important to relate gender to other axes of power: to class, race, age and physical ability. Newman and Williams (Chapter 7) offer a multifaceted model to highlight the interrelated nature of different dimensions of identity and social divisions based on race, gender, class, age, disability and sexuality. The model graphically represents the dynamic relationship between the individual, structure and power in time and over time, and the compounding effects of oppression.

Above all we started with the belief that gender (inequality) matters, that (unequal) power relations matter, that what happens to women matters, and that experience is the essential base on which to build knowledge, theory and change. In this context it is important to make explicit some of the gendered characteristics and experiences of the contributors. Most of the contributors are women and many would regard themselves (or be regarded) as feminists. Two of the contributors are men who have a track record in their work and lives of challenging gendered and other power relations. Many of the contributors combine academic work with activism in their involvement in action to improve the situation of women. The women contributors include lesbians and heterosexual women, ranging in age from their twenties to their fifties: with children and without, single, married and co-habiting. Contributors represent a range of races and cultural and ethnic backgrounds including black Afro-Caribbean and Asian.

Most of the contributors are women whose mothers experienced similar difficulties, obstacles, choices and lack of choices in relation to childrearing and paid employment. This book is about change and the possibilities of change, and we take an optimistic stance, but this needs to be put in the context of the limits to change within organizations, given the inequalities that exist in the wider society and the limited changes that have, in fact, taken place (postfeminism notwithstanding) in achieving equality for women in the labour market or the workplace. This book is about what is possible and why and how. What can be achieved depends largely on men's willingness to move over, to make room for women and to share – in the public sphere – social, political, economic and institutional power, and – in the private sphere – the cooking, cleaning and childrearing. It also depends on women's willingness and capacity to continue to make change happen.

Catherine Itzin and Janet Newman

REFERENCES

Davidson, M. and Cooper, C. (1992) *Shattering the Glass Ceiling*. London: Paul Chapman.
Hearn, J., Sheppard, J., Tancred-Sheriff, P. and Burrell, G. (eds) (1989) *The Sexuality of Organization*. London: Sage.
Mills, A. J. and Tancred, P. (1992) *Gendering Organisational Analysis*. London: Sage.
Savage, M. and Witz, A. (1992) *Gender and Bureaucracy*. Oxford: Blackwell.

Part I

Gendering organizational culture

Chapter 1

Gender and cultural change

Janet Newman

This chapter provides frameworks for exploring the gender dynamics of organiza-tional culture, and identifies ways in which these dynamics are shifting as public sector organizations respond to external change. It explores some of the tensions in theorizing culture, and in bringing about cultural change.

The focus on culture in this volume signifies an increasing recognition of the importance of the cultural practices through which gender relations are both reproduced and changed. 'Organizational culture' is usually defined in terms of shared symbols, language, practices ('how we do things around here'), and deeply embedded beliefs and values. Each of these domains has to be understood as gendered, and together they constitute an important field in which gendered meanings, identities, practices and power relations are sustained. Culture has become a salient issue for analysing gender relations and organizations for several reasons.

First, organizational cultures have been highlighted as a significant barrier to change. Even in organizations where equal opportunity initiatives are well de-veloped, their cultures may be resistant and intractable. The informal organization may continue to transmit cultural messages about the 'proper place' for women; and a gendered hierarchy, with men mainly at the top and women mainly at lower levels of an organization, may be sustained and reproduced through cultural messages about the value of male and female labour. Other informal hierarchies are held in place alongside those of gender. Culture is the site where, for example, the wider ideologies of racism and homophobia become lived out in organizational discourses and practices. Interventions which stop at the level of the formal organization (for example the production of new policies and procedures) are, as a result, likely to be limited in their effectiveness.

Second, experience has shown that a focus on 'numbers' alone is not enough to bring about organizational change. The appointment of more women to senior levels, or the recruitment of women to non-traditional areas of work, is only part of the solution. Where women face hostile cultures, the pressures are great and an undue amount of energy has to be expended in developing strategies for survival.

There may also be hard choices to be made about how far to adapt to the 'malestream' culture which they face, rather than developing alternative ways of working and opening up the possibilities of change for other women.

At the same time, public-sector organizations have been going through a period of massive cultural change, attempting to become more 'responsive', 'flexible', 'customer oriented' or 'businesslike' in their approach. This has a number of implications for women as both users of, and employees in, public-service organizations. Such changes can transform existing structures and hierarchies, and open up spaces in which women can seek to influence the organization of the future. Women often articulate strong support for many of the values which (at least on paper) underpin change: for example, those of developing a stronger service orientation, empowering 'front line' staff, and developing flexible and creative responses to new agendas such as the environment, health and community safety. They are also committed to the more effective management of change, based on better communication, longer-term planning and greater involvement of staff and users in decision-making. Other aspects of cultural change may, however, create new barriers to women's voices being heard, and will certainly disadvantage women as the prime users of many public services.

These changes, partial shifts and combinations of cultures mean that any agenda for change needs to reflect the particular cultural configurations of an organization at a given moment in time. Analysing its cultural patterns is an important starting point; and I want to give a brief account of some approaches to cultural mapping which have been developed with women staff in workshops and training programmes.

DECODING THE SYMBOLS: MAPPING AND UNDERSTANDING CULTURE

Cultural mapping can be based on surveys, questionnaires, interviews and group discussions, producing a mix of quantitative and qualitative data. Other chapters of this volume (e.g. Itzin; Parkin and Maddock) outline formal and broad-based approaches through 'equality audits', surveys and interviews. Here I want to focus on qualitative techniques which produce rich and illuminating data.

Cultural imagery

Culture is slippery and elusive; because it is part of taken-for-granted, everyday reality, it is hard to see. To capture it, one has to draw on the senses, to 'tune in' to the sounds, to bring the chaos of images into some kind of focus, and to use intuition to produce some kind of *Gestalt* from a host of fragmented incidents and impressions. These can be surfaced through collecting anecdotes and stories, exploring language, studying informal routines and work practices, and analysing the 'high-profile' symbols of corporate imagery and official statements. When groups of women are asked to capture their experience of their culture visually, they have produced a host of powerful images: for example, gardens in which some flowers are watered but others left to wither; peacocks which strut grandly and make a lot of noise but which have no brain; octopuses with most of their limbs lopped off or with stunted growth; and multitiered edifices with foundations built on women's labour, with isolated women teetering precariously on their fragile foothold near the top.

Brainstorming

Another approach is to brainstorm a list of ways in which the gender dynamics of an organization are experienced, and how these are changing. A list produced by women in one local authority is shown in Figure 1.1. Each item was written on a

---

Women are now being appointed to middle-management posts, but many are having to struggle to gain acceptance.

There are few women job-sharing above a certain level.

There is only one black woman at middle-management grade, and no senior black women have been appointed.

The new chief executive has stated that he aims to promote more women.

One of the senior women doesn't want to be identified with women's issues.

Cost constraints mean that work at the 'front line' of service delivery seems to be getting harder, especially in services exposed to external competition.

There are new job opportunities for women in areas such as customer care and quality.

Competition is giving more scope and visibility for some 'enterprising' women.

Positive action training is now supported in some departments.

There is only token support for flexible working.

The 'community safety' project means we are starting to respond to some issues of concern to women in the community.

One woman appointed to the directorate team last year is finding life tough, and she may not stay long.

The equalities unit seems to be losing power to enforce policies because of the devolution of staffing issues to business unit managers.

The management style is getting more macho.

The personnel officer is talking about adopting the Investors in People strategy, and is known to favour more flexible working.

More women are now in traditionally male jobs such as finance.

Figure 1.1 Brainstorming the culture

separate 'postit', and these were grouped to show the interrelationships and connections between them, and to highlight recurring patterns.

Many of these items reflect the division of labour and typifications of 'women's work' of traditional public-sector bureaucracies, in which women's work is less valued than men's, but in which some women, as well as men, support the traditional divisions of labour. Other items show lines of movement, with more women gaining entry to jobs previously held by men, and more women coming through into middle management. Some items seem to reflect the emergence of a more 'competitive culture'. This is reflected in comments such as 'Work at the "front line" . . . seems to be getting harder' and 'The management style is getting more macho', but is also evident in the notion that there is more scope and visibility for some 'enterprising' women, many of whom, however, do not want to be identified with 'women's issues' because they are managing to succeed on male terms.

Other items from this list seem to reflect something rather different, arising from contemporary patterns of change. The new chief executive has stated his support for the promotion of women to senior levels; there is some positive action training; new agendas are emerging about services to women in the community; and importance is being placed on the development of new human resource strategies.

While most of these sound positive, other aspects of change are less so. The power of the centre to enforce and regulate equality policies is declining, and it is evident that change has led to great increases of pressure on women (and men) in senior posts at the centre. Other potentially positive aspects are limited in their effectiveness because of the legacy of the traditional culture. Newly appointed women managers have to fight hard to gain acceptance, despite support from the top. There is still a belief that managment is essentially a male function. In other areas, the emergence of a competitive ethos means that the chief executive's support on women's issues may not be enough to 'transform' business managers (although they may well learn to speak the right language).

This analysis suggests that, on the one hand, change is not impossible. There are lines of movement, and new spaces are opening up in which women may be able to shape some of the organization's change agenda. On the other hand, it underscores the message that change is unlikely to progress smoothly.

The next section suggests how this kind of work can be built into an analysis of new cultural forms and configurations of gender cultures.

GENDER AND CULTURAL CHANGE: THE 'NEW MANAGERIALISM'

Shifts in the managerial regimes of public-sector organizations have had profound implications for gender relations, and for the patterning of male and female identities. I want to explore the gender relations of three cultural forms. The first is the *traditional culture*, based on a mix of administrative and professional regimes; the culture which characterized many of the old public-sector bureaucracies. The second is the *competitive culture*, resulting from the introduction of a competitive and business ethos into the public sector, in which parts of an organization are exposed to external competition and/or are set up in relations of internal competition. The third is the *transformational* culture, based on the application of a 'new managerialist' ethos to the public sector. None of these exists in pure form in any one organization; they are overlaid on each other in complex ways. But before exploring such patterns of intersection, I want to suggest the different ways in which these three cultural forms are gendered.

The gender relations of 'traditional' cultures

The traditional culture is based on a mix of administrative and professional discourses, each delivering its own language, imagery, values, relationships and ways of doing things. Each offers particular identities within a hierarchy. Administrative discourses offer functionally specialized identities (finance, personnel) and a hierarchy of clearly defined grades and status positions. Professional identities are tied to the profession itself (social worker, doctor, etc.) and through a hierarchy of expertise and experience within an organization.

These cultures are organized around gender in two ways: hierarchically, with women at lower grades and tiers; and through the definition of jobs as 'women's work' or 'men's work' (across both horizontal and vertical divisions). The gender typing of jobs has traditionally been fairly strong, with women occupying the functional specialisms (such as personnel) or service professions (such as nursing, social work, teaching of young children) most closely associated with female roles. This strong gender distinction between jobs has, traditionally, meant that women were frequently found in senior positions in some settings (such as hospital matron, infant school head, personnel manager). However, there was always an invisible hierarchy operating between sectors, with male-dominated professions generally accorded more pay and status than traditional female professions, whether occupied by men or by women. Similarly the male-dominated function of financial management has tended to be accorded more pay and status than personnel management. This is not, however, just a matter of occupations being based on gender stereotyping (number focus for men, people focus for women), but one of the value placed on different kinds of work. As 'people' management has become linked with resource use ('HRM'), and has become part of larger departments associated with more strategic roles, so it has tended to become the province of male rather than female managers.

'Traditional' cultures, then, have tended to be based on a sexual division of labour reflecting traditional views about appropriate male and female roles. They have also tended to be hierarchical, with strong degrees of role distance and expected deference between high- (typically male) and low- (typically female) status jobs – for example between medical consultant and nurse, between manager and secretary. But the gendered basis of this culture goes far beyond the sexual division of labour. It is also built on sets of gendered and sexualized meanings operating within the workplace, which set up 'invisible' hierarchies between male and female roles and the men and women who occupy them.

Women in traditional regimes are offered quasi-familial roles and identities around a core of male hierarchies and privileges. Women managers, for example, can act as 'mothers' (the kindly personnel officer or line manager concerned with staff welfare); as 'aunts' (the older, probably single, woman allowed senior status but little real power); as 'wives' (the supportive secretary or assistant); and as 'daughters' (allowed some privileges on the expectation that they will eventually 'leave home' and therefore present little real challenge). A few women may be admitted to the ranks of the 'lads', and can be found in more collegial roles: as ''fun-loving sister', or as 'tomboy', able to join in and laugh with the lads (even if sometimes at other women's expense).

Those who take on any other kind of role (for example those who adopt a more sexualized, un-daughterly presence, or who break the rules of permitted sisterly behaviour by talking about 'women's issues') are seen as troublesome and 'difficult'. Black women are rarely admitted to the family at all; but many occupy positions outside these Anglocentric familial relationships. Black and white working-class women occupy an organizational sub-class (perhaps below stairs?) in typing pools, print rooms, canteens and other predominantly female collective spaces – all, of whatever age, consigned to the status of 'girls' and addressed only by first names. Class, race and generation, then, underpin the hierarchy of female roles in the traditional regime of public-sector bureaucracies. But these bureaucracies have themselves been the target of change, and these social divisions are being realigned in complex ways.

The gender relations of 'competitive' cultures

A decade of change has led to the emergence of new elements of organizational culture in the public sector. The form these take, however, has depended on the way in which organizations (and units within them) have responded to the restructurings and changes of recent years. We can, for example, identify different responses to exposure to external or internal competition. 'Being competitive' is not an objective set of attributes, but depends on subjective understandings of how the business world works. Much of the public sector has so far tended to operate on images of that world as requiring hard, macho or 'cowboy' styles of working. It is as if the unlocking of the shackles of bureaucratic constraints has at last allowed managers to become 'real men', released from the second-class status of public sector functionaries through exposure to the 'real world' of the market place. The focus is on cutting costs rather than adding or retaining value; the approach to change is that of 'slash and burn'; people are seen as costs rather than assets; and the dominant management style tends to result in an impoverished organizational culture.

The gender relations of the macho cowboy regime are less familial than those of the traditional bureaucracy. Many of the old patriarchs and benevolent paternal figures are being dethroned (made redundant) or depowered (through restructurings which break up some of the old fiefdoms and power bases). In competitive cultures, power lies where the action is – where people do business. Informal hierarchies develop around the jobs that are seen to be most 'sexy' – those linked to dynamic, thrusting entrepreneurialism. Being an individual or team charged with delivering fast results in strategically important change areas tends to bring fast career rewards. Running a hospital trust, forging big bucks in private-sector partnerships, doing deals with European money and so on are all seen to require a very different style of operating – go-getting, insurgent, and ruthless, tough on both competitors and one's own staff.

These cultures are based on internal as well as external competition. Women are allowed to join if they can prove that they can deliver, and are tough enough to stand the pace. Power is more fluid, and there are fewer rules about how it should be exercised, so women may have a tough time. As men jostle with each other for organizational space, they may be trampled underfoot. Cynthia Cockburn's study of men's responses to women in organizations captures something of the style emerging in parts of the public and private sectors:

> What distinguished him was an overt and confident machismo. Women every-where made reference to the 'cod-piece wearing jocks' of the policy unit, the 'new men' of the advertising department. This masculinity does not share the women's-place-is-in-the-home mentality of the old guard. These men expect to find women in the public sphere. Nominally at least they welcome women into this exciting new world because their presence adds sexual spice to the working day.
>
> (1991: 156–7)

This is a heterosexual culture in which, as in modern marriage, there is a notional equivalence between male and female roles. But this equivalence depends on women taking on roles in which they compete with men (and with other women) in the battle for resources and jobs. Success depends on access to the informal clubs and networks where the 'real' business goes down; clubs largely controlled by white men jealously guarding their power base. Exceptional women may be permitted entry, in a similar way to that in which 'sisters' were allowed into the sub-cultures of 'lads' within the traditional culture. But here entry depends less on 'being a good sport' and more on proving (and continually reproving) your worth. Those women that succeed are likely to attract the scorn of men, and of other women, due to the hardness or 'unnatural' competitiveness they have shown. Machismo is not seen as an appropriate female characteristic, even though the women who use it may be admired for their achievements. Those that fall, fall hard; and the media are always more than gleefully ready to pick the bones.[1] Women who fight rough are also not seen to make positive role models for other women, and they may pay an extreme cost in personal terms.

This is, of course, a stereotypically drawn culture which probably exists only at the margins of public-sector organizations, being more developed among providers than purchasers, contractors than clients. This margin is shifting as organizations are split into 'business units', leading, in many cases, to high levels of internal fragmentation and competition. At the same time, no organization has completely lost its traditional culture. It sits beneath the competitive culture and informs the hidden domain of gender relations. Women, then, have to live out the contradictions between these cultures, in a climate which is rife with mixed messages resulting from the interplay between old and new regimes, and between the gender and racial stereotypes underpinning each. At one moment you must be daughterly and decorous; at another, tough and pushy. To succeed, you have to join in the competitive ethos, but you have to retain your womanly characteristics and remain 'nice' while doing so. But the competitive culture is not a place where 'nice' women thrive.

The gender relations of 'transformational' cultures

There is, however, an alternative model: that of the 'new managerialism' based on the idea of transformational change. It focuses not on short-term competitive success but on building long-term strength. It is culture and value based; the leader's role is to communicate missions and visions, and to build a 'strong' culture around a set of guiding principles through which those visions can be realized. It recognizes the value of people, and talks of the need to 'empower' staff. This is a model which is gaining greater salience in the public sector as some organizations are moving beyond the impoverished efficiency frameworks of the Thatcher years and are attempting to build quality public services.

The emphasis on cultural change offers new ways of doing things, and the possibility of new organizational space for women. This arises partly from increasing emphasis on the importance of 'soft' skills, such as communicating with staff and customers, at which women are seen to excel. At the same time, the emphasis on valuing human resources and 'empowering' lower-level staff requires that organizations address the barriers to women's effective contribution to the workplace. The growth of service and quality orientation seems to offer a greater alignment between the values which many women express and the organizational cultures within which they work.[2] There is even talk of organizations needing more 'feminine' management styles, and of a 'feminization' of management, though this tends in practice to refer to the need for men to change rather than for women to be given more power.

An optimistic reading of the gender relations of the 'transformational' culture suggests that it may be good news for women. Organizational change may lead to better training and development opportunities for women staff, and a more sympathetic climate for 'female' values and ways of working. It seems to offer women the opportunity to become more active partners in the reshaping of cultures and in the delivery of new styles of interface between the organization and its customers. Their communication and collaborative skills may become more valued as organizations recognize the need to build relationships with partners, stakeholders and communities. However, let us not be beguiled by the rhetoric of transformational change. It is often very different from the reality of how women experience their work. Few organizations which talk about new (women-friendly) ways of doing things are prepared to unlock the (male) power bases in which old ways of doing things are entrenched.

The gender relations of the transformational culture are less familial than those of the 'traditional' culture. Women are seen to have been 'liberated' from their traditional sex roles, and are no longer constrained by the old-fashioned, hierarchical patterns of power and authority. At the same time, it is less overtly sexualized than the 'competitive' culture: women are to be respected as people (because they form part of the 'human resources' of the organization), and their contribution is to be valued (because their skills are needed). The model on which it is based is one of partnership: horizontal patterns of working in which all are formally equal. In the transformational culture, women must be 'free' to contribute on equal terms. Their contribution is, moreover, seen to be an essential component of the building of happy, harmonious and productive teams and workplaces.

There are, however, specific sets of difficulties for women within such cultures. First, they are gender (and racially) blind. The acknowledgement of difference (beyond respecting individuality or the uniqueness of each individual) would undermine the consensual values which are seen as essential. All are to be equal partners in the wider project of change; specific interests and agendas are viewed at best as a wasteful diversion, at worst as disloyalty. However, the dominant notion of equality (based on liberal notions of fair access) is illusory rather than real. The gender and 'racial' inequalities of power operating beneath the surface of the seemingly consensual teams and workplaces remain. Women are again, then, operating with contradictory sets of meanings: 'Contribute fully, as equal members of the team', but 'Remember your real place'. A further consequence of the ideology of partnership is that women willingly take on much more than they are paid for; they may be the most junior members of the team, but are expected to carry a full share of responsibility. This may be good for the career development of some women, but is exploitative of many.

A further difficulty with the 'transformational' culture lies in the ideas of leadership on which it is based. The emphasis is on inspiration and vision, and leadership is assumed to be based on affective (rather than cognitive) modes of interaction. This has resonances with the mythic and heroic imagery of 'charismatic' leadership, derived from military and political models, though the new heroes are the business leaders who have become 'champions' of change, entering popular folklore by turning companies round and transforming failure into success. Leadership of this type is portrayed as mysterious and elusive, based on the unique qualities of exceptional individuals. Leaders, we learn, are always born not made; and they are nearly always born male. Tom Peters suggests that leaders should be heroes; but there is little mention of heroines. The imagery of leadership in Western culture in any case tells us that while male heroes lead men into battle, heroines give devoted and selfless service – hardly the qualities needed to bring about transformative change.

There are, then, few points of identification for women in this imagery of heroic leadership (and even fewer for black women, older women or women with disabilities). This does not mean that women do not make effective leaders. But women pioneers in leadership roles in organizations traditionally led by men are isolated and highly visible, and so have to make hard choices about how far to adapt to the prevailing culture, and how far to try to change it. To join the all-white, all-male clubs of senior management it has usually been necessary to conform to the rules and to learn white male values, norms and ways of doing things. There will be little space or support for doing things differently until the power relations within organizations become part of the transformational agenda.

However, the ideology of the new managerialism will militate against the possibility of such an agenda. The ideology emphasizes corporate consensus, and promulgates the view that old lines of conflict are no longer relevant in the new world of change. This is most significant around class, with the weakening of trade-union power across the public sector. But it also has powerful messages about gender. We have, the message runs, now entered a 'postfeminist' world in which the battles have been won and it is possible for women to gain senior positions. At the same time, we all need to pull together in the face of the major external threats to the public sector, declining resources and cuts in service provision. Internal conflicts are viewed as diversionary at best, and at worst destructive. Any residual problems (such as the under-representation of women at senior levels) can be solved by the use of managerial programmes such as Opportunity 2000. In other words, there is nothing we need to worry about any more, and if we continue to complain and struggle we will divert important energy and resources away from the wider project of organizational success.

The three different cultural formations I have described do not, of course, ever exist in isolation. Any organization going through change will contain some kind of mix, though the balance will be different depending on two key factors. The first is where women are positioned in the fragmented organizations which are emerging. While women in the 'core' may be more likely to experience a mix of traditional and transformational cultures, women on the periphery may be faced with more overtly competitive cultures. Similarly there will be differences between client and contractor, or purchaser and provider roles. The second factor is the change trajectory of a specific organization: that is, how it has responded to external change in the past and what kinds of new change agenda are emerging.

Such transitions are not neat or tidy processes. Older and newer sets of gendered messages are overlaid on each other in complex ways. Just as we have learned strategies for dealing with one set of rules, the rules change. However, they only change in part. There will be a persistent underlay of older forms in new contexts, with older messages, injunctions and disciplines lying beneath the surface to trap the unwary.

Shifting patterns of culture mean that we have continually to reshape strategies for change. For example, in traditional cultures with a strong sexual division of labour, equality policies rightly focus on challenging gender stereotypes (ideas of what are seen as appropriate male and female jobs) through 'fair recruitment' procedures. As change occurs, these stereotypes are sometimes rewritten and women gain access to jobs previously seen as 'men's work'. But this does not necessarily challenge the basis of male power; indeed in competitive cultures, male power is being reinforced at a number of levels. If the 'traditional culture' I have described corresponds in part to Charles Handy's (1985) 'role culture', with power resting with formal authority, the competitive culture corresponds more closely to Handy's notion of 'power culture', with few rules and little respect for formal authority. Power operates in a more personal and elusive manner, and is maintained through informal practices of exclusion. Some women may be allowed to join the club, but joining is highly conditional on adopting the assumptions and practices which pervade it. In this context, challenging cultural norms (for example about what 'good business practice' actually means) takes on a new significance.

For women in a 'transformational' culture the priorities are rather different. Women may be sympathetic to the project of transformational change (with its agenda based on developing staff, improving services and building links with customers and communities). However, becoming committed to the wider organizational project can often mean relinquishing the right to challenge practices which disempower women. It is possible to 'come on board' as long as you do not 'rock the boat'. This tendency is reinforced by the consensual ideology which pervades the 'new managerialist' ethos (Newman 1994a).

The shift towards new managerial cultures can, however, re-energize strategies to enhance the position of women. It does so by offering the possibility of setting out a 'business case' for change – that is, one based on arguments that organizational effectiveness will be improved if more women are promoted to senior levels, and the potential of the whole 'human resources' of the organization is realized. One of the priorities in the transformational culture, then, is to assess the possibilities and pitfalls of developing strategies based on such arguments. I return to this theme in the final chapter of this volume.

MODELLING CULTURAL CHANGE

At this point, I want to explore how we might develop models of change which can enable us to address some of the deep structures of experience which characterize organizational change. Initially, I turned to management texts on cultural change to see what they had to offer. In the 1980s there was a proliferation of business and managerial literature on 'corporate cultures' (Peters and Waterman 1982; Deal and Kennedy 1982; Tichy 1983). The concept of culture appearing in this mainstream managerial literature is, however, relatively unsophisticated, and certainly undertheorized. Two important factors give rise to this poverty of cultural theory.

The first is that the managerial texts have tended to be preoccupied with the function of culture in building consensus and legitimacy. Diversity, difference and dissent are treated as problems to be ironed out rather than as issues to be explored or as positive sources of change. In order to bring about change, the texts draw heavily on the rational-mechanical perspectives which have dominated management. Culture is presented as yet another 'lever' which those engaged in managing change must pull. The model remains that of organizational engineering, with clear linkages drawn between strong cultures and organizational performance. As a result, the model of cultural change in the business literature is often inadequate, and is divorced from other change perspectives and strategies (Newman 1994b). Secondly, many of the sociological and anthropological perspectives on which the culture literature has drawn are themselves inadequate. As a result, the models of culture which are found in management texts are based on a number of assumptions which it is worth making explicit.

Assumption 1: Cultures are 'closed societies'

Many of the problems of the literature stem from the anthropological traditions on which the study of culture has drawn. This tradition is based on the study of closed, small scale groups or societies on which the outside world has little impact. But, of course, organizations cannot be treated as if they are sealed from their environment. The internal focus of the managerial literature on culture does not enable those working in the public sector to identify the importance of the external context of change. This is of critical importance to the analysis of gender: gender relations in the wider society clearly impact on the internal gender relationships within organizations.

Assumption 2: Cultures are integrated wholes

Most texts talk of organizations having a 'corporate culture'. That is, an organization's culture is seen as an integrated and undifferentiated whole. This ignores the multidimensional and cross cutting cultures present within any organization. In both the public and private sectors most organizations are strongly divided along departmental, functional and professional lines, each of which has its own sets of values and practices, with different messages about, and consequences for, women. At the same time, change leads to new lines of fragmentation, with new forms of culture emerging as parts of the organization develop responses to new imperatives and demands.

Assumption 3: Cultures are consensual

Organizational cultures are usually depicted in terms of 'shared values'. Culture is seen as the site of consensus, somehow separated from the worlds of organizational politics; however, much organizational politics is in practice played out through the mobilization of cultural values and norms. For example, there is often cultural conflict between those defending traditional values against 'new' (business or market-based) values. Cultural change is a source of potential conflict and division as well as of consensus. 'Resistance' can often be understood in terms of the defence of what used to be held as basic beliefs. Again, this has significant implications for the politics of gender. Where organizations attempt to give a higher profile to equal opportunity issues, powerful strategies of resistance may arise (see Cockburn 1991; Salaman 1992; French and Itzin in this volume).

Assumption 4: Culture is objective reality

Culture tends to be viewed as something which an organization 'has', as a distinct set of attributes or characteristics (Smircich 1983). As such, the notion of culture becomes reified and seen to be something apart from human identity and agency. Workers or employees are viewed as passive recipients of culture rather than its active creators. But work on culture is important precisely because it allows links to be made between organizational processes and individual identity, enabling us to explore the complexity of identity and the factors which influence the patterns of differentiation within an organization. These include differentiation between women, who take on different kinds of gender identity and who deal with the gendered cultures in a host of different ways, drawing on a range of strategies.

Assumption 5: Culture is static

Notions of culture are often static. In the managerial literature, culture is depicted as a passive field waiting for managers to act on it. This means that it is difficult to explore the dynamic qualities of cultural change and the tensions these produce. This is particularly significant in a period in which most organizations in the public sector are undergoing substantial cultural change, in which older messages about gender may be eroded; or, alternatively, may be transmuted into new forms. Unfortunately much of the 'women in management' literature tends to replicate this view of cultures as static. The very notion of the 'glass ceiling' is problematic; barriers to women are more fluid and plastic than this imagery suggests. Rather than barriers being 'shattered,' they are capable of being reshaped and remoulded in different forms as change occurs.

This does not mean that culture is not resistant to change. Cultural norms and values are deeply embedded, and tend to reproduce themselves even after the context has changed significantly and they are no longer appropriate responses. But rather than seeing culture as static, it is more helpful to identify the active processes which prevent change occurring. It may be possible to do this by identifying the 'vicious circles' through which behaviour is replicated and cultural patterns reproduced (Hampden-Turner 1990; Newman 1993). One example from work in a local authority can illustrate the basic technique. This organization wished to promote more women, but found that few women actually put themselves forward when senior posts were advertised internally. I was approached to see whether some kind of programme to 'build confidence and career aspirations' might help. Suspicious of statements which pathologize women in this way, I explored some of the cultural

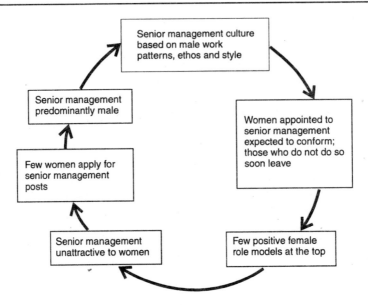

Figure 1.2   The vicious circle of cultural barriers

factors at work and, through discussions at different levels, the vicious circle shown in Figure 1.2 was discovered.

The problem lay not with women themselves, but with the cultural norms of the mainly male senior management group, and the isolation and visibility of women within it. Until the management group changed its ethos, style and behaviour, it was unlikely that more women would wish to join it. Similarly, until senior women felt more supported in challenging the dominant culture at the top, they were unlikely to be seen as positive role models for other women. A range of strategies arose from this work, including work on new leadership styles with the management group, the recruitment of more senior women, mentoring schemes for middle and senior women managers, and a women's network. The point about 'vicious circles' is that it is always necessary to find multiple points of intervention; single interventions will not break the cycle, and may even make the situation worse since they enable organizations to relax and say 'We tried this, and it didn't work'.

Assumption 6: Culture can be changed through new symbols

Prescriptions for cultural change tend to assume that culture is generated by, and centred on, the leader; and that new values can be injected more or less at will through the manipulation of symbols (the production of new values, visions, missions and the like, changing the appearance of buildings, of publicity materials, of reception areas, and even of staff with new uniforms and name badges). While symbols are important, the manipulation of surface appearances can achieve little on its own; and may even be counter-productive by inducing deep cynicism among staff.

Organizations need to pay attention to the symbolic messages which are sent out (often inadvertently) and which affect perceptions of what is, and is not, important. The kind of environment women work in, their physical position in the building, their membership of important groups and high status training events, all carry messages which reinforce deeply held values. But change cannot come about simply by manipulating the symbols. There is, for example, sometimes an assumption that the appointment of a few women at senior level can in itself bring about change through some kind of 'trickle down' effect. In practice this often works at the expense of the senior women themselves, who become overburdened and overexposed (and it does not help black women if all the role models are white). It may also not help women lower down the organization who are blocked by actual practices and behaviours, rather than by the absence of appropriate symbols.

There is a need for a model which draws attention to the different levels and sites at which action may be needed to bring about cultural change. I use a model which analyses culture in terms of three levels. The first is the *symbolic* level, which sends signals about what is important and valued in the organization. But beneath this come two further layers: the layer of *organizational practices* (norms of behaviour embedded in systems and structures); and the layer of *values* (deeply held attitudes and beliefs). Modelling culture in terms of these three levels enables us to look at what strategies are needed at each level to bring about change. Action at any one level alone is unlikely to be effective, and may lead to a gap between rhetoric and action. Action at the symbolic level (such as the production of a new policy, or the adoption of a new style of language by senior managers) can never be effective unless it is linked to substantive change in behaviours and procedures, structures and systems. At the same time, training which focuses primarily on values – including many development programmes for women themselves, encouraging them to develop their 'career aspirations' – will only be effective if they are part of a much broader strategy for organizational change.

The model also demonstrates that cultural change is not just concerned with the 'soft' dimensions of organizational life; it depends on real changes in structures, systems and the use of resources. Only those with access to organizational power (in terms of formal authority and/or resource control) can bring this about. In other words, the kind of cultural change which will benefit women is not just the business of women themselves; it must be seen as benefiting the whole organization, and those with power (men as well as women) must buy into the changes which are needed. The chapters in Part II of this volume set out some of the ways in which local authorities have been attempting to build support for equalities initiatives by linking change to organizational agendas, and by working with men. They are also very clear about the limits, as well as the possibilities, of change; it is evident from the various case studies that those with power are unlikely to give it up without a struggle.

Developments in cultural theory

In the previous section, I have argued that the managerial literature on culture tends to give an oversimplistic and uniform view of culture, which does not take account of multiple perspectives and identities. In contrast, I want to suggest a view of organizational culture as fluid, dynamic and fragmented. To do this it is necessary to draw on some of the rich tradition of contemporary cultural studies in the social sciences, and on developments stemming from feminist and other critical perspectives. Following Meyerson and Martin (1987) and Frost *et al.* (1991) I want to group approaches to the study of culture into three categories: an *integration perspective*, a *differentiation perspective*, and a *fragmentation perspective*.

The *integrationist perspective*, drawn from anthropology and some kinds of sociology, can be valuable in providing a holistic sense of an organization; in providing a feel for the *Gestalt* of organizational behaviours, values and assumptions. Anthropologically based accounts of culture (Jelinek *et al.* 1983; Schein 1985; Ott 1989) provide a very rich picture of organizational life. This approach can provide practitioners with understandings of how their own cultures tend to reproduce themselves in their own image; and can offer guidance to 'outsiders' (marginal or traditionally excluded groups) on how to read and adapt to the culture when permitted entry. But this kind of analysis provides a very limited analytical tool for understanding the internal richness and diversity of organizations.

Sub-cultural theory within sociology gives a view that can be developed to provide a more *differentiated perspective*, offering an understanding of variability within organizations (e.g. Gregory 1983). Organizational subcultures relate to specific variables such as department, function, profession and work groups. Each depends on geographical or social boundaries within an organization (groups of co-workers or colleagues sharing an informal set of meanings, understandings, values and recipes for action). Notions of resistance are made thinkable by the introduction of *counterculture* as an analytic tool (e.g. Martin and Siehl 1988). This suggests a less homogeneous and monolithic view of culture. But 'sub-cultures' and 'countercultures' are still treated as closed entities; the emphasis is on analysis of the sense of belonging and psychological security which membership brings. Individual identity, attachment to culture and group membership are linked in an unproblematic way.

Meyerson and Martin's third perspective, the *fragmentation perspective*, sees organizations as cross-cut with multiple sets of meanings and lines of cultural identification; and it offers a framework for analysing the ambiguities that arise when contradictory sets of meaning (or prescriptions for action) intersect. While the integration and differentiation perspectives are well established, the fragmentation perspective is as yet undeveloped in work on organizational culture. It draws on postmodernist approaches emerging within the social sciences, which are concerned with analysis of the differentiation and fragmentation of the social world (and of individuals within it), and with the dislocation of traditional lines of social cohesion and division.

This model and its possibilities and limitations are explored more fully in Chapter 7 of this volume. Here, I want to summarize briefly the relevance to analysing the gender dynamics of organizational culture of each of the three perspectives outlined above. The *integration* perspective directs attention towards the culture as a whole – to the traditions, beliefs and practices specific to a particular organization, and the ways in which these are gendered. The culture of British Rail will clearly be different from that of a Civil Service department, and the gender dynamic of each needs to be understood in terms of the history and pattern of development of these organizations (although each will be framed by wider social patterning of gender). The *differentiation* perspective can help us explore how the gendered culture takes different forms in different parts of the organization. This may be linked to profession, function or division. It may also be linked to the ways in which the 'new managerialism' has led to new lines of fragmentation, and has transformed different parts of an organization in different ways.

The *fragmentation* perspective can enable us to explore ambiguities and tensions in women's roles and identities within a particular gendered cultural configuration. It can help us to explore the tensions for a women operating in a number of cultural domains: as part of the dominant gender culture, in a managerial or professional culture, as a black or white worker, as a younger or older woman, and as a member of family, community and network. Each of these cultural domains will offer its own language, beliefs, rules and appropriate identities. This perspective can also help us to understand in part the kinds of division between women that may become significant within organizations. Women learn gendered cultural messages early in their career when they have little power to change them; and inevitably they carry some of this with them through their working lives as they move through or between organizations. These may fit uncomfortably with the ways in which other women, working alongside them, may have adapted to or challenged the prevailing culture. We can also consider how the cultures of gender, age, class and 'race' interact with each other in a dynamic way across an organization. So the fragmentation perspective enables us to develop better understandings of the complexities of gendered cultures, and the 'mixed messages' for women which pervade them.

However, none of the typifications of culture I have discussed so far really gets to grips with the dynamic and changing basis of culture. Writings within the integrationist perspective tend to view culture as somehow 'naturally' evolving in response to external change; but the process of change and transition is never as smooth or unproblematic as the idea of 'evolution' suggests. Culture is a site where meanings are contested. The dominant gendered messages can change as a response to women's actions in challenging or reshaping the culture. They can also change in response to other types of pressure, ranging from new organizational imperatives to the effects of ideological shifts in the wider society. Earlier I explored some of the issues arising in the shift towards the ideology of the 'new managerialism' in the public sector.

This brings me to a final point about ways of theorizing culture. In building new models, we need to recognize the limitations of the ways in which existing models of culture deal with power. Power tends to be neglected altogether in many representations of culture, and indeed is positively avoided in the consensual orientation of the integrationist perspective. Power is recognized to a greater extent in the differentiated perspective in its acknowledgement of plural cultures (sub-cultures and countercultures), each the site of its own meanings which may be in tension with the 'corporate culture'. But the dynamic relationship between these is not well theorized, and we are offered little understanding of how power and conflict between sub-cultures, and between countercultures and the dominant culture, is played out. The fragmentation perspective, on the other hand, tends to treat power as too fluid and transient – it exists everywhere, and therefore perhaps nowhere. Forms of power based on racism, homophobia and patriarchy are some-how dissolved into fragmented and individualized discourses.

An understanding of power is crucial to an understanding of the ways in which dominant cultural meanings are sustained and reproduced: meanings which are gendered (whether women are present or not) and racialized (whether non-white people are present or not). Cultural power exists through meanings which are held in place by a plurality of relationships and practices within an organization. It is these relationships and cultural practices which establish and maintain consent. In other words, women continue to help support organizations in which they are marginalized because of the ways in which gender relations are inscribed and 'naturalized'. It is in the domain of culture that meanings are established and work identities formed.

However, these power relationships are rarely absolute or permanent, but can be seen as a set of dynamic forces through which meanings are contested and the struggle to establish consensus is made. As organizations change, we need to explore the shifting dynamics of power, looking at how new meanings emerge, how they are overlaid on older meanings, and how contested meanings are negotiated.

In this chapter, I have explored three different sets of gender relations which can be identified in public-sector organizations as they experience change. The conti-nuities between these are perhaps more significant than the differences. But the differences are significant for a number of reasons. Firstly, 'mixed messages' occur in the overlaying of old and emergent gender identities. These give rise to contra-dictions and tensions which greatly add to the stresses women experience in their organizational lives. Secondly, the dynamics of change will open up new agendas for action and will point to the limitations of some older ones. The 'transformation-al' culture, for example, is undoubtedly beneficial to some women; but it has its own limitations (such as the models of leadership on which it is based). Finally, cultural change is never a smooth or unproblematic process. As it proceeds, old alliances crumble, old power bases are eroded, and new spaces are fleetingly opened up. The dynamics of cultural change, then, potentially open up the space for women to define new meanings and reshape organizational cultures in a way which can benefit women as both workers in, and users of, public service organizations.

NOTES

1   At the time of writing (April 1994) there was considerable press coverage of the suspension of a woman from her post as the chief executive of one of the new NHS trusts. Her suspension was linked to difficulties with her 'management style'.
2   There are, of course, problems of identifying women with values based on sex-role stereotypes, or with a distinctly 'women's way' of doing things. Nevertheless, research on women managers does tend to suggest that women often do not identify with cultures based on stereotypically male styles and values (e.g. Young and Spencer 1990; Allan et al. 1992; Davidson and Cooper 1992).

REFERENCES

Allan, M., Bhavnani, R. and French, K. (1992) Promoting Women. London: HMSO.

Cockburn, C. (1991) In the Way of Women: Men's Resistance to Sex Equality in Organisations. London: Macmillan.

Davidson, M. J. and Cooper, C. L. (1992) Shattering the Glass Ceiling: The Woman Manager. London: Paul Chapman.

Deal, T. E. and Kennedy, A. (1982) Corporate Cultures: The Rites and Rituals of Corporate Life. Reading, MA: Addison-Wesley.

Frost, P. J., Moore, L. F., Louis, M. R., Lundberg, C. C. and Martin, J. (eds) (1991) Reframing Organisational Culture. London: Sage.

Gregory, K. L. (1983) 'Native view paradigms: multiple cultures and conflicts in organisations'. Administrative Science Quarterly, 28, 359–76.

Hampden-Turner, C. (1990) Corporate Culture: From Vicious to Virtuous Circles. London: Hutchinson.

Handy, C. (1985) Understanding Organisations. 3rd edn. London: Penguin.

Jelinek, M., Smircich, L. and Hirsch, P. (1983) 'Introduction: a coat of many colours'. Administrative Science Quarterly, 28, 331–8.

Martin, J. and Siehl, C. (1988) 'Organisational culture and counterculture: an uneasy symbiosis'. Organisational Dynamics, Autumn, 52–64.

Meyerson, D. and Martin, J. (1987) 'Cultural change: an integration of three different views'. Journal of Management Studies, 24, 623–47.

Newman, J. (1993) 'Women, management and change'. Local Government Policymaking, 20 (2), 38–43.

Newman, J. (1994a) 'The limits of management: gender and the politics of change'. In Clarke, J., Cochrane, A. and McLaughlin, E., Managing Social Policy. London: Sage.

Newman, J. (1994b) 'Beyond the vision: cultural change in the public sector'. Public Money and Management, April–June, 59–64.

Ott, J. S. (1989) The Organisational Culture Perspective. Chicago: Dorsey Press.

Peters, T. J. and Waterman, R. H. (1982) In Search of Excellence: Lessons from America's Best Run Companies. New York: Harper and Row.

Salaman, Graeme (1992) 'The management of staff: the case of the London Fire Brigade'. In Pollitt, C. and Harrison, S. (eds) Handbook of Public Services Management. Oxford: Blackwell.

Schein, E. H. (1985) Organisational Culture and Leadership. San Francisco, CA: Jossey-Bass.

Smircich, L. (1983) 'Concepts of culture and organisational analysis'. Administrative Science Quarterly, 8, 339–58.

Tichy, N. (1983) Managing Strategic Change: Technical, Political and Social Aspects. New York: John Wiley.

Young, K. and Spencer, L. (1990) Breaking the Barriers: Women Managers in Local Government. Luton: Local Government Training Board.

Chapter 2

The gender culture in organizations

Catherine Itzin

This chapter uses the findings of research carried out in a local authority to illustrate the many dimensions of sexism and sex discrimination in organizations and how gender interacts with race to disadvantage women. It develops a concept of 'gender culture', and analyses the role and significance of gendered power relations in shaping organizational culture.

> Why should half the population have to go through life like hobbled horses in a steeple chase?
>
> (The Right Hon. John Major, launching Business in the Community's Opportunity 2000 Campaign 1991)

In 1990 I carried out a major research project in a local authority as part of a long-term initiative to improve the position of women within the organization. The results of the research were used to support a range of proposals designed to change the culture, structure and practices of the organization. How the research was used as part of this process of gender and organizational change is described in Chapter 8.

This chapter focuses on the methodology and the findings of the research itself, using the data to build up a picture of the culture of the organization from a gender perspective, drawing on the experiences and observations of both women and men. It relates the research findings to some of the literature on organizational culture and gender in organizations. It uses the research findings to develop a concept of 'gender culture' and considers the possibilities of change in the context of a culture of gendered power relations.

METHODOLOGY

A five part methodology was used to explore the culture and the practices of the organization and to collect data that could be used to support proposals to create a more women-friendly workplace. Three departments were 'researched': the housing and development departments included a range of occupations in which women are generally under-represented, and the social services department was chosen for the range of its work traditionally done by women.

Group interviews

Group interviews were organized with women in different grades and kinds of work in the social services department. There were eight groups covering basic professionals, home care organizers, home helps, under-5s' workers, day nursery staff, administrative and clerical staff grades 1–6, administrative staff in senior officer grades, and senior managers. Participants were selected randomly from printouts from the council's computerized personnel information system. Letters were sent out inviting participation in group discussions about the barriers to women's employment and career progression. The purpose of the group discussions was to identify key issues which could be explored in more detail in a survey questionnaire and individual interviews.

'Postal' survey

A self-completion questionnaire was sent to all women in the social services, housing and development departments in September 1990. Questionnaires were attached to monthly payslips for officer (APT&C) staff, and were handed out by managers with wage packets to manual staff. A reminder letter was sent to all respondents in November 1990. Within the deadline period 487 questionnaires were returned, producing a response rate of 40 per cent. Data were analysed using the SPSS social survey analysis package. The questionnaire contained 57 questions covering personal details, education and training, work history, career progression, caring responsibilities and discrimination.

Management interviews

In-depth interviews were conducted with most first, second and third-tier officers and with a selection of women and men in middle management (Grades PO1A–C) in the housing, social services and development departments. These interviews were designed to collect information on work history and career development, women's career progression, domestic roles and responsibilities, division of time between home and work, childcare responsibilities and sexism in the organization. The interviews were tape recorded and transcribed.

Equal opportunities monitoring data

Data were also collected on the racial and gender composition of the workforce to establish where women and black staff were located in the structure of the organization.

Participant observation

A further dimension of the methodology was my role as a 'participant' in the work of the organization in senior management positions at second and third-tier levels, and my 'observations' and perceptions of the organization at work: in effect my role as 'participant observer'.

THE RESEARCH FINDINGS

The gender and race profile of the workforce

Gender

As one of its 'equal-opportunities' initiatives, the organization collected data on the gender and racial composition of its workforce. A survey of non-manual staff showed that nearly two-thirds of the total staff were women (63.8 per cent) and one third (36.2 per cent) men. Of these women, nearly two-thirds (63.3 per cent) were located in the administrative and clerical grades. Women were massively over-represented in the lower grades, and massively under-represented in senior grades by comparison with men. There were, for example, nearly twice as many men as women in the senior officer grades, and in principal officer grades 20 per cent of men were located in grades PO1 A–C as compared with only 6 per cent of women: over three times as many men as women. Eight per cent of men were located in grades PO2–3 as compared with 1 per cent of women: eight times as many men as women. Only a tiny fraction of 1 per cent of women were located in chief officer grades (0.2 per cent) as compared with 3.1 per cent of men: fifteen times as many men as women. The chief executive and all directors were male, and had been for the previous six years.

Race and gender

The survey produced an unexpected picture of the position of black and Asian women in relation to black and Asian men in the organization. It was widely believed and frequently stated that black women 'did better' than black men. 'Black women get jobs more easily than black men', reported women in the group interviews. The statistics, however, told a different story.

In administrative and clerical grades 1–3, while white staff were under-represented by comparison with black staff, white women were in fact over-represented by comparison with men, as were Irish, black and Asian women. And in grades PO1 A–C, although black staff were under-represented, it was in fact black women who were under-represented rather than black men. The same was true of Asian, Irish and white women by comparison with men in the same racial groups. The workforce profile showed that black men fared significantly better institutionally than black women, and that black women had more in common with white women in terms of their organizational position.

Although black, Asian and Irish men were always under-represented in senior positions in relation to white men, the position of women in all racial groups always compared unfavourably with the position of men, and women were massively over-represented in the lower grades and under-represented in the higher grades by comparison with men, whatever their race.

Survey results

The sample

Of the sample, 76 per cent were 'officer' staff (local government terminology for professional, managerial and senior administrative staff) and 24 per cent were manual staff. This was consistent with the relative proportion of manual and officer staff within the three departments surveyed.

Why women work

Contrary to popular opinion (and also to the organization's mythology, mentioned frequently by women in the group interviews and by men in the management interviews), the majority of women were 'breadwinners', either solely supporting themselves and their families, or joint earners of the family income. Only 8 per cent said their earnings were 'extra to essential family income'. The majority also gave as their reason for working 'to pursue a career' and 'self-fulfilment', characteristics more commonly associated with men than women. This suggests there may be little difference between the reasons why women and men work and the economic and emotional significance which they attach to their work.

Reasons for choosing their work

Seventy-four per cent worked full-time, 20 per cent worked part-time, and 6 per cent were job-sharing. Part-time workers were over-represented in this sample compared with the council as a whole, but this reflected the larger proportion of women part-time workers in the social services department. Of the women who worked part-time, 74 per cent said they did so for 'domestic' reasons (to care for their partner, children or other dependants).

Fourteen per cent of women actually said they chose the work they did because it enabled them to work part-time. Twenty-six per cent said they chose the work they did because it fitted in with their caring responsibilities. Most of these were home helps. Twelve per cent said it was the only work they were able to do or the only job they could get, and 22 per cent said they just happened to get into it. Thirty per cent said it was 'what they'd always wanted to do', 38 per cent said it 'was what they wanted to do now', and 34 per cent said it was what they were qualified to do.

There were no comparable survey statistics for men, but the management interviews with men suggested that men's job choices and career objectives were generally more directed and more focused than women's. Certainly the data suggest that women's choices of work are determined by a variety of external and ad hoc factors relating to domestic responsibilities, assumptions and stereotypes about women's work, and lack of training and low career expectations for women.

Barriers to career progression

Forty per cent of women had worked for the local authority for more than seven years and 21 per cent had been in their current jobs for more than seven years. Fifty-six per cent had applied for a job in the past two years and 78 per cent of those had failed to get it. While there were no comparable statistics for men, this appeared to be a very high failure rate, and data from the management interviews showed men to be more successful than women in getting jobs they applied for internally in the council.

Sixty per cent of the women surveyed said they were planning to change their jobs within the next two years, a factor regarded by the Institute of Manpower Studies as one of the more accurate measures of staff turnover in an organization (Bevan *et al.* 1990). It also suggests a likely high level of job dissatisfaction. When asked 'on balance' how satisfied they were with their jobs, 53 per cent said they were very or fairly satisfied, 34 per cent were neither satisfied nor dissatisfied, and 13 per cent were fairly or very dissatisfied. Thirty-seven per cent said they would prefer to be doing a different kind of job. This also suggests a high level of job dissatisfaction.

When asked why they had not applied for another job in the past two years or why they had failed to get jobs they had applied for, women gave the answers shown in Table 2.1 (per cents represent percentage of cases).

Table 2.1   Reasons for women not applying for or not getting another job

Reason	%
At a disadvantage because of job sharing	5
Lack of encouragement	8
Obstruction from supervisors	8
Sexist attitudes	8
Racist attitudes	9
Lack of confidence	24
Lack of interview or job-application skills	28
Lack of skills or qualifications necessary for the job	28

Again, while there were no survey data on the men in these departments, many of the men interviewed had 'leap-frogged' up the hierarchy, skipping grades, or using 'acting up' arrangements as a jumping-off point. The survey data were also validated by information provided by women in the group interviews.

Training

Sixty-nine per cent of women had been on training courses in the previous two years, about half of these (51 per cent) receiving qualifications training and half (49 per cent) having been on in-service training courses. This reflects the high level of commitment within the organization at that time to staff training as part of the council's Equal Opportunities Policy, and in particular the effects of the positive action training programme for black staff coordinated by the Race Relations Unit. However, when asked whether the training had assisted them to progress in their work 24 per cent said no, and 60 per cent said they needed training to do the kind of work they wanted to do.

Women were asked what training they needed in the next year to enable them to progress in their career or in their work and gave the replies shown in Table 2.2 as the areas in which they most needed training (per cents represent percentage of cases).

Table 2.2   Areas in which women felt they most needed training

Area	%
Supervisory skills	39
Senior management	36
Job application and interview skills	31
Report writing	31
Career planning	30
Presentation & public speaking skills	29
Confidence building	27
Financial management skills	25
Time management skills	24
Qualifications	17

There was an apparent correlation between women's inability to obtain the jobs they applied for and their perceived need for training. The areas which large proportions of women identified as training deficits were precisely those that would assist women into the senior management positions in which they were currently under-represented.

Discrimination

Twenty-eight per cent of respondents said they had experienced incidents of racial harassment or discrimination and 27 per cent said they had experienced harassment or discrimination on grounds of sex. However, only 9 per cent of those who had experienced harassment or discrimination had ever made a complaint and half said they had made no complaint because they had no faith that it would be treated seriously. Discrimination took the form of sexist attitudes and behaviour, some-times covert and sometimes explicit.

Childcare responsibilities

The survey showed that 68 per cent of the women who responded had children and 28 per cent were single parents. 25 per cent of women had children under the age of 5, 16 per cent had children aged 5–11, 12 per cent had children aged 11–16, and 47 per cent had children over the age of 16. For under-5s the most popular form of childcare currently used was childminders (35 per cent) and family members (26 per cent). Nineteen per cent used nurseries, 8 per cent used friends, 7 per cent nannies or au pairs, and 5 per cent used some other form of care. For after school and holiday care for over-5s, 37 per cent relied on family members and 11 per cent used childminders. In 26 per cent of cases the children went home from school alone and in 16 per cent of cases women worked part-time or flexitime in order to collect their children themselves.

Care of adult dependants

Eleven per cent of the sample said they were responsible for caring for dependent people other than children (defined as adults who cannot look after themeselves). This was consistent with national statistics available from carers' organizations on the proportion of women who were providing care for elderly and/or disabled people at that time. This was prior to the implementation of the NHS and Commu-nity Care Act 1990, following which the number of 'informal' carers increased, the majority of them being women.

Group interview findings

The group interview discussions focused on issues of childcare and the care of elderly and disabled people, on barriers to career development and promotion, on sexism, sex discrimination and the sexualizing of the workplace.

Childcare/eldercare

Concerns were frequently expressed about the quality and standards of childcare provision and the costs of childcare. Many women said that it was not financially worth coming to work and that they could earn more working as a childminder. Women on the lowest grades could not afford the weekly average of £55 (in 1990) for childcare. Women identified a need for workplace nurseries, for after school and holiday provisions. They commented on the lack of management support for women with childcare responsibilities: 'Men don't listen to the problems', they said. 'Mothers need to conceal their feelings about their children at work.'

Lack of management sympathy for child sickness and the discretionary status of special leave for sick dependants was a problem. Special leave was often not sanctioned or allowed only grudgingly, and women were forced to take annual leave or use flexitime to care for sick children. There was insufficient flexibility in hours of work, not enough flexitime, and core hours were 'too late' to enable the collection of children from school. Women said they could not 'plan their time as a parent', that there was a tension between mothering and work: that 'mothers were forced to stay at home or to put their career first and then drag the family along.' It was pointed out that 'Women take responsibility for children, men only help out.' Care of elders was an increasing problem for women and they felt the need for organizational recognition of the legitimacy of eldercare.

Problems were also identified for women without children, in particular the view held by men in the organization that women are not the breadwinners. Single women and women without children felt they were expected to make sacrifices to maintain their jobs and received contradictory messages from men: 'You work too hard, do too many hours', but 'I'm passing on this work, I need the report by tomorrow morning, reorganize your diary.'

Promotion/career development

There were many observations on sexism in the organization, such as comments from male bosses: 'If you don't flirt you won't get on', or 'Will you use your beautiful hands to type this up for me?' There was a consensus of view that 'to get on you really need to be a white male – or an honorary white male', and also a 'yes man'. Women who 'got on' were characterized as 'masculine' or aggressive. Women made it to middle management without difficulty, but then hit the 'glass ceiling' and found it hard to move beyond the lower principal officer (middle management) grades.

Women identified conflict between promotion and childcare responsibilities. More women would go for promotion, they thought, if there were suitable childcare facilities, and arrangements for school holidays. It was difficult for women with children to get promotion because of (male) management fears that they would take time out for childcare. They felt there was an assumption that women cannot combine motherhood and a career, and that women at work are seen as only second earners. 'Work is seen either as men's work or women's work and women are regarded as second earners.'

Managers do not encourage women to go for promotion, they said, or administrative staff to cross over into professions. They drew attention to the fact that 'admin. is dominated by women, but men are at the senior levels.' They thought women were better organizers and lateral thinkers than men, but management jobs were less attractive to women because they 'take you away from dealing with people' and consequently provide less job satisfaction. They believed that women did not find the 'politicizing' attractive and did not want to be in the role of 'talking down' to people.

A range of double standards was identified:

- Women have to be better than men to get the same job, so they hang back until they are really confident. Men go after jobs because they are after power.
- Women have to work harder to get to the same position as men and to maintain their position once there.
- When they are there, they are less powerful than men in the same position.

Male culture and sex-role stereotypes

Men at the top were described as white and able-bodied: 'The old school tie and the old boy's network operates.' 'There are cliques and politics', they said, and 'It's a question of who you know.' They referred to the 'all-male director's group': some, they said, were incompetent and maintained in their position by the women beneath them.

Women were 'cut out': they often did not receive key information, or information was shared elsewhere, and when women asked for information or challenged the missing information, men denied the issue of exclusion. 'Goalposts suddenly change without women being told,' they said. 'Women are not listened to in meetings', they observed. They felt that women talked in a different style, so their responses were edited out, and their comments were shot down, and that all the normal intercourse and interaction were between men.

Men, they thought, liked to keep women in certain 'servicing' roles: 'making the tea', a 'dumping ground for admin.' and 'bad news'. Men were often 'asking to be rescued'. Women were patronized: called 'darling' and 'love'.

They observed that women and black people were 'picked on' for not doing things, although lots of men were not doing the same things, and they were not picked on: 'Men could coast, women and black people couldn't.' The behaviour of women and black people was labelled and stereotyped to disempower members of these groups: there was always a focus on negatives not positives, and women rarely got a pat on the back. Women were labelled as aggressive if they asserted any right to the same entitlements as men.

Administrative work was downgraded, they thought: 'It's only admin.' There was no recognition of the skills and experience required for different kinds of work. Women's expertise – whatever it might be – was not respected, they thought: good communication skills, for example, were seen as 'only being friendly and sociable'. A skills analysis for home helps would be interesting, they thought, making explicit the often invisible and undervalued skills involved in the caring work women usually do. Transferable skills should be identified, and the supervisory process needed to recognize and encourage women's skills.

Work practices

Job-sharing was felt to reduce stress and was regarded as good in practice for women with childrearing responsibilities who could afford a period of time on a reduced income. But they felt there was only theoretical support for job-sharing in the council and, no will to make it work. Job-sharing was a barrier to getting on training courses. It was difficult for job-sharers to go for promotion; and there was a management belief that women would not do the job properly as job-sharers. They felt that expressing a desire to job-share was a disadvantage at interview even though adverts said 'Job-sharers are welcome.' Job-sharing was seen as 'skiving', they thought; 'not carrying your weight, not committed to the organization', even though in their experience job-sharers generally worked more hours than they were paid for without reimbursement.

There was a need, they thought, to re-examine how work is done and in particular where. They referred to the 'jacket on the back of the chair syndrome'; that is, the need to be seen at your desk to be regarded as working, and their perception that a man's jacket was evidence in itself of work. Working at home could be an advantage for women (though care needed to be taken to avoid the negative consequences of exploitation, isolation and lack of visibility), but there had been guidelines saying staff 'cannot work from home unless there are exceptional circumstances'.

Discrimination in recruitment

There was a general feeling that the recruitment procedures were corrupt: 'a question of who you know' and a belief that 'things are fixed before interviews put women off from applying.' They had observed that coaching was offered informally to some people for job interviews, providing practice in answering likely questions: these 'people' were rarely women. Interviews, they thought, were 'play acting' and depended on an ability to perform. Women lack confidence and needed training and opportunities to role play in preparation for interviews. Women were not prepared to 'creep', and wanted to be appointed on professional criteria. Often interview panels were all-male, and women saw this as a problem.

'If a panel was known to be racist, I wouldn't go for the interview', said one woman who felt that most recruitment panels were racist. Black people were regarded as being appointed for political purposes and not recognized for their skills. Some black people who were not competent were given jobs, they said: this was regarded as another aspect of racism and reflected negatively on the abilities of black people generally. They were cynical about the council's equal opportunities policy: 'Managers know the right things to say on equal opportunities, but don't mean it and don't implement it'.

Management interview findings

The interviews conducted with women and men managers in the three departments produced a wealth of information to support the data collected in the group interviews and the survey, and the material that emerged from the work history interviews revealed many obstacles facing women at work.

Women's work histories

Women with children had generally left full-time employment during the early childrearing years, returning part-time, often in 'home-based', child-related areas of work: to community work, childcare or playgroups, or as home helps. In the social services department, in particular, the 'career break' had provided an avenue into a first-time 'career' or an opportunity for a career change. A number of women, and particularly black women, had come into social services via nursing. Women's work histories were also characterized by the pursuit of qualifications. Women in management tended to be more qualified than the men, and to believe that they needed professional and management qualifications in order to get on. Continued pursuit of professional study was particularly noticeable amongst black women.

This study showed that women were very serious indeed about their careers and their career development, even if their 'careers' had been interrupted by childrearing and even though their career development had been 'irregular'. Although the men in this study did not, in fact, rigidly conform to conventional career paths, the women's career paths were much more fragmented due to managing work, childrearing and domestic responsibilities, and the women had generally done a much wider variety of different kinds of work prior to settling into a career path or professional area of work.

Men's career patterns

When it came to 'career development', men's progression appeared to be much faster and higher than women's. One senior male manager in the social services department had been promoted over and over again without ever being interviewed, although he had always worked in local authorities which purported to be 'equal opportunities employers'. In his words:

> In 1975 I was promoted to Team Leader. Just offered the job, no formal interview, no competition. Director called me in, 'You've done well! We've had our eye on you.' Offered another promotion in 1977: 'How would you feel about taking over Jane's job? Can you start next week?' Then later on, here, the informal pattern of my career continued and I was 'seconded' to a higher post, and then was promoted as part of 'interim management arrangements' and then 'acting up' – I can't remember ever having an interview.

While men 'leap-frogged' up the hierarchy, women did indeed conform to the adage: 'having to work twice as hard to get the same level'. 'They said I wasn't ready', said one woman who had failed to get the job she had been acting into, 'but in the same circumstances, they give the men the benefit of the doubt.' 'I've been here for three years', said another woman, 'and I'm still on grade PO1C, while a man who started at the same time as me at Scale 5 is now on PO1C.'

In the social services department, while the man quoted above rose to second-tier level without ever being interviewed, a woman in his department had acted into a second-tier post for two years 'working 90 hours a week', as she put it, but when it came to the permanent appointment, it went to a white man.

Sex discrimination

In one department, there were cases of a man and a woman both of whom had started at a similar age at the bottom (scale 1/2 in local government), both of whom had progressed fairly – and equally – rapidly to middle management level. Then they both 'acted up' into the same kinds of post in different parts of the department. When it came to permanent appointment, the man was selected straight away. But although she tried three times, the woman was rejected on each occasion.

On one of these I was present at the interviews in an observer capacity, and found that although she met all the criteria and clearly came out in front of the other candidates, the panel obstructed her appointment. Other members of the department confided (when interviewed as part of this research project) that it had been decided in advance that she should not get the job: 'A decision had been made not to appoint her before the interview was held.' It was 'rumoured' that she had had an affair with one of the councillors and it was said that she dressed 'like a tart'. These are crude but classic sexualizing and sexist stereotypes, and it seemed almost unbelievable that they were being used successfully to block a competent woman's career progression.

Sexual divisions of labour

Men confirmed the difficulties women experienced in combining family commitments and childrearing with 'getting on' at work. 'Having children hasn't been a barrier to my career, but it has to my wife's', said one. 'It is easier for me than my wife', said another, 'because of expectations of her.' And another: 'It's regarded as a hassle to accommodate women's needs.' A number of women said what they needed to be as successful as the men was a wife.

Certainly when asked who in their households took responsibility for cooking, cleaning, shopping, childcare and child sickness, all of the women said they did (in addition to their full-time employment), and all but one of the men said they did not. The one man who did share these domestic and childcare responsibilities did so 'as a matter of principle' but felt it put him at a disadvantage and under stress in his job.

Sexism

The men themselves – all first, second and third-tier officers – described a closed male culture at the top with very few 'windows of opportunity' for women. In particular, they identified 'blockages at the middle'. One said he could not account for why there were not more women at senior levels: 'Some of the most competent officers in the council are women in middle management, often much better organized than men', he said, and added without a trace of irony that 'Perhaps it is because male senior officers tend to protect their power base to a certain extent.' 'Women are judged quite differently in all aspects', said another. 'If I was asked to advise a young woman entering the department how to get to the top', said one, 'I would have to say "Don't bother".' Many of the men said they believed sexism was a serious problem in the organization.

One of the questions in the management interviews was: 'What advice would you give to the chief executive for dealing with sexism in the organization?' This produced many suggestions for positive action measures, but a (male) deputy director in one of the service departments simply said 'Resign', and a senior woman thought he needed to examine his own attitudes and behaviour. Someone described the management style at the top of the organization as a mixture of Billy Bunter and Basil Fawlty, and someone else refered to the 'Boys' Own' philosophy of management at the top. Some described the senior men as macho: others just called them cowboys. None of the analogies was complimentary, and all were descriptions of some version of masculinity.

Participant observation findings

My role as 'participant observer' in the organization over a period of five years provided a further source of data on the culture of the organization as experienced by women.

Women's networks

At one stage women in senior management took steps to counteract the effects of the male culture by establishing a caucus of 'senior women' within the organization, meeting as women for mutual support, and to develop initiatives to improve the position of women in the organization. The group met informally for a period of months (over lunch, bringing food to share) and drafted a formal 'constitution' with a view to obtaining recognition and 'approval' for the Senior Women's Group from directors, and their permission for the group to participate as part of the formal decision-making processes. It was proposed that committee reports and papers be sent routinely to the Senior Women's Group for comment on gender implications, and that the group might put forward its own proposals on gender initiatives in report form to directors. It was a modest proposal. A small delegation of women (carefully selected to avoid conveying any 'radical' messages) took the proposals to the chief executive. The meeting was polite, but the group was never included on any internal mailing list, never integrated into the system and never consulted.

Experience has shown that women's networks and support groups are an effective way for women to counteract both institutional sexism and some of the effects of sexism they have internalized. But they are notoriously difficult to maintain: although the men themselves meet together formally and informally all the time (in corridors, lavatories, clubs, pubs and sports grounds), women meeting together is regarded as threatening to men. The senior women's initiative failed to introduce the voice of women into the male discourse at decision-making levels in the organization, and eventually even the 'conversation' of women over lunch was silenced.

The 'glass ceiling'

The senior women's network also lost momentum as senior women left or lost their jobs. A number of women in senior positions left the organization having reached the 'glass ceiling' of promotion and been unable to break through. This would not, in itself, be an indicator of institutional sexism: there will always be people who find promotion by moving to other organizations. But women in this local authority almost never moved above the 'glass ceiling' and women were almost never appointed from outside the organization to fill the top jobs.

There was, for example, a third-tier woman in one of the departments who was not appointed to a deputy director post, but who was then immediately snatched up for the same post in another local authority. One of the women described earlier who failed to be appointed to the post she had been 'acting into' for several years, left to become the director of a national charity. Some women left 'under a cloud', with unsubstantiated, rumoured reputations for 'not being very good'. That two of these women went on to become a director and an assistant director in other local authorities, and others to 'good' jobs elsewhere, suggests that the rumours were unfounded and their 'poor' reputations undeserved.

A white male in his 'golden decade' of 30–40 was recruited to head a new unit. There was an excellent woman on the shortlist, but she was not expected to get the job. It was said that 'he would fit in nicely', and he did. His boss was known to feel 'uncomfortable' around women, and described by one senior woman as 'pathologically unable to interact socially or professionally with women'.

Divisions between women

The senior women's network also highlighted – and fell victim to – some of the ways in which divisions between women can operate against women's interest. There was, for example, some reluctance to agree and to adopt leadership roles within the group in an effective way, and there were key women who did not participate. These included the minority of women who had been successful in the organization or in their careers without apparent difficulty, who did not feel they had experienced any discrimination and did not believe 'gender' was a problem. There were also some senior women who had succeeded by adopting male modes of identity and behaviour and consequently did not identify 'as women' with other women in the organization (neither their peers, nor women lower down in the organization). Their philosophy might have been described as 'Every man for himself, be he male or female.'

Institutionalized sexism

There were pockets of extreme sexism in the authority which were well known but about which nothing was done, and some women left as a result of experiences of sexual harassment and sex discrimination. As a senior manager with designated responsibility for women's employment, I had contact with a number of women who left the organization, many of whom had previously taken out grievances about their treatment without success.

There was a woman with a PhD in her field, and well qualified for the relatively low-level post for which she had been recruited, who was told her work was not regarded as up to standard and forced to leave. Another woman left quietly without making a fuss, having resigned without another job to go to at the height of the recession. A keen, enthusiastic and talented young woman with a range of professional qualifications in her field had a 'breakdown', went on extended sick leave, and refused to return to work in the department she had left. She returned to work on a secondment in another department where she produced work of a consistently high and highly regarded standard. She finally left with the offer of two new jobs to choose from.

Another woman with an excellent track record in her work found herself increasingly overlooked in the allocation of high-profile work projects and felt that she was belittled by her boss in front of her staff. She had taken out grievances without success and was preparing a case for the Equal Opportunities Commission claiming sex discrimination when she obtained a new job, a promotion to a senior position with another authority. She had been labelled a 'bad employee': she excelled in her new appointment. These 'cases' included black, Asian and Irish women.

Women who used the sexual harassment procedures also came to grief. One, having brought her case with the support of her director, resigned her job after the man was found guilty of harassment because she was expected to resume working with him. He was 'popular' with the male managers in his department and regarded as 'good at his job', and had therefore received a lenient response to his sexual harassment. But she too – a woman in a senior position in a non-traditional area of work – was universally regarded as an excellent performer and high flier. She left. He stayed.

In another case of sexual harassment and sex discrimination, the perpetrator was found guilty at the investigation stage. Between the investigation and the disciplinary hearings, the woman was victimized in the workplace and many of the witnesses against the perpetrator changed their stories or refused to testify against him (absenting themselves on the day of the hearing through sickness or annual leave). This tactic was so obviously obstructive that it worked against their intentions and the perpetrator was found guilty at the disciplinary stage and sacked. But the woman suffered from stress and depression as a result of hostility at work and was forced to take long-term sick leave. She felt she would have to find another job rather than return to work.

Although there was a formal organizational policy and a procedure for dealing with sexual harassment, it was not in women's interests to use them. In spite of the many informal complaints and formal grievances, most of the victims left their jobs, while the perpetrators remained 'in post' and usually very highly regarded by their male peers.

GENDER AND ORGANIZATIONAL CULTURE

The results of this research provide an empirical account of organizational life as experienced by women. It is a detailed and graphic picture of routine discrimination and disadvantage based on gender at every level and in every dimension of attitude, belief and behaviour in the organization. There is now a substantial literature on gender and organizations consistent with the results of this research, and a number of explanations have been offered to account for these gender factors.

Gender in organizations

Clegg (1981) includes gender in the 'category of extra-organizational rules' that govern behaviour: attitudes about the nature and relative social worth of women which are reflected and reinforced within organizations in such things as low pay, processes of deskilling, the construction of dual labour markets and low status work. Women's domestic responsibilities are the 'category of extra-organizational rules' most often used to account for the sex-segregated and 'inferior' position of women in organizations. This study has certainly shown how 'shoppping, cooking, cleaning and childcare' do pose real restrictions on women's ability to work full-time and participate fully in organizational life. It has also shown the freedom men have (whether they are single or with wives to carry out their domestic responsibilities for them) to work long and inflexible hours.

But a recent British study by the Institute of Manpower Studies of women managers and career progression showed that women's 'careers fall behind those of men quite early – certainly too early for it to be blamed on having children' (Jackson and Hirsh 1991: 12). The study drew on a number of sources to show that 'women graduates underachieve in the labour market compared with men,... had low status jobs, more limited promotion prospects and earned significantly less than men.' In the Civil Service 'even "fast track" women are promoted more slowly than their male peer group' (p. 13). This suggests that 'extra-organizational' explanations are insufficent to account for women's organizational status.

Clegg (1981) also sees gender as an integral factor within organizations. Women may be excluded or undervalued through the definition and value attached to different skills and through 'the social-regulative rules' of organizations. Morgan identifies some of the ways that gender operates within organizations to the disadvantage of women:

It often makes a great deal of difference if you're a man or a woman! Many organisations are dominated by gender-related values that bias organisational life in favour of one sex over another. Thus . . . organisations often segment opportunity structures and job markets in ways that enable men to achieve positions of prestige and power more easily than women, and often operate in ways that produce gender-related biases in the way organisational reality is created and sustained on a day-to-day basis. This is most obvious in situations of open discrimination and various forms of sexual harassment, but often pervades the culture of an organisation in a way that is much less visible.

(Morgan 1986: 178)

Mills (1988a) sees gender as a 'crucial yet neglected aspect of organizational analysis' (p. 351), 'permeating not only extra-organizational rules, but each and every area of rule bound behaviour' (1989: 33). He cites male domination of the organizational world in the form of ownership and control (Bilton et al. 1983), positions of status and authority (Wright et al. 1982), cultural values (Morgan 1986) and hegemony (Mills 1988b) as 'restricting the entry of women into the labour force', filtering women into a narrow range of occupations, channelling them into low pay/low status work, and overall reinforcing notions of female inferiority (p. 35). Ferguson (1984) describes how in the context of male organizational power 'women learn the role of the subordinate, and that role can easily become self perpetuating' (p. 94). Mills (1989) argues that women's roles as wives and mothers are used to restrict/throw doubt upon women's ability to be organizationally effective. Mills describes how the 'social regulations of organizations may edit women out of the frame of someone who fits in or is fully committed' because, as Barrett (1988) argues, women are viewed as having a primary commitment to a domestic life outside the organization.

And yet a British Institute of Management study of UK managers found that there appears to be little foundation for the popular myth that women are less ambitious and career oriented than men, and that if anything women appear to be more ambitious and committed to their career than many men (Metcalfe 1989). The authors of the study (Bevan et al. 1990) found that older women who had taken career breaks and whose children were older showed a strong interest in career progression again. They also observed that this ambition was not fully appreciated by the managers of such women.

Lemmer (1991), in a small-scale study of married women aged 35 and older, who had interrupted employment for a minimum period of two years for the purpose of family formation before re-entering the labour market, found that:

Although the women did not regard the years at home as part of an unfolding career, in many cases a vocational career was evident in their exceptional commitment to voluntary activities, in providing back up to a husband's career, in part time work or in a successful return to further education. The importance of work in their lives increased significantly after re-entry, when a clearer and more stable pattern of career progression began to emerge with an accompanying commitment to work. At this stage, notwithstanding the irregular nature of career development, the women perceived themselves as having careers. Although their career development failed to conform to the standard pattern based on the male model, they regarded themselves as involved in the process of their own career development, took their work seriously and planned to continue working until retirement age. This picture of women's careers endorses the call for a wider conceptualisation of 'career' from a female perspective.

(Lemmer 1991: 14–15)

Mills (1989) refers to the variety of organizational practices that can 'signal to females that they are not regarded as full organizational members' (p. 39) and cites a number of sources to illustrate these. Simpson *et al.* (1987), for example, show how women are denied access to important organizational networks, especially where these are rooted in male-centred extra-curricular activities. Crompton and Jones (1984) identify organizational belonging as depending upon involvement in officially sanctioned but male-oriented social activities. Noe (1988) points out that the availability of mentors may be largely confined to males. Riley (1983) refers to the motivating language of the organization in terms of male-oriented metaphors. Mills (1989) reviews this literature and concludes that sex discrimination is embedded within the cultures of organizations. Smith (1992) describes how this in turn creates inequality of access for women to employment at senior levels in organizations.

Culture theory

Culture theory has been a useful way of understanding what happens in organizations and specifically in local government. It has been used to explain some of the dynamics and mechanisms of organizational behaviour and how organizational culture influences the practices and values of organizations (Hampden-Turner 1990). Most of Handy's (1985) categories of organizational culture can be found in local government. Primarily it is a role culture (bureaucratic, based on procedures and position power), but there are also power cultures (control exercised by individuals at the centre), person cultures (when the organization is subordinate to the individual) and task cultures (influence based on expertise).

What has not been made explicit is that all of Handy's cultural categeories are in fact also gendered. Men are largely in the roles and positions of power, where they often operate as an exclusive and closed male club. The power culture replicates itself, with men choosing the 'right people', who can think in the same way they think, and exercising control largely through the selection of key individuals: ones like themselves. The operation of an 'old boy's network' within the organization may be seen as another example of power culture within the role culture. Person cultures are peopled by men and produce policies, procedures and practices defined by male values, experience and expectations. Task culture, operating within the role culture, is often based on competition and male bonding.

Role culture itself has often been characterized in male terms. Hofstede (1984) describes 'masculinity' as a characteristic of corporate culture, an analysis based on gender stereotypes which in practice function to exclude and to subordinate women. Handy (1985) gives an illustration of the ideal corporate highflier as needing 'to proceed intuitively, to know by instinct' what to do (p. 204). It is only possible to know by instinct what one is 'born to' or 'bred for' and familiar with. Men will be more comfortable in institutional roles, not because these come 'naturally' to males, but because they will have more experience in those cultures, which have been constructed around the 'male chronology' of full-time, uninterrupted employment and freedom from domestic responsibilities. Maccoby's four corporate types – the 'Jungle Fighter', the 'Company Man', the 'Gamesman', the 'Craftsman' – are all masculine stereotypes (Maccoby 1976), as are Kanter's corporate characters: the 'organization man', the 'corprocat', the 'maverick', and the 'cowboy', in particular, who 'lives in a world of immediate action... wants to seize every opportunity, betting big... strains limits... breaks rules and gets away with it' and 'shoots from the hip' (Kanter 1989: 360).

Conceptualizing the gender culture

The literature provides a picture of organizational culture as gendered and discrimination based on gender as embedded in organizational culture. But it falls short of conceptualizing a 'gender culture' *per se* within organizations and fails to capture the systematic power relations which are gendered and which permeate the culture and practice of organizations. Role culture – the dominant, visible, formal framework of local government within which task and power cultures operate on an informal, ad hoc, acknowledged basis – is governed by 'rules and regulations'. Gender culture by contrast is unarticulated and usually rendered invisible by virtue of being regarded as perfectly 'natural'. Its rules and regulations do not have to be written down and published: the gender culture is just one of 'the ways they do things' in organizations.

This study identified the many ways 'things were done' in the organization which account for why women fail to achieve their potential, their ambitions and parity with men in senior management positions. These included:

- the long hours expected and required of senior managers, which were incompatible with women's domestic responsibilities;
- lack of encouragement for women from male managers and sometimes positive obstruction (one male manager had withdrawn a woman's application for a new job within the organization without consulting her);
- women's lack of confidence to go for positions of power;
- the ways that the interview process disadvantages women;
- the way that women are handicapped by the withholding of information (one confessed to keeping abreast of information crucial to her work by snooping around on her boss's and other senior male managers' desks);
- women's isolation and lack of support;

- the suspicion and hostility towards women networking;
- the prevalence of sexual stereotypes;
- the incidence of sexual harassment;
- the closed, hostile and indifferent male culture at the top of the organization.

There was also evidence of the unequal sexual division of labour in the home, with women carrying out the majority of domestic labour as well as paid employment. The culture of this organization was characterized by its cowboys on the one hand (the macho culture), and on the other by its 'hobbled horses' (representing the position of women).

The data leave little doubt about the nature and extent of discrimination and disadvantage experienced by women working in organizations. The data also make explicit the cultural as well as structural and practical obstacles that exist, and the extent to which gendered power relations determine the practices and culture of the organization. Taken together, the literature on gender and organizations and the results of this research suggest that there is a 'gender culture' common to organizations, which has a number of characteristics relating to both 'extra-'and 'intra-'organizational factors, and to the complex and dynamic relationship between these 'public' and 'private' spheres.

Characteristics of the gender culture

The 'gender culture' is characterized by a number of distinct and interrelated features.

Hierarchical and patriarchal

Men are hierarchically in the positions of power and influence. They control information and access to information, the decision-making processes and the decisions that are made. Women are organizationally subordinate and socially, politically and economically subordinate within the organization. Men are the gate-keepers and control the access of women to training, promotion and career progression. In this study, although men were numerically in the minority, they were positionally dominant, whatever their race. Hierarchically within the organization, women were located in the lower-grade administrative, clerical and secretarial posts.

Sex-segregated

Women are generally to be found in the low paid, low status sex-segregated work. In this study women were located in the cleaning, catering and caring areas of work: social work, home care, teaching. Men were found in the 'macho' world of housing and in the traditional areas of male work such as architecture, engineering and planning in the development department. Within the areas defined traditionally as women's work, where men were a numerical minority, as in the social services department, they were still to be found in the senior positions of power.

Sexual divisions of labour

Sex-segregated work is one reflection of the sexual division of labour within organizations. Another is the impact of such 'extra-organizational' factors as childcare, eldercare and women's domestic responsibilities on their ability to work full-time, on their continuity of employment and on their career opportunities. This study showed that women undertook the majority of the domestic labour and childcare responsibilities and the men did not, leaving them free to focus their time and energy on work and to progress their careers with the 'extra-organizational' support of their wives.

Sex-stereotyped

Consistent with, and also no doubt as a consequence of, their roles and responsibilities in the sexual division of labour and their largely sex-segregated work and subordinate status, women are perceived, characterized and stereotyped as inherently fit for their sexually determined roles and status and unfit for the positions of power and influence held by men. In this study, women were commonly found to be, in the organization as in the home, in roles of servicing men: sex role stereotyped as the tea makers or helpmates or adornments.

Sex-discriminatory

Women are denied access to and prevented from achieving parity with men in positions of power and influence in the organization. Barriers operate at points of entry (recruitment), in selection for training and the provision of appropriate training, and in career progression. Sex discrimination in employment is illegal. This study documented a number of cases of women who experienced discrimination on grounds of sex, both covert and overt, in recruitment and career progression.

A sexualized environment

The use of pornography and 'pin ups,' and sexual and sexualized language, creates a wider social and a workplace culture which sexualizes women. This inhibits their ability to be treated as fully human, equal and competent, diminishes their opportunity to be taken seriously in their work, and makes them vulnerable to sexual harassment and assault. In this study, information was not sought directly about sexual violence or abuse, but evidence was volunteered of sexualized 'banter' and of sexual harassment.

Sexual harassment

Sexual harassment is usually defined as repeated, unwanted and unreciprocated sexual contact, which can take the form of leering, ridicule, embarrassing remarks or jokes, unwelcome comments about dress or appearance, deliberate abuse, demands for sexual favours or physical assaults. In this study women experienced sexual harassment in various forms relating to comments on appearance and dress, and unsolicited sexual attention.

Sexist

Sexism is reflected in attitudes and behaviour, in language and practice. In this study, inappropriate emphasis on aspects of femininity and sexuality was commonly used in ways that defined and maintained subordinate and servicing roles, and women and men alike described the sexism that operated in the organization, whereby women were regarded as inferior to, less valuable than men, and less valued by men.

Misogynist

Misogyny is usually defined as hatred of women. It has become acceptable to talk about 'sexism' and 'male culture'. It would probably be regarded as 'extremist' to talk about the culture of this organization as misogynist, but in this study, there was evidence that women were positively disliked, invisible as 'people' and regarded negatively as 'women'.

Resistant to change

Cockburn (1991) found in her study of four large organizations (an industry, a trade union, the Civil Service and a local authority) that men's resistance to sex equality had effectively subverted the objectives of the equal opportunities agendas and maintained the obstacles 'in the way of women'. In this study, the failure of the senior women's network to have even the slightest influence on the male leadership cabal was one example of the power of the male culture to resist change and to protect itself from including women or women's issues.

Power is gendered

Whether power in an organization is determined by role, position, person or task, it is always gendered; and however it is exercised, the power in organizations is male. Ironically, men appear to be oblivious to the power they have and paradoxically appear to feel powerless to address and redress the subordination of women at work.

Individually there were men in this study who indicated that they would like to make changes, but the rituals and practices of male bonding and the ethos of the male culture made collective male action against sexism and sex discrimination very difficult indeed.

One very senior male manager in the organization was unusual in the many ways that he demonstrated that he was principled, committed to equal opportunities, astute in his awareness and understanding of the origins and negative effects of sexism (and racism), and active in supporting women to overcome institutional barriers. But, he confessed, it was in fact the case that he was often in the company of men at the top of the organization where sexist, sex-stereotyped and sexualized remarks about women were not uncommon. He was, he said, ashamed to say that he never – absolutely never – challenged these attitudes, beliefs and behaviour. And he knew that he never would. If he did, he would in effect cease to be 'one of the boys', and much as he wanted to take a stand on behalf of women, he could not bring himself to break ranks, and could not bear the thought of being on the outside of the charmed circle of men. In this moment of unguarded honesty, he captured the essence of male power (and powerlessness) at the heart of the gender culture.

The gender culture in other organizations is unlikely to take precisely the same form as it did in this local authority, but it is likely to include all of these characteristics in some form, mediated by other local, cultural and institutional factors and the leadership values that direct and contribute to shaping each individual organization. It is most unlikely that an organization exists without a gender culture characterized to a greater or lesser extent by the features identified in this research. Acknowledging and articulating the rules and regulations of the particular gender culture in an organization is probably a prerequisite of successful organizational change.

REFERENCES

Barrett, M. (1988) *Women's Oppression Today*. London: Verso.

Bevan, S. (1990) *Staff Retention: A Manager's Guide*. Institute of Manpower Studies Report No. 203. Brighton: IMS.

Bevan, S., Buchan, J. and Hayday, S. (1990) *Women in Hospital Pharmacy*. Institute of Manpower Studies Report No. 182. Brighton: IMS.

Bilton, T., Bonnett, K., Jones, P., Stanworth, M., Sheard, K. & Webster, A. (1983) *Introductory Sociology*. London: Macmillan.

Clegg, S. (1981) 'Organisation and control'. *Administrative Science Quarterly*, 26, 545–62.

Cockburn, C. (1991) *In the Way of Women: Men's Resistance to Sex Equality in Organisations*. London: Macmillan.

Crompton, R. and Jones, G. (1984) *White Collar Proletariat*. London: Macmillan.

Ferguson, K. E. (1984) *The Feminist Case Against Bureacracy*. Philadelphia, PA: Temple University Press.

Hampden-Turner, C. (1990) *Corporate Culture: From Vicious to Virtuous Circles*. London: Hutchinson.

Handy, C. (1985) *Understanding Organizations*. London: Penguin.

Hofstede, G. (1984) *Culture's Consequences*. London: Sage.

Jackson, C. and Hirsh, W. (1991) 'Women managers and career progression: the British experience'. *Women in Management Review and Abstracts*, 6(2), 10–16.

Kanter, R. M. (1989) *When Giants Learn To Dance*. New York: Simon & Schuster.

Lemmer, E. M. (1991) 'Untidy careers: occupational profiles of re-entry women'. *International Journal of Career Management*, 3 (1), 8–16.

Maccoby, R. (1976) *The Gamesman: The New Corporate Leaders*. New York: Simon & Schuster.

Metcalfe, A. B. (1989) 'What motivates managers? An investigation by gender and sector of employment'. *Public Administration*, 67, 95–108.

Mills, A. J. (1988a) 'Organization, gender and culture'. *Organization Studies*, 9(3), 351–69.

Mills, A. J. (1988b) 'Organizational acculturation and gender discrimination'. In Kresl, P. K. (ed.), *Canadian Issues X(1) – Women and the Workplace*. Montreal: Association of Canadian Studies/International Council for Canadian Studies.

Mills, A. J. (1989) 'Gender, sexuality and organization theory'. In Hearn, J., Sheppard, J., Tancred-Sheriff, P. and Burrell, G. (eds), *The Sexuality of Organization*. London: Sage.

Morgan, G. (1986) *Images of Organization*. London: Sage.

Noe, R. A. (1988) 'Women and mentoring: a review & research agenda'. *Academy of Management Journal*, 13(1), 65–78.

Riley, P. (1983) 'A structuralist account of political culture'. *Administrative Science Quarterly*, 28, 414–37.

Simpson, S., Mccarrey, M. & Edwards, H. P. (1987) 'Relationship of supervisors' sex role stereotypes to performance evaluation of male and female subordinates in nontraditional jobs'. *Canadian Journal of Administrative Sciences*, 4(1), 15–30.

Smith, L. (1992) 'Banging your head against the glass ceiling'. *Guardian*, 16 September.

Wright, E. C., Costell, C., Hacken, D. and Sprague, J. (1982) 'The American class structure'. *American Sociological Review*, 47(6), 709–26.

Chapter 3

Men and locations of power
Why move over?

Kate French

This chapter, based on an action research project in a local authority (see Chapter 8), identifies the ways in which senior male managers contribute to the shaping and continuation of an organization's culture. It explores the relationships between organizational culture, the structural arrangements of bureaucracies and the organization of work, and goes on to assess the possibilities of change.

Do men want to share their locations of power and influence with women? A large scale research project was under way in a local authority when an invitation by senior men in the housing department offered an opportunity to extend the research on women's employment and career prospects. The senior team of that department were all men and they were concerned that women were stuck at middle management levels. They wanted to know why. The results of the council-wide local authority research project are recorded elsewhere in this volume (Itzin, Chapters 2 and 8). I want to focus here on some of the themes that emerged from the in-depth interviews with male senior managers.

Before I do so, I want to comment on my personal perspective and the experience that I brought to this work. I had had senior management experience in an embattled local government department in the throes of radical change. I was highly committed to effecting change in the department and I worked long hours in my attempts to do so. I was the only female manager in that senior management team, and previously I had worked for another local authority where the gender balance of the middle-management team was equal. I was divorced and I had chosen not to have children. Much of my satisfaction from life was derived from the public sphere of work. In this way I was typical of the senior managers in social services departments at assistant director level, who from recent research findings are single in status and do not have children (Foster 1987). I had a powerful role model in my mother, who had been the main family breadwinner as a headmistress (at an exceptionally young age) and who did everything else besides. I was expected to follow suit.

From my own life and career experience, I have been left with the problem of of how organizational change can be achieved in a way which maximizes both the experience and skills of women at the same time as maximizing organizational performance. As a management consultant and researcher over the last seven years I have worked extensively on management performance and gender and organizational change issues. A large area of this work has been with women managers, both working on their management development needs, and researching into barriers in organizations that affect opportunities for women.

Many women have utilized training and management development programmes to initiate change for themselves and have developed a political awareness of the need to manage up and out in order to succeed. In terms of achieving incremental change through individual and group actions by women themselves, women have reported that the impact of this work has encouraged them to think strategically and politically about their futures. Yet we know from a review of equal opportunity policies in the 1980s (Coyle 1989) that the impact of those policies and the training and development work stemming from them has failed to make any significant impact on organizations and the position of women in them.

I remain dissatisfied with progress. I am left with the question of what to do about men. They remain in the predominant locations of power and I wonder whether there are sufficient levers for change to alter this position. What, if anything, would motivate men to develop and change organizations into more women friendly places? Women may manage up (where most men are) and manage around men and sometimes manage in collaboration with men to develop their working potential. Yet by and large men continue to dominate organizations through positions of power and mechanisms of influence. Organizations in their structures, working arrangements and modes of service delivery continue to serve the interests of men's lives. These were some of the questions and dilemmas that the research project gave me an opportunity to explore. The particular interviews with men in control of the housing department presented an opportunity to explore how they were contributing, if at all, to the existence of the glass ceiling phenomenon. The themes that did emerge from this small part of the overall research project indicated some ways in which a group of men, highly committed to concepts of social justice and equality of opportunity, constructed and operated a glass ceiling.

There are three major themes that emerged from the interviews. The first concerned the way in which the senior men influenced the culture of the organization, 'the way we do things around here' (Schermerhorn et al. 1985: 103). The second concerns the nature of status and power afforded by participation in the public sphere of work, and the perceived lack of status of the private sphere of domestic life. The third concerns the apparent rationality of structure and processes in the organization and its relationship to the sexuality of organizational life. All themes are considered in relation to the impact on opportunities for women.

In the final section of this chapter, I want to pose some questions about implications for change with particular reference to the radical reform of public sector service provision.

The research was an action research project and the interviews were conducted using a semi-structured questionnaire. The in-depth interviews with the seven most senior managers of the Housing Directorate formed a small part of the overall study. One manager was black, the others white. They were all male.

THEMES FROM THE RESEARCH

How senior men influenced the culture of the organization and its implications

Organizational culture is a term used to describe 'systems of shared values (what is important) and beliefs (how things work) that create behavioural norms (the way we do things around here) to guide the activities of organizational members' (Schermerhorn *et al.* 1985: 103). The type of bureaucratic structure of the department and council, with its rational and formal processes and procedures, in part determines one aspect of the culture. People who have a stake in the department, the members of the council, the managers, staff and users all create a culture through their attitudes, actions and opinions. This creates another aspect of the culture. Those in positions of leadership and power have much influence on what is and is not done, and how things are done.

There were several noticeable aspects of how things were done that emerged from the interviews. The men conveyed a strong sense of commitment, energy and enthusiasm for their work and the services that they produced. There was a powerful sense of belonging to a team and an enjoyment of the crises, problems and pace of change they encountered. This was in strong contrast to other senior managers and teams in the rest of the council. In individual interviews several of the men talked of the shared values that had motivated their careers and their commitment to the work. They spoke with passion about their desire to achieve greater equity and social justice. There was a missionary style of dedication and two members of the team had in their distant past had strong religious commitments. There was, in fact, the embodiment of what some management writers have prescribed for new management teams: strong shared values, highly motivated, fast and fluid communication between them, love of the challenge of change, hard work and task centredness (Kanter 1989; Peters 1987). What kind of culture did this produce?

The aspect most of the interviewees mentioned was the exceptionally long hours that team members put in. One team member described his life as akin to that of a 'travelling salesman': although he returned home to his partner and children late every evening, he regarded his time from Monday morning to Friday night as totally committed to work. He was not 'present' in the domestic sphere during the week. In recognition of this, he gave his time fully to his family at weekends and severely limited any weekend working. Some reported an implicit sense of competition around the hours worked ('You should speak to B., he virtually lives here!'). There was pride in this style of working, although the most recent recruit to the team was less enthusiastic about its impact on his domestic life. The common practice of putting in exceptionally long hours (plus extensive travel on top for some) in addition to some weekend working seemed to be part of the notions of what it takes to work in housing. Several of the managers commented that you had to be hard and tough to work in the department, both out at the area offices dealing with tenants with complaints, and at the corporate centre. Some of the senior managers had chosen housing to work in rather than social work, describing it as the 'hard' end of that sort of social market. One interviewee described the culture as 'combative and competitive and macho in language'.

The rigour of long hours had some positive side effects for the team members. One was the sense of camaraderie amongst the team, another the strong sense of belonging to the 'club'. Stories were told with warmth of take-away meals at unsocial hours shared across the conference table littered with papers. One had the sense of a constant social drama taking place, the team being a close knit core.

The dynamism, pride and sense of belonging were strongly conveyed by all the individual managers. The ways in which the team related to each other to achieve organizational purpose and tasks can be said to constitute the 'social regulative rules'(Clegg 1981). Clegg found that what was at stake in being a fully accepted member of an organization was doing the job in the accepted mode rather than having the skills to do a job:

> For managers of organisations this is usually stated as a problem of commitment, of morale and of motivation and this colours attitudes to recruitment, training promotion and involvement in the organisation. To enter, prosper and survive in the organisation can be dependent on how one is viewed by decision makers – who will 'fit in' and be a committed person.
>
> (Clegg 1981)

To be 'full' team members, women would have to fit in with the social regulative rules. One interviewee reflected in a frank way that although interviews were run on equal opportunity lines, in the back of his mind he would silently scrutinize all women applicants as to their age, likelihood of marriage and childbearing status. He said he thought his colleagues did the same, but would not tell me so. He would be anxious about the impact of a woman's partner's or her children's demands on her potential work performance, motivation and commitment. In the light of the hours dedicated by these managers to their job and their assumption that this was the way to work in housing, this attitude does not come as a surprise. Implicit in this is that women would be reluctantly appointed or encouraged for promotion opportunities and that the equal opportunities interviewing methods did not stand as a barrier to discriminatory practice.

Other aspects of the wider research project, and other research sources, have shown that many women are deterred from moving to senior management by this style of working by both male and female senior managers who are at the top of organizations. Many women cannot see how to balance multiple demands from the domestic sphere with those on senior managers. In addition, the quality of life of those in senior management roles appears poor to others.

Power and the senior management role

Like most organizations, the housing department reflected in microcosm the gender bias of society as a whole. In other words, the sphere of public work and activities is deemed of high status and cultural value, and the domestic sphere of low status. Hence men's activities have a higher status than those of women. From these interviews there was no evidence that men were queuing up to enter the domestic sphere in preference to their roles in the public sphere. There were, however, several concerns expressed by the men about their way of life; concerns about isolation outside the work team, fears of their relationships foundering (one had), and anxiety about the individual sense of emptiness experienced in their current lifestyle. One interviewee feared that without the constant adrenalin from the excitement of crisis-ridden work, he would fall into complete apathy and not know what to do with his time. He wondered if he would stay in bed all day. Others expressed tension between the demands of work and their parental roles.

This was the downside of their mode of work. Asked whether they would want to spend more time at home, most responded positively, particularly so that they could see more of their children. When asked how much time, most wanted an hour or two more a day. When presented with the findings from the interviews, they were all very clear that they would not wish to swop roles with their partners, and recognized that they were in a much more exciting, stimulating and challenging place at work than they would be at home. They enjoyed the power afforded by their roles at work. Women as well as men who are senior managers have noted the pleasure that this can bring (Rabbats 1993).

The contributions of their partners in the support given to sustain their career development and current working practices were warmly acknowledged without exception. Those who had partners all said that their partners either worked part-time in paid employment or worked full-time in their household. It is perhaps not coincidental that senior women managers, when asked what they need to support them in their careers, have looked towards the male model of management and said 'I need a wife!' (Allan *et al.* 1992).

The men simply had no experience of trying to juggle roles between the two spheres, and reported that they did not want it. They were asked if they would like to work part-time or on a job share basis. They said they would not, and certainly did not see how it could be worked. When specifically questioned on the barriers that they thought women faced, the interviewees apart from one interviewee with a partner pursuing her career, had no reported perception of the difficulties that women may encounter.

Women seeking to be 'full' organizational members in this department were faced with a problematic situation. The difficulties of balance between the public and domestic spheres of activity were seen as belonging to women and being largely up to women to solve. Any tension experienced by women would at the same time risk them being discredited as competent organizational managers. There was no discussion by the men interviewed of altering their own working practices to create a more equal balance of time between the two spheres, in spite of their acknowledgement of some problems for them. Indeed, they reported a dislike of any job share arrangements and were concerned about maternity leave absences in the department. As already noted, they did not want such options for themselves. Their focus was single minded. They were concerned with coping with the workload and turning the department around to improve services, which a recent Mori poll had highlighted as being poorly regarded by the tenants. They wanted full-time workers who could be there on a reliable basis to shift the workload; in other words, people working as they did for long hours.

It had appeared that they might have wanted to create more flexible working practices initially, because they had advertised one set of professional jobs for term-time working only in order to attract women into these posts. When this was explored in the interviews, it proved to be a measure introduced in response to a national shortage of those professionals. The motivation was related to organizational efficiency, not to enabling women with children to gain access to employment opportunities.

Some understanding of the dilemma for women was encountered by the one interviewee who had a partner who wanted to return to full-time work, by a black manager who drew parallels between the discrimination faced by women and that faced by black workers, and elsewhere in the larger study by a male manager who had several years' experience as a single parent. The last of these was noted by staff for his ability to create flexible working practices for those with childcare responsibilities.

The bureaucratic structure as asexual

The housing department at that time typified a bureaucratic organization. Such organizations are noted for rationality; for fairness in their systems, with agreed codes of practice, job specifications and job descriptions; and for an emphasis on rules of procedure and contractual arrangements.

Arguably this would be the ideal type of organization within which women and other people who suffer discrimination should flourish. There is an emphasis on the post holders, not the people themselves; an emphasis on skill and experience, not on whom you know and interpersonal influences. One would expect that the structural arrangements and rules would transcend any 'cultural' factors, the attitudes and preferences brought to their roles by individuals at all organizational levels. Yet in this department, women did not flourish. To quote Pringle from her work on secretaries in organizations:

> It can be argued that the rational-legal or bureaucratic form, while it presents itself as gender neutral, in fact constitutes a new kind of patriarchal structure. The apparent neutrality of rules and goals disguises the class and gender interests served by them.
>
> (Pringle 1989: 88)

To this needs to be added race interests.

Was this true of the housing department, whose managers were seeking to find the barriers preventing women moving into senior management level?

In the interviews, I explored how they developed their careers to get to their current positions of power and how they had used the formal procedures and processes to do so. Their accounts pointed less to a deliberate planning of their careers than to a crafting approach, whereby they had been encouraged to take opportunities afforded by chance and circumstance. These men, in contrast to those in other studies, had not planned their careers specifically but had crafted them with the help of several factors.

Important influences had been both men and women, either line managers or mentor figures, who had noted their potential. They had been encouraged to take on additional work and projects created by vacancies where work needed to be covered. They had been encouraged to 'act up' into more senior positions on a temporary basis. They had been seen to be 'in the frame' for managerial positions. They had the capability afforded by using time as a resource to take on additional workloads. The importance of encouragement by line managers and mentors has also been noted by women managers in their own career development in other research (Allan *et al.* 1992).

The question is whether this is different for women, and whether women are less likely to be identified as natural role occupants for management positions. A body of research has contested the notion of bureaucracies as being asexual places and has pointed to the nature of gender-based expectations that abound in the workplace (Gutek 1989). Gender-based expectations are rooted in stereotypes about men and women. Stereotypes of men revolve around the dimension of competence and activity (Deaux 1985). Gutek (1989: 60), in her review of recent research on heterosexual social-sexual behaviour at work, notes that:

> . . . these stereotypes include the belief that men are rational, assertive, tough, good at maths and science, competitive and make good leaders. The common view of the male personality is the picture of asexuality . . . the carry over of sex role stereotypes into the workplace enforces this view of men as organisational beings: as active and work orientated.

Women, on the other hand, are seen as sexy, affectionate and attractive. If one takes the view of Pringle (1989), that bureaucracies or large corporations are places where there is a separation of the public world of rationality and efficiency from the private sphere of emotionality and personal life, then women are not likely to be perceived as potential for management. Gutek (1989) notes that the sex role of women interferes with and takes precedence over the work role, and Kanter (1977) refers to the fact that the perceived sexuality of a woman can 'blot out' all other characteristics. It has also been noted from research by Les Back (1990) that Afro-Caribbean and Asian men are sexualized in the workplace as are women. Research has shown that these stereotypes have remained stable over the last two decades. This occurs even though it is generally assumed that men are more sexually active than women (Glass and Wright 1985) and that they are the initiators of sexual encounters (Kinsey *et al.* 1948; Grauerholz and Serpe 1985; Zilbergeld 1978).

Morgan noted that:

Many organisations are dominated by gender related values that bias organisation life in favour of one sex over another. Thus . . . organisations often segment opportunity, structures and job markets in ways that enable men to achieve positions of prestige and power more early than women, often operate in ways that produce gender related biases in the way organisational reality is created and sustained on a day to day basis. This is most obvious in the situations of open discrimination and the various forms of sexual harassment that often pervade the culture of the organisation in a way that it is much less visible.

(1986: 178)

There is evidence from these interviews that this stereotyping was still in place. One female interviewee outside the management team noted that women who did get promotion from first-line management positions did so according to the length of their skirts and the shape of their legs. The men considered themselves not to be sexist but said that the issue of discrimination against women would not be taken seriously until people were disciplined for making sexist remarks. The order had to come from 'the top', by which they meant the members of the council, the Housing Committee and the chief executive.

Disciplinary action was taken in the case of racist remarks being made because the council had required this. Until there was a similar requirement on sexist remarks, the management team did not report that they intended to use their power to challenge sexist attitudes. However, overt sexual harassment was seen to be a disciplinary offence. One interviewee did note that he had been educated on issues affecting women by hearing a grievance on a sexual harassment case, which was the one instance of sexism being acted upon by the woman concerned. He said that he understood now why women did not want 'girlie' calendars in the building, whereas previously he had been impatient with this perspective.

From these themes emerging from the interviews, one can see the beginnings of some possible explanations of how the glass ceiling was operating in this particular location in the council.

First, the style of working long hours, and the single-mindedness the managers were able, with the support of their partners, to bring to the job, combined with an unstated assumption that this constituted effective working practice, meant that women were unlikely to be seen as possessing the 'competence' required to fit in. Secondly, there was no personal motivation to change the situation for women, as the men did not wish to spend much more significant time themselves in the domestic sphere. They were grateful and happy that their own partners took the primary responsibility in the domestic sphere, which they saw as unenviable. Thirdly, their thinking about women reflected sex role stereotypes, and the sex role of women predominated when it came to recruitment and to the encouragement of women to broaden their experience so that they might be better placed to gain promotion.

The management team were presented with a report on the interviews. At that meeting there was recognition and acknowledgement of the position of power they wanted to retain *vis-à-vis* their partners. They agreed to act as mentors in facilitated mentoring groups with women in the department, with the aim of sharing their expertise and views with women. Mentoring was also intended to bring about a cultural shift by putting the men at the top in direct touch with the issues and barriers blocking women. It was hoped that this would be a two-way educative process and would bring about the beginnings of a culture change in and from the top of the department. This was a project that was to take place over the following twelve months.

This project did not proceed. There was a dramatic change in the control of the council, resulting in a large number of senior managers leaving the council, including key managers from the housing department. In view of this change, the mentoring group plan was shelved. Resources were not available subsequently to fund it, and at the same time the senior managers were leaving the team. It felt like an opportunity lost, not only for the women in the department, but for that particular management team. A subsequent attempt to resurrect the programme of work failed due to funding constraints, and it was considerably later and long after most members of this senior management team in the housing department had gone that a council-wide mentoring scheme was introduced (see Chapter 8).

IMPLICATIONS FOR CHANGE

There are times when the odds seem so stacked against change that personally I can feel overwhelmed by the huge agenda and the multiplicity of obstacles to greater equality of opportunity in society. What are the prospects, therefore, of changing organizations so that women have equality of opportunity and equivalence to but difference from men?

These interviews point tentatively to the diverse ways in which an agenda of change can be blocked successfully, at best unknowingly, at worst deliberately. They also point to ways in which men may be influenced to change themselves (which has to be part of a long term agenda) and the levers and forces for change that women, and some men, can use to chip their way towards change in the shorter term.

What evidence do we have of these?

Impetus from the 'top'

The managers in the housing department would have responded to taking issues for women at work more seriously if there had been an impetus for change from the top of the organization, in this case from members of the council and the chief executive. They did want to demonstrate to their 'employers' the ways in which they were implementing change with regard to racism. It was in their interests to do so. This did not necessarily change attitudes, although it may have done, but it had affected observable behaviour. There was no such drive from the top in relation to sexism, and this was known and acknowledged as not being a serious issue by the managers interviewed. To get such a change at the top of local government requires women in the local community mobilizing their power to pressurize council members from outside the organization. At the same time, women and men inside local government and other organizations who have sufficient leverage to affect the policy and rule making levels need to pursue an agenda of change consciously and actively.

Formal rules and the threat of disciplinary action may force people to change their behaviour, but they do not necessarily alter attitudes and can make discrimination even harder to deal with. The example of shared and unspoken views about avoidance of the recruitment of younger women, who would be likely to have other demands on their time, would be hard to identify. It is inevitable that the way women 'scored' in the formal recruitment process is still essentially subjective, and may reflect unspoken anxiety about hiring women who have roles as cooks, cleaners and carers back home. In this sense the formal rules can be subverted to support covert prejudice in relation to racism, sexism and other forms of discrimination.

Impetus from men

There appeared to be some awareness by these men of the limitations imposed on their lives by a lifestyle dedicated to work and predicated on overworking. They expressed concern about their own wellbeing, both emotionally and physically, and that of colleagues. Recent work by Warren Farrell (1993) on the statistics of health risks to men points to the fact that men lived one year less than women in 1920 but seven years less in 1990, as well as to the other factors such as the higher suicide rate of men.

The interviewees cited examples of these risk factors and anxieties. One had neglected a hernia for eighteen months. Another was concerned about the premature death of a former boss who had been the youngest ever chief officer, somehow putting into perspective a life in which this man had never had the opportunity to enjoy his children. Another had spent six months apart from his partner and family to try to get things in perspective, and he said he tried now to get a greater balance in his work and domestic life. (There was little practical evidence of change, but a greater awareness of the issues.)

They were critical too of the organizational chaos that demanded the kind of performance that they felt they had to give it: unreasonable demands for delivery of work with impossible time targets, requiring excessive overtime. Their mode of working may well have been influenced by their employers, the council members, who were responsible for these demands. I have noted previously their reluctance, however, to give up even partially what amounted to an addiction to the pace, power and prestige of work, or to influence upwards to get change in the work process. There was no sign of radical rethinking of the place of work in their lives.

With future limited access for both men and women to full-time careers, and with the increase in redundancies, early retirement and limited term job contracts, the relationship between activities in the public and domestic sphere is likely to become increasingly a key issue. Men may need to seek other forms of identity beyond those associated with domination in the sphere of work. There is also the question of whether men may 'take over' and command in other spheres. The work of Farrell and others, for example, can be viewed as an attempt for men to gain equal status as 'victims' with women, blacks, homosexuals and people with disabilities (Grant 1994; Farrell 1993). This serves to obscure the differential power locations occupied by men and women.

The public sector reforms

Men's anxiety about their health and quality of life in this study seemed outweighed by their job satisfaction and need to work in the way described. Whether the restructuring in the public sector offers opportunities for change is uncertain. Certainly, from my current work across the whole range of the public sector, women managers are finding the situation more problematic than before. Fewer senior managers are working increasingly longer hours, under tighter work contracts. Anxiety about the threat of redundancy, 'delayering' of middle management, and the introduction of social market mechanisms all seem to focus the minds of managers on accepting more onerous work schedules. Entry for women under these conditions appears more, rather than less, prohibitive.

Thus the organizational climate is characterized by fear of job loss, uncertainty of the future and a loss of 'identity' with organizations whose value systems appear under threat, or lost. Women are concerned that there will be greater reliance on the club-like culture between men to stitch up the fewer job opportunities available, and to position themselves for their own development into the newly emerging locations of power.

Women managers question, for example, where the power will lie in the new commissioning/providing arms of local government and health service provision (Allan *et al.* 1992). Fears have been expressed that men are moving into those positions of perceived power, leaving women in culs-de-sac of professional provision in low-key areas of service delivery.

With the changes and the introduction of market mechanisms into the public sector, it is vital that work opportunities and the gendered location of work are monitored. This needs to occur by pressure from men and women within and outside organizations, from women active in organizational networks, and from women and men in the unions. The Equal Opportunities Commission have been monitoring the impact on new pay and conditions brought about by restructuring in the public sector, and it is clear that women have lost out (EOC 1993). Women managers, working together in action learning groups and through mentoring arrangements, can offer both support and strategic development ideas to each other.

Gearing change to the business agenda

Getting other people or organizations to change can often mean gearing what you want to the concerns and interests of those who are in a position to provide what is required. It was undoubtedly true that any argument for change would have been listened to by the men in this study if it would have furthered the aims of the organization. There was evidence that one impetus for change in term-time working contracts was implemented due to the shortages in the labour market, and hence the attempt to recruit women caring for children back into the organization. Economic and social trends may create more leverage for women in this respect, with women likely to fill the skills gap that is prevalent in this country, particularly through part-time work. With women comprising a cheaper alternative in this mode of work, there may be more entry for women. Whether this will serve to create women friendly organizations is another matter.

Women, the domestic sphere and the public domain of work

Opportunities for greater equity between men and women in both the public domain of work and the domestic sphere seem limited from this study. Across all the staff that I interviewed in this local authority, there was little evidence of this type of shift occurring. It appears that women will be increasingly in demand in their domestic role as carers, and at the same time be required to fill the skills shortages by taking on flexible working hours, possibly home-based to facilitate or retain the primacy of their role in the domestic sphere.

To gain greater equity and opportunity for choice is part of the longer term agenda described by Cynthia Coburn (1991). She suggests that an economic policy is needed providing a 30-hour working week as a standard for both sexes. Backed by the unions and through legislation, these approaches would create new ways of working that would challenge the existing social order. Patricia Hewitt (1993) describes a new model of working time in which only a minority of people work a 'normal working day' or a 'normal working week', and the organization of working time is becoming more flexible, varied and individualized. This, she argues, creates the opportunity to exploit flexibility and to encourage a variety of working-time arrangements relevant not only to days and weeks but to lifetimes – flexibility that would benefit men and women alike.

This does not seem an area where men will be willing to change, in spite of their recognition that there is a downside to their work patterns. Women will need to continue to challenge the existing order, from both within and outside organizations. In spite of the decline in an active feminist movement, there may be changes in the expectations of both young women and men in how they achieve balances in their lives in the public and domestic spheres. This remains to be seen.

Cultural change

There is a view that only when there is a critical mass of women of at least 30–35 per cent of a group can women set their own terms. It would seem that the critical mass often has to be located in positions of some power, or be active in a trade union that has such power. The present mass of women is by and large at the bottom of organizations, and this in itself has not been a force for change. In the public sector, the newly created union Unison with its majority of women members does have such an opportunity to take a leadership role, even in a time of reduced union influence and power. This will be a formidable task.

We can look to, but cannot rely on, the few women at the top of organizations to be able to change much. Their power is limited. Equal opportunities policies and initiatives such as Opportunity 2000 have assisted some women to reach the top of organizations in the public sector. They have not had a significant impact on the large majority of women, many of whom are working class and black and remain at the bottom of organizations or in ghettos of work which are culs-de-sac for women workers. Those women who have succeeded have often adopted male management methods and approaches to work that fit into the existing culture and enable them to survive. One participant on a management development course for women noted bitterly to me that her female boss, who had had a meteoric career path, was a 'lousy' role model for her. She saw that with her childcare responsibilities she could not put in the length of day that her boss did. Her boss saw no alternative to her mode of work, as indeed the housing managers in this study saw no alternative either. Some women managers have helped others through individual encouragement, the provision of management development opportunities for women, and raising the level of debate. I would count myself as one of this number. But we have not created a critical mass of women in key leverage positions in organizations, and we have had little, if any, impact on transformative change.

WHAT OF THE FUTURE?

I have not addressed many of the issues facing men and women in future organizations. The interviews I have focused on were part of a limited study of issues primarily facing white, middle class men in relation to white and black women managers. I have tried to identify some of the positive and negative factors that have bearings on change. The fact that the public sector is in the throes of radical reform, with the introduction of market mechanisms, needs assessment in terms of the place women will find within it. The noted demographic shifts in this country will bring to the fore the question of how the increasing number of elderly citizens and our children are to be cared for, within the context of a diminished labour force. The changing structure of jobs and of lifelong, full-time work patterns may cause men to reassess the mode through which they gain prestige, power and self-recognition. It may also promote a reappraisal of the emotional and physical risks to men of their current lifestyles.

Cynthia Cockburn (1991) suggests that today men have a choice: to accept the patriarchal system or to work collectively to challenge it. I remain unclear about what will motivate men to take on an agenda of challenging the patriarchal system. I interviewed twenty-three men across the council altogether. Only one white man with childcare responsibilities, and three black men in relatively senior positions, had actively promoted greater opportunities for women to gain equivalence with men. Women will need to continue to organize for change both consistently and persistently, even in an era where feminism is decried. I am left with the question: why move over?

REFERENCES

Allan, M., Bhavnani, R. and French, K. (1992) *Promoting Women: Management Development and Training for Women in Social Services Departments*. London: HMSO.

Back, L. (1990) 'Racist name calling and developing anti-racist initiatives in youth work'. Research paper – *Ethnic Relations*, 14.

Clegg, S. (1981) 'Organization and control'. *Administrative Science Quarterly*, 26, 542–62.

Cockburn, C. (1991) *In the Way of Women: Men's Resistance to Sex Equality in Organisations*. London: Macmillan.

Coyle, A. (1989) 'Implementing equal opportunities'. *Public Administration Journal*, Spring.

Deaux, K. (1985) 'Sex and gender'. *Annual Review of Psychology*, 36, 49–81.

EOC (1993) *Equal Opportunities Commission Research Review: Women and Men in Britain 1993*. Manchester.

Foster, J. (1987) 'Women on the wane'. *Insight*, 15 (11/12).

Foster, J. (1990) 'Women's careers – challenges, choices and constraints'. Unpublished paper, cited in (1991) *Women in Social Services: A Neglected Resource*. London: HMSO.

Glass, S. P. and Wright, T. L. (1985) 'Sex differences in type of extramarital involvement and marital dissatisfaction'. *Sex Roles*, 12 (9/10).

Grant, L. (1994) 'Troopers in the sex war'. Interview with Warren Farrell. *Guardian*, 22 February.

Grauerholz, E. and Serpe, R. (1985) 'Initiation and response: the dynamic of sexual interaction'. *Sex Roles*, 12 (9/10).

Gutek, B. (1989) 'Sexuality in the workplace: key issues in social research and organisational practice' In Hearn, J., Sheppard D., Tancred-Sheriff P. and Burrell, G., *The Sexuality of Organization*. London: Sage.

Hewitt, P. (1993) *About Time: The Revolution in Work and Family Life*. London: IPPR/Rivers Oram Press.

Kanter, R. M. (1977) *Men and Women of the Corporation*. New York: Basic Books.

Kanter, R. M. (1989) *When Giants Learn To Dance: Mastering the Challenges of Strategy, Management and Careers in the 1990s*. London: Simon and Schuster.

Kinsey A. C., Pomeroy, W. B. and Martin, C. E. (1948) *Sexual Behaviour in the Human Male*. Philadelphia, PA: Saunders.

Morgan, G. (1986) *Images of Organisation*. London: Sage.

Peters, T. J. (1987) *Thriving on Chaos*. London: Macmillan.

Pringle, R. (1989) *Secretaries Talk: Sexuality, Power and Work U K*. London: Verso.

Rabbats, H. (1993) Speech to Office for Public Management Conference on 'Managing Across Cultures', November.

Schermerhorn, J.R., Hunt, J.G. and, Osborn, R.N. (1985) *Managing Organisational Behaviour*. New York: John Wiley.

Zilbergeld, B. (1978) *Male Sexuality*. Boston, MA: Little, Brown.

Chapter 4

A gender typology of organizational culture

Di Parkin and Sue Maddock

This chapter demonstrates how organizational cultures can be revealed through the use of 'equality audits'. It draws on the results of work on gender, race and disability in a number of public sector organizations, and identifies a range of gender characteristics typical of organizational culture.

This chapter sets out a way of exploring women's perceptions of organizational cultures through conducting 'equality audits' among staff. We outline the approach and methodology, and then go on to identify key findings from the equality audits we have conducted in a range of public sector organizations. We also suggest a typology of the gender characteristics of organizational culture which emerged from the audits.

Both of us have been actively concerned with equalities issues: with women's development projects and as a women's officer in local government. In our work, we have become increasingly aware of the limitations of equality agendas which focus on structural changes alone. For years, structural changes – the introduction of job-share, flexible working, harassment policies and so on – have formed the main agenda of equality work on gender issues. But fitting these structures into diverse organizations is like slotting a grid over a jelly – the reality of white, male dominance continues to ooze around it. That reality is sustained, we believe, through organizational culture. But while it is moderately easy to propose structural changes which benefit women, grasping the slippery nature of organizational culture is more complex.

How can we understand what is going on? How can we make proposals for change which are based on a fuller understanding of cultural issues? To answer these questions we have developed a form of attitude survey we call an equality audit. Now working as management consultants, we have conducted equality audits across a range of public sector settings (for example, a county council, a metropolitan borough, a regional health authority, and a fire authority).

The idea of using equality audits arose from our work as consultants providing equalities training. We were aware that training alone seemed only the tip of the iceberg; or, more accurately, a shifting of the deck chairs on the *Titanic*. We wanted to find out what was really going on below the water line. We also wanted the findings to be *heard* by today's organizations. Couching the issue in terms of audit seemed to have a satisfying number crunching ring to it, like a car MOT or body health check. The idea of audit, we felt, was compatible with the new management language and approach being adopted throughout the public sector, and was therefore more likely to be heard and seen as valid by senior management. This approach is also recognized within the equalities literature as helpful in identifying the reasons for inequalities within a specific organization, and as suggesting what might produce the quickest results in reducing gaps and changing the levels at which women, black and ethnic minorities, and people with disabilities are employed (Coussey and Jackson 1991).

THE EQUALITY AUDIT PROCESS

The starting point for conducting equality audits has usually been the recognition by a senior member of staff that there are particular cultural problems which are blocking organizational development. Yet senior staff cannot put their finger on exactly what is happening, perhaps because they are defended from the reality of racism or sexism by a filtering process:

> I know something is going on, but I don't know exactly what it is. I want to find out, and, if necessary, bang their heads together.
>
> (Director, competitive services)

> I know there is a lot of sexism here. I want to be able to prove it.
>
> (Personnel officer, local government)

> We know a lot of horrible things are going on; we want to find out about them.
>
> (Equal opportunities officer)

Alternatively, equalities staff may be seeking outside help in bringing about change:

> We have an Opportunity 2000 target to meet and this may help us do so.
>
> (Personnel officer)

These internal organizational change agents were seeking to draw on external support to diagnose the nature of the problem, and to identify the particular forms of organizational resistance they were faced with. Once agreement to conduct an equality audit was reached, we designed an approach to fit the requirements (and budget) of each organization we worked with. The scale and focus of the audits differed (some concerned gender, some focused on disability and some on race), but the basic methodology was similar and consisted of a number of stages. As equality audits are, above all, about finding out what people think and feel, the first stage necessarily involved a number of days of in-depth qualitative interviews, identifying the particular concerns within an organization. These explored issues included areas such as access to training and promotion, treatment by male colleagues and peers, attitudes to women's domestic and caring responsibilities, sexual harassment and so on. The first stage of an audit, then, is talking to people about their feelings on the issues.

We then used the concerns raised as the basis of a questionnaire, and conducted sample surveys, usually of around 1000 people. The samples for gender audits were structured in a way which reflected the specific concerns which had emerged from the interview stage and other research. For example, in one local authority, analysis of the staffing profiles indicated where the barrier of the 'glass ceiling' occurred, with few women occupying posts above a certain grade. It was, therefore, seen as important to survey a greater percentage of the few women above and just below the ceiling to find out what was happening at that particular point in the organization, and to explore what could change it. In the fire brigade it was important to study the views of a high proportion of the few female firefighters.

The questionnaires were distributed by personnel officers inside the organization and returned, unopened, to the consultants. Analysis was conducted using SPSS computer packages. Cross-tabulations were made for significant factors: full-time v. part-time staff; managers v. non-managers; mothers v. childless women.

One audit of people with disabilities proceeded slightly differently, as the numbers employed were, typically, small. In this audit, qualitative face-to-face interviews were conducted with as many disabled people as possible. The interviews were designed to find out what the key barriers they faced were, including the prejudices of other workers as well as physical obstacles. In many cases it was the first time that the views of disabled workers (especially those with learning difficulties) had been taken into account.

OUTCOMES OF EQUALITY AUDITS

The audit process itself works at three levels. The first level is that the very act of talking to women about their concerns begins to open up the organization. People respond to being listened to, and see it as an indication that the organization cares about them. We found that our methods of asking people about their perceptions of how the organization treated them were supremely relevant. One cook supervisor in an education department said:

I've worked here for 27 years and no one has asked me before what I think.

In addition, the concerns raised can be fed back to other women during later stages of the audit process. The audit itself, then, becomes integral to the management of change process.

The second level at which the audits work is that of establishing how women perceive the organization, and of identifying the barriers they experience. The results of equality audits sometimes produce surprises, challenging previous assumptions about the most significant issues facing women. As well as perceiving barriers to *progress up* an organization, the results of our audits suggested that women are very concerned about barriers to doing their *current job* effectively.

Many women we interviewed did not want to move from their present job, but they did want their work to be valued more. They wanted to be listened to and taken seriously:

> They don't ask our opinion, they just impose changes and then are surprised when they don't work.

> They treat me as if I'm stupid; I can see ways things could be done better, but I don't have a say.

Interestingly, we found that women currently employed on administrative and manual grades were more likely to feel undervalued in organizations which had not tackled the problem of changing the balance of women at senior grades or in non-traditional areas. Undervaluing women on low level grades seems to go hand in hand with not wanting women at senior levels. This qualitative outcome of equality audits can help organizations to shape their equality strategies, basing them on the specific barriers experienced by women at different levels rather than by adopting 'off the peg' solutions.

The third level at which the audit process works is that of quantitative data. A number of key statistics emerged from each audit (see appendix to this chapter). These quantified results reflected the issues emerging from the qualitative material gathered during the initial interviews, and from the 'comments' section included in each questionnaire. The data gathered were particularly helpful in enabling equalities staff to build a case for change in each of the organizations we worked with. The audit process, then, benefits organizations in a number of ways. It helps them to see what is going on, so they can begin to identify where the problems lie. Sometimes, of course, organizations do not really want to know; they are scared of lifting the stones because of what they might find lurking beneath them. Once they know about the real consequences of prejudice and discrimination they are expected to act: not knowing can be a cosy defence.

The things which are discovered through an audit may be structural – there may be no job share or flexitime scheme, and women see these as necessary. But more usually the outcomes concern cultures rather than structures. The culture of an organization may be hostile to women, at worst, or at best indifferent to their needs. Even in organizations which have taken some steps to address barriers to women (through, for example, the provision of part time, flexible work or a crèche), the culture may define women in terms of their motherhood, thus excluding them from 'high flying' or non-traditional routes.

The cultural pictures which emerged from our audits were very rich, and we feel that perhaps the most valuable outcome of equality audits can be the process of cultural mapping.

'Gender typology' of organizational culture

The audits we conducted enabled us to help women within organizations build up a picture of the specific cultural barriers they faced. From these qualitative findings we were able to develop a gender typology of organizational cultures operating in public sector organizations, using the following categories (Parkin and Maddock 1993):

- the gentleman's club, with its paternalist overprotection;
- the barrack yard, with its bullying hierarchy;
- the locker room, excluding women, using sexuality;
- the gender blind, pretending differences between men and women do not exist;
- the feminist pretenders, men assuming the mantle of feminism;
- the smart macho, where profit is all that matters.

The gentleman's club

The gentleman's club is polite and civilized. Women are kept firmly in established roles by male managers who are courteous and humane and patronize in the nicest way. The old paternalist is one of the few men who will ask after employees' welfare and remembers when a secretary's child is sick:

> It's so difficult asking Mr... about promotion or regrading, he's always so sweet and friendly, I think he may be upset and think I'm unhappy here.
>
> (Secretary)

> The chief education officer is always very polite and is embarrassed if anyone swears in front of me.
>
> (Principal officer, education)

Older men frequently say they feel it is their duty to restrict younger women in order to protect them. Overprotected women frequently conform to type. The 'gentleman' expects women to be 'caring and moral' at work, and if they behave appropriately, they are rewarded by warmth and concern. Women recognize that, if they become too demanding or too assertive, and ask for change and promotion, they will lose the friendly, 'gentlemanly' boss and instead he will become difficult and they will become outsiders. These cultures rely on women understanding what they have to lose if they seek to challenge common practice. In this way women are warned that if they seek less traditional work or more decision-making power, men and women may become antagonistic towards them. In this culture, women are valued in the jobs they do, but they are not expected to break barriers and move outside traditional women's work.

The gentleman's club reinforces the notion that a woman's role as mother and homemaker, and a man's role as breadwinner, are natural and preordained:

> I think women like running the home; they only want part-time work – not all women want to be managers.

This perspective creates a myth about women and hides the reality of black women, single parents and those people in need of full-time employment irrespective of domestic arrangements. This type of working environment clearly determines women's expectations, sense of possibility and general confidence. Ideas that women 'lack ambition' are culturally biased. A survey in one authority revealed that male managers thought women lacked ambition, while the majority of women said they lacked encouragement and were waiting for the 'green light' to contemplate promotion as a possibility.

Three examples of the gentlemanly culture were found in a metropolitan authority where:

- one woman trainee surveyor was not allowed on site during two years of training because managers wanted to protect her from male highway workers' attentions;
- women landscape architects were not asked to go to 'rough' estates;
- women mechanical engineers were not asked as frequently as male colleagues to go out to make inspections (involving crawling behind dirty boilers).

Women may be overprotected from possible violence, sexual danger, dirt or physically arduous tasks. Gentlemanly overprotection, with which some women can collude, leads to women gaining less experience even where they have crossed the barriers and are performing 'men's jobs'. They are protected from the defeminization of doing the job fully. Thus, women become less competitive for promotion because their experience is less. The kindly overprotection can easily extend into more explicit exclusion. Our audit of a fire brigade reveals that protecting women from physical danger or dirt is one of the rationalizations for a women-excluding culture.

The barrack yard

This culture dominates in hierarchical organizations where a chain of command exists from top to bottom. The barrack yard characterizes organizations modelled on the military, such as the fire brigades. It is a bullying culture where subordinates are shouted at and rarely listened to. It leads supervisors and managers to bawl at people when they make mistakes and to despise those beneath them. Juniors are frequently women, manual workers or black people, for whom managers have little respect:

He shouts at everyone, he's known as the Fuhrer.

We ask for training, but never get it. We can't do what they want without it. Then we make mistakes, but when we try to explain they don't listen.

It's not just the women who are scared of him, so are some of the managers – but he *blocks* women and says things such as 'no women will work above scale 5 in this department'.

The barrack yard can hide a real hostility toward women, black people, manual workers and anyone 'weak' or possessing little institutional power, but it tends to be led by a few people and most other employees are merely responding to them out of fear. The barrack yard can be vicious and is basically an authoritarian culture where abuse of power coerces compliance. As women rarely have senior status within organizations, their interests and comments are ignored and they are rendered invisible.

In fire brigades, there is a need on the fireground, at incidents, for an immediate response to commands. In training, officers shout 'Uncouple the hose' and trainees bawl back 'Uncoupling the hose, sir'; this mode of a 'command culture' is extended to other aspects of brigade life where it is quite inappropriate.

The locker room

This is a culture in which men actively exclude women, building relationships on the basis of common agreements and common assumptions. It is a culture where men frequently talk about sport and make sexual references to confirm their heterosexuality:

> I would learn about the sport and talk about it, then they would change the subject – they didn't want me, a woman, in the group.
>
> (Chief officer, northern authority)

> Men still exclude women from 'drinks-in-the-pub' and evening socializing. It's difficult asking a woman because everyone assumes you must fancy her even if all you want to do is talk about work.
>
> (Male director of housing)

A man who is comfortable within the locker room culture may justify 'pin-up' calendars as harmless and fun, but then he puts them in full view to intimidate younger women. Although 'girlie' pictures and calendars are more rare in public sector organizations than in private companies (policy statements have made it clear that they are not endorsed by management), even today some men in local government have them in filing cabinets and behind doors. The illegality of sexual harassment, and the high costs to organizations losing in tribunals, may confuse us into thinking this culture is waning. Yet, both in the northern authority, where a number of women reported groping, leering and offensive remarks, and in the study of women hospital doctors, where 71 per cent of women had experienced overly familiar comments and behaviour such as putting arms round shoulders, patting on the head, we found the locker room alive and well.

In the fire brigade, the situation is more extreme:

> I've lost count of the men I'm supposed to be having affairs with.
>
> (Woman manager)

> They watch pornographic videos on the station and talk about women in a pornographic way.
>
> (Female firefighters)

You can't have a man and a woman alone on a station, they'll be at it.

(Male firefighter)

The gender blind

The gender blind ignore a woman's identity and experience, and they probably also deny racial differences and disabilities. Such blindness usually grows out of an illusion that everyone is white, able-bodied and male. Gender blind persons may not want to discriminate, but instead they deny reality and difference.

One manager organized 24-hour shifts for all employees in the computer pool without any reference to the difficulties that most women had with this in working late, being alone in buildings or walking to car parks at night. A gender blindness to the reality of women's lives ignores the fact that domestic responsibilities, sexual violence and social realities do affect the choices women can make, and women's ability to attend training courses or events which involve leaving home earlier.

Such an avoidance of the reality of women's lives is also convenient for management; it creates an illusion of 'sameness' between men and women and denies the obstacles and difficulties many women face, especially when they seek to break with traditional practice. A female surgeon pointed out the gender blindness of things like the height of operating tables:

I had to get a box to stand on.

It means that organizations can pretend that it is unproblematic to treat everyone *as if* they were men, can avoid facing up to diversity and people's different needs.

In our study of the fire brigade, this gender blindness was being challenged as senior officers became aware that the way fire appliances are built and the reach necessary to pull down equipment was not a static given, but itself gendered:

Fire appliances can be designed differently, so ladders are not carried so high.

(Senior officer)

Paying lip-service and the feminist pretenders

Some public sector organizations, which have well developed equal opportunities policies, have also developed a new breed of men: men who are well versed in feminism and think of themselves as non-sexist. There are those who pay lip-service to equality programmes and declare themselves to be equal opportunities employers, but do little to promote or develop women or black people. As equality work becomes more respectable, the number of people espousing support for equal opportunities policies grows. Those who pay lip-service produce policies and charters and then ignore them.

There are also those who are adept at manoeuvring around equal opportunities policies. They have learned the 'politically correct' language and how to use it to their own advantage. Highly politicized organizations have developed highly politicized administrations, and officers criticize and judge each other on the basis of their political perspectives, their 'equality' behaviour and their own identities.

The culture of the 'feminist pretenders' or equality 'experts' is moralistic, where men and women will attempt to out-do each other over the 'correct way to deal with equality issues'. Hierarchies of oppression have developed where a person's status is determined by his or her position on the ladder of oppression – female, black, gay, disabled, working class, etc.

New forms of oppression develop in such a culture. Individuals who do not conform to the alternative radical stereotypes are belittled and patronized. Instead of men assuming women will get pregnant, there is a tendency to think all women must speak in meetings and be confident, or that all black people must have a position on black politics: 'I think Mary should be more assertive, I've suggested she reads . . .' This culture is prevalent in parts of academia.

The smart macho

The current commercial climate in the National Health Service, and in local government with compulsory competitive tendering, encourages economic efficiency at the expense of all other criteria. It is a breeding ground for smart macho managers.

Managers dominated by the 'smart macho' culture feel under such pressure to reach performance and budget targets that they have no desire to block or obstruct employees who can work 80 hours a week and deliver on time. These new managers are driven by extreme competitivity; they discriminate against those who cannot work at the same pace or who challenge the economic criteria. If you cannot keep up, you are likely to be sacked, demoted or passed over, whoever you are. Superficially, this appears not to be a gendered culture and many women managers are known to be as ruthless as male managers, sometimes more so:

> She was known throughout the region as focused totally on objectives and meeting them within deadlines. There was no point in explaining difficulties to her, she wouldn't listen.
>
> (Woman director, NHS)

> They sacked the old gentlemen in cardigans, replacing them with young ruthless yuppies, and most of them are male with no domestic responsibilities or interest in staff development.
>
> (Woman in education department)

What many of these cultures have in common is that at worst they *exclude* women and at best they *discourage* them.

In the women hospital doctors study we found that *discouragement* was the prevalent factor:

- 52 per cent of all the women doctors in the study had been actively discouraged from taking up a career in surgery or general medicine;

- 71 per cent said that male doctors had been overfamiliar with them;
- the majority said that they had been asked personal questions during interviews.

Women doctors were also discouraged by the widespread patronage system, which allows informal lobbying and support of favoured candidates and the pressure to do well to keep good references.

THE PROSPECTS OF CHANGE

Each of the cultures identified in the typology operates in a different way to disadvantage women. However, we also identified some emergent patterns which seem to offer something different.

One opening lies in the process of cultural change itself, in which women may be used as change agents. This seemed to have been occurring in three of the organizations we have studied or worked with. These had adopted an agenda or radical change in order to become more effective, outward looking and customer oriented. They were led by dynamic figures who, while often operating with a somewhat similar agenda to the 'smart machos', saw that increasing effectiveness would come from working with people rather than through ruthlessness. They often found women to be useful allies in breaking up habitual ways of working and traditional power cabals; women were seen as less wedded to tradition. In addition, women were not, in the main, holders of the old patterns of inward looking organizational power: at its most overt, women could not be Masons and did not have corrupt links to local networks of patronage.

The difference between this type of culture and that of the 'smart macho' is a recognition that organizations will not succeed if they do not value the people who work for them and the people whom they serve:

> Before he came, I had no scope to make decisions, I had to refer everything to the boss. He's given me my head. If I ask what to do, he says 'Well, what do you think?' I've been given a chance to develop.
>
> (Female manager, local authority)

Sometimes there are vestiges of the gender blindness found in more traditional cultures:

> He's not interested in gender, his concern is that the service be improved. He recognizes the way that will happen if he lets me get on with it. He's not hung up on power and is able to consult people, involve them and then take decisions. This means that the female admin. staff are consulted as much as the academics, on matters that concern them.
>
> (Woman academic, university sector)

But in other cases, women are viewed as a positive asset:

> Women are not tied into traditional notions about how work should be done.

They are not as defensive as men and they are more open to customers and new ideas.

> (Male general manager, local authority trading association)

This type of change oriented culture clearly offers new opportunities to women, both in career terms and as shapers of new styles of organization and new ways of working. However, promoting women at a time of change can also carry risks. Jackson (1993) suggests that women may be brought in because they can be identified with the new, and then when perhaps things go wrong and mistakes are made, it is the women who have taken the risks who can be blamed.

More positive prospects of change are offered in an emergent cultural form we term 'egalitarian humanist'. This is linked to organizations or units which take a holistic approach to the person:

> Working in a women-led environment, I am recognized as a whole person with whole needs. I can leave early to pick up my child.

> (Male trainer)

> He has always talked to me in an open fashion. It is liberating being in a gender neutral environment.

> (Female hospital doctor)

There is a recognition of the reality of people's whole gendered lives where work and the domestic world are less segregated from each other, and where female strengths are recognized. At present, this characteristic of culture is rare, and is associated with female leadership or with men committed (or not hostile) to gender equality.

The signs of change are promising. The need for organizations to be more responsibe to their staff and customers is gaining increasing recognition following the work of Peters (1981, 1985) and with the development of quality initiatives across the public sector. There are now more explicit links being made between organizational effectiveness and equality. Management 'gurus' such as Drucker (1989) and Handy (1992) recognize that women in particular have a part to play in transforming organizations; women can juggle multiple demands and can cope with high levels of uncertainty, and so can help organizations respond to diversity. As more organizations have women in senior positions (for example, the increased number of women chief executives in local government), there are developing seed beds of a cultural change towards a more holistic recognition of the gendered person.

The difference between a local authority corporate management team where one of us was the lone woman in 1986 and the same team in 1990, with a majority of female members, is marked. In 1990 a topic concerning childcare for staff was hotly supported by the female directors, while to the men its significance had been invisible. Women-led teams are not a sufficient condition for cultural change; yet they can be its beginning, and can actively assist the process.

CONCLUSION

Our studies revealed that organizational effectiveness and equality can be seen as essentially linked. In one organization a manager who was a dictatorial 'barrack yard' boss did not listen to, or respect, his female staff. He also managed in a 'fear and command' manner so that other, white, male managers were scared to take responsibility or risks, to innovate or develop. This was as much (or more) a problem for organizational effectiveness as for equality, and contributed to the changes which ultimately led him to leave.

The future of organizational effectiveness is to be seen in openness, being able to adapt to change, and being able to respond to what the users of an organization want. Organizations need to face outwards to meet the needs of their customers and users, not inwards to traditional pyramids of power and bureaucratic rule-following. In local authorities, which we know best, central government has legislated for increased competition and more responsiveness to the views of users. This has understandably been resisted as being driven by the ethos of business and the market place, rather than by a commitment to public sector values of fairness, account-ability and equity. Yet changing 'town halls' from the old-style, grey, unresponsive monoliths involves genuinely listening to, and taking account of, the views of users who are female, black, from minority ethnic communities, old, gay, working class and disabled. Only a small proportion of users are white, heterosexual, able bodied, middle class males.

Organizations who do not listen to front line staff cannot listen to the customers whom staff talk to. If the people on the reception desks, the servers of the meals and the cashiers are mainly women, and the people emptying the bins, cleaning the streets or schools are working class, then organizations managed by white, middle class men need to know what the customers are saying to these staff. The people on the front line cannot respond to the needs of diverse customers if they are not empowered to take decisions to meet customers' wishes. Empowering the front line, outward-facing, lower grade parts of the organization means empowering women, black, disabled and working class staff. This is perhaps a more radical agenda for organizational equality change than the agenda of enabling women to break through the 'glass ceiling'.

However, our audits found that organizations which do not enable women to get to the top do not value women and other powerless groups wherever they are. The two prongs of equality change have to go together. Equality audits can reveal the different ways in which organizations operate to the detriment of equality and effectiveness on both dimensions: blocking women's career development pros-pects; and undervaluing the contributon of women and other staff in front line, service delivery roles. Equality audits can also reveal the particular pattern of culture within an organization, and suggest appropriate stategies for change.

APPENDIX: DATA FROM THE AUDITS

Hospital study

Of the women surveyed:

- 46 per cent thought girls were not encouraged into surgery and obstetrics & gynaecology;
- 43 per cent said consultants discouraged women;
- 52 per cent had been encouraged to avoid surgery;
- 30 per cent were put off some specialisms by the male culture;
- 66 per cent said surgeons thought women were unreliable because they got pregnant;
- 46 per cent felt nurses treated male house officers better than they do women;
- 58 per cent had been spoken to overfamiliarly;
- 71 per cent had had overfamiliar physical contact;
- 61 per cent thought male consultants liked women SHOs if they were attractive;
- 46 per cent were not satisfied with their training.

Metropolitan borough study

Of the women surveyed:

- 49 per cent agreed that other people thought women were unreliable because they had children;
- 42 per cent agreed that people thought many jobs required physical strength which women did not have;
- only 8 per cent job shared;
- only 35 per cent had been offered training;
- 26 per cent felt that they had been treated as inferior by male workers;
- 23 per cent felt that they had been treated as inferior by male supervisors;
- 21 per cent had experienced 'unfair' remarks by other staff;
- 12 per cent had experienced sexual harassment;
- 26 per cent had experienced problems with safety.

REFERENCES

Coussey, M. and Jackson, H. (1991) *Making Equal Opportunities Work*. London: Pitman.
Drucker, P. (1989) *Adventures of a Bystander*. London: Heinemann.
Handy, C. (1992) *The Age of Unreason*. Pan: London.
Jackson, C. (1993) *Celebration of Success*. London: NHS Management Executive.
Parkin, D. and Maddock, S. (1993) 'Gender cultures'. *Women and Management Review*, 8(2).
Peters, T. (1981) *In Search of Excellence*. London: Collins.
Peters, T. (1985) *A Passion for Excellence*. London: Collins.

Chapter 5

Gendered ageism

A double jeopardy for women in organizations

Catherine Itzin and Chris Phillipson

Drawing on research carried out in local government and in the private sector, this chapter describes the combined effects of ageism and sexism on women's conditions of employment and career opportunities. It explores the possibilities of change through attitude change and positive action, but also identifies some of the limits of organizational strategies in the context of wider social divisions.

In 1992 we carried out a major study of 'age barriers at work' in the public and private sectors sponsored by the Metropolitan Authorities Recruitment Agency (METRA), the Institute of Persnnel Management (IPM) and the Local Government Management Board (LGMB). The study included a survey of 449 local authorities, case studies in 11 selected local authorities and 3 private-sector companies, and an attitude survey of 476 local government line managers.

The case studies included a sample of 350 men and women who were interviewed individually or in groups. These group interviews were held in most of the local authorities with senior managers, with administrative and clerical staff and with manual workers. On average 6–8 individuals participated in each group interview. In addition there were three individual management interviews in each local authority: with the head of personnel, with the equal opportunities manager (where these existed), and with a director in one of a range of service departments including housing, social services, personnel, community and environmental services, direct labour/works, information technology, leisure, planning and technical services, and chief executive's.

There was a specific focus in the study on gender. The management and group interview schedules included questions about women and gender issues. In addition, there was a subset of group interviews with what we called 'women in the middle', which targeted middle-aged women in middle management.

The results of this research illustrated the ways in which age discrimination operates with respect to recruitment, career progression and retirement, and were published as a research report with a section on gender and age (Itzin and Phillipson 1993). In this chapter we will draw on the material collected from women and about women from the survey of local authorities, from the line-manager attitude survey, and from the management interviews and group discussions in the local authorities and private-sector companies, to consider how age impacts on women's experience in organizations.

MANAGEMENT PERCEPTIONS OF AGE AND GENDER

The glass ceiling of age

In general terms women were perceived as being 'older earlier' than men and it was generally men rather than women who thought this to be the case. 'Women hit their peak younger than men', said the director of personnel in one authority. 'Women get where they are going by the age of 35', he added.

The line manager attitude survey revealed a tendency for line managers to regard women rather more than men in their forties as being 'older workers'. The gender difference in perception was most pronounced for women in their fifties. There were even a few respondents who categorized women as 'older workers' as young as 30. That women are perceived as being older (and categorized as 'older workers') at a relatively – and sometimes ridiculously – early age was supported by the qualitative data in this study. This perception is likely to have a negative impact on women's employment and career opportunities in organizations that increasingly regard anyone beyond their forties as 'past it' for senior promotion.

'There is now a culture that our top managers come in at around 40 and we tend to appoint people in their golden decade of 30–40', said the head of personnel in an authority with a high-profile commitment to countering age discrimination in employment. 'Chief executives are appointed at 45–ish', said one manager, 'and most chief officers by 40.' He added: 'Members just aren't prepared to contemplate anyone over the age of 40.' A chief personnel officer put it quite bluntly: 'The cut-off point for women's career progression is ten years younger than for men.' 'If there is a general perception that you need to "make it" by 40, this will clearly discriminate against women', said one service director.

The golden decade favours men, and appointments made on this basis are almost certainly a form of indirect sex discrimination. The result of appointing 'people' in their golden decade in one authority was to introduce a 'batch of new young men and make the council quite male dominated', thus reinforcing the under-representation of women in senior positions. 'There is an age ceiling in local government and in general it is 50, going down to 45, so it could get more difficult for women', said one service director. 'In local government you rarely see senior women', said another, who added that he 'went to many conferences and rarely found women attending'.

Broken careers

In addition to the discriminatory potential inherent in the perception of women as ageing earlier and being older at a younger age than men, there is the reality that the majority of women (80 per cent) will at some time in their reproductive life bear and rear children, many taking a break from employment for part of the childrearing years. One manager described women as, 'five to ten years late in their careers if they have taken a break, perhaps having spent their golden decade at home with children and ready for a golden decade at work a decade later than the men'. A service director in an authority committed to age equality referred to a woman assistant director 'who took maternity leave one year after appointment', and said 'This wasn't well received.' Another service director said, 'Career breaks can adversely affect women depending on how long they decide to stay out of work. If for many years, it is difficult to get back in. Women's careers are fragmented and do not follow the straighter path of men's.' The service director of one authority described the career break as 'a handicap for women', while another said he 'would like to think the career break wasn't a barrier, but it is'.

Women in senior positions spoke of the pressures they felt not to take career breaks, in spite of their entitlement and the provisions made by their employers to enable them to do so. One woman assistant director had a child, but had only taken a three to four-month break and was 'wary of taking a longer break as it makes such a lot of difference'. She had had her child 'late' and 'would advise women not to break their career in the first ten years. Establish your background and experience first and take a break when you are fairly high up.' She added that 'there was really not ever a good time to break' because 'the higher up you get if anything takes you away, you are perceived as not committed.' She said she 'had doubts about taking maternity leave – a matter of confidence, of losing track, of not being in the know'.

A male personnel officer described the situation of senior women in his authority as very difficult: 'If they are going to play the male game, and at the moment they have no choice, women have to put off having children until they are 30.' One of two women chief officers had two children, but used nannies to enable her to return to work. The other had no children. A woman deputy chief officer in another authority was single. A career-minded female head of personnel in one authority said she and the other two 'women at the top' all had caring commitments but they had not taken a break from work in spite of the authority's positive and encouraging policy on career breaks. They recognized that a break in career was a liability: 'The golden decade can't apply to women if they have had a break.' They were aware that when women who have taken a break from paid employment to have children return to work, they usually have to start at a lower level and have less time to progress.

Age as a factor in low-status work

In response to a question in the local government survey asking managers to indicate whether they regarded specific kinds of job as more or less suitable to older workers, most of the answers reflected sex-segregated work and gender as well as age considerations. Women were regarded as more suitable for clerical, caring, cleaning and catering work, and less suitable than men for chief executive and senior management jobs as well as for heavy manual work and for jobs as porters, caretakers, and road workers. Predictably the majority of women in both the public and the private sectors in this study were located in the positions that were regarded as most suitable for them.

One (male) manager described the over-representation of women in lower grades in his authority as 'a traditional ladies' horror story of 60 per cent plus of the women in clerical jobs with little prospect of progression'. One manager observed that it tended to be older women who were located in administrative and clerical posts, while another commented that the 'council has a hard core in administration, often long-serving "middle-aged" women who are seen as set in their ways'. When another authority had set up a development programme for the lower administrative grades, over 90 per cent of these were women over 40. 'It's clear that something is operating to keep women in lower grades and it's both age and gender issues that affect where and when women plateau in an organization', said one female head of personnel.

A service director in another authority put a different construction on the congruence of age and gender in the administrative grades when he said that 'women are in jobs where ageing is less significant to performance, in repetitious and menial work where issues of concentration and pressure don't come up.' At the large private sector company, where, typically of the finance sector, 63 per cent of staff are women concentrated in the lower grades and 80 per cent of administrative staff are women, the equal opportunities manager observed that it appeared to be acceptable to be older and female in the lower but not the higher grades. However, since senior management positions have traditionally been held by older men, the implication must be that menial work is more suitable for women than men, and management more suitable for men than women.

The position of women in these lower grades and the difficulties they experience in moving up, in spite of their potential, was graphically illustrated in one authority. There, the service director had worked for thirty years in local government and had become a director on a high salary with the power, status and pension that was attached to the job. His secretary had forty-five years' service with the council since leaving school and had risen to administrative/clerical grade 6. He said she had 'seen off seven directors', that she 'ran things' in the department, and that she was the 'real director'. One of the glass ceilings based on age-related barriers for women is situated between the administrative/clerical grades and the officer grades.

Age/sex stereotypes

Whatever their level in the organization, women work in an environment which ranges from hostile to unfriendly to just tolerant of women generally, and specifically of the 'uppity' women who try to enjoy the same opportunities as men. One head of personnel described his as a 'very sexist authority' where a significant number of 'senior people believe women shouldn't work'. Women in senior positions were often described as 'being expected to be surrogate men', having to act as if they were 'men in frocks' and forced to fit into the male culture or to fail.

According to one manager, 'Age is always linked to male perceptions of women. There is always a sex stereotype for the age a women is: she is a "flighty young piece", or "hearing wedding bells", or "raising a family and not really committed to her work" or "it's that age – the change".' The head of personnel in another authority, a woman in her thirties, mentioned that councillors would comment on her age, and there was a recognition that some men would only appoint young women as their secretaries – the 'dolly birds'. Another head of personnel (male) referred to 'the psychological dislike of appointing older women – aged 40–45' – to any post! This was 'not spoken about', he said, 'but to do with those women being seen as less sexually attractive – as spinsters'. At the same time, a woman chief officer who was described as 'young and attractive' was 'perceived as being younger than she is'. There was one woman who had become a director in her golden decade at the age of 35. Unlike men of a similar age in a similar position, 'She is seen as an "upstart".' In the view of the (male) manager who made this observation, her age compounded with her gender to disadvantage her in relation to her male peers.

THE EXPERIENCE OF WOMEN

Institutional barriers

'Whatever age they are, women's age is held against them. They are never the right age, they are either too young or too old', said one woman in a statement which seems to epitomize the general attitude that had emerged from the management interviews. Data collected from women age 35–50 wholly reinforced the picture of stereotyping, bias, barriers, obstacles, harassment and discrimination based on age and sex reported in the management interviews. From the perspective of women's experience there seemed to be a great deal of truth in the observation that women are never the right age.

Institutional age-related beliefs had a negative influence on women's conditions at work and on their career opportunities. 'Men don't take you seriously as you get older', said another woman. 'They see you as you were ten years ago. I'm still asked to do routine tasks, even though I have obtained qualifications and am in a much more senior post.' 'I went to an interview', said one woman, 'and it was quite evident that they wanted a young attractive woman.' According to another woman, 'Men want dolly bird secretaries, not old girls.'

From another authority, a woman said: 'Men don't want women at the top. They pay lip service to equal opportunities, but they think if you are a woman you are only good for pushing pens and making tea.' In one authority the women spoke of the male assistant director 'who won't employ women of childbearing years'. One woman had been asked when she applied for a post at the age of 24 whether she was in a steady relationship and planning to have children. This is sex discrimination and unlawful under the 1975 legislation.

Internalized barriers

The institutional attitudes and beliefs and the age-based organizational practices associated with them appeared to have a profoundly negative effect on women's own attitudes, beliefs and behaviour. 'Women tend to look at their disadvantages rather than what they have to offer', was how one woman put it. In the words of two others:

> Women are made to feel they have not done things at the right age. Not married at 30? No children at 40? These pressures affect women's self-image. Women feel obliged to dye their hair. Age is a visible issue, others define you negatively if you look older, women much more so and much earlier than men. Women can overcome some of the disadvantages of age-stereotyping at work by looking younger as long as they can.

> You don't want to look like you are past your sell-by-date.

One woman said she saw herself as 'too young' for a management post, and even though she had plenty of relevant experience she did not apply. The successful candidate was a man, younger than she was, whom she had trained. She also said she did not feel she would 'fit into the prevalent male environment'. It was observed in another authority that even in social services with predominantly female staff, the 'very top management are men'. 'You do get the feeling that women might be kept out', they said, and told the story of a young woman colleague whom they all agreed should 'go far'. But 'She is put down as too young – as a "too young woman" as well.' A slightly older woman would be allowed to the top. Although younger men are allowed to the top, 'You can be "too young" as a woman at the same age as the man.'

Speaking of training and promotion, one woman said, 'They wouldn't think of us', and another replied, 'I wouldn't think of it for myself.' At the lower level, one woman said: 'I wish the department would pay for me to go to tech to learn something else but only the youngsters get day release. If you're mature you don't get the backing.' Women are not expected to go for training and they are not selected: this then leads to self-deselection. One older woman had decided not to go for a promotion opportunity because it was advertised as 'a post with training'. She felt training equated with being young so did not put herself forward for it. Personnel staff encouraged her to apply and supported her: 'She got the job and the training and has not looked back, but without someone else pushing her she would have deselected herself.' One local authority's recent management development programme had no women on it. 'We don't put ourselves forward for management', said one woman in another authority, and there was a consensus of opinion that women had to 'be pushy' and 'clone themselves as men' to compete with men at the top in their 'male culture'.

'Women need to be better qualified and work harder than men to get to the same level', observed one group. This created problems of motivation. 'I imagine', said one service director, 'if you had to slog away as a woman every step of the way and fight overt or covert prejudice you would get to a point where you might say "I can't go any further".' This was certainly the case with a number of women. There was a female deputy director in one department about whom it was said: 'She could have been director but didn't particularly want the hassle.' Another manager commented on the 'reluctance on the part of women to go for top jobs because they know they will get a hard time in senior posts and that holds them back'. One woman had been the only female officer among fourteen men for two and a half years. 'They often referred to me as one of the boys', she said, 'and I still don't know if I felt insulted or complimented.'

Women also talked about the high level of stress in senior management and the excessively long hours that the local government culture expected from first, second and third tier officers. These hours were incompatible with family responsibilities and therefore operated as a barrier to exclude women from senior posts. A number of women questioned whether the long hours characteristic of male culture did, in fact, represent good management practice.

THE COMBINED EFFECTS OF AGEISM AND SEXISM

The effects of sex discrimination on the employment of women is well documented with respect to low pay, low status, sex segregation, part-time work, the absence of employment protection, pension inequalities, sexual harassment and the under-representation of women in senior positions. The majority of women are located in a narrow range of sex-segregated occupations (Dex 1987; Beechy 1987; Walby 1988; Cockburn 1988). There has been little change in the earnings differentials between women and men since the Sex Discrimination Act came into effect in 1975, and women's earnings are still only three-quarters of men's (Department of Employment 1991). A survey by the Institute of Directors in 1992 found that three-quarters of women company directors believed inequality at work was widespread and 36 per cent of senior women executives said they had suffered discrimination.

Women are massively over-represented in the sex-segregated occupations (constituting three-quarters of catering and clerical workers), and in the lower-grade administrative and clerical levels in organizations (Reskin and Padavic 1994). Women are overwhelmingly under-represented in senior positions by comparison with men (Jackson and Hirsh 1991; Allan *et al.* 1992). A typical local government workforce profile showed that 90 per cent of chief officer posts were filled by men, while 90 per cent of staff in grades 1 and 2 were women (Itzin and Phillipson 1993).

In recent years, partly in response to demographic changes and the increase in the proportion of older people in the population and in the labour market, age discrimination in employment has become a focus of both research and political interest (Naylor 1990; Thompson 1991; Taylor and Walker 1992; Itzin and Phillipson 1993). Studies have addressed employment (LGMB 1991; Casey *et al.* 1993), training (Plett 1990; Plett and Lester 1991), retirement (Laczko and Phillipson 1991; Walker 1992) and 'the role of work in the third age' (Trinder *et al.* 1992).

There has also been some recent work on gender, age and employment (Arber and Ginn 1991; Bernard and Meade 1993).

This study illustrates the extent to which the organization of work is structured to accommodate a male chronology of continuous employment, and not the female chronology, which combines childrearing and domestic responsibilities and the discontinuity which follows from moving in and out of paid employment. In this context the 'glass ceiling' can be seen to consist of a combination of age as well as gender factors. The particular disadvantage of age for women is partly the result of being 'later' and 'older' in the organization's male-based and male-biased chronology because of taking time out of paid employment for childbearing and childrearing. It is also partly the result of the sexualizing of women's value in youth.

In addition, this study illustrates the prejudice that operates against women as women, which, as a result of the sexualizing of women's value, is compounded by age. Negative attitudes and beliefs about the abilities and value of women were communicated in the form of classic sexist sterotypes. It is possible to see here how attitudes and beliefs based on age and gender stereotypes defined the culture of these organizations and functioned to justify and perpetuate structural inequalities.

It is also possible to see how women as well as men have internalized age and gender-based 'attitudes and beliefs, and how women operate these 'attitudes of subordination' against themselves and each other as routinely as men exercise their 'attitudes of dominance'. Feeling less competent and less confident, self-deselecting for training and promotion, putting themselves down, putting (less competent) men first, the resigned acceptance of their subordinate status are all examples of this 'internalized oppression'. In other contexts this can take more positively unconstructive forms as, for example, when women in senior positions sometimes place obstacles in the way of other women or behave in unsympathetic or unsupportive ways towards other women (usually below them in the hierarchy).

This study suggests that gender on its own is an insufficient explanation of the discrimination experienced by women in organizations. The extent to which ageism is a factor in sexism and sex discrimination has been insufficiently theorized. And yet on the evidence of this research, age and ageism appear to be factors whose importance has been under-rated. It would appear that ageism is in fact significantly gendered and that sexism operates always with a dimension of ageism within organizations for women of all ages. What we would conceptualize as 'gendered ageism' appears to be a significant aspect of organizational culture.

CONCEPTUALIZING 'GENDERED AGEISM'

This chapter has illustrated some of the pressures on women to conform to the male chronology of employment and career progression, the 'gendered ageism' that operates in the culture of organizations, and the combined effects of age and gender and in particular ageism and sexism on the organizational status and opportunities of women.

The reality of women's potential is of course quite different. The demands of the female chronology (with its career breaks, and its domestic and caring responsibilities) are quite compatible with the requirements of work – with a change of attitude and flexibility in workplace practice. Childbearing and childrearing represent a very small proportion of any woman's total working life. It is a feeble excuse for discrimination, for which she pays a heavy penalty in economic disadvantage throughout the lifecycle by comparison with men, and which represents a significant loss of resource to the organization.

Despite the disadvantages of lower grading, lack of up-to-date training and reduced career prospects, a number of managers commented that women who have taken a break may return with 'more vigour' and 'more energy than the men who have been working in the same area for twenty-five years without a break and who are beginning to get tired': that 'Women returners want to come back and make a go of things in a short time.' This perspective on the female chronology was put most strongly by the 57-year-old female director in the private sector housing association when she said: 'Men haven't got as much staying power. Women become ambitious in their late thirties, early forties. Women come into their "work prime" when men are on the decline.'

There is potential for change in the organization of work: in job design, flexible hours, job share, structured career break and return-to-work provisions, and 'positive action training' to increase the representation of women in areas where they are currently under-represented. Most of these measures have been adopted within both the public and the private sectors and individual women have benefited.

But these measures do not seem to have changed the culture of organizations significantly: and that may be explained by the kinds of deeply embedded attitudes and beliefs revealed in this study, which render women invisible, which rationalize and justify women's existing position, which maintain women cannot or should not do what men do, which define women's potential in terms of age and sex stereotypes, and which enable men to exclude women on grounds of age or sex or both. Those implementing change strategies within organizations would be wise to take account of the ways that age and gender intersect and interact to the disadvantage of women, and the importance of the internalized attitudes and beliefs of both dominance and subordination in determining the culture and values of an organization and in sustaining the subordinate status of women.

REFERENCES

Allan, M., Bhavnani, R. and French, K. (1992) *Promoting Women: Management Development and Training for Women in Social Services Departments*. London: HMSO.

Arber, S. and Ginn, J. (1991) *Gender and Later Life*. London: Sage.

Beechey, V. (1987) *Unequal Work*. London: Verso.

Bernard, M. and Meade, K. (1993) *Women Come of Age*. London: Edward Arnold.

Casey, B., Metcalf, H. and Lakey, J. (1993) 'Human resource strategies and the third age: policies and practices in the UK'. In *Age and Employment*. London: IPM.

Cockburn, C. (1988) 'The gendering of jobs: workplace relations and the reproduction of sex segregation'. In Walby, S. (ed.), *Gender Segregation at Work*. Milton Keynes: Open University Press.

Department of Employment (1991) *New Earnings Survey*. London: HMSO.

Dex, S. (1987) *Women's Occupational Mobility: A Lifetime Perspective*. London: Macmillan.

Institute of Directors (1992) *Members' Opinion Survey: Women's Participation in the Workforce*. London: IoD.

Itzin, C. and Phillipson, C. (1993) *Age Barriers at Work: Maximising the Potential of Mature and Older People*. London: Metropolitan Authorities Recruitment Agency.

Jackson, C. and Hirsh, W. (1991) 'Women managers and career progression: the British experience.' *Women in Management Review and Abstracts*, 6 (2), 10–16.

Laczko, F. and Phillipson, C. (1991) *Changing Work and Retirement*. Milton Keynes: Open University Press.

LGMB (1991) *Age Discrimination in Employment*. Luton: LGMB.

Naylor, P. (1990) *Age No Barrier*. Solihull: Metropolitan Authorities Recruitment Agency.

Plett, P.C. (1990) *Training of Older Workers in Industrial Countries*. Geneva: International Labour Office.

Plett, P.C. and Lester, B.T. (1991) *Training for Older People : A Handbook*. Geneva: International Labour Office.

Reskin, B. and Padavic, I. (1994) *Women and Men at Work*. Thousand Oaks, Calif.: Pine Forge Press.

Taylor, P. and Walker, A. (1992) 'What are employers doing to "defuse the demographic time bomb"?' *Skill and Enterprise Briefing*, 21/92, 1–4.

Thompson, M. (1991) *Last in the Queue: Corporate Employment Policies and the Older Worker*. IMS Report 209. Brighton: Institute of Manpower Studies.

Trinder, C., Hulme, G. and McCarthy, U. (1992) 'Employment: the role of work in the third age'. Research Paper No. 1. The Carnegie Inquiry into the Third Age. London: Public Finance Foundation.

Walby, S. (ed.) (1988) *Gender Segregation at Work*. Milton Keynes: Open University Press.

Walker, J. (1992) *Preparing for Retirement: The Employer's Guide*. London: Age Concern/Pre-Retirement Association.

Chapter 6

Gendered noise

Organizations and the silence and din of domination

Elizabeth Harlow, Jeff Hearn and Wendy Parkin

This chapter reviews previous work on gender and culture, exploring different facets of gender power, and then looks at how the 'silence and din' of domination and subordination operate in various groups and organizations. While the primary focus is on gender power, the chapter also considers differentiation by age and race.

Din and silence, silence and din, are part and parcel of the gendered domination of organization. In this chapter silence and din are considered in relation to the domination of organizations and domination within organizations. While most of the emphasis is on gendered domination, there is a general recognition that this is only one aspect of domination and power relations. Other examples of oppression are therefore also acknowledged. Throughout the chapter silence and din are treated both as literal terms and as metaphors. Noise itself is usually taken for granted and only becomes din when it is displeasing. Any noise can therefore be identified as din if it is perceived from a particular standpoint to be negative. It might even be possible to describe, in a metaphorical sense, an oppressive or negative silence as din. Hence terms which might appear to 'speak for themselves', on closer examination may become complex and perhaps contradictory, particularly when they are applied to the domination of and within organizations.

In a literal sense din includes the sound of imposing loud voices, interruptions and put-downs as well as the clatter of machinery. Silence might mean absence of noise but it can at the same time be full of significantly meaningful content. Although metaphorically din most readily equates with domination and silence with the passivity of the oppressed, silence can be the response of management to the din of demands for change, and hence a tool for the maintenance of domination. Both din and silence then can metaphorically represent the means of domination, the response to domination, and a means of subversion and change to and within organizations. In one sense organizations are in constant change, but despite this some features particularly of domination and oppression appear to remain constant. These relations do not exist without struggle, as domination has to be recursively produced. Strategies for changing power relations may be macro, micro, conscious and unconscious. They are equally relevant to the development of equal opportunities policies or the subtle dynamics of interpersonal relations. These are the themes that will be explored throughout the chapter.

A broader macro-perspective marks the start of the chapter. The focus then changes towards a narrower micro-perspective. The chapter is divided into four sections. The first provides the general context of how organizations are gendered. Five different but interacting ways in which organizations can be gendered are considered. These are the dominance of the public sphere over the private; the division of authority within organizations; the dominance of the centre over the margins in organizations in both a literal and metaphoric sense; the relationship of organizational participants to their domestic responsibilities; and finally, the operation of sexuality within organizations. The significance of silence and din is then considered in relation to the structure and construction of organizations. In this second section, attention is paid to the gendered relationship between the public world of the organization and the private domestic world as well as the gendered interactions which take place within organizations. Specific examples of both literal and metaphoric silence and din are considered. These illustrations are drawn from a variety of different organizations and settings. The third section considers how silence and din both inside and outside organizations contribute to the construction of gendered subjects. It is argued that subjects are constructed and gendered by means of language, conscious and unconscious processes and power relations. This construction is only ever temporary and the need for its constant re-creation opens up opportunities for subversion and change. Lastly, the conceptualization of organization itself is reviewed from the perspective of silence and din. For example, silences exist in organization theory on who holds power and who is excluded from power within organizations. There are relative silences on topics such as 'race', sexuality and violences within organizations, as well as on the gendered nature of particular theories. The din in organizational theory comes from the dominant perspective.

Throughout each of these sections the implications for change in organizations are acknowledged. Change itself is recognized to be complex and paradoxical. Ready, easy solutions for change are unlikely as there always exists the risk of change bringing with it the importation of new and unintended oppressions.

The conclusion pulls together the various theories that have been drawn upon during the course of the chapter, but there is also recognition of the limitation of this particular application of the concepts of silence and din.

THE GENDERED ORGANIZATION

Silence and din in organizations, however conceptualized, defined and categorized, occur within the context of organizations that are gendered. What this means is that not only are silence and din gendered processes, but the very fabric, texture and existence of organizations, and all aspects of organizations, are gendered. This is demonstrated in the very construction of organizations, both in their formation in the context of external social relations and in their internal writings and structure.

Thus most organizations are doubly gendered, in the sense that the public domains and the organizations within them are valued over the private domain, and also within organizations the structure and processes are themselves gendered.

The internal workings of organizations are gendered in both the distribution of women and men, and the distribution of gendered practices. Thus it is important to recognize the gendering of organizations even when they totally or almost totally consist of all women or all men.

While the number of different ways in which organizations can be gendered is immense, it may be helpful to build up a picture by focusing on a limited number of some typical differences.

1 First, there is the question of the gendered division of labour, both formal and informal. Women and men may, through processes of inclusion and exclusion, specialize in particular types of labour, thus creating vertical and horizontal divisions within organizations.
2 Divisions of authority are typically gendered, with men exerting more authority over both women and other men. These interactions of gendered division of labour and gendered divisions of authority produce, when consolidated in a formalized structure, what might be called the gendered bureaucracy (Ferguson 1984; Bologh 1990).
3 Gendered processes also occur between the centre and the margins of organizations. These may be literally or metaphorically spatial in terms of the distribution of power and activity between the centre and the margins of organizations. The central 'main aim' of organizations tends to be dominantly defined by men and in men's interest (Cockburn 1991). 'Front-line' activities are often staffed by women, while 'central' activities may be more often performed by men. The casualization, and hence implicit dispensability, of employment may also affect women workers more just as it may also affect black workers and, in different ways, younger and older workers.
4 A further gendered set of processes concerns the relationship of organizational participants to their domestic and related responsibilities. Women typically continue to carry the double burden of childcare and other unpaid domestic work. In addition, there may be a triple burden of care for other dependants, including parents and older people, and people with disabilities.
5 There are gendered processes in the operation of sexuality within organizations, including the occurrence of sexual harassment and the dominance of various forms of sexuality over others. Sexual processes may also interrelate with the occurrence of gendered violence in organizations.

These five elements can be understood as part of a picture of how the gendered organization, silence and din are constructed. In particular organizations these elements interact with each other in ways that may reinforce or contradict each other. Frequently these interactions are ambiguous, paradoxical and amenable to multiple interpretations. Additionally, these gendered processes and their interrelationships should not be seen as monolithic.

Indeed, of particular importance is the impact of atypical gendered positionings, either in terms of women or men occupying atypical positionings or in the use of atypical gendered practices. While atypical gendering may be a means of organizational change, not least in the transformation of silence and din in organization, the positioning of 'women managers', 'women doctors', 'men secretaries', 'male nurses' and so on should not be seen as necessarily subversive. Indeed it is quite possible that the production of atypical gendering can reproduce dominant gendered patterns within organizations, albeit in more subtle ways.

This leads to a final issue in this section, namely how gendered processes are reproduced in organizations. The elements and their interactions are above all occurrences in change, flux and becoming. Thus, while men's dominance is profound it is neither monolithic nor unresisted. It has to be continually re-established, and in the process it can be challenged, subverted and unestablished. For these reasons, linguistic and discursive processes of differencing in organizations, for example, in definitions of what is and is not 'legitimate' or 'illegitimate', are crucial (Cockburn 1990). These are also silences and dins.

Thus, to change organizations effectively and fundamentally it is necessary to avoid simply replacing one set of structures with another. The 'iron law of oligarchy' (Michels 1968) applies not just to political hierarchy but also to the very structuring of organizations, and specifically their gendered structuring (Ferguson 1984, 1987). More generally, political change is always liable to be reincorporated into fixed structures and ideologies (Griffin 1982).

SILENCE, DIN AND THE STRUCTURING OF ORGANIZATIONS

While silence and din occur differentially between women and men, both as organizational participants and as members of their different genders, the formations of organizations themselves are fundamental ways of constructing silence and din in the first place.

There are two major and intricately connected ways in which silence and din are structured by the very existence and presence of organizations: first, organizations can be constructed as din; second, they can be constructed as silences.

Organizations themselves can be din(s) in two ways: through the inclusion of participants – workers, managers, members – as accumulations of power, resources and people; and through the exclusion of others who are not members. In the first inclusive model the din is between those in the organization, usually dominantly between men, the loudest voices. In this sense the voices, usually men's, recount 'offers' to talk to and support them. In the second, exclusive model the din is of those inside over those outside the organization. It is a bit like the organization operating as a loudhailer, which broadcasts its message over those not in the organization. This can of course be literally the case with media organizations, like cable TV, or it can apply metaphorically to clients, users, and other members of the public who employ the 'services' of the organization. In this view men may be making the din over women who are both excluded and yet defined by those noises.

This model might apply, for instance, to women clients who seek services from state welfare organizations.

Organizations can be silences in two further ways: first, through the inclusion of participants, and second, through the exclusion of non-members. In the first of these two cases organizations are silences when, through their corporate organizing, they bring people together to silence them. This is most graphically seen in coercive and custodial organizations. In some organizations the silencing is not just the silencing of voices, so that members (or inmates) have to be silent, but also the silencing of bodies. Thus silence may equal death. This is clear in the concentration camps, the Gulags and similar total institutions. These organizations exist in and through silences. Sometimes the organization is reproduced daily through the prohibition of speech, as in schools, monasteries and other religious institutions. Needless to say, organizations as silence are not necessarily unwanted by participants. Some may indeed seek the silence of organizations, as in meditation and retreats. Furthermore, while such silencing may often involve men's silencing of women, some of its most brutal forms also involve men silencing men.

The second of the two cases conceptualizes organizations as silences through the exclusion of other people. This kind of silence is the obverse of the din of the loudhailer. Those outside are silent and silenced, and through their absence the presence (din) of the organization is confirmed. This may apply not just to women, but also to young people, older people, people with disabilities, and many others. In this view the silence is for them not even being part of the conversation in the first place. They may be excluded from being in certain public domains of certain organizations and may not yet have been 'allowed' to join the debate about their exclusion.

Silence and din: gendered interactions

Having outlined the way in which silence and din are fundamental to the structured relationships between gender, power and organization, we now explore large-scale and small-scale interactions in organizations. The interaction processes will be perceived as the area for the maintenance and reinforcement of a number of interconnected oppressions through the use of din and silence, and hence an important focus for change. Though our theme is gender we acknowledge that it is linked with other oppressions, including that of disability. As we focus on noise in organizations we recognize how they are sites for the able-bodied and fit, with the majority of disabled and profoundly deaf people confined to the private realm and having no actual or metaphoric voice in organization, and thus being silenced politically.

A gender analysis of silence and din leads to questions about who makes the most din, who is silenced. This alerts us to further dimensions of oppressive gendered power relations. Noise is so much a part of life that it is frequently perceived only when it becomes intolerable or offends. It is also perceived in its absence, as when intolerable noise ceases or there are uneasy silences.

Our concept of 'din' is literal and metaphoric, with the literal din of machinery being enhanced by the metaphoric din of ownership and supremacy through numbers and structures. Silence too is literal, though it is important to separate out silence through choice from being silenced through intimidation, threat, exclusion, marginalization and put-downs. Din and silence are not seen as exclusively opposite, for silence can be imposed through silent bullying and coercion, which is really din, and the din of oppressed groups whose grievances fail to be heard is actually silence.

Applying this understanding in practice needs first a recognition of the processes, secondly a willingness to intervene, and thirdly a way of evaluating any changes. For us, fundamental change will occur when men silence their din and truly listen to the voice of women and other oppressed groups.

The din of power, in one sense, is literal and obvious in the clatter of machinery and drills, the roar of rockets, the explosion of mortars and guns, the shriek of high-powered aircraft and the thud of marching armies. This is the din of production and control, and is to be contrasted with the processes of reproduction, when women may be told they are making a fuss if they fail to control the scream of giving birth. The 'good mother' is told she has done well if she puts on a brave face and keeps as silent as possible. The din of production and silence of reproduction are both a literal and a metaphoric representation of the relationships of class, labour and gender (Hearn 1987).

The din of production is also part of the interaction between the public and private domains, with the majority of production in public organizations. Ownership of this din is ownership of the means of production and inextricably linked with wider 'ownership' of the public world by men (Clark and Lange 1979) and through public men, public masculinities and public patriarchies (Hearn 1992). Part of the metaphoric silence of the private is its diminishing size and task in relation to the public. Other silences are the silences of oppression as men dominate in families, with the silent screams of women subjected to violence, and the silence of children frightened by the threats of further harm if they speak of the abuse they have suffered. Not only do men have control of both public and private realms, but the public realm and its organizations also control and scrutinize the private, whether through, for example, the benefit system or through ideological moral panics about single parents. In this there is double domination of the private realm by men (Hearn and Parkin 1987).

Women located in the private realm by domestic responsibilities are seen as apolitical, along with other groups with little voice. The private realm is the world of dependent children, dependent older people, disabled people, sick people, unemployed people. None of these groups has a part in the noise and din of production, and their metaphoric silence is further compounded when they have little or no say in organizational policy making on their behalf. The din of their grievances is transformed into silence by the din of the mobilization of bias, whereby powerful groups ensure that their issues are organized out of politics and the issues of the powerful are organized into politics (Bachrach and Baratz 1962).

The din of the meeting will be the din of the agenda items. The silent agenda is the one that is not heard, as voices are excluded.

The transition from public to private and private to public also involves noise. The din of traffic, tubes, trains, buses is there for all, whether male or female. However, for women the hazards are greater through the din of male violence, which makes walking in the street, breaking down on motorways, or travelling alone an area of potential threat. Women, not men, were advised to stay indoors or seek protection at the height of the Yorkshire Ripper scare. Women can be subjected to 'tailing' by lorries or horn-sounding, light-flashing, fast-revving cars wanting to overtake. A woman in a first-class railway compartment several times found herself the only woman and was made to feel she did not belong. The steward called her 'sir' and then 'lovey' when he discovered his mistake. Men travellers complained with loud voices or used portable phones with loud voices. In the travelling, mobile organization there is the replication of din, silence and gendered interactions around noise that are found in the public and the private domains.

In the public world of paid work there are numerous constructions and reconstructions of gender powers in the daily interactions between women and men.[1] Women continue to be perceived in terms of the domestic and as representatives of the private, both in the work they do and in the qualities they possess. The work they do continues to be lower paid, lower status work than that of men. Although women are rising in management and in 'top' professions such as law, accountancy and medicine, they continue to hit 'glass ceilings' and find the 'goalposts' are moved to prevent further promotions (Cockburn 1991). When women do achieve management and leadership roles they are often in semi-professional settings where the agenda, language and power relations are already set. Their behaviour in male dominated management settings is interpreted through male norms and values. Essentialist assumptions are made about the qualities they will bring to the management role (Hearn and Parkin 1988). In this there is the din of male leadership, management, rules, power, and decision making structures. Through this there is the din of male control of organizational space and time and male control of theory, as men's accounts of what constitutes organization and management prevail. This interaction of public and private helps construct and is constructed by the structures of the public world, which in turn are constructed and reconstructed by the processes of interaction between women and men, silence and din.

To develop this further, the din of machinery contrasts not only with the silence of the private but with other dins such as the din of the domestic in the organization. The clatter of buckets and noise of vacuum cleaners and emptying bins could arguably be seen as silence, as it usually does not impinge on 'normal' working time. The male caretakers work throughout the day but the female cleaning staff come in early and leave as other members of staff arrive. In one work setting where car parking spaces were at a premium, staff would try to time their arrival as women cleaners with cars were leaving. This gave rise to the sick joke of 'Adopt a cleaner as the answer to your car-parking problems.' The women cleaning staff were further marginalized and silenced through their pay and conditions. Their work was contracted out, wages reduced, work increased, and union rights lost. The abolition of the Wages Council further eroded their position and further silenced them. Their grievances rarely, if ever, reached the organizational agenda. In one sense they were hardly in the public world, as their contribution was not recognized until it was not made. The domestic cleaning task in organizations is thus a mirror of the domestic cleaning task in the private domain: predominantly performed by women, undervalued, and remunerated by low pay or no pay. Its din is silence as it is marginalized, ignored and devalued. In one Health Education Council (n.d.) booklet on keeping fit at work, one identified stress was that of noise, with the din of women talking/gossiping and the clatter of tea trolleys seen as contributing to the stress of suited, white males sitting at desks. This example of women's work in organizations is one of many we could have chosen to illustrate the din of male work and the marginalization and silencing of women and their work.

Some organizations or parts of organizations have written rules on silence, but in this section we focus on unwritten rules and norms around noise. The gendered nature of who speaks, who is heard and how speaking is interpreted starts early. Grandparents meeting their new grandson for the first time heard him crying and commented on his fine pair of lungs, whereas the grandparents of a new baby granddaughter saw her crying as an appeal for help (Giddens 1989). This gendered interpretation of noise sets a very early silence/din agenda.

Some men are slowly learning politically correct language and beginning to avoid blanket use of words such as 'chairman', 'manpower'and 'craftsmanship', recognizing them as an imposition of 'malestream' language and theory. In this context there is the din of male harassment through language. Within language, other dimensions of male control can be recognized when the sexualized language of the organization demonstrates the interconnections of sexuality and gender powers (Hearn and Parkin 1987). The language of male heterosexuality is that of 'goals', 'scoring' and 'policy thrusts', and the din of this language can silence women who feel harassed by it; but it also effectively silences gay men and lesbian women from stating their sexual stance. Challenging this language quickly challenges the merely 'politically correct', as does recognition of other interactions around speech and language. It is not only a matter of what is said but of who says it and how that contribution is perceived. Male voices dominate in boardrooms and management meetings, where they are in the majority. This, when linked with male gendered language, amplifies the din.

The din of management is replicated in other settings in organizations. There are a number of reasons for having mixed gender groups, both formal and informal. What is of interest is the gendered interactions and who again makes the most noise.

Moyer and Tuttle (1983) suggested the following 'common pitfalls' for men in mixed gender groups:

- 'hogging the show';
- being a continual problem solver;
- speaking in 'capital letters';

- defensiveness;
- task and content focus, to the exclusion of nurturing;
- put-downs and one-upmanship;
- negativism;
- transfer of the focus of discussion;
- holding on to formal powerful positions;
- intransigence and dogmatism;
- listening only to oneself;
- avoiding feelings;
- condescension and paternalism;
- using sexuality to manipulate women;
- seeking attention and support from women while competing with men;
- running the show;
- protectively storing key group information for one's own use;
- speaking for others.

Our own observations lead us to concur with this list but also add to it. In one instance in a leaderless group, the only man assumed he would chair it. In another group of four women and one man, it was his stated intention to listen to the women's views and plan future work with them. He was a colleague and not hierarchically superior to the women, yet he did 90 per cent of the speaking, spoke for the women, dictated what the future work would look like and did not listen at all.

Another instance was on a training day where small-group discussion took place in one group with seven women and one man who was also a manager. He stood up, commandeered a writing board and told the group how to proceed with the task. He chaired the group without consultation, he told one of the woman to take notes, told her what to write and ignored any contributions with which he disagreed. He laid down procedures, reworded women's contributions and directed rather than interacted. When forced to include feedback with which he disagreed, he announced he could be arrogant and looked for approval. Two of the women subsequently discussed why this behaviour had not been challenged and both found they had previously challenged similar behaviour and been silenced by the strength of the attack on them. The din continued when the man fed back to the whole group. He stood up when others had remained seated, he raised his voice, overrode other contributions and stressed the important committees of which he was a member. Wider discussion elicited the fact that many women had found his behaviour arrogant, but some did not perceive it as harassment or silencing, whereas others did in this context.

By contrast, another small-group discussion comprised women only. They quickly did the task amid laughter and interchanges, and were 'reprimanded' by men for 'making a din'. A group of women meeting in one of the women's rooms were involved in a mixture of sorting out some work and also supporting each other. Again there was laughter and noise, with one man feeling it acceptable to come into the room and comment on the noise. It would appear that when the powerful are literally or metaphorically noisy, it is not called din. Din is used for noise perceived as dysfunctional and possibly part of resistances in the context of women refusing to be silent or silenced.

Silence and din as harassment

The incidents described add to the growing catalogue of sexual harassment in its many forms. The din of harassment includes unwanted touch; unfunny jokes or accusations of being unable to take a joke; pin ups; pornography; initiation ceremonies; sexual advances; and being called 'love', 'girl' and similar names. However, analysis of silence and being silenced revealed a further dimension to harassment. A woman had two apparently contrasting experiences. She went to a second-hand car dealer to reclaim some money on a faulty product and was shouted at and pushed by three men, who made systematic threats of what they would do to her and in fact caused some bruising. She found this a very intimidating experience, but less of an ordeal than when a self-described 'new man' attacked her credibility publicly after she had disagreed with him in a discussion group. The metaphoric din of harassment in the second incident effectively silenced her more than the literal din of the threats in the first.

This led to consideration of other parallel experiences, as when four women working together in a small office with one male manager arrived early. They talked of the weekend and of the coming day's work. The man arrived, barely responded to greetings, and sat at his desk in silence. The women were gradually reduced to silence. He did not say a word, but the din of his presence, maleness and intimidation created a silence which was uneasy. The women felt they had been bullied. This leads to considerations of other forms of bullying, including the behaviour of men who refuse to acknowledge women in corridors, refuse to respond to women's greetings, and refuse to acknowledge women's raised hands in plenary sessions, thereby refusing a voice to the women. In all these instances women are silenced through male power: men's silence towards women, either individually or collectively, can be another form of bullying and harassment of women.

These examples of harassment exemplify the role of silence and din in interactions. Many of the men involved in these interactions use 'politically correct' language on gender, which is demonstrated to be no more than 'lip service' when their behaviour is observed. Language and structures can be changed, but it is in the daily interactions that there are the possibilities for fundamental change. These areas, however, are also the most problematic.

Men need to be aware of their conduct in groups (Moyer and Tuttle 1983) and how it harasses women. The first requisite is that they silence their din and listen to the voice of women. It is more than reducing the din so it is not displeasing and being pleasant or nice. This fails to redress power imbalances. It is a fundamental 'tuning in' to women's grievances and altering behaviour accordingly. The din of bullying through imposition of silence is one of the hardest to redress. It is difficult to complain that a person will not speak to you or acknowledge you, and it would be impossible to legislate for this sort of behaviour. Women who do challenge can be humiliated and made to feel foolish. Challenging silence or lack of noise is difficult when only the recipient experiences it as overwhelming din.

Part of men's 'backlash' to such critiques is often to cite instances when women have been intimidating and powerful. They can be immune to the recognition of how sexism as a system can devalue both men and women, but women are the major victims of it. The difficulty for women in such an asymmetrical situation is their vulnerability to the various forms of counter-attack which can victimize them further. Nevertheless, we suggest that interactions are the arena for change, with a focus on the deconstruction of the various forms of intimidation reconstructed into non-threatening situations. The pace of change is slow. It will concentrate on challenging din in its many forms, but using the analysis of silence and din and pointing out not only the din but its ability to silence. When we are silenced we are powerless. The uneasy silences need reconstructing into a confident voice which will not be silenced. This is not women making a din, but silencing the din to create mutuality.

These gendered interactions do not leave subjects untouched. Practices do not occur outside subjects as if they are hermetically concealed biological entities. Men and women are not isolated individuals but subjects who exist and are constructed in relation to one another (Hollway 1989).

SILENCE AND DIN: CONSTRUCTING THE SUBJECT

Unconscious processes and linguistic, discursive and behavioural practices construct men and women as different both within and outside the organization. The characteristics/constructions of men and women might be seen in terms of binary oppositions, but also of complementarity. Dominant discourses of science and nature deliver these constructed, characteristic differences of men and women as 'truth'. Furthermore, this truth is widely known through and as common sense. 'Man' and 'woman', however, do not stand alone, but are pivotally connected to one another in a relationship of power. These linguistic and discursive constructions of men and women can be seen in terms of silence and din both literally and metaphorically.

In a literal sense women might be silent as a result of their oppression. Jean Baker Miller (1988) describes women in this way. She argues that the silence arises from being a subordinate group. Women are not the only group of subordinates. Black people might also be silent as they share a similar position. The dominant group (white, able bodied men) have most opportunities to construct and validate discourses which have the status of defining reality. Subordinates such as women and black people, who may have a different construction of reality, may be violently opposed if they attempt to break the silence. The disciplinary activities of organizations, such as courts, clinics and hospitals, may be brought into play in order to sustain the acceptable level of noise. Subordinates' silence conceals their active watching of and listening to the din of the dominants. This is essential to survival, as noisy confrontation is best avoided. Retaliation from the dominants can mean for women extreme hardship, social ostracism and psychological isolation. As Jean Baker Miller says, 'Subordinates won't tell' (1988: 10).

Women may in this general sense be constructed as silent, but when women are acknowledged as breaking the silence the language used to describe this is often derisory. Women's talk is identified as 'prattle, babble, chatter, jabber, blather, hot air, small talk, rubbish, gibberish, verbosity', according to the poem 'Women's Talk' by Astra (Spender 1980: v). Schulz argues that all language is systematically sexist, thus reflecting the patriarchal power relations (Schulz 1975, quoted in Spender 1980: 16).

In a metaphoric sense din might signify action and silence might signify passivity. Even from this perspective women remain silent, being constructed as submissive, passive, docile, lacking in initiative and unwilling to act. Women are constructed as similar to children – immature, weak and helpless. Men, in opposition, are not silent; they are active, rational, scientific and instrumental. Women, constructed as emotional and nurturing, offer support from the private, while men pursue active rationality in the public work of organizations. Ferguson (1984) argues that bureaucracies as 'scientific' and 'rational' constructions have a crucial role in constructing subjects. For Ferguson, society is permeated by both the institutional forms and the language of rationality. Inequalities such as race, sex and class are perpetuated within bureaucracies, which categorize subjects into hierarchies with the rationalization of scientific organization. Bureaucracies control directly and indirectly by legitimizing certain kinds of gendered language, motivation and behaviour, all shrouded in the necessity of scientific rationalization. Hence organizations and bureaucracies are defined and constructed in the same or similar linguistic terms and discourses as men. Not surprisingly, men's dominating position in bureaucracies gives them a voice while women are to a large extent excluded from public speech.

Within both the public and private spheres, women are constructed as the carriers of emotion and as the carers and nurturers of others. To be a woman is not to voice one's own needs but to subsume these needs in concern for and caring for others (Lawrence 1992). But this construction does not endear men to women. On the contrary, whatever women do will be met with dissatisfaction from men, because, according to Jean Baker Miller (1988), men deny and reject the emotional aspects of humanity which they fear, such as vulnerability and weakness. Women voicing, expressing or working with these human characteristics/constructions are then derided for doing so. While Lawrence and Miller apply a psychoanalytical analysis and conclusion, theories of linguistics and discursive power relations can make valuable use of psychoanalytical insights. Psychoanalytic processes can provide content to discursive positions and practices, and can contribute to the construction of gendered subjects (Hollway 1989). Unconscious desires and defences can be in play as part of the discursive practices which render women as silent.

Women in this general sense might be constructed as silent, but according to poststructural theorization, gendered power relations are not given but require constant reconstruction. The 'microphysics of power' is in play at all times. Despite the possible and potential consequences, women do break the silence and challenge dominant constructions. Women, amongst others, do in fact tell. The idea of one universal, rational, scientific truth is under threat as the different voices of women, black people, gay and lesbian people and those with disabilities emerge, each challenging the din of domination.

Challenge and subversion may take a variety of forms. Attempts at change may occur on a daily basis inside and outside of organizations, as subjects struggle to assert their differences and resist hegemonic constructions. Strategies developed by subjects acting together may aim to overturn hegemonic practices which silence and deny. The patriarchal conceptualization and construction of the subject itself is challenged by theorists and writers such as Irigaray and Kristeva. According to Irigaray (1985) language itself can be a space for change, and Ferguson supports the principle as attempts are made to 'loosen the hold of universal male discourse in order to let differences be (either the difference of women or the multiple diversities of a differently gendered world)' (Ferguson 1985: 76).

Language and discourse can contribute to the construction of subjects as silent and submissive or noisy and dominating. The matter does not end there, though, as these constructions need to be renewed and reinforced, constantly making the opportunity for challenge ever present. Language itself can be a space for challenge and change. This is not to say that change is easy and automatically follows conscious, 'rational' decision making. Unconscious, psychodynamic processes, which are in play and contribute to the power relations between gendered subjects, also affect the structuring and processes within organizations (Menzies 1970). Change for subjects, subject relations and organizations is a complex phenomenon which defies simple explanations and solutions.

SILENCE, DIN AND THEORIZING ORGANIZATIONS

The ideas of silence and din can also be applied to the processes of theorizing organizations – the socially sanctioned ways of making sense of organization and organizational workings that have been described. Thus, in simple terms dominant organization theories and theories of organizations are dins, while those that are subordinated or absent are silences. These dominant processes can refer to the form, politics or methodology of theories, or to the domination of certain topics or even certain theorists. In each case these dominant processes are gendered, most obviously by men.

Dominant theories include bureaucratic theory, systems theory, contingency theory, technology theory, and a host of organizational psychologies and motivational theories. In this there is usually a male or supposedly agendered centre, both to the theory and to the organization. There is usually a 'something' that explains, or is supposed to explain, the way organizations are. This is most obviously the case in management theories, where the 'reality' of organization is defined from the point of view of the perspective of men/managers. The mutual associations of men, management, and organizational/managerial theories are intense. There are often male dominated, male centred and supposedly non-problematic discourses.

The silences of organization theory are several. Just as there are silences about that which is not talked about within organizations, so there are silences in theorizing. These include knowledge from the perspective of those with less power or those excluded from organizations. There is also knowledge that concerns the subtexts of organizations, such as the ways in which men may prefer men's company even where a heterosexual, or heterosexist, culture dominates.

There are also significant silences in organizations theory around particular topics: 'race'; disability; the bodily experience of organizations; sexuality; love and affection; violence, coercion and humiliation; indeed silencing itself. These might be seen as not just absent or neglected topics, but absent or neglected bases of further theories. They are part of the decentred margins that are excluded by the dominant centres of 'malestream' theoretical discourses on organizations.

Perhaps most significant is a further set of silences on the very nature of theory and theorizing. Poststructuralist and postmodernist approaches to knowledge not only deconstruct the subject, they also deconstruct theory, including what is meant by theorizing in and on organizations. Thus, what counts as theory, what is called theory at all, needs to recognise and address silences and absences, along with otherness and paradox, as equal in importance to presence, din and the centres of discourses. Such a 'direction' needs developing so that the centrality of oppression, including gender oppression, is elaborated. Rather than using poststructuralism and postmodernism to exclude 'feminism', 'women', 'gender', 'sexuality' and 'violence', as has been done by some male theorists (see Hearn and Parkin 1993), such 'othered' approaches may be a way of understanding and changing gendered power and gendered oppressions in more far reaching ways. In short, the deconstruction of the din and silence of gendered power cannot be reduced to the formal and informal structures of 'the gendered organization'. Gendered power is much more complex, subtle and paradoxical. And accordingly, theorizing organizations to change needs to be equally complex, subtle and paradoxical.

In this section we have noted some of the major silences and dins of dominant theorizations of organizations. Dominant theories neglect certain aspects of and perspectives on organizations, particularly the ones that represent those interests which are dominated in organizations. This in turn suggests the need not just for changing organization theory, but for theory and theorizing that lead to change. In producing such theory/theorizing for change, it is constantly necessary to avoid it working against change by the obscuring of issues (Hearn and Parkin 1993). There is no point in developing theories that theoretically 'open up' spaces for voices that have previously been excluded if that theorizing is itself so exclusive and exclusionary as to close off those very voices simultaneously.

CONCLUSION

During the course of this chapter we have tried to show that organizations can be considered as structured in a number of different ways. Whichever way is considered, men dominate. The metaphorical use of the term 'din' means this domination is deafening and defining for the women (and other marginalized groups) who by their oppression are metaphorically and often literally silenced. Despite the hegemony of seeing organizations and their structure as inevitable, challenge and the expectation of change do exist (for example, Kanter 1977). Fundamental structural change of organizations might be seen as the long agenda (Cockburn 1989), but the fact that alternative, subversive visions of organizations exist gives us hope for the potential of change. However, the consequences of structural change would have to be thoroughly considered, as change leading to even greater oppression or different kinds of oppression would be no solution.

Women are silenced by the structure of organizations, but also through interactional processes. Men dominate in meetings, interrupt and talk over women, silence women with subtle put-downs, ignore contributions made by women and even attribute them to men. The physical dominance of men through the unwanted touch of harassment and the more subtle social exclusion of women takes place within organizations. Examples such as these have been given in an attempt to show how, through interactional processes, men's din dominates and silences women and others who share a similar social location.

Some mechanisms for change are in place in some organizations with the introduction of personal and sexual harassment policies. The more subtle forms of exclusion by humiliation are less easy to legislate against, but women in some settings have formed themselves into support and action groups where these interactional processes are explored and exposed, and strategies for challenge and change are developed. Attempts towards such change are few and far between, however, and the task of making them is not insignificant, given the crucial role that relations between men and women have in constructing and reconstructing gender. Consideration of such issues highlights the complexity and enormity of the task of making fundamental change.

Potential for change within organizations is to a certain extent confused by the way organizations are theorized. The din of certain kinds of theory and the silence of alternatives leads to conceptual and practical constraints. Poststructuralist and postmodernist approaches, however, may be ways of changing discourse so that previously silenced voices can be heard.

Silence and din have been the conceptualizations used to consider overt and covert gendered domination within organizations. The possibility of and challenge to change has been acknowledged within each section, and what has been revealed is the amount and range of change required for the noise of gendered mutuality as opposed to the silence and din of organizational domination.

While the concept of silence and din with both literal and metaphorical meanings has provided a vehicle for exploring gendered oppression within organizations, the conceptualization has its limitations. Domination cannot only be equated with din and silence with oppression. Silence can also be dominating, while din can literally be the noise of the oppressed. Using these terms with both literal and metaphorical meanings could lead to some confusion and perhaps a dilution of the power of specific meaning. Silence and din as concepts are audio based and do not encompass the visual or other sensory media. These concepts are based on the word. According to postmodernists the word is part of a modernist narrative – to put it crudely, relying on the word is old-fashioned. But the postmodernist concern with medium might reduce concern for the content. The content with which we have been concerned is the silence and din of oppression within organizations, and the potential and limitations for change.

NOTE

1   Hearn and Parkin (1987) describe gender power in organizations as part of the gendered structures and power relations of organizations. They also see gender powers linked with sexuality in terms of:

- the power of men (over sexuality, and over women);
- the power of the public realm (over sexuality and over the private);
- the power of production (over sexuality and over reproduction); and indeed
- the power of reproduction (over sexuality)

REFERENCES

Bachrach, P. and Baratz, M. S. (1962) 'Two faces of power'. *American Political Science Review*, 57(3), 632–42.

Baker Miller, J. (1988) *Toward a New Psychology of Women*. Boston, MA: Beacon Press. (1st pub. 1976.)

Bologh, R. W. (1990) *Love or Greatness? Max Weber and Masculine Thinking – A Feminist Inquiry*. London and Boston: Unwin Hyman.

Clark, L. M. G. and Lange, L. (1979) *The Sexism of Social & Political Theory*. Toronto: University of Toronto Press.

Cockburn, C. K. (1989) 'Equal opportunities: the short and long agendas'. *Industrial Relations Journal*, 20(3), 213–25.

Cockburn, C. K. (1990) 'Men's power in organizations: "equal opportunities" intervenes'. In Hearn, J. and Morgan, D.H.J. (eds), *Men, Masculinities and Social Theory*. London and Boston: Unwin Hyman.

Cockburn, C. (1991) *In the Way of Women*. London: Macmillan.

Ferguson, K.E. (1984) *The Feminist Case Against Bureaucracy*. Philadelphia: Temple University Press.

Ferguson, K.E. (1985) 'Subject-centredness in feminist discourse'. In Jones, K. B. and Jonasdottir, A.G. (eds), *The Political Interests of Gender: Developing Theory and Research with a Feminist Face*. Beverly Hills, CA: Sage.

Ferguson, K. E. (1987) 'Work, text and act in discourses of organization'. *Women and Politics*, 7(2), 1–21.

Giddens, A. (1989) *Sociology*. Cambridge: Polity Press.

Griffin, S. (1982) 'The way of all ideology'. In Keohlane, N.O., Rosaldo, M.Z. and Gelpi,

B.C. (eds), *Feminist Theory: A Critique of Ideology*. Brighton: Harvester; Chicago: University of Chicago Press.

Health Education Council (n. d.) *Stay Fit in the Office*. London: HEC.

Hearn, J. (1987) *The Gender of Oppression*. Brighton: Wheatsheaf; New York: St Martin's Press.

Hearn, J. (1992) *Men in the Public Eye: The Construction and Deconstruction of Public Men and Public Patriarchies*. London and New York: Routledge.

Hearn, J. and Parkin, W. (1987) *'Sex at Work': The Power and Paradox of Organization Sexuality*. Brighton: Wheatsheaf; New York: St Martin's Press. 2nd edn. (1995) Hemel Hempstead: Prentice Hall.

Hearn, J. and Parkin, P. W. (1988) 'Women, men and leadership: a critical review of assumptions, practices and change in the "industrialized nations"'. In Adler, N. J. and Israeli, D. N. (eds), *Women in Management Worldwide*. New York: M. E. Sharpe.

Hearn, J. and Parkin, W. (1993) 'Organizations, multiple oppressions and postmodernism'. In Hassard, J. & Parker, M. (eds), *Postmodernism and Organizations*. London: Sage.

Hollway, W. (1989) *Subjectivity and Method in Psychology: Gender, Meaning and Science*. London: Sage.

Irigaray, L. (1985) *Speculum of the Other Woman*. Ithaca, NY: Cornell University Press.

Kanter, R. M. (1977) *Men and Women of the Corporation*. New York: Basic Books.

Lawrence, M. (1992) 'Women's psychology and feminist social work practice'. In Langan, M. and Day, L. (eds), *Women, Oppression and Social Work*. London: Routledge.

Menzies, I. E. P. (1970) *The Functioning of Social Systems as a Defence Against Anxiety*. London: Centre for Applied Social Research, the Tavistock Institute of Human Relations.

Michels, R. (1968) *Political Parties*. London: Collier Macmillan.

Moyer, B. and Tuttle, A. (1983) 'Overcoming masculine oppression in mixed groups'. In *Off their Backs ... and On our Own Two Feet*. Philadelphia: New Society Publishers.

Schulz, M. (1975) 'The semiotic derogation of women'. In Thorne, B. and Henley N. (eds), *Language and Sex: Difference and Dominance*. Royley, MA: Newbury House.

Spender, D. (1980) *Man Made Language*. London: Routledge and Kegan Paul.

Chapter 7

Diversity and change

Gender, welfare and organizational relations

Janet Newman and Fiona Williams

This chapter assesses the significance of gender as a social division in the restructuring of social welfare, and in the pattern of change in public sector organizations. It explores the relationship between gender and other lines of social division and identity, and considers the implications for the politics of change.

The current patterns of economic and political change are having profound consequences for women as both users of, and workers in, public sector organizations. In Britain, almost every area of state provision has recently seen massive change. In this chapter we are concerned to place the issues around gender and organizational change in the wider context of an understanding of fundamental shifts in the provision of welfare that are taking place in the 1990s. We examine the relationship between three areas of change: the social relations of (and within) gender; public sector organizations; and the restructuring of welfare provision. In attempting to make sense of these changes we look, in particular, at the extent to which explanations of changes in organizations and in welfare can account not simply for gender relations, but for a more multifaceted and fluid understanding of the category 'woman' arising from changing social divisions and the destabilization of social and political identities.

The chapter is based on research in different areas: work on social change, social divisions and the welfare state (Williams 1989, 1992, 1994), and work on gender, organizational change and managerialism (Newman 1993, 1994). In bringing these together we attempt to synthesize a number of ideas. First, we suggest that changes in welfare in Britain – a 'new welfare settlement' – can be understood in terms of a dovetailing of three dynamics: the 'logic' of post-Fordism, the neoliberal ideology of welfare of the Conservative administrations since 1979, and the influences of managerial discourses. Second, we argue that the social relations of and around gender need to inform the analysis of these dynamics. Third, this understanding needs to be informed by the ways in which other social identities, social divisions and inequalities cut across gender – especially those around class, 'race', disability, sexuality and age. Fourthly, we suggest that it is necessary to acknowledge the specific relationship between gender and welfare in terms of women's role as users of services, as providers of welfare – both as paid and unpaid workers (in the voluntary sector and as carers) – and as agents of change. Finally, these ideas can provide us with a framework to assess the impact of changes in organizational culture upon women and their possibilities for action. The chapter is structured around these five sets of ideas.

THE DYNAMICS OF CHANGE: THE LOGIC OF POST-FORDISM

'Post-Fordism' has become a way of understanding and explaining changes in welfare provision taking place not just within Britain, but internationally. It is a conceptual term referring to the process of industrial change, characterized by a trend towards differentiation in both production and consumption. The mass, large scale production of the assembly line (Fordism) has given way to the disaggregation of semi-autonomous work groups held together by new information systems. Standardized products have been replaced by diverse products aimed at diverse groups of consumers, and this is accompanied by a move towards a situation where consumers and retailing lead production rather than the other way round. Alongside this the workforce too has changed its nature and form, no longer dominated by a unionized and skilled (and white, male) workforce, but fragmented into a smaller (and white, male) multiskilled workforce and a peripheral workforce of low-paid, part-time workers, often black and white women and black men.

The analysis of economic change in terms of a shift from 'Fordism' to 'post-Fordism' is usually based on a series of dichotomies:

Fordism	*Post-Fordism*
Mass production	Flexible production methods
Mass markets	Niche markets
Mass labour force	Flexible labour force
Functional specialization	Multiskilling

Each shift, it is argued, is based on the search for more flexible regimes of accumulation in response to problems of profitability. There is considerable debate about how far this is happening in the private sector (Whitaker 1992), and we should certainly be cautious about a direct transference of ideas from the private to the public sectors. However, there are some key trends in the pattern of public sector organizations which are of great significance to women both as 'workers' in, and as 'customers' of, the welfare state.

One of the basic principles underpinning the restructuring of public sector organizations has certainly been the search for flexibility. We can see the emergence of more flexible patterns of provision across the public, private and voluntary sectors in the emerging 'mixed economies' of service provision. Flexibility has also been a key principle underpinning a succession of internal restructurings designed to introduce greater levels of devolution and decentralization. These have been linked to the idea of providing a more flexible pattern of services, more precisely 'tailored' to specific needs (such as individual community care packages) or more tightly 'targeted' at a particular market (such as women-only swimming sessions).

Underpinning such changes has been the search for ways of introducing greater flexibility into the labour process itself, through the increase in part-time work, the introduction of short term contracts, and the erosion of national pay-bargaining structures, in order to introduce 'local' flexibility for employers. Organizations are also searching for 'functional' flexibility within the workforce, with employees being increasingly expected to deploy a range of skills and a flexibility of approach to their working roles, for example in nursing (Walby 1992).

However, the reasons for these changes are more diverse and complex than a simple transition from Fordist to post-Fordist systems. In order to avoid economic determinism, we need to ask ourselves how far these changes can be understood as a 'natural' spin-off of the economic shift from Fordism to post-Fordism, and how far they have been influenced by other social and political realignments.

To begin with, the nature of and explanations for these changes have all been contested. The consequent critiques stem from different theoretical and critical positions. Some concern the extent of change, and the failure to take account of the diversity of (non-post-Fordist) responses to the crisis in Fordism (Clarke 1991). Others concern the problems of transferring the argument from the sphere of production to theories of social welfare (Clarke and Newman 1993). Many analysts point to the failure of the Fordist/post-Fordist dichotomy to explain the dynamics of change (e.g. Cochrane 1991). It has been argued that the 'post-Fordist' thesis is reductionist: it reduces changes in welfare (or social and cultural change) to economic and technological imperatives and ignores the significance of political struggles and shifts in the balance of power in generating, resisting or permitting change (Rustin 1989).

Williams (1994) argues that most post-Fordist analyses have emerged from an unreconstructed political economy approach to the organization of labour – that is, one which fails to account for the significance of social relations other than class, particularly the social relations of gender and of 'race'. She suggests that the main criticisms of the applications of the Fordist/post-Fordist dichotomy to welfare are that first, they have focused on the relationship between the state, production and class relations to the exclusion of the relationship between the state, production, the domestic sphere and other significant social relations of power, most notably gender and 'race'. Second, there has been a tendency to generalize and conceptualize from the basis of the white, male experience of work and of welfare. Third, in so far as gender or 'race' relations are brought into the picture, then these references tend to be non-specific (using general terms such as 'family' or 'inner city'), ahistorical and class determined. In particular, no power of agency is given to either gender, 'race' or other social relations.

Williams' argument extends that of Pollert, who suggests that the post-Fordist model, in its focus on change, fails to identify the continuities in labour processes. In particular, it confuses what is in effect a 'repackaging of well worn employment patterns and practices' (Pollert 1988: 310) aimed at raising productivity and profit, with a conscious management strategy aimed at developing flexibility through a core and peripheral workforce. Instead, she suggests other factors need to be brought in to account for these developments: intensified employment inequalities around 'race', gender and age; new social forces like the feminization of the workforce; and new right policies in employment, such as youth training schemes and weakening of trade-union and wage-bargaining powers.

In relation to the public sector, she also claims that here employment restructuring may be more developed than in the private sector, not merely following it. This is a consequence not of economic or technological change, but of budgetary constraints, uncertainty over future funding, and new right policies aimed at encouraging a mixed economy of welfare, especially private welfare. Whilst this last point may underestimate the extent to which similar processes are being followed in other European welfare states not led by neoliberal administrations (see Baldock 1993), nevertheless Pollert's analysis is important for several reasons. First, she brings in the relevance (within production) of other social divisions. Second, she suggests that since the post-Fordist model is drawn from the experience of manufacturing it tends to universalize a white, male experience of work; it assumes a gender neutrality in its use of terms like 'core', 'periphery' and 'skill', which are in fact profoundly gendered and racialized. In common with many labour-market theories, it provides no adequate conceptual bridge to allow an understanding of the relationship between the production and the domestic sphere (Beechey 1988). And third, by bringing in the possible factor of the 'feminization of the workforce' she gives gender a power of explanation in the argument.

These points suggest that we should be wary of explaining changes in the position of women in the labour force, in organizations, or in the pattern of social welfare provision simply in terms of the shift from Fordism to post-Fordism. We want now to sketch out some of the issues which we see as relevant to the debate about the gendered dynamics of change, firstly in social welfare, then in organizational analysis.

THE MIXED ECONOMY OF WELFARE AND NEO-LIBERAL IDEOLOGY

Over the last decade, there has been much greater acknowledgement and promotion of a 'mixed economy' of welfare. The traditional pattern of state provision has been fragmented along the lines suggested by a Fordist/post-Fordist shift. However, this has to be understood in terms of the changing political terrain in Britain. Whilst the development of a 'mixed economy' of welfare has had support from the political centre, it has also provided an opportunity for the new right to exercise ideological principles in relation to welfare. These include the aims to break up the monolithic power of the public sector and to encourage a diversity of provision from public, private, voluntary and informal sources. Thereby, it is claimed, the expression of a diversity of individual choice can be enabled.

One outcome has undoubtedly been an increasing fragmentation of provision. Examples include the separation of purchaser/commissioning and provider/service delivery roles in health and community care, with increasing fragmentation of provision across different sectors. As already discussed, fragmentation of the workforce is also occurring, with many 'low skilled' jobs being contracted out, and an increasing use of flexible (that is, insecure and badly paid) forms of labour. Fragmentation is also occurring in voluntary and grass roots provision, with growing divisions between large, relatively securely funded voluntary organizations participating in the new 'contract culture' and small scale or localized projects meeting specific needs (including those of women or of minority ethnic groups).

A second outcome is the attack on 'universal' forms of state provision and state benefit. Universalism is not a gender-free notion – it is built on a particular model of the white family, centred on a male 'family' wage earner. But its demise has significant implications for women as workers in public sector organizations, and for women as the users of services and the recipients of benefits. The decline of universalism has also led to increased uncertainty for many of those who use welfare services or receive benefits. The increase of discretionary benefits, the streamlining of existing benefits, and the threat to established ones like child benefit create an atmosphere of insecurity. So too do pressures to move from long-stay hospitals into often temporary and insecure accommodation in the community. There is, in other words, a diminishing certainty that what is will be.

However, these changes are also marked by an uncertainty of a different sort: of ethos or purpose for state welfare. This is not to say that there is a 'crisis' of state welfare, but to say that whilst many of the universalistic policies and assumptions of the post-war period have been eroded, they have not been replaced by an overarching commitment to individualism, family, self-help and the market. The situation is more fluid, more complex and more contradictory.

Fragmentation in the form of greater diversification, differentiation and lack of coordination represents one aspect of the changing pattern of welfare provision. However, this change is not linear or straightforward, but embodies a tension between two contradictory processes: on the one hand, towards fragmentation; on the other, towards centralization. The fragmentation of state provision has, in most cases, been accompanied by tighter control of resources by central government; the setting out of centrally determined national standards and the publication of league tables of performance; and a stronger emphasis on central inspection and regulation of services. Local autonomy and accountability have been eroded by centrally determined 'rules of the game' (for example, setting out criteria against which local authorities can compete for special funds, such as those linked to the 'City Challenge' initiative, where urban funding had previously been based on universal, needs led criteria).

The last decade, too, shows other contradictions. On the one hand, there has been a worsening of the material conditions in which many people live. The impact of the new right's social policies has been to intensify inequalities of gender, race, disability and age, particularly where these are compounded with class inequalities or with marginalization from paid work. For example, whilst more women are being drawn into the labour market, the pay, conditions, associated benefits (health insurance, pensions, etc.) and access to childcare have deteriorated. Indeed, for black women in manual work this deterioration has been greater (Bruegel 1989). This has been accompanied by the erosion of trade union power and of local authority power and funding; the tightening of law and order policies in inner cities, and of immigration controls; and an attempt to discredit anti-discriminatory strategies by local authorities. Through all of this, the new right have attempted to appeal to notions of traditional family responsibility, British cultural tradition and national unity to justify the maintenance, even the desirability, of continuing inequalities and divisions (Williams 1989).

On the other hand, the past decade has also seen a growing awareness of inequalities of race, gender and disability in particular. The influence of equal opportunities demands has left very few areas of welfare provision untouched. At the same time, the Citizen's Charter, together with structural changes in the state (especially 'contracting out' and the exposure of public services to market forces), has led to an increased emphasis on quality in the delivery of public services. While much of this is tokenistic, in some areas the focus on quality has led to greater responsiveness to the diverse needs or requirements of different groups of service users. Examples include responsiveness to different dietary needs in hospital catering and school meals services; responsiveness to women's concern over safety issues in the design of public spaces; and the development of more sensitized responses to users with 'special needs'. The dominant impact of quality management has been an attempt to standardize, and consequently moves to assess quality often fail to be responsive to diverse requirements.

However, the beginnings of change are apparent as some groups of users develop stronger self-advocacy movements, and as managers begin to talk of 'niche marketing' in relation to particular groups of customers. But in the new market place for public services, it is evident that some groups will have less leverage than others. Many women, black and ethnic minorities, the elderly and people with disabilities will not be in a position to buy private health care, private pensions, private schooling and so on. What we are witnessing, perhaps, is the emergence of a two-tier welfare system, with more and more groups being targeted as 'niche markets' for private provision, leaving large numbers of the population dependent on residual public welfare.

MANAGERIALISM, WELFARE AND LABOUR FORCE RESTRUCTURING

The fragmentation of public sector organizations has partly been through the application of market or quasi-market principles, leading to the separation of 'purchaser' and 'provider' roles within organizations; the contracting out of services; and the partial dismantling of organizations which played coordinating and planning roles (such as regional health authorities and local education authorities). These changes have clearly been political in nature. However, the political conditions are themselves not straightforward. One thrust has been ideological, and has been dominated by new right theories of the state and the need to limit its collective role in providing for social needs. The language of the market place – of 'customers' and 'choice' – has had a transparently ideological slant. But we have also seen a much more pragmatic political struggle to secure and ensure Conservative dominance of the political landscape. There has been a clear imperative to break, or at least curtail, the power of local authorities, one of the few sources of resistance to conservative dominance of the political terrain of Britain through the 1980s and 1990s. However, from a different perspective, it could also be argued that the radical attempt to transform the public sector around market/quasi-market principles has been led by a necessary concern to seek new solutions in an economic environment of reduced resource base (because of recession and a declining industrial base) and a social environment of increasing demands (linked to spiralling demands for health care and an increasingly elderly population), an environment faced by all European welfare states.

This process of restructuring has been accompanied by a search for a more 'flexible' labour force, based on the reorganization of labour around the separation of 'core' and 'periphery' (Pinch 1992). This resonates with Charles Handy's (1989) model of the 'shamrock' organization, with three separate but interrelated leaves. At the centre is a small core of highly qualified professionals, managers and skilled workers. These are well rewarded, but are expected to work long hours and have a high degree of commitment. The 'contractual fringe' consists of self-employed professionals and consultants paid fees for delivering specified services as and when the organization needs them. The 'flexible labour force' is the third leaf of the shamrock, and consists of low skilled, part-time or temporary workers who provide basic services to the organization.

While these models can be understood in terms of a basic Fordist/post-Fordist economic shift, they can also be seen as matching the political agenda of realigning state organizations around quasi-market principles. As restructuring takes place, many organizations are contracting out many of their activities to the private and voluntary sector contractors, and are retaining only a small core responsible for strategy and the purchasing or commissioning of services. The exact form this is taking varies across sectors – for instance between local government and the health services – and is more developed in some than in others. Sometimes the model is one of 'externalization', and sometimes it is based on an internal replication of the model, with splits between purchasing and providing roles within a single organization.

At the same time, however, many of these internal changes can be seen as managerially driven. Organizations have been setting their own agendas for increasing the degree of internal flexibility. Devolution, decentralization, the setting up of business units and the change in internal patterns of coordination and control have been driven as much by managerial preoccupations as by political ideology (Clarke *et al.* 1994). We can attempt to explain some of these contextual and organizational changes in terms of a dovetailing of the logic of post-Fordism, new right ideology, welfare pluralism and managerialism. Separately and together, we have indicated, these have particular implications for women. We now want to focus on the gender dynamics of organizational change.

'Flexibility' undoubtedly has a positive ideological gloss. Indeed, as women we have been arguing for some kinds of flexibility in our relationships with employers for years. In managerial terms, flexibility is usually identified as a positive virtue in comparison with the stultifying inflexibilities of bureaucracy. However, this ideological gloss masks a profound deepening of inequalities in the labour force and in the experience of work. These inequalities are both gendered and racialized.

Pinch (1992) points to a general polarization and segmentation of the public sector workforce in terms of pay rewards, working conditions and employment prospects. This segmentation and polarization have led to increases in the pay and rewards for senior managers (in return for performance), at the same time as cost pressures are driving down pay and leading to 'flexibility' strategies at lower levels, with substantially worsening conditions of service in the contracted out and flexible sectors. Given that the organizational core is largely made up of men, and women are frequently found on the organization's periphery, in part-time, low-paid jobs with little job security, this polarization must be seen as profoundly gendered. But there are parallel polarizations taking place around 'race', class and age; so the polarization process does not affect all women in the same way. These flexibility strategies apply differentially to middle class women and working class women; to black women and to white women.

We can also see variations in degrees of security and protection for women and men of different ages. For employers seeking flexibility, older staff at higher points on a pay scale may be seen as more expensive and so less desirable. Older staff are also more subject to redundancies. There is, furthermore, a growing practice of offering short-term contracts to new, younger staff at lower points on pay scales, thus reducing opportunities for older women who may be seeking to develop careers after childrearing. The effects of flexibility strategies are particularly sharply felt by black women. While in some organizations with strong equality policies black women now occupy professional or managerial roles in the core, in most they are found in the traditional support roles of cleaning, catering and low grade clerical and care roles – precisely those areas most likely to be based on part-time or contracted out labour. At the same time, equalities initiatives are being weakened through internal restructurings and the devolution of responsibility for staffing issues to 'business managers' within a fragmented organization, with less strong lines of control by the centre of policies affecting employment conditions.

In Chapter 1 of this volume, Newman explored how the new managerial culture of public sector organizations can be understood as a gendered domain. Women's experience will depend on the nature of the managerial regime within which they work; different types of managerial culture will inscribe different sets of relationships between women and men, and will offer different patterns of roles and identities for women. But the place of gender and 'race' in this analysis is not just about women, members of black and ethnic minority groups and so on as the recipients of change. Shifts in the social relations of gender and of 'race' play a role in the reshaping of organizations around new patterns of control. These shifts have other significant consequences. They are accompanied by a realignment of social divisions within organizations between centre and periphery, redefining the boundaries between labour which is 'inside' (part of the core) and that which is 'outside' (part of the contractual arm of production). This means that many women are losing their valued 'insider' status, and relinquishing the benefits which working for a large state organization with good employment practices may have brought. At the same time, women's labour and skills are being used in new ways as jobs themselves change under the rhetoric of 'flexibility', with increased pressure on staff to become multiskilled and to take on multifunctional roles. The argument that this is all 'caused' by a universal imperative of fragmentation built deep into the processes of the restructuring of the economy around post-Fordist principles ignores, and indeed masks, the significance of the social divisions on which processes of fragmentation and flexibility are built.

SOCIAL DIVISIONS AND SOCIAL IDENTITIES

Earlier we suggested that post-Fordist accounts of changes in social welfare and in organizational restructuring are limited by their failure to take account of both gender and 'race'. They are limited in several important ways: first, no power of agency is given to gender, 'race' or other social relations in the development of explanations for change. Secondly, the differential consequences of change for different groups – for male and female, black and white – are not sufficiently acknowledged (though they tend to have a stronger research base within social welfare, in terms of differences between 'users' of welfare, than in organizational studies).

In particular we need a more complex and multifaceted approach to both social policy and organizational analysis. More sensitized approaches are needed around issues of gender, 'race', disability and their relations to class. In addition, these differences should not be seen as permanent, essential or uniform, but as shifting, various and interrelated. Nor should they be seen as being determined through distinct categories of need or distinct modes of discrimination – they must be seen as being defined by the subjects themselves as well as shaped by the social, cultural and material conditions around them.

We draw here from work by Williams which explores issues of 'race', gender and class in the British welfare state. In this a framework is developed for understanding these issues – as both separate and interconnected – through the discourses of family, nation and work. These discourses can be seen as both central and interconnected themes in the development of welfare (Williams 1989). These interconnections are, however, not straightforward, but embody tensions and contradictions. One source of tension lies in the fact that the realities of work, family life and nationhood often do not accord with political discourses. Whilst the new right have espoused a commitment to traditional forms of work, family and nation, the very conditions of each have undergone changes which challenge the new right's reliance on them as the basis for welfare provision. So, for example, there have been changes in the organization of work (increases in part-time, low paid and casual work) combined with an ageing population and an increase in families dependent on a female income. These have all exposed the inadequacies of the post-war social security and insurance system. However, recent reforms in social security serve to reinforce the changes in work organization and intensify inequalities in inefficient ways (Deakin and Wilkinson 1991). In relation to the family, while there has been an increase in the diversification of family forms, government policies have attempted in different ways to reinforce a particular patriarchal family form (see Wicks 1987; Langan 1991; Williams 1992). Similarly, the issue of 'nation' reveals a conflict between government statements which reassert sentiments of nationalism, or of traditional British culture (in debates over Europe or the teaching of history) and the reality of multiracial Britain or the tendencies towards Europeanization.

It was suggested that these three interconnected discourses of welfare reflected shifting social relations of gender, race and class. And although these themes could be applied to most industrialized societies, in the context of Britain they provide the basis for analysing the place of the welfare state within a patriarchal and racially structured capitalism. Whilst this may define the structural context, we need also to take account of the further myriad forms of identity, difference and inequality, in particular, disability, age and sexuality (Williams 1992), and the ways their significance changes over time. For example, in recent years there has been an increase in inequalities amongst young people structured particularly along 'race' and class lines (Solomos 1988). This inequality is also reflected amongst older people where gender and disability play a more significant role. The multifaceted and interrelated nature of these forms of identity and social division are represented in Figure 7.1.

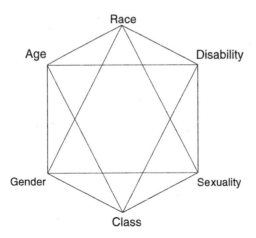

Figure 7.1 Identity and social division

At a simple level, the figure is a series of axes which represent different social relations of power; but imagine the figure as a three-dimensional polyhedron reflecting different and changing experiences. The multifaceted nature of such a model is that, first, it poses a dynamic relationship between the individual, power and structure. Its multiple facets reflect the fact that social divisions impact upon people, singly or in groups, in different ways, at different times, in different situations. At one or many moments, in one or many places, issues of disability may be heightened; at another moment the inequalities of class may predominate for the same person or group. The focus shifts over time: new axes of power – religion or nationality, for example – may be important at a given historical moment.

Second, the image emphasizes the interrelatedness of different forms of power and oppression, and therefore the compounded or contradictory nature of oppression. 'Race', gender and class have a compounding effect on the experiences and life chances of a black, working class woman. Similarly, the class position, as well as the age, 'race', and sexuality, of a disabled man will affect the nature of support he needs and receives.

The model is not, however, intended to suggest an evenly distributed and balanced terrain. It should be seen as prismatic rather than fixed; and will reflect different patterns over time. Some lines of interaction within the model will have greater salience at a particular historical moment, or within a specific organization, or to an individual woman. In this way the image should suggest a greater sense of interaction than the 'rainbow' image which is often evoked to represent the alliance between different social movements. At the same time, it does offer a way of seeing 'diversity' as a series of interrelationships, rather than a group of separate categories.

How might this model help us to understand organizations? In the same way as Williams attempted to elaborate welfare theory which focused primarily on the sphere of work, and had been developed from theories of class, so too we need to shift the preoccupation with class relations in the sociology of work and occupations. However, where gender has entered the debate on the social relations of the workplace, class has tended to disappear. In much of the literature on gender and organizations, women have tended to be regarded as a universal category, defined by their exclusion from the mainstream of organizational life by a combination of female biology (childbirth and childcare) and male discrimination and practices of exclusion (embedded in the processes of selection, recruitment and advancement). However, class and 'race' have operated as a set of 'invisible presences' in the debate. One group of studies – and certainly the largest group of writings – have centred on women and management: that is, the difficulties which women face in gaining management positions. This work has tended to focus on the position of professional or business women, who have tended to be largely middle class and white. Thus (middle) class and (white) 'race' have usually been implicitly assumed rather than explicitly addressed.

At the other end of the spectrum, studies of low paid areas of women's work have sometimes addressed issues of class but only rarely dealt with issues of 'race'. 'Race' tends only to be evoked as a category when studies deal with 'exceptional' groups (black or other minority ethnic workers) rather than with the 'normal' (which is assumed to be white). When black people are not the focus of discussion, life is assumed to be non-racialized. For example, 'race' as a social category is generally absent from studies of the working experience of older women, and of women with disabilities.

The absence of social categories other than gender is partly due to the ways in which studies of gender are organized around 'male' and 'female', 'women' and 'men' as oppositional categories rather than as facets of real and complex identities. In other words, texts which are organized around difference frequently do not help us to explore the dynamic interrelationships which constitute human life and experience. In both studies of women and management and studies of women as low paid workers, issues of difference between women and men have been the main focus of analysis – differences of pay and conditions, differences of status, differences of access to jobs categorized as 'men's work' or 'women's work', differences of occupational stress levels, differences of management style and so on have all been fully explored. However, differences *between* women have been dealt with much less adequately.

Does this matter? Some of the ground that has been won in profiling gender issues within organizations has been precisely because of the success in drawing comparisons between the working conditions, experience and opportunities of women and men. But we think that there are now a number of dangers which could block the development of the analysis of gender in organizations. First, differences of class and 'race', disability and age, impact on the structures of opportunity open to women. With the patterns of change leading to increased polarization between different groups, the interplay of different lines of social division becomes increasingly significant (see Mayo and Weir 1993). Interpretation of the polarization of the labour force discussed above needs to be sensitive to the relationships between different patterns of discrimination and processes of marginalization.

The interplay of differences also helps us understand the ways in which organizations define and police the boundary between 'safe' and 'dangerous' agendas for change. It is no accident that lesbian and gay agendas constitute the most marginal and vulnerable area of organizational politics, and are usually excluded from equality policies. All women, then, are organizationally constituted as 'heterosexual' women. In delimiting the terrain of legitimate struggle, class can be understood as a category which interacts with all the other lines of difference. Middle class women's demands for access to managerial jobs are more easily accommodated than the demands of low paid, black or white, working class women, which would require a more wide-ranging restructuring of pay and conditions. This is evident in the ways in which employers have tended to resist the implementation of equal value legislation (Cockburn 1991).

The model set out in Figure 7.1 is also helpful in unravelling some of the tensions which have emerged in equal opportunity struggles within organizations. The use of categories (women, black workers, people with disabilities) has underpinned the way in which equality agendas have been set, and has sometimes led to the development of competition between different equality issues for declining resources (see Itzin, Chapter 8 in this volume). This model perhaps provides a framework for moving beyond the 'category politics' which has sometimes dogged equal-opportunity policies where groups are often represented as discrete and sometimes competing entities.

Finally, we would argue that to understand the gender dynamics of organizations, we have to build theory out of women's actual experience of organizational life. Perspectives which foreground diversity can enable us to explore ambiguities and tensions in women's roles and identities within a particular, gendered, cultural configuration. At one moment, a black woman may define herself as a professional or manager; at another as a trade unionist; at another as a member of a women's group or network. Some experiences (such as racial harassment) will foreground her identity as black; others (such as lack of access to childcare) as a woman. It is the relationship between these different elements of identity that constitute women's experience. If we want to understand that experience, we have to take on the complexity of issues of identity.

THE LIMITS OF DIVERSITY

So far in this chapter we have been exploring 'top down' change – that is, how change at the level of the state, and in the structuring of organizations and the workforce, is having effects *on* women. We have argued that we need to understand the diversity of women's experience of change by exploring the interaction of gender and other social divisions such as class, 'race' and age. But women have never been merely the passive victims of their fate, and the changing dynamics of welfare which we have traced have brought with them multiple pressures for change from women themselves, as users of services, as 'carers' for others, and as the shapers of emerging political agendas (for instance on environmental issues, and on the design and safety of public spaces and buildings). At the same time, other agendas are emerging as disability groups and others argue for self-advocacy and the control over resources, in order to shift from being the objects of welfare to the subjects of 'choice'. Agendas around age are becoming better established (see Itzin and Phillipson, Chapter 5 in this volume).

From a radical perspective, then, notions of diversity signal the development of a new form of politics. Lines of political identity and struggle have shifted, with the fragmentation of traditional forms of protest around social class and the emergence of political movements based on 'race', gender, sexuality and disability. At the same time, many 'progressive' companies and public sector organizations are becoming increasingly aware of the value of diversity within their organization. A diverse workforce can increase the responsiveness to multiple groups of customers and users, and can help an organization achieve quality improvements. It can improve organizational effectiveness by widening the pool of talent on which the organization can draw, and can broaden management styles and approaches. But 'diversity' is a term which has resonances across the political spectrum; and rather than setting out a radical agenda for change, it can imply a shift towards individualism and can signal the further impoverishment of equality policies in the new managerial culture. Diversity can also appear as a seemingly 'progressive' notion in the new right ideology of the market for welfare. In the rhetoric of the market place, choice is seen as best provided though market mechanisms. Post-Fordist notions of the fragmented market place suggest the development of a multiplicity of 'niche' markets responding to a diversity of needs and requirements. Here notions of agency are conflated with market preference, and choice is individualized.

Notions of diversity, then, can militate against our understanding of the conti-nued salience of social divisions. While there are significant differences between women, gender as a social division undoubtedly continues to structure our experi-ence in important ways, and it is important that women continue to transcend differences in order to develop affiliations across different patterns of experience and around different political agendas.

A further problem with notions of diversity is the danger of blurring different patterns of social division. There is a danger of lumping everything together in a series of 'isms' which give no acknowledgement of the specificity of different lines of exclusion and of social action (for example, statements which go 'This is about sexism, but we mustn't forget racism, heterosexism, able bodyism, ageism, etc.'). This is problematic because it defines the different patterns of oppression as equivalent, thus decontextualizing each one from the specificities of the social, historical and economic forces that have shaped it. Racism and sexism are not equivalent, and each has its own lines of development and focus of political struggle which have to be understood. It is only by collective action around specific patterns of oppression, each of which develops its own perspective, that change is energized.

The development of ideas of diversity also has implications for theories of change, and for lines of political and social action. As well as the fragmentation of identity, diversity signifies the fragmentation of power, an observation also made in postmodern approaches to organizational theory (e.g. Hanssard and Parker 1993), which portray power as multifaceted, fluid, fragmented and transient. In Chapter 1 of this volume Newman discussed some of the strengths and limitations of this perspective. Seeing power as fragmented and transient enables us to understand the current transformation of the public sector as containing contradic-tions and tensions rather than as being global, overarching and fixed. Such tensions give rise to myriad spaces in which women are acting to reshape organizations and to set out demands as citizens of the fragmented state. But as they do so, let us not be bewitched by the attractions of new theories and new ideas of politics – much of the old structures of power remain in place, but under new guises and new managerialist ideologies.

In arguing that we need to take greater account of diversity among women, it is important not to lose the commonalities of gender as a social division (Soper 1990).

Some usages of the idea of diversity have been dislocated from the values of equality, from the politics of collective solidarity, and from the need to challenge the unequal relations of so-called diversity or difference. But the developments around feminist politics, especially the assertion of both the specific needs women have as *women* (as different from men) and the differences that exist *between* women, have led to a reappraisal of the meaning of all-encompassing notions such as equality, justice, universalism and citizenship. What is necessary is the development of a concept of equality that can incorporate difference and diversity not just in an individualized sense, but in its collective sense – around a politics of difference that exists to assert identity and to challenge inequality and exclusivity.

REFERENCES

Baldock, J. (1993) 'Patterns of change in the delivery of welfare in Europe'. In Taylor-Gooby, P. and Lawson, R. (eds), *Markets and Managers: New Issues in the Delivery of Welfare*. Milton Keynes: Open University Press.

Beechey, V. (1988) 'Rethinking the definition of work: gender and work'. In Jenson, J., Hagel, E. and Reddy, C. (eds), *Feminisation of the Workforce*. Cambridge: Polity Press.

Bruegel, I. (1989) 'Sex and race in the labour market'. *Feminist Review*, 32, 49–68.

Clarke, J. (1991) *New Times and Old Enemies: Essays on Cultural Studies and America*. London Harper Collins.

Clarke, J. and Newman, J. (1993) 'Managing to survive: dilemmas of changing organizational forms in the public sector'. In Deakin, N. and Page, R., *The Costs of Welfare*. Aldershot: Avebury.

Clarke, J., Cochrane, A. and McLaughlin, E. (eds) (1994) *Managing Social Policy*. London: Sage.

Cochrane, A. (1991) 'The changing state of local government; restructuring for the 1990s'. *Public Administration*, 69 (3), 281–302.

Cockburn, C. (1991) *In the Way of Women: Men's Resistance to Sex Equality in Organizations*. London: Macmillan.

Deakin, S. and Wilkinson, F. (1991) 'After deregulation: social and economic rights in the labour market'. Paper presented at the Anglo-German Social Policy Conference, Nottingham.

Handy, C. (1989) *The Age of Unreason*. London: Hutchinson.

Hanssard, J. and Parker, M. (eds) (1993) *Postmodernism and Organizations*. London: Sage.

Langan, M. (1991) 'Who cares? Women, social work and the mixed economy'. In Langan, M. and Day, L. (eds), *Women, Oppression and Social Work*. London: HarperCollins.

Mayo, M. and Weir, A. (1993) 'The future for feminist social policy'. In Page, R. and Baldock, J. (eds), *Social Policy Review 5*. Canterbury: Social Policy Association.

Newman, J. (1994) 'The limits of management: gender and the politics of change'. In Clarke, J., Cochrane, A. and McLaughlin, E. (eds), *Managing Social Policy*. London: Sage.

Pinch, S. (1992), 'Labour flexibility and the public sector'. Paper presented at the conference 'Towards a post-Fordist welfare state?', University of Teesside.

Pollert, A. (1988) 'The "flexible firm": fixation or fact'? *Work, Employment and Society*, 2 (3), 281–316.

Rustin, M. J. (1989) 'The politics of post-Fordism: or, the trouble with "new times"'?'. *New Left Review*, 175, 54–77.

Solomos, J. (1988) 'Institutionalised racism: policies of marginalisation in education and training'. In Cohen, P. and Bains, H. S. (eds), *Multi-racial Britain*. London: Macmillan.

Soper, K. (1990) 'Feminism, humanism and postmodernism'. *Radical Philosophy*, 55, 11–17.

Walby, S. (1992) 'Professionals and post-fordism: the NHS in transition'? Paper presented at the conference 'Towards a post-Fordist welfare state?', University of Teesside.

Whitaker, A. (1992) 'The transformation of work: post-Fordism revisited'. In Reed, M. and Hughes, M., *Rethinking Organizations: New Directions in Organization Theory and Analysis*. London: Sage.

Wicks, M. (1987) 'Family matters in social policy'. In Loney, M., Bocock, R., Clarke, J., Cochrane, A., Graham, P. and Wilson, M. (eds) *The State and the Market*. London: Sage.

Williams, F. (1989) *Social Policy: A Critical Introduction. Issues of Race, Gender and Class*. Cambridge: Polity Press.

Williams, F. (1992) 'Somewhere over the rainbow: universality and diversity in social policy'. In Manning, N. and Page, R., *Social Policy Review 4*. Canterbury: Social Policy Association.

Williams, F. (1994) 'Social relations and the post-Fordist debate'. In Burrows, R. and Loader, B. (eds), *Towards a Post-Fordist Welfare State?*. London: Routledge.

Part II

Strategies for organizational change

Chapter 8

Crafting strategy to create women-friendly work

Catherine Itzin

This chapter describes the process over a five-year period of putting strategic change theory into practice to change the culture of an organization to create more 'women friendly work'. It shows how strategies were 'crafted' to take account of the changing priorities and agendas of a local authority as it responded to external pressures. The chapter is based on analytical work in the same organization described in Chapters 2 and 3 of this volume.

This chapter provides a case study of a 'gender and organizational change initiative' carried out in a local authority over a five-year period between 1987 and 1992, and describes a process of 'crafting strategy' with a view to achieving changes in the culture, structure and practices of the organization aimed at improving the position of women.

When the gender and organizational change work started, the case study local authority was Labour controlled and had a long history of developing race equality initiatives in a borough with a large black and minority ethnic population, and a mixture of poverty and affluence. It was, in the early 1980s, one of the first local authorities to establish a Race Relations Unit and had placed race 'advisers' in the social services, housing and education departments.

In the mid-1980s the Labour administration undertook an expansion of the council's equal opportunities resources, establishing a Women's Unit, a Disability Unit, and race, disability and women's advisory posts at a senior management level in the personnel department. It was in my capacity initially job-sharing as Women's Officer, and later full-time as Assistant Director of Human Resources, that I undertook the gender and organizational change initiative.

The Women's Officer job description contained responsibility for developing equal opportunities training and casework, but the major brief was 'to develop, implement, evaluate, analyse and monitor policies and procedures to promote genuine equality of opportunity for all existing and potential employees of the council with specific responsibility for women'.

From the beginning I defined the job in terms of trying to achieve fundamental change in the organization by developing a strategic policy framework within which steps could be taken to improve the position of women in the organization:

to enhance the recruitment, retention and career progression opportunities of women at all levels in the organization, including women manual workers; to improve the working conditions and the working environment for women at all levels in the organization; and to increase the representation of women in senior positions.

There were a number of fluctuating and competing variables within the organization which influenced the level of commitment and resources available to support the gender objectives. Frequent changes in political control created a tenuous balance of power, ideological tensions, and constantly shifting agendas and priorities for the delivery of services. Over the five-year period political control ranged from left-wing Labour to right-wing Conservative, with at one stage, a 'hung council' in which the Liberal Democrats mediated the overall control, followed by a Conservative majority obtained mid-term as a result of a change of political allegiance by individual Labour councillors.

During this time there were major reductions in public expenditure, organizational restructurings, and staff reductions. The attention of staff at all levels was, therefore, frequently focused on day-to-day issues of survival: responding to political pressures and trying to deliver services with ever-decreasing resources, and within constantly changing structures and arrangements, driven by central government legislation.

This chapter starts with a review of the organizational change theories that were used to analyse the culture and structure of the organization and guide the gender and organizational change initiative, including the diagnostic and analytical techniques that were used – and found to be useful – in deciding on and designing 'change strategies'.

A key dimension to the strategy was the use of research to identify cultural and structural barriers to equality of opportunity for women in the workplace and to underpin the change initiative. This chapter explains how research can assist the process of organizational change and describes the changes that were managed within the organization, using the results of the research and the heightened awareness that the research process itself had achieved. The research findings are analysed and discussed in Chapter 2.

This chapter shows how strategy was 'crafted' from internal and external factors to influence the views of senior managers and politicians, responding to and taking advantage of the political, financial, economic and institutional changes which occurred in local government during this period. It includes details of the various policies, schemes and provisions that were proposed, drafted, negotiated and agreed upon, and the process of developing a package of integrated, off-the-shelf provision aimed at providing a range of choices to meet the needs of the organization and of women with domestic and caring responsibilities both *in* time and *over* time.

The chapter concludes with an account of what the gender and organizational change initiative did and did not achieve, and an evaluation of what is and is not achievable within an equal opportunities context in a large organization, taking into consideration the gendered power relations that exist in the organization and the wider society.

THE THEORY

Strategic change theory

The gender and organizational change initiative drew on a number of models for implementing strategic change in organizations. These provided a theoretical framework within which to plan and execute – and the practical tools for designing and implementing – an organizational change strategy.

Schein's (1980) 'planned change theory' derives from 'the common observation that people resist change, even when the goals are apparently highly desirable' (p. 53). Schein therefore proposes a model of planned change that addresses three basic human needs: the creation of a motivation to change; developing new attitudes and behaviours on the basis of new information and cognitive redefinition; and the stabilizing of the changes once they are made. A number of assumptions underlie his model:

i)   Any change process involves not only learning something new, but *unlearning* something that is already present and possibly well integrated into the personality and social relationships of the individual.

ii) No change will occur unless there is motivation to change, and if such motivation to change is not already present, the induction of that motivation is often the most difficult part of the change process.

iii) Organisational changes such as new structures, processes, reward systems, and so on occur only through individual changes in key members of the organisation; hence organisational change is always mediated through individual changes.

iv) Most adult change involves attitudes, values, and self-images, and the unlearning of present responses in these areas is initially *inherently* painful and threatening.

v)   Change is a multistage cycle... and all stages must be negotiated somehow or other before a stable change can be said to have taken place.

(Schein 1980: 53)

These points highlight the importance of leading people through the process of change, of targeting key individuals and enlisting their support, of overcoming resistance and helping people to unlearn old ways and to deal with perceived threats and real pain.

Pugh (1978) also recognizes that 'a real change proposal, that will almost inevitably change the current balance, is ... likely to encounter resistance' (p. 29). He defines an 'effective manager' as one who:

a) *anticipates* the need for change as opposed to reacting after the event to the emergency, b) *diagnoses* the nature of the change that is required and carefully considers a number of alternatives that might improve organisational functioning, as opposed to taking the fastest way to escape the problem; and c) *manages* the change process over a period of time so that it is effective and accepted as opposed to lurching from crisis to crisis.

(Pugh 1978: 29)

Pugh reminds us that organizations are organisms not mechanisms, that it is individuals within it who must change if the organization is to change, that members of organizations operate simultaneously in rational, occupational and political spheres (to which could be added the 'emotional' sphere), and that people are likely to be more receptive to change if they are already doing well in their work. He provides six rules for managing change effectively:

1. Work hard at establishing the need for change.
2. Think *through* the change – what it will mean for all parties involved.
3. Initiate change through informal discussion to get feedback and participation.
4. Positively encourage those concerned to give their objections.
5. Be prepared to change yourself.
6. Monitor the change and reinforce it.

(Pugh 1978: 30–1)

Schein's 'planned change theory' and Pugh's 'rules for managing change effectively' became the guiding principles and operational guidelines for the gender and organizational change initiative. Waterman *et al.* (1991) provided another way of identifying the various aspects of the organization that had to be addressed for change to be successful. Their '7–S' change framework model assumes 'a multiplicity of factors that influence an organization's ability to change and its proper mode of change' (p. 309), and an interrelationship between 'structure, strategy, system, style, skills, staff and superordinate goals'. Most useful were the concepts of systems (and the importance of being systematic) and superordinate goals (which give the organization meaning).

Diagnostic tools

Of great value in developing a change strategy were Bryson and Roering's (1987) guidelines on applying private sector strategic planning to the public sector, in particular their strategic planning process based on the Harvard Policy model of identifying an organization's strengths, weaknesses, opportunities and threats (SWOT analysis). A SWOT analysis of the specific local government situation in which this work was done identified the opportunities and threats presented by the external environment (political, economic, social and technical forces; clients and customers; mandates; competitors and collaborators), and the strengths and weaknesses of the internal environment (the mission and values of the 'stakeholders' and the resources of the organization). A separate SWOT analysis of the equal-opportunities implications for local government was also carried out. The SWOT analysis technique was useful, particularly in highlighting the importance of demographic trends in creating opportunities for women at work and identifying women themselves as stakeholders (representing two-thirds of the total workforce and half the population of the community the local council serves).

There were also other useful diagnostic strategies. Through a process of 'key relationship mapping' it was possible to identify the 'winners' and 'losers' in the change process, to consider who had power in the organization and who had hard and soft information. There were at that time, for example, no reliable data on where women were located in the organization or their racial classification. The exercise also highlighted the fact that there were, ultimately, no real losers: that men would benefit from a more equal and women-friendly organization. A later 'winners and losers analysis' assisted the completion of the change process, identifying key individuals with expertise and decision-making power and mapping the end-game stage of the project.

Force-field analysis was helpful at an early stage in addressing the problems of obtaining and presenting information and persuading councillors to take action, and at a later stage in implementing change initiatives. This involved identifying 'pushing forces' and 'restraining forces' in the organization, evaluating their likely power and effect, and considering how to increase the positive forces and to decrease resistance. This produced a number of practical ideas and solutions to problems: from finding resources for analysing survey data, to obtaining support from race equality staff in targeting black women for career development. A later force-field analysis assisted in identifying how to 'pitch' the proposals within the changing culture of the organization, and even produced draft outlines for the two major committee reports that would persuade the organization to adopt new policies and procedures.

Crafting strategy

Useful as all these tools were, by far the most relevant account of organizational change was Mintzberg's model of 'crafting strategy'. 'Strategies', writes Mintzberg, 'can form as well as be formulated ... A realized strategy can emerge in response to an evolving situation, or it can be brought about deliberately through a process of formulation followed by implementation' (Mintzberg 1987: 68). In fact, argues Mintzberg, 'all strategy-making walks on two feet, one deliberate, the other emergent' (p. 68). Complementary to Mintzberg's theory of crafting strategy is Miller and Friesen's (1984) 'quantum theory of strategic change': this sees change as not necessarily linear, deliberate and continuous, but sudden and built on 'potentials' within the organization that have been latent or peripheral because they have not been central to the objectives of the organization in its original 'stable' form, but which emerge when needed in times of change, ready to be developed to become dominant in the organization (p. 72).

Mintzberg describes emergent strategies as 'growing like weeds around the organisation':

> What the quantum theory suggests is that the really novel ones are generally held in check in some corner of the organisation until a strategic revolution becomes necessary. Then as an alternative to having to develop new strategies from scratch or having to import generic strategies from competitors, the organisation can turn to its own emerging patterns to find its new orientation. As the old, established strategy disintegrates, the seeds of the new one begin to spread.
>
> (Mintzberg 1987: 72)

Mintzberg's 'emergent strategy' theory is closely related to the 'grounded theory' model of social research developed by Glaser and Strauss, which assumes that concepts and theory emerge *from* data rather than being imposed upon them, and even that theory itself is developed as an active process in the relationship between the researcher and the researched (Glaser and Strauss 1967). The gender and organizational change initiative involved the development of emergent strategy in the organization and the use of emergent theory in the development of the project itself. Grounded theory has been popular in feminist sociology, and was particularly appropriate, therefore, as the methodological approach to a change project concerned with counteracting discrimination against women in the workforce.

The 'key to maintaining strategy', says Mintzberg, 'is the ability to detect emerging patterns and help them to take shape ... The job of the manager is not just to preconceive specific strategies but also to recognise their emergence elsewhere in the organisation and intervene when appropriate' (Mintzberg 1987: 74). The 'story' of this change project is really an account of 'crafting strategy': a combination of formulated strategy and emergent strategy, of fixing aims and objectives and working out a number of strategies for achieving them, but then responding flexibly – and patiently over a period of time – to changes in the internal and external environment, taking advantage of opportunities and turning threats to positive advantage. Using Mintzberg's metaphor, it proved to be a combination of some vision and considerable cultivation of organizational weeds: doing some groundwork, seeding, weeding, watering and nurturing the project along its way, but also making use of whatever happened to sprout in the constantly changing landscape of the local authority over a period of years.

PUTTING THEORY INTO PRACTICE

The equal opportunities context

The gender and organizational project originated and developed initially in an equal opportunities context. On the basis of legislation passed in the 1970s, local authorities had been developing work in the field of equal opportunities. The Sex Discrimination Act 1975, for example, made it illegal to discriminate in employment – either directly or indirectly – on grounds of sex or marital status. It legislated for equality in recruitment, promotion, dismissal, redundancy and fringe benefits, and made provisions for positive action to increase the representation of women where they were under-represented in the workforce. The Equal Pay Act 1970 stipulated equal treatment in pay and conditions of employment for women and men doing the same or broadly similar work.

The Race Relations Act 1976 made it illegal for employers to discriminate in recruitment, promotion, training and transfer, terms and conditions of employment, or dismissal on grounds of colour, race, nationality or ethnic or national origins. In addition, Section 71 of the Race Relations Act placed a special duty on local authorities to ensure they performed their functions 'with due regard to the need to eliminate unlawful racial discrimination and to promote equality of opportunity and good relations between persons of different racial groups'.

The Disabled Persons (Employment) Acts 1944 and 1958 placed a statutory obligation on employers with more than twenty staff to employ at least 3 per cent who were disabled. Although most employers – including local authorities – apply for exemptions from this requirement on the grounds that disabled people do not apply or that the jobs advertised are not suitable for disabled people, this legislation has underpinned equal opportunities employment initiatives for disabled people in local government.

Throughout the 1980s, many local authorities adopted equal opportunities policies covering race, sex, marital status and disability (Stone 1988). Sometimes the policies would also cover discrimination against lesbians and gay men and discrimination on grounds of age, although there is no legislation against discrimination in employment in these areas. In 1991, three-quarters of local authorities had equal opportunities employment policies and some had policies on equal opportunities in service delivery. Most advertised themselves as 'equal opportunities employers', and some had established posts or units and allocated resources to implement equal opportunities initiatives in advertising, recruitment and selection procedures, setting targets for increasing the representation of under-represented groups, creating more flexible and family-friendly working conditions and improving provision for childcare (Itzin and Phillipson 1993).

Although the case study authority had expanded its equal opportunities initiatives and resources in 1986 to include gender and disability as well as race (setting up a Women's Unit and a Disability Unit alongside its Race Equality Unit), there was throughout this period an ideologically driven, 'hierarchy of oppressions' dimension to the culture of the organization, which regarded racism as the main oppression, with gender and disability as secondary and subsidiary. It was assumed, for example, that black women had more in common with black men than with white women, and that black women would identify primarily as black and secondarily (if at all) as female; and the sexism and gendered power relations of black men in relation to black – or white – women were unarticulated. Race was not only the most highly resourced equal opportunities 'issue' in the council, but for a period the use of the words 'equal opportunities' was officially banned by committee. Disability equality ranked below race and gender, and although the council's equal opportunities policy specifically mentioned lesbians and gay men, the level of homophobia in the organization was so great that most gays and lesbians were not 'out' and the 'issue' was rarely mentioned.

In 1987, an opportunity arose to enhance the status of gender on the organization's equal opportunities agenda with the establishment of a 'Women's Officer post' in the personnel department and a senior management decision to revise and update the council's Equal Opportunities Employment Policy. The drafting, re-drafting, consultation, negotiation and agreement of this document by the various equal opportunities 'interests' (trade unions, directors and councillors) eventually took four years, but in the process gender and disability achieved parity with race at the level of policy in the organization, a formal Positive Action Programme with specified aims and objectives was agreed, and, as part of a new Equal Opportunities Employment Code of Practice, a manual of detailed recruitment and selection procedures was produced to underpin the implementation of the policy. Strategically it was important to establish a policy on gender and to generate organizational commitment to gender equality as well as race equality prior to and as a prerequisite to attempting any systematic changes in the organization to improve the position of women. It was also desirable to have a procedural framework for recruitment and selection as a foundation for change.

Another strategic objective was to try to obtain agreement to an 'equal opportunities targeting policy' as a basis for increasing the representation of women in senior positions. The aim of this policy was to identify areas and levels of under-representation of women and black and disabled staff in the council, with a view to setting 'performance' targets for increasing their representation. Given the 'hierarchy of oppression' tensions in the authority, it was important to try to take the major equal opportunities issues forward together. An ad hoc Equality Targeting/Positive Action Strategy Group was set up, including officers with responsibility for race, disability and gender, chaired by the Positive Action Officer in the Race Equality Unit. This group produced a policy document that was eventually agreed by directors in a context of performance indicators, which included equality targets alongside budget and performance targets. The Equality Targeting Report failed to obtain committee approval, however, due to a disagreement between Asian and Afro-Caribbean councillors over the level at which targets should be set for the representation of their respective groups. Eventually, at a much later stage, it became possible to use the Equal Opportunities Employment Policy as a vehicle for achieving agreement on an equality targeting and equal opportunities monitoring policy.

The political commitment to gender equality proved to be shortlived and the Women's Unit was abolished in 1988, literally overnight, just over a year after it was established, leaving just the one personnel post dedicated to gender issues. Limited resources and the low priority accorded to women's employment issues demonstrated by these decisions (taken by a Labour administration) determined the subsequent shape and form of the gender and organizational change initiative, and the strategy was reviewed and revised with a view to enabling a single officer to drive through change in a cultural environment that was largely indifferent to the situation of women.

At this stage it had become clear that if any gender change was to be generated it would have to be 'officer-led', but whether any change would ultimately be carried out depended on political decisions over which there was little, if any, officer control. A strategic decision was therefore made to define 'the job' in terms of what could be controlled and what could not. It would, for example, be possible to provide, in as authoritative and persuasive a way as possible, information about the current position and needs of women in the organization, and concrete proposals for different ways of meeting those needs, with details of costings and how to implement them. It would then depend on a variety of constantly varying – and competing – organizational and political variables whether any action was taken. In order to achieve the gender and organizational change objectives, it was necessary to start by persuading people in positions of power of the need for and value of making changes, and by making the culture more receptive to change.

It was at this stage that research came into consideration as a possible means of effecting some of the desired change in the organization. Research produces information that can be used as a basis for persuading people to adopt new policies. At the same time, the very process of collecting information can lead key individuals – and the organization – in the direction of the desired change. 'It is possible', according to Hampden-Turner, 'to intervene to change a corporate culture ... The method involves a cumulative investigation into values, myths and rituals, using interviewing and group discussion' (Hampden-Turner 1990: 185). The interviewer, he says, 'is at the heart of the process of investigating culture' (p. 189). 'The essential point to remember about a culture', he writes, 'is that you cannot study it without already starting to change it' (p. 204).

Some thought was given to the value and practicalities of 'researching the organization'. There was, increasingly, information available about women and employment (Dubeck 1979; Borisoff and Merrill 1985; Beechey 1987; Beechey and Perkins 1987; Spencer and Podmore 1987; Walby 1988; Hunt 1988), but if information could be collected about that particular local authority it was likely to carry more weight in persuading managers and politicians of the need for change, and to contribute to a sense of ownership of the problems. It would be possible, for example, to collect information from departments which would identify, illustrate and evidence the typical institutional barriers that exist in organizations, including barriers to women in non-traditional areas of work. The process of collecting information could also be targeted to departments with senior managers who might be interested, committed and helpful, bearing in mind Schein's strictures about influencing – and using – key individuals. The process might also generate support from managers in the second and third tiers of each department, who, through participating in and contributing to the research, might acquire the motivation and commitment to pursue – and participate in – finding solutions. Eventually the process might assist in attracting the agreement and, if possible, the blessing of directors – at officer level the ultimate decision makers. Hampden-Turner's model of organizational intervention, using interviewing and group discussions, became the basis of an idea for a workforce research initiative to produce information that would underpin proposals, influence decision makers and make all staff more receptive to any changes that might be implemented. There were, however, no resources at that time to undertake a major piece of workforce research.

At this point 'emergent strategy' came into the ascendency. The 'demotion' of gender equality as a political priority and the reduction in resources marked by the closure of the Women's Unit coincided with the rumour of a contingency fund in the chief executive's department, some of which had been earmarked for equal opportunities. A successful case was made – in the context of the competing 'hierarchy of oppression' culture – for a proportion of this meagre contingency to be directed towards gender, and specifically to 'buy in' external consultancy to assist in developing initiatives for women. At this stage the project was redefined more 'narrowly' (due to limited resources and political pressures) as 'researching, developing and making proposals to Members for strategies to increase the representation of women in senior positions'. The major focus of this phase of the change initiative was to be workforce research in selected areas to support the case for increasing the representation of women in senior positions, and persuading senior management and councillors to take action.

Decisions on whom to target and where to intervene were influenced by Pugh's analysis of the need to overcome resistance and Schein's advice on motivating individuals and making the environment receptive to change. Three departments were selected to participate in the research project. The development department was chosen because of its range of work not traditionally done by women (planning, architecture, engineering) and because it had already demonstrated a commitment to career progression for lower graded staff with proposals for an in-house, competence-based training programme. The social services department was chosen as representing one of the largest areas of traditional women's work (home helps, childminders, social work with children, families and elderly and disabled people). It also had a newly appointed female deputy director with a track record of work on problems facing women in social services. The housing department asked to join the project. They had identified difficulty in recruiting women above the lower grades of middle management and had a reputation in the council for being a bulwark of male chauvinism. The director and his senior managers had decided to do something about it, and were looking at the possibility of establishing a workplace nursery for staff in their department. (For a detailed account of the 'research' in the housing department of the case study authority, see Chapter 3.)

The demographic context

The context in which the 'change project' was developing changed during the period of its progress. In 1988/9 the importance of the equal opportunities context (both positively and negatively) diminished as interest focused on the impact of the demographic downturn: that is, the anticipated effects of the 25 per cent reduction in the birth rate in the 1970s and the resulting skills shortage this heralded for the 1990s, with significantly reduced numbers of young people entering the labour market. With the prospect of a skills shortage, local government (together with the private sector) began to take a renewed and enthusiastic interest in the needs of women, driven by the economic imperative of being able to recruit and retain staff during the predicted labour market shortages (METRA 1993). Women represented the largest pool of untapped labour: women were now – just as they had been in the Second World War – on the political and economic agenda, as 'the reserve army of labour' (Bruegel 1979).

Senior managers now wanted – and requested – proposals on the recruitment and retention of women in the 1990s, and it became possible – even necessary – to recast the original gender and organizational change objectives in a new mould. As a first step, a briefing was prepared for directors explaining why women were now an important focus for a recruitment and retention strategy and setting out a range of ways of attracting and keeping women. These included: workplace childcare, childcare subsidy, after-school and holiday provisions, flexible working hours, homeworking, career breaks, term-time working, flexitime to correspond with school hours, reduced hours (a '24–hour week'), job-share, a maternity returners induction, a women returners programme, and enhanced career development opportunities.

From the point of view of long term changes in the gender culture of the organization, it was important to present these not as ad hoc, one-off options, but as an integrated package of provisions designed to meet the needs of women *in* time and *over* time. The briefing was careful to explain that:

> These proposals are put forward as a *package* – with the intention that the council should implement *all or most of them*. No single provision meets all the needs of women with children. No single provision would meet the Council's objectives of retaining staff during the period of skills shortage. Women with children have very different needs in time and over time, e.g. for nursery and/or child care allowances *and* after school provisions *and* term time working *and* career breaks *and* returning part time or job sharing *and* flexible working hours. Both the organisation and the individual have a need to *plan* for their future needs. A package of child care and career development provisions enables that planning to take place.

The briefing also emphasized that, although this package of provisions was vital in supporting women at work, for any individual woman the intensive childrearing years represented only a small proportion of her whole working career, and that her career potential far outweighed any perceived inconvenience to the organization during the childrearing years. Any provisions, therefore, represented a long term investment for the organization.

The briefing outlined the range of proposals – with provisional costings – that would be developed and put forward over the next period of time. It was intended only to inform directors of possibilities at this stage, to influence the direction of their thinking and to get their general support without forcing any final commitment, especially of a financial nature: part of a deliberate strategy to educate and influence decision makers without posing any real threats. The briefing also went to committee as part of the budget making process. There was no requirement – or request – for immediate funding, but the costs of a recruitment and retention programme were set out as a signal to councillors of what they would need to consider at a future date if they were to take any specific action, with a view to paving the way for eventual agreement.

At this stage, in response to demographic and economic factors, the gender and organizational change initiative moved from the margins of equal opportunities to the mainstream of strategic human resources management, thereby acquiring a stronger power base within the organization. In the meantime the workforce research was being implemented, the results of which were intended to support the eventual change proposals.

The economic context

The re-emergence of economic recession in the early 1990s eventually masked the effects of the demographic changes, and the opportunities to promote women and the interests of women in response to the predicted skills shortages did not materialize. For local authorities generally, and this case study authority in particular, the climate became one of retrenchment and cutting back. The focus moved from 'recruitment and retention' to 'downsizing': to staff reductions, voluntary and compulsory redundancy, and early retirement. As the recession took hold, women ceased to be the 'flavour of the moment', and the demographic factors that were driving the gender and organizational change initiative at this stage ceased to have any power to influence the position of women in any positive sense. There were also other major political and economic changes impacting on local government at this time.

Privatization of local government services

There had been some fifty pieces of legislation affecting local government since 1979, aimed at restricting or controlling expenditure, privatizing services, and creating an enterprise culture in the public sector. In the area of housing, the building of council housing had been virtually curtailed, the sale of council houses had been encouraged, capital receipts had been diverted to cover debts rather than create new housing, and council tenants were able to opt out of local authority management. This had greatly reduced the quantity of subsidized local government housing stock and created a multi-million pound market in bed-and-breakfast accommodation for homeless families. In education, the Secretary of State for Education obtained the right to determine teachers' pay and conditions of service. The Education Reform Act 1988 delegated financial management to individual

schools (local management of schools), allowed schools to opt out of local government control, and required a core curriculum, achievement tests at specified ages,
and the publication by schools of performance indicators. The direction of the
legislation was to reduce the power, influence and control of local government in
education. In social services, the Children Act 1989 and the NHS and Community
Care Act 1990 were designed to shift the role of local government from service
provider to service assessor and service purchaser, with the expectation that local
government would buy cost-efficient services from the voluntary and private
sectors, and also develop those sectors as alternative service providers (Phillipson
1992).

Throughout this period, local government finance was undergoing changes
which reduced income from both central government and the local collection of
taxes, and increased central government control, limiting grant levels and revenue
and capital expenditure. There had been specific legislation requiring the privatization of local government services, in particular the 1980 Local Government
Planning and Land Act and the Local Government Act 1988. These placed a duty
on local authorities to put many of their services out to tender. Compulsory
competitive tendering (CCT) had a major impact on services predominantly provided by women manual workers, and generally worsened pay and conditions,
especially for mature and older women workers. The compulsory competitive
tendering of blue collar work was the first major stage in creating a market economy
in local government service provision, establishing a split between the client
function of the council and the contractor function of the service providers. CCT
was a statutory requirement of the Local Government Act 1988 to enable external
labour market competition for the provision of local government services.

Creating a local government business culture

CCT also created a model for the 'privatization' of internal labour market services,
with many local authorities establishing service level agreements as the contractual,
financial and accounting framework for the purchase of services by and between
departments within an authority. These 'internal services' did not have to compete
with external commercial businesses, although with the implementation of white
collar CCT this would change in specified service areas. But the internal services
operated as businesses with trading accounts, charging mechanisms and cost centre
management. They also involved quality assurance guarantees, performance standards, appraisal, review – and the potential for reward (performance related pay or
promotion), 'punishment' (discipline or dismissal) or improvement (with training
or support).

During this period, there was a change in political administration in the case-
study authority, from Labour to Conservative, and steps were immediately taken
to establish a new 'business culture' to replace the old 'role culture', with the
creation of eighty devolved business units within the shell of the old local government bureaucracy, with financial and personnel powers delegated to business unit

managers, and a brief to operate as fully fledged independent businesses in open competition with the external market place at the earliest opportunity.

Business objectives and cash limited budgets can – and did – lead to streamlining, staff reductions, short-term contracts, temporary or part-time employment, and the contracting out of work to external consultancies. All of this can – and does – impact negatively on the employment of women. The devolution of responsibility to line managers in service departments or business units places women (and other groups who are subject to prejudice and discrimination) at the mercy of line manager attitudes, which can, when bias exists, lead to discriminatory practices, whatever the corporate policies of the organization.

The introduction of a market economy in local government has had a major impact on both organizational structure and culture, with largely negative implications for women. It has marked a shift away from the bureaucratic structures which have traditionally offered reasonable job security and career opportunities. In its place there is now a tendency towards the corporate model which developed in the 1980s, characterized as a 'shamrock organization' (Handy 1990). This consists of a 'core workforce' of highly qualified professionals, managers, technicians and skilled workers. These employees receive good pay and conditions in exchange for long hours, hard work and flexibility with respect to the demands and needs of the organization. The 'core workforce' are likely to be white males in their thirties and forties operating as a club culture, the 'people', in Handy's own words, 'who do not see their home in daylight for half the year, whose children remember them as the person who comes to lunch on Sundays, who wonder what has happened to the leisure society they keep reading about' (p. 204).

There is also a 'contractual fringe' of self-employed professionals who are paid on a fee basis for delivering specified results. The 'contractual fringe' includes 'former permanent employees made redundant in the slimming down of the core, sacrificing job security for the freedom of self-employment' (p. 205). Handy describes it as 'one of those rare cases in business when no one loses under the new arrangements': the organization gets them 'off the premises and off the pension scheme' and is 'able to pay such people much more per day or per week than they were earning as employees' (p. 206). There have also been opportunities for women to form their own businesses or consultancies and to compete on the contractual fringe. But the 'freedom' also involves substantial *losses*: of job security, of pension, and potentially, in a retracting labour market, of earnings.

Then there is the 'flexible labour force' of low skilled and unskilled, part-time and temporary workers on low pay. The 'flexible labour force' consists largely (as it always has done) of women, who work part-time with low pay and limited employment protection: without choice. Handy makes no pretence about this: 'it has', he says, 'the sound of exploitation about it, of getting labour cheap', and it will be 'women with children at school' who 'like part time work' (p. 206). But he shows no recognition of the fact that women with children 'choose' part-time work because they need to, because it is the only way many women can manage the combination of domestic work and childrearing with paid employment. There is no acknowledgement that these women would almost certainly prefer a permanent job with security, benefits, employment protection and opportunities to develop their careers, but with the flexibility of hours and conditions that would enable them to meet their domestic commitments.

OUTCOMES

Initial achievements

All of the factors relating to the new 'enterprise economy' affected the gender and organizational change initiative, both positively and negatively. In an immediate cost-cutting exercise, the council decided to get rid of its enhanced maternity provisions for new employees, although the costs were demonstrably negligible in the short term and a proven investment for the long-term retention of staff. A Maternity Returners Survey, for example, of women who took maternity leave under the previous relatively generous provisions had shown that there was a 70 per cent return rate. Rank Xerox found that when they offered only statutory maternity pay their return rate was 25 per cent, and when they offered enhanced maternity provisions, including a return to part-time work, the return rate rose to 75 per cent (Ford 1991: 29).

But largely the new business culture created opportunities to take forward a whole range of initiatives that had been in the pipeline for a long period of time. This was primarily due to increased flexibility in the decision-making mechanisms, whereby the long and tortuous process of trying to persuade boards of directors and committees of politicians to make major organizational changes was replaced by more immediate, operationally oriented decisions by local business managers. It was also due to the shift from having to make a case for treating women well and fairly on grounds of equal opportunities (always a struggle at the best of times) to the 'business case' for equal opportunities generally and gender equality specifically (far more palatable). In the context of the enterprise economy, it became possible to make the business case for gender equality initiatives with more success than had been possible in an equal opportunities context.

An equal opportunities employment policy and procedures

After five years, and nearly a year after it was finally agreed, the council published 10,000 copies of its revised Equal Opportunities Employment Policy for distribution to all existing and new staff. The new Recruitment and Selection Procedures were published and eight days of intensive training were designed and delivered to 160 second and third tier managers and personnel officers, including the 80 Devolved Business Unit Managers. A package of proposals for recruitment and retention provisions was put together, which included a career break scheme, a term-time working scheme, proposals for a private sponsored workplace nursery with an option of childcare vouchers, and self-financing extensions to the existing after school and holiday provisions provided by the education department.

These proposals drew persuasively on the results of the workforce research and were presented as a framework 'within which a variety of provisions can be introduced locally by managers when they are relevant to the efficient management of business' and as 'a range of tools which can provide greater flexibility in the management of staffing requirements with respect to meeting operational and financial objectives'. The package was based on a 'menu approach', with a range of provisions that could be taken 'off the shelf' and used when managers needed them. Strategically – and sometimes cynically – employee entitlement was replaced by market forces and management expediency.

The Opportunity 2000 campaign

A major impetus towards achieving the gender and organizational change objectives was the Opportunity 2000 Campaign launched in 1991 by 'Business in the Community' to increase the quantity and quality of women's participation in the workplace, encouraging companies to take up the challenge and set the programmes and goals necessary for improvement. The campaign (which continued in 1994, supported by 267 public and private sector organizations) is based on the belief that businesses will be best served by a balance of women and men in the workforce in all areas and at all levels, and especially in management, that reflects the abilities of the labour force as a whole. John Major launched the campaign with the question, quoted at the start of Chapter 2 in this volume, 'Why should half the population have to go through life like hobbled horses in a steeple chase?'

It was Opportunity 2000 that finally, after nearly five years of failed attempts, provided an organizationally 'acceptable' framework within which efforts could be made to try to increase the representation of women in senior positions in a way that was compatible with the new business culture and also enabled the council to promote itself as a 'leading edge' authority. In this context, initiatives were specifically designed to try to change the 'gender culture' of the organization at the top gradually over a period of time: breaking down the barriers that had been identified by the research for women between middle management and senior management by enabling women to gain access and experience of the male culture with the active support of the men who were there (see Chapters 2 and 3).

The case study authority joined the Opportunity 2000 Campaign with a commitment to developing corporate and departmental action plans, to setting targets for women in senior positions, to a senior secondment scheme, and to accelerated management development schemes for women. An Opportunity 2000 Steering Group was formed, chaired by a male director with a hand-picked group of sympathetic men in second tier positions and key senior women, to oversee the drafting and implementation of the action plan and pilot schemes. The council committed itself in a committee report agreed by directors and councillors to a 'public launch of its campaign initiatives with a conference in which other businesses in the borough who are members of the campaign would be invited to participate' (Itzin 1992).

Equal opportunities monitoring: setting gender targets

As part of the workforce research, a profile of the organization's racial and gender composition was collected. The survey of non-manual staff showed that just over one-third (36.2 per cent) were men, and nearly two-thirds (63.8 per cent) were women. Of these women, nearly two-thirds (63.6 per cent) were located in the administrative and clerical grades. Women were massively over-represented in the lower grades and massively under-represented in senior grades by comparison with men. (For a detailed analysis of the monitoring data, see Chapter 2.) These 'equal opportunities monitoring data' were initially used to prepare a committee report to establish the regular collection, reporting, reviewing and monitoring of the representation of staff by grade with respect to race, gender and disability, and to set targets to increase the representation of women, black and disabled staff where they were currently under-represented in the organization. Within the equal opportunities context, the report with these proposals again failed to obtain the approval of councillors because of disagreements between different racial groups about the levels at which targets should be set for each group.

Within the Opportunity 2000 context, however, it was possible to use the monitoring data to obtain agreement on an 'Opportunity 2000 Target Setting' proposal. This undertook to establish annual 'gender audits' of the organization and the use of a 'performance indicator' to measure success in achieving the objective of increasing the representation of women in senior positions. The 'success criteria' for gender targets were defined as follows: 'By 1995 – ie in 3 years' time – there will be significantly more women managers in post in principal officer grades than there are at present in 1992.'

A Women in Middle Management Mentor Scheme

The results of the workforce research had shown that not only were women under-represented in senior positions, but there was a 'glass ceiling' at middle management level beyond which women failed to progress, and a culture at the top of the organization that was male oriented and not very women friendly (see Chapters 2 and 3). If the representation of women was to be increased in senior positions, it would not be enough to recruit or promote at that level: the 'male culture' at the top had to be made less hostile and more welcoming and conducive to women.

A Women in Middle Management Mentor Scheme was proposed and agreed with a view to 'moderating' and 'mediating' the male culture and making it more accessible to women. The Mentor Scheme would involve chief officers and senior management teams in each department acting as mentors to women in middle management for an initial period of one year, providing career advice and guidance, information on 'how things are done around here at the top', coaching in leadership and managerial skills, pointing women in the right direction, and providing tips on career development and a sympathetic ear to discuss problems, concerns and aspirations. Following a successful pilot, it was intended to extend the Mentor Scheme throughout the council, to assist the career development of women both vertically and laterally within the organization.

A Shadowing Scheme was also considered as an opportunity for women at all levels in the council to spend a limited period of time seeing what was involved in someone else's job, 'shadowing' and observing how the person did it. It was suggested that two weeks in a year might be designated as 'shadowing weeks' and departments were asked to put forward proposals for how they intended to manage and promote shadowing.

Using the workforce research results

All of the change proposals went in the form of reports with recommendations to directors for their agreement and then to committee for political ratification. The reports quoted extensively from the results of the workforce research to support the case that was being argued. Thus, for example, in the Women's Employment Survey (completed by 476 women in the housing, social services and development departments), women had been asked to indicate which 'schemes' they would take advantage of if they were available to improve their working conditions and career opportunities. Their responses indicated a high level of demand for the schemes shown in Table 8.1.

Table 8.1　Demand for schemes shown by responses to the Women's Employment Survey

Scheme	%
Senior secondment	60
Acting up	58
Career counselling	56
Shadowing	55
Job rotation	42
Mentoring	39

With respect to children and childcare, the survey had shown that 68 per cent of the women who responded had children and 28 per cent were single parents. Of the women with children, 25 per cent had children under the age of 5, 16 per cent had children aged 5–11, and 12 per cent had children aged 11–16. Asked which, if they had a choice, they would prefer, 56 per cent nominated a workplace nursery and

44 per cent childcare allowances. Asked which of various provisions they would use 'right now' and 'in the future', women gave the responses shown in Table 8.2.

Table 8.2 Demand for provisions shown by responses to the Women's Employment Survey

Provision	Now		Future	
	Nos	(%)	Nos	(%)
Nursery/crèche	138	(18)	198	(15)
Childcare subsidy	106	(14)	101	(8)
After-school care	56	(7)	87	(7)
Holiday care	77	(10)	99	(8)
Career break	20	(3)	76	(6)
Job-share	31	(4)	71	(5)
Term-time working	59	(8)	92	(7)
24-hour week/reduced working	44	(6)	77	(6)
Homeworking	64	(8)	74	(6)
Flexitime to correspond with school hours	68	(9)	108	(8)

The data indicated that there was sufficient demand to warrant the provision of a variety of schemes to assist women to maintain paid employment and career continuity during their childrearing years.

The committee reports also drew on data collected in a Workplace Nursery Feasibility Study completed by 580 employees (male and female) who were currently working at seven different council sites. Asked if they would consider using a crèche/nursery at work if provided and operated by the council, 221 said 'yes within the next 2 years' and 195 said 'yes within the next 2–5 years'. The Maternity Returners Survey of 223 women who had taken maternity leave between January 1988 and January 1990 had identified 38 women who would have used a council nursery on their return to work. The Women's Employment Survey had found 27 women in the housing department alone who would have used a council nursery 'now' and 24 'in the future'. This information suggested the council could easily have filled places in a workplace nursery if it wished to consider such provision a priority. These and other results of the workforce research were used to support recommendations for a workplace nursery and a wide range of other proposals, such as career breaks, term-time working and the mentor scheme, all of which were agreed by directors and councillors.

An evaluation of the gender and organizational change initiative two years later

When I left the local authority in 1992 many things had been agreed in principle, but most had yet to be implemented. At a time of continuing cuts in budgets and staff, I was not confident that the change momentum could be sustained. Nor was it clear how much of what had been achieved depended on the continued input and persistence of one individual. I returned two years later in order to evaluate the implementation of the organizational change initiative for the purposes of this book, and discovered that:

- the management framework that had been established to oversee the change programme was not only still in place, but expanded;
- the policy framework and in particular the business case for equal opportunities had been tested over time and proved to be relevant and sufficiently flexible to survive the continuing organizational upheaval;
- some initiatives that had been proposed had taken root and blossomed, with some notable successes;
- some initiatives had not flourished, but 'lessons had been learned' and other initiatives had been developed;
- the 'core leadership' of selected individuals had not only retained and developed their commitment, but new 'leadershp' had also emerged.

The council was still a member of the national Business in the Community Opportunity 2000 Campaign, which promotes the view that a solid senior managerial commitment is a prerequisite for success in achieving organizational change objectives. Within the council the Opportunity 2000 Steering Group was still leading the local campaign in the authority 'to promote the quality and participation of women in the workforce' and ' to make it easier for women to combine working with their domestic and parenting responsibilities'. The group consisted of male and female managers who had shown an interest in the 'campaign', and met on a regular basis to discuss and work on campaign initiatives. But another council-wide management framework, in the form of a Service Improvement Team (SIT) for Equal Opportunities in Employment, had also been established to support the gender initiatives and to develop a broad-based equal opportunities strategy for devolved business units. The Opportunity 2000 Group was operating effectively, but outside the formal organizational management structures. The new Equal Opportunities Employment SIT, however, was given the same structural strategic and operational status as the Commissioning, Devolution and Members' Induction and Training SITS. There was also a new SIT for Equal Opportunities in Customer Services.

The cross-departmental mentoring scheme had been developed, matching senior managers of one department with more junior women managers of another to improve the career and management development opportunities available to women middle managers across the council. Evaluation of the views of the first thirty mentors and mentees had indicated that the scheme was proving highly successful, and the Women Managers' Mentorship Scheme had been chosen as a model of best practice in a study on mentoring by Ashridge Management College, and had been nominated for an award from SOCPO (the Society of Chief Personnel Officers). All mentees had found the scheme beneficial in terms of personal and career development. Regular mentoring sessions had helped to develop self-confidence, business skills and a wider span of knowledge about the council, and to identify areas where the enhancement of skills would assist with future work assignments. Mentees referred to the benefits of having an independent adviser to discuss work or career development issues. Mentors felt they had a better understanding of the gender specific issues that women managers are confronted with. Mentoring had enhanced their communication skills, and the mentoring relationship had enabled them to revisit their own experience to find relevant situations and examples to illustrate points and give advice to mentees.

The national Opportunity 2000 Campaign is very clear that, unless organizations succeed in developing targets for progress and action plans arising from them, the chances of success are very limited. The organization had not only retained but renewed its commitment to setting and meeting targets to increase the representation of women in senior positions: what the council now called its 'glass ceiling' work. The authority was continuing in its endeavours to meet the targets that had been set in the original proposal: that by 1995, there would be a significantly greater proportion of staff graded at PO2 and above who are women. To enable the council to 'act on the facts' (as they put it), another monitoring exercise had been undertaken in July 1993 to produce 'baseline data' to identify the progress of various departments towards the council's Opportunity 2000 objective. The 1993 data showed a marginal improvement in the representation of women within a number of departments.

A workplace nursery had not been established, but it had been found that the social services and education departments had a number of spare places in council nurseries and teacher's crèches, which had been made available to council employees at a significant subsidy, and greater than that likely to have been available for a workplace nursery. The providers of these services had publicized the availability of places to council staff.

The original proposals had included a conference to launch the council's Opportunity 2000 initiative. This had not taken place, but two innovative series of seminars had been organized. One was aimed at persuading managers to increase their interest in taking positive action, and the other was a six module programme, to cover topics such as auditing and target setting to increase representation, recruitment and retention initiatives, and drawing up equal opportunities action plans.

There was also a new initiative to develop the concept of creating a Women-into-Management Assessment and Development Centre. This was to have two purposes. First, it would help identify the potential in women staff which for various reasons (referred to as 'probably family-centred') had not yet been fulfilled. Secondly, success within the centre would be linked to opportunities to participate in a springboard-type women-into-management training and development programme.

Proposals that fell by the way

A number of the original proposals did not receive support. These included: homeworking, a 24-hour week, an improved job share policy, and making core time in the council's flexitime scheme compatible with school hours.

A Homeworking Feasibility Study was attempted, but encountered considerable management resistance. During that period a neighbouring local authority had advertised two posts as suitable for 'homeworking' and had received over 1000 responses, most of them from women. But the general view in the case study authority was that homeworking would be abused by women: this was the prevailing mythology then with regard to special leave, reflected in the belief that large numbers of women used their children's sickness as an excuse to abrogate their work responsibilities. There was no sense of moving on from the 'jacket on the back of the chair syndrome' to the prioritizing of productivity and the recognition that there might be some jobs or parts of jobs that can be as easily, or better, done from home in terms of 'outputs'.

Although there was a council job sharing policy, and job sharing was identified in the workforce research as one of the single most useful provisions for women with young children for short periods of time during the early childrearing years, it had always been regarded with hostility by male managers. They saw it as only suitable for lower graded posts, and believed it could not work at senior decision-making or supervisory levels, and certainly not for directors. They saw it as a nuisance, and as too complicated to manage, without realizing that most of the 'difficulties' applied similarly to 'normal' management situations.

Interestingly, the greatest resistance arose with respect to moving the core hours of the flexitime scheme (then 10 a.m. to 4 p.m.) by one hour in the afternoon – from 4 p.m. to 3 p.m. – to enable women to collect their children from school. A belief was often expressed that 'everyone abuses the flexi system', notwithstanding the fact that everyone still 'clocked in' at this case study authority, punching time cards rather than filling in their own time sheets, thus significantly limiting the actual potential for abuse. It was argued that if the core hours were changed to benefit parents, the system would be even further abused.

The '24-hour week' was a proposal that I had developed, based on research carried out by the Department of Employment and the OPCS showing that women usually left full-time employment when they had children, returning to part-time employment when their children were young, and later returning to full-time employment (Martin and Roberts 1984). This research had shown that of those women who returned to part-time employment, the majority worked five hours a day five days a week (that is, during school hours). This was translated into a proposal for a '24-hour week' (the reduction of one hour would entitle those working 24 hours a week to family benefits). In a climate unsympathetic to flexible working hours, this 'idea' never progressed beyond proposal stage.

In the two years following the agreement of the original proposals, there were some initiatives that had proved to be unpopular. The term-time working policy, career break agreements and holiday play scheme were described as 'by no means well received'. The organization was described as having 'learned the lesson' that, because of the diverse needs of devolved business units, 'corporate schemes had not been welcomed' and 'giving corporate-wide staff rights had not been a realistic or successful proposition'. 'Shadowing' was not implemented and the council had also got rid of the job sharing policy which had been in existence for many years.

CONCLUSION

Unexpected successes

It was the workforce research conducted in this organization that provided the graphically detailed picture of 'the gender culture' described in Chapter 2. This was the organization which produced examples of the whole range of characteristics from hierarchy and patriarchy through sex segregation, sexual divisions of labour, sex stereotyping, sex discrimination, sexual harassment and sexualizing of the environment to sexism, misogyny, gendered power relations and resistance to change. I was genuinely surprised, therefore, to find some two years later such a high level of continued commitment amongst key individuals in the organization to improving the position of women, such a relatively high degree of sustained momentum still to the gender and organizational change initiative, and so much progress on specific initiatives.

In a sense it was most surprising that monitoring and targeting were the two most successful initiatives, because they required the greatest commitment of 'time', 'self', 'effort' and engagement on a personal and individual level (mentoring) and organizationally (targeting) over an extended period of time. These were also the initiatives that were likeliest to have a lasting effect, to change significantly the culture and practices of the organization, and to make it a more women-friendly place to work.

The relative success of the gender and organizational change initiative was unexpected, and can largely be explained as a credit to the soundness of the theories that guided and supported it, and to the fact that theory was translated (almost literally) into and tested in practice. This experiment in putting theory into practice suggests that Schein (1980: 53) was right that 'organizational changes occur only though individual changes in key members of the organization', that 'no change will occur unless there is motivation to change', that if 'such motivation to change is not already present' it needs to be 'inducted', and that this might be 'the most difficult part of the change process'. Pugh (1978: 30–1) was right about the need to 'work hard at establishing the need for change' and 'to initiate change through informal discussion to get feedback and participation'. Hampden-Turner (1990: 204) was right about the possibility of changing corporate culture through intervention, 'using interviewing and group discussion' and 'starting to change a culture' through the process of 'studying it'. Waterman et al. (1991: 310) were right about paying attention to the 'superordinate goals' of the organization (in this case, for example, equal opportunities and the enterprise economy).

Being aware of systems and in turn being systematic in the approach to change paid off. The use of diagnostic tools – SWOT analysis, key relationship mapping and force-field analysis – was decisive in how well the change strategy was operationalized. Above all it was putting into practice the concept of 'crafting strategy' which proved to be the key success criterion. Mintzberg's (1987) concept of 'emergent strategy' made it possible to recognize and to make use of the potential for change that already existed in the organization, and the success of the change initiative suggests there is some truth in Miller and Friesen's (1984) 'quantum theory of change'.

In general, adopting a strategic approach enabled and facilitated the process of change. Use of organizational change theory enhanced the effectiveness of the change initiative. In particular, the process of researching the organization developed some interest in, commitment to and ownership of the specific initiatives; and the decision to 'develop leadership' and to 'hand over responsibility' to selected key individuals, and to leave behind an institutional infrastructure and management arrangements for taking the initiative forward, contributed signficantly to under-writing continued commitment and impetus.

The limits of equal opportunities

Important as it is to acknowledge the possibilities of change demonstrated by this work, it is equally important to be clear about the limits of the success and of what is possible. What has occurred is 'only' the motivation of some key individuals and the establishment of some mechanisms that might enable a shift in the gender inequality that is institutionalized in the organization and internalized in the attitudes, beliefs and behaviours of individuals. The gender and organizational change initiative established the potential for change and a more positive and hopeful climate for change than might have been considered possible. But gender equality or parity in this organization is still a goal, yet to be realized.

And there are limits to the extent equality can be achieved within organizations, whether it is gender, race or disability equality. The limits are determined by the inequality which exists in the wider society, by the hierarchies, divisions and competition which exist between and within groups that experience discrimination, by the power relations that are institutionalized in the organization of work as well as in work in organizations and in the sexual divisions of labour, and by the lower value and status of women as women, and of work when it is done by women in all spheres. In this context the outcomes so far of the gender and organizational change initiatives were encouraging: they demonstrated some small progress and the potential for more.

REFERENCES

Beechey, V. (1987) *Unequal Work*. London: Verso.

Beechey, V. and Perkins, T. (1987) *A Matter of Hours: Women, Part-time Work and the Labour Market*. Cambridge: Polity Press.

Borisoff, D. and Merrill, L. (1985) *The Power to Communicate: Gender Differences as Barriers*. Illinois: Waveland Press.

Bruegel, I. (1979) 'Women as a reserve army of labour: a note on recent British experience'. *Feminist Review*, 3, 12–32.

Bryson, J. M. and Roering, W. D. (1987) 'Applying private sector strategic planning in the public sector'. *American Psychological Association Journal*, Winter, 9–22.

Dubeck, D. J. (1979) 'Sexism in recruiting management personnel for a manufacturing firm'. In Alverez, R. *et al.* (eds), *Discrimination in Organizations*. London : Jossey-Bass.

Ford, V. (1991) 'Thinking outside the sphere'. In Schlesinger, H. (ed.), *Work Versus Family*. London: Dawlish Hall Educational Foundation.

Glaser, B. G. and Strauss, S. (1967) *The Discovery of Grounded Theory*. Chicago: Aldine.

Hampden-Turner, C. (1990) *Corporate Culture: From Vicious to Virtuous Circles*. London: Hutchinson.

Handy, C. (1990) *Inside Organizations*. London: BBC Books.

Hunt, A. (ed.) (1988) *Women and Paid Work: Issues of Equality*. Basingstoke: Macmillan.

Itzin, C. (1992) 'Hobbled horses: gender and organizational change'. *Local Government Management*, Summer, 18–20.

Itzin, C. and Phillipson, C., (1993) *Age Barriers at Work: Maximising the Potential of Mature and Older People*. London: Metropolitan Authorities Recruitment Agency.

Martin J. and Roberts, C. (1984) *Women and Employment: A Lifetime Perspective*. London: Department of Employment/OPCS.

METRA (1993) *Women and Local Government: A Directory of Local Authority Initiatives*. London: Association of Metropolitan Authorities.

Miller, D. and Friesen, P. H. (1984) *Organizations: A Quantum View*. Englewood Cliffs, NJ: Prentice Hall.

Mintzberg, H. (1987) 'Crafting strategy'. *Harvard Business Review*, July–August, 66–75.

Phillipson, C. (1992) 'Challenging the spectre of old age: community care for older people in the 1990s'. In Manning, N. and Page, R. (eds), *Social Policy Yearbook No. 4*. Coventry: Social Policy Association.

Pugh, D. S. (1978) 'Understanding and managing organizational change'. *London Business School Journal*, 3 (2), 29–31.

Schein, E. H. (1980) *Organisational Psychology*. New York: Prentice Hall.

Spencer, A. and Podmore, D. (1987) *In a Man's World: Essays on Women in Male Dominated Professions*. London: Tavistock.

Stone, I. (1988) *Equal Opportunities in Local Authorities: Developing Effective Strategies for Implementing Policies for Women*. London: HMSO.

Walby, S. (1988) *Gender Segregation at Work*. Milton Keynes: Open University Press.

Waterman, E. H., Peters, T. J. and Phillips, J. R. (1991) 'The 7–S framework'. In Mintzberg, H. and Quinn, J.B. (eds), *The Strategy Process: Concepts, Contexts and Cases*. Englewood Cliffs, NJ: Prentice Hall.

Chapter 9

Working for equality in the London Borough of Hounslow

Munira Thobani

This chapter describes the author's experience as a black woman working for equality in the London Borough of Hounslow. It looks at the origins and development of equality initiatives, and provides an important link between the traditional focus on employment issues and the emerging agenda of equality issues in service delivery. It explores the role of an equalities unit in influencing change, and describes the challenges and opportunities presented by the changing context in which local authorities work.

My understanding and analysis is guided by my experiences as a black woman working in Hounslow as Head of the Equal Opportunities Unit, and as a recipient of local services. In this chapter I will share with you what it has been like to try to put equality principles into practice: the excitement and the frustrations. This work has been motivated by the passion and commitment of people who believe in changing practices to benefit people just like themselves, and in the process exactly for themselves. I am committed to an integrated approach to equal opportunities and believe that the struggle for race equality, women's equality, disability equality, age equality and all other struggles against discrimination, are all part of the same struggle, just on many different fronts. I have acknowledged and faced the tensions that exist between equalities target groups, especially in relation to race and gender, and have managed to synthesize the work, thus avoiding destructive debates on the hierarchy of oppression. The experience has been truly enriching, and often I have felt privileged in leading the work.

Local authorities have the power to control employment practices; to use their purchasing power to encourage other employers to adopt fair policies; to promote cultural diversity; and to introduce policy initiatives that directly benefit the most oppressed groups within society. The struggles and demands of oppressed groups in some places received the support of socialist politicians who, during the 1980s, introduced equal opportunities policies within local government. Implicit in this agenda for change is the necessity to challenge existing structures, to improve them in order to make the organization more responsive. Like most institutions, they are male dominated and consequently work to men's advantage. Within this setting there is nothing you can do to achieve equality on the ground without the support of white, able bodied, heterosexual males. Nevertheless, much has been achieved by local authorities that have a political commitment to equality in the provision of employment and in service delivery.

Hounslow Council first declared its commitment to equal opportunities in 1982, but it was not until the 1986 administration that the commitment was backed by resources and actively supported by politicians. This time some councillors were clearer about what they wished to achieve, particularly in changing the workforce profile to represent the local community better. Hounslow joined the 'equality game' late in the day, especially in relation to equality in employment, but has ended up leading the field in changing mainstream service delivery.

A number of authorities had invested resources to promote equality in employment both by improving recruitment procedures and in positive action training programmes designed to advance the careers of black and women staff. The pioneering work of the Greater London Council to tackle institutional discrimination had inspired many. Authorities set up structures to support their policy commitments, which varied considerably depending on how they believed they could achieve change. Some councils set up new departments, others set up specialist units to promote race, women's and disability equality, some also set up specialist posts to work on equality for lesbians and gay men.

Local authorities in themselves are large employers and Hounslow provides municipal services to around 210,000 people. Services provided include planning and transport, consumer and environmental services, social services, education, housing and leisure. A local authority may be providing as many as three hundred different services: some universal, such as refuse collection and street lighting; some driven by choice, such as leisure facilities; some targeted, such as meals on wheels; and some which protect individuals or the public interest, such as child protection and weights and measures. Many of the services are statutory requirements, whilst others are discretionary. The sheer diversity of services presents difficulties in defining equality outcomes in service delivery, but it is fair to say that women are the main providers and consumers of local authority services. They are also grossly under-represented in management at both political and officer level.

Until recently, most of the decision making meetings in local government would have been all white and mainly male. Millions of pounds' worth of services serve particular sections of the community whilst ignoring the needs of others. Services mirror the people who provide them and embody the values of those that manage them. Where groups that experience discrimination get services, the provision is often paternalistic, patronizing or so culturally inappropriate as to result in no services.

Equal opportunities work in local government is not about changing the world: it is about touching the lives of people in a way that enhances their quality of life. At a practical level, equal opportunities objectives have to be addressed in the context of quality, economy, efficiency and effectiveness in the delivery of services within finite resources.

Meeting the objectives of equal opportunities has also come to be recognized as good management practice, and new practices relating to customer care, citizens' charters, consultation and rights to information have been very much what equalities staff have been working to achieve over the years. Equal opportunities work in local government has blazed the trail for 'people centred' service delivery which meets individual needs. The statutory requirements of the sex discrimination and race relations legislation have provided the opportunity for these developments, but ironically it has been the market-oriented policies that have given this work a legitimacy and priority it lacked simply as a response to discrimination. Over many years, equal opportunities work has been taken forward against the tide. Politicians and public servants have not been able to see the benefits of practising equal opportunities and so sacrifice the talent, the creativity and the knowledge that different people have, together with the chance of getting the services right for the community.

Most equalities officers will know the pain and heartache involved in working to shift mainstream organizations. It is not simply a matter of winning or losing an argument to influence people who have executive power. We are acutely aware that when successful the concessions are small and seldom about redress, and when unsuccessful the injustices are very visible and consolidated further.

So, why start or continue to press for equality through local government? One reason is that local government is an important instrument for social policy and public services. The public service sector employs huge numbers of women and so equality in employment and pay is very important. Secondly, the sexual division of labour puts the primary responsibility for unwaged work on women especially as carers. Women's participation in the labour force is thus hindered and they are unable to participate effectively in the economy. Public services are therefore extremely important for women's struggles for equality. But the main reason is that local government, unlike any other provider of services, is a democratic institution. What women lack in economic power they may make up for in voting power, and women's needs and aspirations can find expression through local government. In response there is an awareness amongst politicians of the need to secure the support and the votes of women.

GETTING STARTED

Before the Hounslow Equal Opportunities Unit was set up, the committee held consultation meetings with all 'target groups'. Open public meetings were held with women, black people, people with disabilities, pensioners, unemployed people, young people, lesbians and gay men. From these meetings, a number of issues were raised in relation to employment and access to council services. People did not have information about what was provided by the council, nor did they feel involved in decision making. In addition to identifying specific service needs they called for more information and greater consultation. They also requested more financial support for voluntary organizations meeting their immediate needs. Although there was a departmental response to service needs, there remained a policy vacuum, as it was still unclear how the council could operate dynamically to respond to different and changing needs in the community.

Hounslow decided to have a modest structure. Unlike many councils at the time, it created an Equal Opportunities Unit with a focus on service delivery, comprising a Head of Unit, one Principal Race Adviser, one Principal Women's Adviser and one Principal Disability Adviser. Responsibility for equality in employment was given to the Director of Personnel. The Equal Opportunities Committee also had a capital budget of £250,000 and a small revenue budget of £100,000 to fund additional staff, plus funds to carry out research, information and educational projects. Work on age equality developed later, with Hounslow as one of the first local authorities to employ a Principal Older People's Adviser, having recognized that people are discriminated against and have their opportunities and choices limited on account of their age. Project officer posts were also set up for each of the equality target groups to develop close working relationships with community organizations.

How then could a centrally based Equal Opportunities Unit have any influence or impact on all the services provided by various departments? The challenge was going to be to find a way to secure the cooperation of chief officers, the major stakeholders and power barons. Otherwise the politicians would have to instruct departments and the Equal Opportunities Unit would lose the ability to work with other professionals on the basis of mutual trust and respect.

I believed always that there were political, professional, legal, social and moral dimensions to our work and that we would have to find strategies on all these fronts. Different people who could affect change would respond at different levels to these imperatives. If change was to be sustained it needed *not* to be enshrined in policies but grounded in practice.

With our small staff team, we began to tackle how we could possibly shift the ethos, the priorities and the resources to implement the council's equal opportunities pledge. We were expected to provide leadership to develop equal opportunities work in service delivery, but we were outside the departmental structure and our status within the organization was unclear. Everything had to be negotiated.

We had to identify areas where we had power and to use it strategically. We had access to and support from politicians, and we also had our small budget. But there was a great deal of suspicion amongst senior officers as to the purpose of the Unit. This left us feeling we had to justify our existence and prove our professional capability before there was the remotest chance of being accepted as doing legitimate local government work.

A discussion document was produced for chief officers to begin a dialogue about how the work could be organized, how a policy statement could lead to a clear definition of tasks, and how strategies for implementation could be worked on together. This was to help us to define the respective roles of the Unit and the departments.

A policy statement for service delivery linking to a policy statement for employment was developed to provide a framework for the work being done and to guide the organization on its aims and objectives. The policy aim for services set out how departments were to comply with legal obligations, acknowledge discrimination and disadvantage, identify the target groups, ensure equal access, meet special needs and encourage regular consultation.

What emerged from the early discussions was a clearer rationale for the Unit as a focus for change. The Unit would be linked to departments in a way that could influence change whilst maintaining independence from them. Two key roles for the Unit were identified:

1   to encourage departments to provide services to the target groups in a manner that genuinely recognized their needs and interests, and where staff understood and respected their wishes;
2   to respond directly to needs in the community, using our own resources to set up new services.

As it turned out, this gave us the opportunity to prove our leadership qualities in the field and made it easier to work with departments.

In order to develop and implement equal opportunities in the council, the following tasks were identified:

- *policy development* – developing specific corporate policies that would promote the interests and concerns of target groups, in areas such as domestic violence, racial harassment, integration, access, etc;
- *training and education* – providing training and information necessary to influence change in decision making and in professional practice;
- *policy implementation* – promoting, enabling, and ensuring implementation by producing procedure and practice guidelines;
- *policy monitoring* – evaluating the effectiveness of policies;
- *policy review* – periodic assessment of progress and strategies;
- *research and information* – ensuring that the work was well informed and relevant to Hounslow;
- *advising, negotiating, confronting and challenging* – establishing priorities and appropriate responses;
- *community contact* – creating rapport with community groups and involving them in policy development;
- *coordination* – of equal opportunities work in the authority.

The Unit was created in the recognition that the organization was neither geared up to respond to new and changing needs in the community, nor equipped to deal with conflicting priorities. It needed specialist advice and expertise, and so the role of specialist officers was to be to:

- participate in decision making;
- sensitize staff and their activities;
- add their perspective to problem solving;

- be consulted in long term planning;
- recognize and suggest action to overcome discrimination;
- share knowledge and motivate others to practise the policies;
- model a different way of working.

The ultimate responsibility for change rested with the chief officers as did the bulk of the work required to achieve change. However, the development of policies, procedures and practices on equal opportunities were to be delegated to the Unit in recognition of its corporate role, its expertise and its interface with the Equal Opportunities Committee. It was necessary for the Unit to establish a relationship of trust and a partnership with chief officers and departments, but it was also necessary for it to be given status and a degree of power within the organization in order to achieve change.

A framework for equal opportunities work was established along these lines within a matter of three to four months, and I was able to participate in the chief officer management team. It was another three to four years before I was accepted as a full member of the team. Involvement at this level proved to be invaluable in ensuring that the equalities work was integrated with the priorities of the whole council.

EQUALITY IN PRACTICE

In most authorities, equality officers are in the business of trying to sell good ideas. They have very little executive power. Much has been achieved through the powers of persuasion, but unless equality is given institutional power in the form of position and resources it is difficult to affect change and then to sustain it. Our strategy at Hounslow was to utilize our small budget to create practical projects giving expression to equality policies. We controlled how the projects were developed and implemented.

The thinking behind the capital budget allocation was to provide security measures to all pensioners in the borough. This proposal had come from the consultation meetings. The sum to do this had been significantly underestimated and also it was hard for me to see how assisting people to lock themselves away was promoting equal opportunities. Instead we wanted to set up projects where people would feel that their needs were being addressed and produce a greater level of confidence amongst the different groups in the community. Safety and security were crucial issues for all the equalities target groups. We felt that our quarter of a million pounds would not touch the tip of this iceberg, but it could assist in small scale projects to give expression to wider equalities principles. We identified key principles that could be addressed through practical projects, such as: identifying and meeting target group needs; promoting integration; information provision; valuing diversity; and promoting positive images. And we set up a range of small projects:

- *Adventure play for children with disabilities*. This facility was built in a park alongside an existing inaccessible construction. Our aim was to promote integration of children with disabilities in a way that extended the debate on access beyond just buildings. We also wanted to complement integration efforts in the education department by extending them into other spheres. This project became a model for another authority, who visited Hounslow and decided to include integrated play in all its parks as part of its programme to refurbish play areas.

- *Crèche provision.* A crèche was set up in the civic centre for service users to improve the quality of service for women users. The crèche helps to communicate a message that the council welcomes children and recognizes the caring responsibilities of people. This small project enabled the Unit to give a higher profile to childcare needs and led to the provision (via portable crèche kits) of childcare facilities at public meetings and community events.

- *Translation and interpretation service.* This was initially funded by the council and was later extended with Section 11 funds from the Home Office. Under Section 11 of the Local Government Act 1966, the Home Office can provide additional monies to local authorities who demonstrate that they have ethnic minority communities whose needs are greater than those of the general population. A remuneration scheme was also established for staff who were asked to use their language skills to deliver services. The job evaluation scheme did not recognize language skills, so an honorarium was introduced. This initiative encouraged departments to monitor needs and reward staff accordingly.

- *Care Giving and Receiving Conference.* This was organized with the Women's and Disability Equality Advisers working in collaboration with carers and disability organizations. The aim of the conference was to look at the issue of 'care' from the perspectives of both those providing care and those receiving it, with the intention of opening up the debate about the rights of disabled people to receive the best quality services. Many lessons were learned in the organization from the conference about the kind of support and outreach work necessary to enable genuine participation; for instance, personal care support both at the conference and at home to enable carers to attend, interpreters, signers, transport, etc.

- *Domestic Violence Action Research Project.* This was developed as part of the process of setting up an Asian Women's Refuge, opened in 1994. An inter-agency forum was established and training was provided for all advice agencies to give effective support to women. The forum also addressed violence in lesbian and gay relationships and the particular issues faced by disabled women. Work is under way with judges and magistrates to raise awareness of domestic violence.

- *Women's Directory.* This was put together with women's organizations in the borough and included information on advice and counselling, childcare, women's groups, health, and services provided by the local authority and voluntary organizations in the borough.

- *Women's health information booklets.* The first booklet on menopause was welcomed by many women's organizations. Another booklet on women's mental health was produced in 1994.

- *European Year of Older People.* Three months of activities targeted towards older people were organized with the participation of most departments. Opportunities were taken to highlight age discrimination, and positive images of older people were profiled. Some seven thousand older people participated in these events, including older people from the council's residential establishments, one outcome of the positive links established between the Unit and the social services department. There is now an annual programme of events.
- *Age discrimination in employment research.* This project was supported by the Unit. As a result Hounslow Council became one of a dozen employers to participate in a major study which identified age discrimination as a substantial problem for people who are 40+.
- *Racial harassment policies.* These have been developed in all service departments with ongoing support to encourage implementation. A special graffiti removal project was set up by the Unit covering the pre-election period, and a staff handbook to support all staff in taking action to tackle harassment was planned for publication in 1995.
- *Adult abuse policy and guidelines.* The policy, developed with other agencies, is aimed at adult protection against abuse in the home as well as in institutions.
- *Race Equality in the 90s Conference.* This was organized in May 1992, planned and run in partnership with local black and ethnic minority organizations. Over three hundred people attended. One of the main aims of the conference was to establish an ongoing dialogue with the council. This has led to the establishment of the Race Equality Community Forum, which meets quarterly: each chief officer, together with the chair of his or her committee, presents a progress report on his or her work on race equality.
- *Handbook for Disabled People.* This was produced to meet the council's obligations under the Disabled Persons Act 1986. The book contains sections on rights, benefits, living independently, services at home, planning and transport, education and training, employment, leisure, health and community involvement.
- *Reflections Project.* This is a project which provides a 'sensory environment' for people with learning difficulties. A soft play area and a 'white room' for relaxation and sensorial pleasure are open to both disabled and non-disabled people. This project is located in the Hounslow Urban Farm, in order to integrate the facility as part of leisure provision.
- *Older People's Handbook.* This provides information on all services available for older people in the borough. The aim is to enable older people to make informed choices to improve their quality of life.
- *Security for older people.* This project has been allocated £50,000 annually to provide free security measures to pensioners on low incomes.
- *Child Care Partnership Project.* This is a joint initiative with Save the Children

to explore the opportunities for increasing the quantity and quality of childcare using a partnership approach.

Many of these projects resulted from consultation with community organizations. In all cases new services were added and resources found from the Equal Opportunities Committee budget. The vast resources and services in departments were hardly touched by these projects except where individual managers showed interest. This is gradually changing as better working relationships are developing with chief officers and staff in their departments. These projects undoubtedly set real, practical models for service delivery to equalities target groups.

Projects aimed at directly meeting the needs of these groups may be seen as making separate and special provisions, for example providing separate residential care for particular ethnic communities or having swimming sessions for women only in leisure facilities. Developing such initiatives is a critical part of the strategy for equality, as it builds a foundation of provision from which people can choose to integrate into mixed provision, and gives them a choice of how their needs can best be met.

STRUCTURES AND STRATEGIES

In addition to progressing these projects, we decided to develop strategy statements for all the target groups. As a support for departments, structures were established to take work forward. Each department was asked to identify a lead equalities officer at second tier level with a brief to influence decisions on services, resources and management priorities, and to provide leadership at a senior level to others to change their policies and practices. In addition to this, each department also identified a member of staff to work on each of the interdepartmental groups on race, women, disability and age equality.

The key objectives in the Women's Equality Strategy Statement are:

- through positive action, achieving a workforce that reflects the community of Hounslow at all levels, in particular at decision making level;
- eliminating sex discrimination in recruitment, training and promotion and in the general working environment;
- ensuring that all council services are accessible to all women and where necessary appropriate services are developed to meet identified needs;
- challenging sexism and developing procedures to deal with sexual harassment;
- establishing effective consultation and liaison with women including Asian, African Caribbean, and other ethnic minority women, disabled women, young and older women, and lesbians;
- providing support to women staff and developing the potential for women to participate more fully in decision/policy making;
- developing mechanisms for ensuring that changes in the authorities work in response to central government legislation, and that local decisions identify and

take into account the impact on women – for example, in community charge, care in the community and transport;
- addressing the specific needs of carers in the borough;
- promoting the above objectives to other voluntary, statutory and public agencies.

The action programme called on departments to take steps to achieve a better representation of women within their departments, start looking at their mainstream services to consider their relevance to women, consult women in the borough and start gathering information on gaps in service provision. Commitment was given to an annual report to council on progress.

The interdepartmental women's group was made up of the most senior officers, although generally women were under-represented at this level. It was a real struggle, however, to get the group to focus on women's equality in service delivery. Despite the corporate women's equality work programme, highlighting domestic violence, safety concerns, access to services, childcare, etc., the group's interest remained with employment issues. Women staff strongly felt that unless the workplace was sensitive to women, valued women and responded positively to their needs, it would be extremely unlikely that services to women would be changed or developed.

There was a problem also in how services were organized. Women's lives are not organized in departments: instead of looking at their services, departments were opting out of doing this kind of work because they saw domestic violence as an issue just for the housing department, or childcare as only for social services and education. The council does not see itself as providing services to women, but to 'people'. Even so, people are not seen in a holistic way and 'customers' remain ungendered. Women may get services because they are battered or have children or are disabled, but not because they are women who would like to participate individually and fully in all spheres of their lives.

The tendency to focus on employment was present in all the equality working groups, but some managed to identify specific barriers or work that was common to all service departments, like physical access, ethnic monitoring, racial harassment, information provision, etc.

It became increasingly obvious that the structure of equality groups was proving to be a cumbersome way of trying to change mainstream services, because:

- it relied on one individual to tackle the work of a whole department;
- our expectations that departments would scrutinize their services (unrealistic in hindsight) were not being realized;
- the work was burdensome and not making sufficient progress;
- major changes were taking place that were significantly altering how the authority was working, with power to make decisions about services shifting away from local politicians, mainly through the Education Reform Act, the Local Government Act 1988, the introduction of compulsory competitive tendering (CCT), the Children Act, the NHS and Community Care Act, and severe budget reductions.

In the Unit we felt we were still tinkering at the margins of the £170 million+ worth of services provided by the council. There were three significant developments which helped to identify the priority areas of work where better progress could be made:

1   We decided to commission a review of the equal opportunities work in the authority. We were prepared to put our work under the scrutiny of external consultants, to assess progress and to assist us to think through the challenges we faced and to map a way forward. This was a high risk strategy as reviews up and down the country were resulting in equal opportunities units or departments closing down or being merged with other structures such as policy units/departments.

2   The Women's Group's concerns with the working environment and the culture of the organization led them to propose an investigation of how far staff in the workforce were aware of the women's equality strategy statement, what their understanding was in employment and service delivery, what level of support there was to address this work in their departments, and finally what they wanted to see done in the organization to progress women's equality.

3   The Principal Women's Adviser set about working with one department to try to develop a service delivery equality action plan. The only guidance given was that it should be linked to the departmental equality action plan (DEAP) for employment.

WOMEN'S EQUALITY QUESTIONNAIRE

A survey carried out by the Women's Equality Group found very little work going on in the council on women's equality, especially in service delivery. Some improvements have been achieved in the workforce profile at the senior levels only. Staff perceptions are that very little resources are allocated to women's equality in the council. The status of women in the organization is a major concern and gets reflected in the lack of legitimacy given to addressing women's equality. The group has highlighted specific recommendations for training, tackling issues important to women like childcare, safety and reasonable working hours, to convey that women are valued in the council. The results of the survey are currently being analysed and recommendations will be made on making a stronger commitment to women's equality in service delivery.

CHALLENGES AND OPPORTUNITIES ALONG THE WAY

During the last seven years, the major challenges being faced by the local authority were also being faced by the Unit. Equal opportunities work has constantly been under threat in the context of compulsory competitive tendering, budget cuts, various restructuring exercises and the Audit Commission's drive for the three Es: economy, efficiency and effectiveness.

Local Government Act 1988

Sections of this legislation were specifically targeted against contract compliance policies. CCT signalled that equal opportunities considerations were anti-competitive and therefore not permissible. Minimal race equality concessions were made by government, but no action was taken to safeguard the interests of women affected by CCT.

We argued successfully that equal opportunities issues were directly relevant to CCT on the grounds that many of the jobs threatened were done by women, and that improved conditions had created better employment opportunities for women and other minority groups. If equalities issues were not integrated in the work on CCT, it would become further marginalized and seen as 'nice if we can afford it'. We agreed to integrate equal opportunities, in so far as we could, with the council's work on CCT. The Unit then produced detailed guidance for departments on tender evaluation and how to ensure that the service specifications addressed the needs of all equal opportunities target groups.

Restructuring

Many restructurings have taken place in the authority, driven by budget cuts, changes in departmental responsibilities, and streamlining the organization. Every time, the merger of the Unit with another part of the council has been raised. Our position has been to remain with the chief executive and continue to be independent of departments. I believe that we have succeeded because of a political commitment to have a visible structure and the value of having an equalities viewpoint put to chief officers in their deliberations. It has also been regarded as useful that our links with the community are not constrained or distorted by a particular service perspective. Also, the value of having a chief executive in Hounslow who is committed to and supportive of equalities work cannot be overstated.

Performance monitoring

All councils are introducing systems for performance monitoring and identifying performance indicators. In the Unit we responded to this by trying to develop equalities performance indicators. In terms of service delivery, it was not possible to produce performance indicators at a general level: they had to be service specific. What was achieved, however, was an equalities process which could give the initial equalities performance indicators: for example, was the particular service or task analysed to identify equal opportunities issues? Was there any consultation with equalities groups? So, for each key task, departments could go through the process of identifying equalities aspects of the task, establish specific goals for the task/service, and then set targets for equal opportunities outcomes. At this stage this was the best that could be done. Even today, the Commission for Racial Equality and the Audit Commission are struggling with adequate performance indicators. The work done by the Principal Women's Adviser on Strategic Equality Plans in Service Delivery (STEPS), described below, provides a model for developing clear performance indicators for each service. It involves auditing the services and producing action plans to make the services more accessible and to achieve equality in service outcomes.

Budget reductions

Ever since Hounslow's Equal Opportunities Committee was set up in 1986, there have been budget cuts. We found it difficult to assess the impact of the cuts on different target groups, and it was the equalities requirements that exposed the poor quality of management information available to guide the decisions of the council. We wanted to ensure that new additions to service delivery targeted to equal opportunities groups were not sacrificed in the traditional discriminatory practice of 'last in first out', as practised in redundancy situations. Similarly, in relation to job cuts, we aimed to ensure that a process of early retirement, voluntary and compulsory redundancy did not impact disproportionately on staff from the target groups. The cumulative impact of cuts in different departments on the equalities target groups was identified, and demonstrated that the impact on older people was disproportionate in both employment and service delivery.

A significant amount of management time is spent on budgets, particularly on cuts. Raising concerns about the impact on particular groups helped to shift attention to the resources left in the council and how they could benefit different sections of the community.

THE REVIEW

The equal opportunities review was useful in confirming many of the concerns we had about progress in the organization. It focused on the management of change, and implementing equal opportunities was placed in the context of delivering responsive services effectively to the community of Hounslow. The report identified strategic blocks and barriers as well as operational inconsistencies between the espoused values and actual practice. The review made explicit the drift in the culture of the organization away from practising equal opportunities, and the need to restate the council's commitment in the context of the challenges of the 1990s. It concluded that:

- there was a need for vision and commitment from the top, from both councillors and chief officers;
- progress across departments was uneven, implementation was patchy, and it depended on individual commitment and voluntary involvement;
- there was a need to gain knowledge about diversity within the community amongst staff at all levels through equalities training;
- current structures for developing and coordinating equalities initiatives were

ineffective, and proposals were made to move towards a more strategic and a more action-oriented approach;

- communications within the organization's centre and periphery needed to be improved to provide for better understanding and support for the policies;
- the culture was perceived to be hostile to equalities issues and there was a sense of fear amongst staff about 'taking risks' in supporting equalities work. This in part was created by the cuts exercise and subsequent restructuring.

The outcome of the review has been to develop a vision for the future, restructure how we take equalities work forward, and place clear expectations on chief officers and councillors. Action plans have been put forward by the consultants, and different staff groups through consultation have added their suggestions. Our aim is to take the work forward in a focused and strategic way through key equalities themes identified annually and backed up by all departments. We will also be investing in direct support to departments in reviewing specific services from an equalities perspective, using the STEPS model created in the Unit.

STEPS (STRATEGIC EQUALITY PLANS IN SERVICE DELIVERY)

STEPS is a model for focusing services onto the community. The method of review for the service(s) is based on the equal opportunities policy statement. The outcomes of such a review produce action plans for redress where there is an over or under-representation of target groups using the services.

The political parameters for STEPS are set by the general themes common to all the equalities strategy statements. These are as follows:

- There should be equality of access.
- There should be equality of treatment, based on equal respect for different social and cultural traditions.
- Services should seek to remove the barriers which deny access to certain groups.
- Services should be based on consultation with those who use them, and positive steps should be taken to include excluded groups.
- Services should be flexible and responsive to the changing needs in the community.
- Information on services should be widely available and where necessary targeted.
- All chief officers are responsible for the overall implementation of the equal opportunities policies in their respective services.
- All staff have a duty to implement the council's equal opportunities policy in service delivery.

The following is taken from the Hounslow STEPS guide:

Developing equality plans in service delivery is a much more complex task than developing equality plans in employment. The employment process is more or less uniform across the council, conditions for recruitment and selection, training and promotions apply similarly in all departments. The added complication in services is that they can be universal to all residents or selectively used by people or targeted specifically at certain groups, and therefore, the equalities implications will vary. Simple exercises of monitoring access to services is insufficient.

A more systematic and qualitative approach is needed to assess access to and experience of services. Also the quality of a service may be different for different groups of 'customers'. For example, car drivers want street lighting to light the roads whilst pedestrians want street lighting to light up the pavements. This illustrates the fundamental point that services impact differently on people. Equal opportunities is not about giving people the same service nor treating people in the same way, it is about adapting services and making conscious choices to meet different needs.

The overall aim of STEPS is to provide a model that can meet the following objectives:

- be effective: too often equalities work has ended up as a paper exercise, filed away in a manager's drawer and resulting in no real change happening at the front line.
- be strategic: equal opportunities in the past has tended to be ad hoc and piecemeal initiatives.
- stay within financial constraints: as local authorities contract equal opportunities can no longer simply be about 'adding on' services.

To meet these objectives the main characteristics of STEPS are to *change* the services rather than add new services. This strategic model can be applied to all services and involves front line staff to ensure effective change. The service requirements are set by users and not providers, front line staff rather than managers and target groups rather than white, able bodied men.

Through this process women and other target groups can say what they want and how it should be provided. The process for STEPS is to work through checklists which help staff to define the service, look at and test out who has access and who *should* have access, explore what needs or interests different groups may have in the service, consult users and non-users, consider how the service could be changed and make specific recommendations in order to meet different needs.

STEPS as a model was developed in the planning and transport department in reviewing their reception and information service. The data gathered for the review revealed unequal access for women, older people and disabled people. Although the staff's perception was that as many women as men used their service, in fact, women represented only 27 per cent of the users. Consultations with the groups confirmed that they were very interested in the services provided by this department but needed more information and wanted to access the department's services via the telephone (direct line) and with visits by the department to their local areas.

People with disabilities found the signposting in the civic centre to be inadequate, particularly for the route that involved using a lift!

Specific changes were proposed to the service in the way that information was provided, where it was provided, and how the customers wanted their needs acknowledged, respected and reflected in the way that they were treated by staff. The action plans included going out to people in their community centres, libraries and group meetings to provide an accessible service.

STEPS are now being carried out in planning applications, housing reception, the customer services section in consumer and environmental services, and in revenues, which includes housing benefits and community charge. Equalities performance indicators are developed for specific services, with clear time scales and lead responsibilities. A regular review is carried out by the team and senior managers to ensure implementation. Using this model in one small but significant access point to the department can show how little the services are based on a clear understanding of people's needs.

The STEPS model assumes a *bottom-up* approach in which the service review is led by:

- front line staff;
- users;
- non-users (potential customers – usually our target groups, exactly the kind of people the council needs to reach).

The review process is supported by the commitment of senior managers and practical help is provided by equal opportunities staff. The review teams, with the participation of front line staff develop 'solutions' where barriers to equalities issues are identified, and consequently own the outcomes of the review. By working in this way, staff get 'on-the-job' equalities training where they can identify their immediate responsibilities in promoting the council's commitment to equal opportunities.

This initiative is going to be developed further to include a kite-marking scheme to acknowledge the work of staff in actively promoting and implementing equal opportunities in the practice of delivering services.

EQUALITIES VISION FOR THE 1990s AND BEYOND

What vision for equal opportunities can be sustained in the context of the future of local government under threat? Constantly in relation to equal opportunities, you hear the question 'Can we afford it?' The real question however, is 'Can we afford not to?'

In April 1994, Hounslow adopted the following vision on equalities:

Local government is unique: it is the only provider of local services which is accountable to those it serves. Numerous organisations provide local services, from shops to quangos. Their success is measured in the market place by a board of directors. The strength of local authorities is that their accountability does not depend on 'purchasing power' (market forces) but on 'voting power'. A local authority belongs to its community in a way no other service provider does. This means that a local authority has two main defining characteristics:

- as a service provider
- as the elected voice of the community it serves

The 1991 census shows that in Hounslow women are 51 per cent of the population, black and ethnic minority people 25 per cent, disabled people ('long term illness') 10 per cent, people over 60, 17 per cent. The estimated figure for lesbians and gay men is 10 per cent. Taken together and allowing for overlaps this represents the majority of the people living in the borough. Equalities is therefore about addressing the needs of the majority and must be central to the work of the council in:

- improving services to target groups
- acting as an advocate for target groups, an advocate for all local service provision – Council run and services run by non-elected bodies.

The introduction of the Audit Commission's performance indicators and the Citizen's Charter's objective is intended to ensure market accountability, but this is not necessarily the same as democratic accountability for target groups. Local government could move towards a partnership approach working with community groups in such a way that people define their own needs not just at election time but also throughout the period of an administration. For equalities to work in practice, the local authority's ear must be constantly tuned into the voice of the community.

In the coming years local government could focus on the following areas:

- *changing services* (as opposed to providing 'more' services – this is no longer an option) by making them accessible, providing assistance where necessary for this to happen and by measuring achievement. The STEPS process is one way of enabling this to happen and ensuring that equal opportunities are consolidated, even in the services that are provided by external contractors.
- *empowering and enabling* the most dispossessed and powerless to have a say in the services they receive, including non council-run services.
- *accountability*. For accountability to work in practice, the council should aim to have decisions made as close to the community as possible.

CONCLUSION

I believe that the council will continue with its commitment to equal opportunities in employment and service delivery, because it embodies principles of social justice and also underpins the principle of quality in public services.

Hounslow's relative success in developing equal opportunities awareness, initiatives and practices is due to three major factors. First, the Unit was resourced to work directly with the community and set up innovative projects. Secondly, the Unit was represented at the most senior management level and ensured that equal opportunities work developed in the direction that the organization was moving in as a result of the many pressures placed upon it. The third factor was the tenacity, resilience and integrity of women and members of minority groups in keeping challenging the macho culture in the organization, which is dysfunctional and wasteful of real talent.

In Hounslow, the stage we have reached in the development of equal opportunities work leads me to conclude that we are in a good position to meet the challenges that face the local authority side by side with other departments. The level of integration of equal opportunities at the corporate level is consistent and comprehensive enough to span the full range of challenges, and we have an effective STEPS model to create a bottom-up pressure (both from the community and from front-line staff) for change. Equalities implications will continue to be important in the following areas:

- budget considerations;
- CCT and services contracted to external providers in the private and independent sectors;
- quality in service provision;
- targeting services where there is greatest need;
- performance review;
- community participation;
- user involvement.

There is growing awareness of the need to move away from trying to mimic the private sector in order to distinguish ourselves from them. As a democratic body, the council needs to be seen to be relevant to and involving all sections of the community. It is only through representing and championing the rights of local people at all levels that the council can secure the support of the electorate. As councillors develop their community leadership role, they need to have strong links with all sections of the community.

The composition of the council itself will keep equalities to the fore in order to ensure better and greater participation of all councillors. In the local elections in May 1994, the Labour Party increased its majority by 38 (49 Labour members in total). The labour group has more Asian members (15), sadly all men, 2 African Caribbean councillors for the first time in Hounslow, and 9 women; yet the majority party hierarchy is dominated by white males. The experience and awareness of discrimination and disadvantage will be mirrored in the majority group as they exist in the organization and within the society.

Whilst power remains concentrated in the hands of white men, it is difficult to think of explanations for the inequality of women and black people other than the conscious and unconscious commitment to preservation of power based on gender and race inequality. What we have done in Hounslow is taken every opportunity to try to move towards goals of equality for women, black people, disabled people, older people, lesbians and gay men, and to model what we believe in as we are working towards real and lasting change.

Chapter 10

Challenging racism
The BBC mentor scheme

Jackee Holder

This chapter complements others by taking race and racism as its primary focus. The author describes the development and operation of a mentor scheme for black students developed within the BBC as part of its Race Equality Initiative, and sets this in the context of her own experiences of racial harassment as a black student.

This account is based on my experience of mentoring and my post as coordinator of the BBC Mentor project. This project matches black students from a local college, Hammersmith and West London, with black professionals working in the BBC. The scheme was introduced as one of a number of Race Equality and Equal Opportunities initiatives within the BBC and is funded by the Network Television and the News and Current Affairs Directorates. This chapter describes the development of the BBC Mentor Scheme's first two years, focusing on what was learned from 1993 to improve the programme in 1994. It provides a picture of achievement, but also deals with problems faced by both mentors and students, and questions how far schemes like this can be successful in achieving large scale inroads into institutional racism. The views expressed here are solely the author's and do not represent those of the BBC.

In 1992 I responded to an advertisement in the *Voice* (the well-known black newspaper) seeking a consultant to the BBC to set up and coordinate a mentoring project for twelve black students. I knew I should apply for this, given my own experiences of mentoring. I applied and was shortlisted. I was very excited at the prospect of a job like this, as it would provide me with the opportunity to put into practice what I had learned. The recruitment process involved devising an outline for the course that I would propose to run, and a five-minute presentation on the key elements of a mentoring project. To prepare for the presentation I allowed myself to reflect back to a number of experiences, both positive and negative, in my own life which helped to shape my ideas and views about the need for mentoring for black students. In particular I was able to draw on my own experiences in higher and further education in the 1970s, 1980s and early 1990s.

At the age of 16 I was verbally abused by a lecturer in my college. I was a student in his law A-level class. I loved the subject and was enthusiastic and eager to go on to study law at degree level. Instead of the support and encouragement from my

172 Strategies for organizational change

lecturer that I expected to receive, all my essays were returned to me with negative comments and low grades, even though I could see that I was in fact producing better quality work than other students. This began to have a negative effect on my self-confidence. The lecturer constantly put me down in front of the class, and I started to attend the class infrequently.

On the particular day of his abuse, I was walking down the corridor on my own. I saw him coming towards me. I stopped to say something to him, probably to explain why I had not been attending his lectures. He glared at me. When he did respond I was not prepared for his onslaught. He moved in closer towards me, pinning me into the corner, forcing me into a very intimidating and compromising position. I could feel his breath on my face. I was wishing for someone to walk along, but no one did. He launched into a verbal attack on me, finishing with 'Why don't you go out and get pregnant like all the other black girls do?'

So much for education being a door to success. How could it have been when it is taught by ignorant racists like him? My parents, who came here from the Caribbean, had drilled into us the importance and value of education. I was given different messages from both of them about surviving in the system. My father taught us to defend ourselves from physical and verbal attacks from other children. However, that message did not necessarily apply to teaching staff. He taught me to tell the time and helped me with my homework through both primary and secondary school. My mother, on the other hand, severely contradicted this message. We should always listen to what the teachers had to say and ultimately they were right and we were wrong. To survive and achieve we just had to keep our heads down. No wonder I did not rush to tell my parents what had happened to me. Nor were there any teaching staff at the college that I felt I could talk to.

That is just one example of my treatment in educational establishments. Not all were as severe and as devastating, but all in some way wore away at and undermined my self-esteem and self-confidence in subtle ways. I spent the rest of the afternoon after that particular incident in the student common room. I became almost paralysed. I remember smoking lots of cigarettes, desperately trying to choke down my feelings. I suspect there was also a lot of anger there but I do not remember ever letting it out. My friends at college listened to what I had to say and then we moved on to discuss other things. We were all busy trying to survive in a system that was attacking us from all sides.

What stuck out for me was the isolation I felt and the lack of support I received. That particular incident is vivid in my mind even today. It confirmed for me the isolation that black students feel in the education system. I had no shoulder to cry on, and no one to offer me support and encouragement or advice on how I could have challenged what he did. Help with the negative impact of the situation would have been very beneficial to me at that time. This experience was to reinforce strongly some years later my support for the notion of mentoring for black students.

In March 1994 I went away on a 'residential' with the fourteen students on this year's BBC Mentor Project, where I shared this particular incident with the students. Most of them were stunned, but began to share similar incidents that they too had experienced. One student asked me why I had let that incident have such a negative effect on me. I thought about what she had said, and the group discussed how they might have reacted. Many thought that they too would have felt hurt at the time, and many black students will have had many more than one incident like the above. The lack of black teachers as positive role models in the education system, and the lack of positive black role models at all levels of society, have been proven to be a factor in the low levels of self-confidence and performance and the underachievement amongst black students. I hoped that mentoring might redress some of the negative aspects of black children's underachievement through supporting and nurturing student skills and developing and increasing student knowledge and awareness around a variety of issues. The mentor would provide support for black students in pursuit of their goals, in attaining achievements and in gaining success, both academically and in their career. Most importantly the mentor would act as a role model, by modelling her or his own career and life history, and through this process help to equip black students with the necessary skills to survive and thrive in organizations like the BBC.

My first experience of mentoring was on a mentor project at North London College in Islington. I was keen to work in an environment that actively provided support and mentoring for black students. I was matched with a 16-year-old black student (Martha) and spent two years as her mentor. Martha was in the process of completing her A-levels. We developed a positive working relationship over the two years which had clear goals and operated within a context of friendship, mutual respect and trust. We met regularly each month and discussed Martha's college work and ambitions. I shared some of my own experiences with her and how I overcame difficult blocks in my personal life and at work. Working with a 16-year-old meant that I had to abandon much of my 'adultist' behaviour, such as thinking that I always knew best; I had to listen and place myself in her shoes, and try to remember what life was like for me as a 16-year-old.

Martha and I still keep in contact and I know that I did have an impact on her life. I was able to open her eyes to a career she had not been familiar with. We explored and discussed my career as a training consultant and writer. We shared our experiences about the education system and black issues. I was able to support Martha with her college work and with a difficult situation with one of her lecturers. What became clearer as our relationship developed was the importance of Martha having an independent person who would listen to her objectively. As an A-level student there were lots of issues she needed help with, such as time management, completion of coursework, and writing and literacy skills. I was able to support Martha confidently with all of this and I could personally identify with many of the issues that she faced.

However, as I became more familiar with my role as a mentor I began to realize that black students also required other forms of support that would nurture their confidence and development. The mentor project team at North London College offered me the opportunity to facilitate a 'black awareness' session with the students on a weekend residential trip away. I was also asked to facilitate a series of seminars in the college on the themes of 'black awareness' and 'assertiveness'. This gave Martha and me the opportunity to explore our relationship in another setting. The main focus of the weekend was a series of outward-bound activities to help develop individual confidence and team-building skills. Unfortunately this was hampered quite considerably by some of the overt and covert racist attitudes of the staff at the centre; so much so that by the Saturday evening, when we were about to begin the session on black awareness, the staff protested, saying 'Why on earth do we have to have sessions like this!' This was clear evidence to us of how the institutionali-zation of racism operates, and how it affects the views and beliefs of individuals on the issue of race.

The session on black awareness was the highlight of the weekend for many of the students. We explored the contributions that African and Asian civilizations have made to world technological and cultural advancement. We discussed the contribution of black people to a wide range of areas of public life. The concept of mentoring was explored through examining student expectations and anxieties regarding the mentoring relationship. The students also participated in a number of practical exercises. I was totally inspired by the work that was completed over that weekend, so much that when I saw the advert in 1992 for the BBC I knew I had to go for it.

THE BBC MENTOR PROJECT

The mentor scheme for black students was introduced in the context of a range of Equal Opportunities and Race Equality initiatives implemented in BBC Network Television and News and Current Affairs Directorates. Some examples of these initiatives include:

- the *Television Production Training Scheme*: a two-year programme of high quality 'on the job' training and work experience in production. Five places are targeted each year for ethnic minority candidates (targeted training is advertised under Section 37 of the Race Relations Act 1976). The 1993 scheme received 3000 applications, from which 100 candidates were chosen for preliminary interviews and 21 candidates for final interviews.
- the *Technical Operations Bursary Scheme*, which seeks to address the under-representation of black and minority groups in technical jobs in television. The training lasts for fourteen weeks and aims to train participants so they can compete for jobs on an equal footing within the BBC and the independent sector.

The BBC Mentor Project was established by the then Community Liaison Officer to meet the BBC's commitment to extend its outreach work in the local West London community. The Mentor Project was aimed at twelve black students from a local college, Hammersmith and West London, who wished to pursue a career in the media. Given the under-representation of black people in the media, one of the preliminary objectives of the project was to increase the access that black students have into an organization such as the BBC. The 'who you know' network still operates widely and it is acknowledged that many black people do not have those contacts or access to those networks. Through the matching of a student with a black professional in the BBC it was hoped to address this (and many other issues) by positive role modelling, providing inspiration and transferring knowledge and experience between mentor and student. The mentor was to work with the student during the year, meeting fortnightly on a one-to-one basis.

In addition to matching students with mentors, the other key elements of the 1994 scheme were as follows:

- A structured curriculum programme combined a modular approach with linked assignments to each subject area, comprising thirty weekly seminars of two and a half hours each, held each week at BBC White City. The students met programme makers from across the BBC and had an opportunity to visit rehearsals and programmes in production. They visited programmes and studios and explored different aspects of equality issues in the weekly seminars.
- Students were expected to complete ten assignments as part of the course requirements. These could be presented in a variety of formats, guiding students away from the traditional methods of writing assignments in the form of essays and encouraging them to become familiar with creative and innovative ways in which to present information.
- The 'video diary' was an ongoing feature over the thirty weeks. Through it, students recorded their experiences on the Mentor Project. Students were given three days' training in video operation, provided by an assistant producer from the Community Programmes Unit.
- During the summer vacation some students were given the opportunity to participate in a four-week work experience placement, providing them with practical, hands-on experience.

As coordinator my first role was to do 'outreach' by going into the college and giving a presentation to interested students about the scheme. Students were invited to complete an application form which would form the basis of their selection. Twelve students from a variety of disciplines were selected to take part in the 1992–3 BBC Mentor Project.

With any new initiative, one never accurately estimates the amount of work a project will require. I felt that the original contact time of one day a week would be sufficient to coordinate the project. I had misjudged this badly. It demanded more time and energy than I would ever have imagined. The sheer scope and potential of the project were huge, and got bigger each time an area of the project was developed.

It was hard work getting the project started. I walked into a massive organization, which I had not been formally inducted into, and learned a lot through trial and error and from working closely with the Community Liaison Officer. It proved at first quite difficult to recruit mentors: a project such as this needs a higher profile than it was given. Some potential mentors were apprehensive about its intentions and purpose. The mentors for the 1992–3 project came from a wide range of careers within the BBC (producers and directors, a graphic designer, a sound operator, and a presenter). Mentors worked in a variety of programme areas from news and current affairs to light entertainment and features.

The mentoring relationship forms a crucial aspect of the scheme. The way in which student relationships with mentors developed proved to have a significant impact on the overall development of the student on the programme. Our evaluations clearly indicated that where students spent a lot of time with their mentor, this significantly improved the quality of the relationship and the student participation on the programme. Where students did not spend a lot of time with their mentor or where contact was irregular, this seriously affected the contribution the student was able to make to the project.

The idea of positive role modelling is fundamental to the successful and positive mentoring relationship. Skills such as effective listening, basic counselling skills, problem solving, sensitivity in giving feedback, picking things out that the student may not be saying, and being able to motivate and encourage an unenthusiastic student and develop creative ways of managing the relationship are all necessary mentoring skills. Their quality should not be underestimated. In addition mentors are expected to reflect to their student a positive self-image and their sense of cultural identity, as well as sharing knowledge and information and teaching the student – but not in a way that reminds him or her of school.

Having time and patience is a must: creating time and space is crucial if the mentor is going to develop a meaningful relationship with the mentee. The reality is that often on a project such as this young adults are exposed to situations where they may feel inferior, vulnerable, uncertain and often in awe of the profession of the mentor. Some students may put on an appearance which suggests that they are not really interested or lack motivation. The challenge for the mentor is to get behind this and find creative ways in which to equip students with skills and knowledge that will help them to survive in the world of employment.

Past and present mentors have shared countless stories of how important 'being determined' has been in achieving success in the media industry. Many applied several times to the BBC before they were shortlisted. Many had several years of other relevant experience before they were given that break. Instilling the importance of determination and persistence and the need for students to have a vision and a plan is paramount in meeting the pastoral needs of the students on the scheme and developing greater self-confidence in them.

The management of the project posed other issues. Even though I was employed in the post of coordinator of the project, many decisions in practice had to be made by the Equal Opportunity Officers in Network Television and in News and Current Affairs, the directorates which were the main funders of the BBC Mentor Project. I was also accountable to a Mentor Steering Committee comprising the Equal Opportunity Officers, a mentor from the 1993 project and the Community Liaison Officer.

It was difficult during the final months of the 1993 project to be accountable to so many people in the context of doing the job one day a week. Simple decisions were often delayed by having to seek approval. Tasks and roles were often confused or duplicated. At times I felt that my position as coordinator/consultant was undermined. This raised a number of questions about the extent to which the issue of race and racism may have impacted on the management style of the project. I felt at times, for example, that it was a battle to get my perspectives and strategies in relation to the project agreed to. A lot of time was spent justifying ideas and actions which I believed to be unproblematic and easily implementable.

Under-resourcing was a problem on the 1994 project, following an increase in intake of students and a lack of adequate administrative support. Administrative support is crucial because the project has a demanding turnover of written information and many dimensions to manage. It is fast paced, and the first two years highlighted the need for the right amount of resources to support an initiative as ambitious as this.

There was no question in my mind about commitment to the project from individuals in the organization, but the success of the project was partly dependent on my own style, assertiveness and strong feeling of personal power. Being assertive was useful in meetings with the steering committee and at times when it was necessary to challenge what was going on. As a team we worked through most issues with a positive outcome, but there were always issues about how black workers can strive to survive when working in predominantly white institutions on all-black projects.

Identifying the needs and cultural aspirations of black young people was often at the forefront of my mind, and I was challenged to find different ways to overcome the young people's blocks and barriers: lack of motivation and different standards and levels of literacy created real, live issues as to what the project should be seeking to address. In the world of employment, particularly in the media, competition is fierce, and this makes demands on presentation skills both in writing and orally. Resources were limited to support students in this area both amongst the mentors and from the project itself.

In evaluating the 1993 project I concluded that the development of the students could have been enhanced with a more structured curriculum. The personal development needs of the students could have been more successfully challenged within a supportive environment to encourage increased self-awareness and understanding. One example of this was the issue of homophobia: encouraging the students to shift from this way of thinking proved almost impossible. In an environment like the BBC, which has a high profile equal opportunities policy, it was my view that homophobia should be addressed on a project such as this. The contribution of black gay men and women should not go unacknowledged, but challenging the barriers that prevent this happening requires the support of both mentors and the rest of the staff team in addressing this issue head on.

In spite of its teething problems this project had many successes. One example of a rewarding mentoring relationship on the 1993 project occurred in the matching of a female student with a mentor who worked as a director/producer in television. The mentor was a very dynamic woman and highly respected in her field of work.

The relationship started slowly but eventually took off, providing the student with a rewarding and challenging experience. With her student, the mentor was able to identify areas of learning and goals she wished to achieve from the mentoring relationship. She then provided the student with lots of opportunities to shadow her at work, in the office and out on location. The student was able to see her mentor working practically on the job, in the studio, in meetings and in the office. The mentor inducted her student into television and the student was interviewed as part of a television series the mentor was directing.

This was an invaluable experience for the student, equipping her with real skills and knowledge and boosting her self-confidence significantly. When the project finished the student put forward a proposal to the steering committee for the development of a post of student liaison officer to act as a link between the project team and the students and to work on special projects with the project coordinator. The proposal was accepted and the student became an active member of the project team. She planned and co-facilitated training sessions with the new mentors and made presentations to various groups on behalf of the project at the same time as embarking on a degree in media and communications.

Another example of a mentoring relationship working well but in a different way was that of a student on the BTEC Engineering course. He was very quiet and shy on the course and at times it proved very difficult to get him motivated to participate actively on the project. Added to this, there did not seem to be an area of broadcasting that he was keen on. His mentor worked very hard at establishing a relationship with him despite some of their own cultural differences. The student had periods of absence on the project. However, this was dealt with positively and it was not just assumed that the student was not interested. The mentor invested time in meeting with the student and discussing his development. Feedback from these meetings identified that the student was giving priority to his college course-work and was not seeing the project as that useful for him at the time. Through these discussions what emerged was the student's love and passion for sport and his wish to have a work placement in this area. After many discussions with both the mentor and the project coordinator the student made the decision that he would no longer continue with the scheme, but he was able to evaluate positively the project and what he gained from it. He was also able to identify new developments and learning for the future. Most importantly, we learned that the scheme needs to attract students who really wish to pursue a career in broadcasting.

The 1994 project took a much more developed approach. We built in most of the recommendations from the previous year's students and mentors, and it had a clearly defined curriculum that operated on a modular approach. A mission statement was developed which outlined clearly the aims and objectives of the project and its purpose. A new development was the introduction of ten assignments linked to the course curriculum, which all students were expected to complete as part of the course requirements. There was also the introduction of a 'student portfolio' and the presentation of work as evidence of learning.

At the beginning of the 1994 recruitment process we introduced much tougher selection criteria. These included more questions on the student application form and an essay on a media-related topic. This strategy worked and we were able to attract students who were committed to the project and who really wanted a place. The 1994 students appeared to have a much stronger connection to the project and a clearer view of what was expected of them. They were completing assignments and arriving for sessions on time and taking the project seriously. On the whole it appeared that the project had recruited students who were more open to developing their potential.

There was a great deal of potential amongst the 1994 students, which needed to be teased out and utilized. This required using a creative and flexible approach to the leadership of the project, and, through a positive personal relationship with the students, securing their trust. Personal development and team building were explored on the residential at the beginning of the programme. Black perspectives and 'black awareness' were useful to the induction, and many students were challenged in a supportive and constructive environment about characteristics of their personal style, and given feedback as a way of positive support and highlighting areas of future development.

The content and approach of the 1994 project has paid off. The students presented and hosted the evening for the matching of the students with their mentors. They came over as confident and positive in their presentation with a maturity that belied many of their ages. Many had shared with me their apprehension about meeting their mentors for the first time. They were anxious about how they would get on with each other and what they would have in common, but walking around during the matching evening it was wonderful to see the aliveness between mentors and students who had just met for the first time. The students could identify with their mentors through their lifestyle and common areas of cultural identity. Students introduced their mentors to their parents, who had been invited to the event. The mentors were enthusiastic about their roles and it showed. Mentoring is about inspiring and nurturing growth and development in a challenging environment. It was clear that these students would be receiving this.

The mentors receive training in all aspects of the project areas and what is expected of them. It can be exciting to see what the road ahead holds for each year's students. The BBC to many students can be a hostile and unfriendly place, but the 1994 students came to feel comfortable enough to visit their mentors on days when the project was not running. One student after first meeting her mentor went straight into the studio with him that same evening.

Coordinating a project like this requires a great deal of energy and vision. I am committed to this work because of the real rewards I know it will bring to both mentors and students. It is a two-way process which requires both individuals to give. Mentors are making a difference by putting some of their skills back into the black community. They discuss and share the real, live issues that they are faced with, such as the 'glass ceiling' which prevents black workers being able to develop their careers, the tokenism that can sometimes be experienced when working on black-only projects, and the issue of where black workers get support for themselves. The 1994 mentors were considering establishing a network of support amongst themselves.

Another issue is the numbers of black people working within the BBC who are located at administrative or researcher and assistant producer level and not at senior level. Inroads are slowly being made, but this needs to be considered in the light of the fact that many black programme makers are entering the BBC either through a Positive Action targeted scheme or an Equal Opportunities Initiative. The BBC is attempting to address barriers such as lack of career progression and the need for wider networking into the organization. Some black workers have successfully navigated their way through the organization and are willing to share their skills, knowledge and information freely with other black workers, while others have adopted more the approach that 'I'm here now and I need to fight this battle on my own'. Many are working in great isolation and tackling issues of discrimination individually within their departments. What is clear from my perspective as the coordinator is that black workers need to share their different experiences and ways of surviving in the broadcasting world, where the tables are stacked against their effective participation and contribution, but where none the less they have proven they are competent and professional enough still to deliver. Sharing these experiences as a mentor can go a long way towards shaping the future generation of young black people moving into the world of the media. Developing strategies for survival for black workers in the media is a significant factor in increasing access and success.

In the future it is hoped that there will be a marked increase in the numbers of black young people entering the BBC through 'normal routes', relying significantly less on schemes such as the Mentoring Project but maintaining the concept of mentoring through networking. For the time being, however, the Mentor Project needs to remain as a Race Equality Initiative that is well resourced, financially viable, and with the appropriate management structure to nurture and realize the potential of the young black talent of tomorrow.

The Mentor Project still remains marginalized on the edge of the mainstream establishment in BBC culture. Extending the scheme to a wider range of other departments would help move it into mainsteam culture. There are still questions as to how much the scheme can expect to achieve. Issues such as management recognition of mentors' involvement on the project and recognized time off to work with students have yet to be formalized, leaving the project to rely mainly on the goodwill of the mentors involved, who are often under a great deal of work pressure themselves.

The evaluation of the project's success will need to be monitored over a period of five years in order to follow the progress of the students. How many will pursue careers in the media? And what will their point of entry be? How far will their participation in the scheme contribute to future employment? Other factors less tangible to monitor include how far the scheme will have affected the students' level of confidence, motivation and media competence. These factors need to be monitored closely. But what has stood out has been the responses from so many people, black and white: 'I wish a scheme like this had existed for me when I was young' is a constant refrain, and a reminder of the need for a strong scheme that effectively equips and prepares young black people with a realistic chance of working in the media in greater numbers.

Chapter 11

Women in social services
Accelerating the process of change

Averil Nottage

This chapter describes a programme of activities initiated by the Social Services Inspectorate directed at managers and trainers in social services agencies. It shows how a range of approaches were used to identify the position of women in social services, to give voice to their experience and provide advice and guidence on how to achieve change. Because of the position of the Inspectorate within the Department of Health, these issues gained additional authority and credibility and were brought directly to the attention of senior managers. This helped raise the profile of women in social services and accelerate the process of change.

A higher proportion of women work in social services than in any other area of the public sector in the United Kingdom, and yet the management of local authority social services departments has always been dominated by men. In 1971, when the departments were established, 90 per cent of the Directors in England were men. By 1990 it was 89 per cent, despite the fact that 86 per cent of all the staff employed were women.[1]

As a woman manager working in social services departments, I experienced the effects of this situation. In moving up the management hierarchy I found that I was increasingly in male, rather than female, dominated groups and that this could be very uncomfortable and isolated. When I was a social worker the fact that I was a woman was unremarkable. As an assistant director I was continually experiencing situations where other people's behaviour to me was influenced by my gender and where my preferred ways of doing things were seen as 'different'.

In 1989 I went to work for the Social Services Inspectorate (SSI) of the Department of Health. This is a professional division within the central government department responsible for policy on social services. The responsibility for delivering the services lies with local authorities and independent sector agencies. The Inspectorate offers professional advice to the government ministers and civil servants responsible for developing policy. It also acts as a link between the Department of Health and the agencies that provide services, undertakes development work to ensure that policies are implemented effectively, and inspects the quality of service delivery. The Department of Health, and therefore the Inspectorate, has no responsibility for the employment policies and practices of these organizations. In this chapter I will describe work I undertook as an inspector to influence the position of the women working in social services agencies.

I was based in a regional office covering London. Before I arrived a colleague, Sandra Walmsley, had undertaken a project with a group of senior women managers. They had met for a series of workshops covering communication and group processes; race and ethnicity; personal career planning; childrearing; opportunities; recruitment and retention and training. The project was written up in a report entitled *Women as Managers* (Walmsley 1989). Sandra moved to a new job before the report was published in November 1989 and I took over responsibility for any follow-up work. Although it had been a London based activity, the issues were seen as sufficiently important to justify circulating the report nationally and running a joint national conference with the British Association of Social Workers. There was a very high demand for the report and the conference was oversubscribed. This highlighted the extent to which women across the country shared experiences and were seeking to address them in their own situations.

In January 1990 it was suggested that the Inspectorate might wish to present the issues from the report at a workshop at the annual autumn conference of the Association of Directors of Social Services and local authority associations. There was heavy competition for these workshops, and no guarantee that even if we applied we would be successful. However, the process of considering whether this was something that the Inspectorate should do, and if so, how we would go about it, provided a useful focus for reviewing the work. It raised the possibility of moving from work that was targeted at women to trying to influence senior managers and local politicians, most of whom were men.

It was an exciting, and daunting, prospect. It made sense to try to influence those who held power and made decisions about key appointments. The Inspectorate was well placed to communicate at a senior level and could potentially give voice to the issues that women were finding difficult to get heard within their agencies. However, I was also aware from my own previous experience of raising these issues with male senior manager colleagues of how easily women's experiences could be discounted. They might be seen as untypical ('Surely that does not happen here?') or typical ('But it is just the same for men') or unimportant ('It is not a priority with all the other pressures on our time'). To counter such arguments it seemed important to build up our evidence about the position of women in social services.

It was agreed that I should draw together all the available information with a view to preparing a further report. Although I was based in the London Region this was designated as national work. The management line for these purposes would be via my local male manager to a woman Deputy Chief Inspector. The equivalent of six weeks of time would be allocated to the task, to be interspersed with my other responsibilities over a number of months.

In preparing the report I had several objectives:

- to address issues relating to all women in social services and not only those in management positions. The vast majority of the more senior jobs are only open to the minority of staff with a social work qualification. For many other women, including most of those from black and minority ethnic groups, there are few promotion opportunities. To concentrate only on women in management would have been unacceptably elitist.

- to describe the position of women in social services agencies, identify the ways in which their potential is restricted and provide practical advice and guidance on how to achieve change. This was to include examples of approaches that agencies had used successfully.
- to write in a way that would be equally accessible to men and women.
- to direct the report at managers and trainers and to identify real advantages for them in addressing those issues beyond the 'feel good' factor.
- to produce a printed report at a price that individuals as well as organizations could afford.

The task of collecting material took me in a number of different directions. There was limited statistical information, but by linking data from several sources some useful headlines emerged. Of the staff employed in local authority social services departments in England and Wales in March 1990, exactly one-third (33.3 per cent) were women who worked full-time and over half (53.2 per cent) were women who worked part-time. Just over an eighth (13.5 per cent) of all staff were men and there were very few male part-time workers (1.7 per cent).

By correlating information about part-time staff with more detailed Department of Health data collected by job category, it became clear that part-time women staff worked predominantly in low-paid jobs that did not require formal qualifications, mainly as home helps or care assistants in residential homes for older people. There were significantly fewer part-time staff in jobs that required a professional qualification and hardly any in management posts. With the help of colleagues in other regions of the Inspectorate, I was able to collect comparative information about senior managers. In 1990, 89 per cent of the Directors of Social Services in England, 90 per cent of the Deputy Directors and 80 per cent of the Divisional/Assistant Directors were men.

These stark figures did not do justice to the range of occupational groups employed in social services agencies and their diversity in terms of age, ethnicity, educational backgrounds, qualifications, working patterns and career opportunities as well as gender. I used a combination of a literature search, contact with training bodies, employers' associations, trade unions and professional organizations, and discussion with women to identify the key issues for each of the occupational groups. There were significant variations in the amounts of information available and the ease with which it could be accessed, which highlighted marked status differences between the groups.

I found out about two surveys of staff attitudes to equal opportunities in employment. One had been undertaken in Cheshire, the other in three Scottish regions. They provided evidence about how women combined employment with family responsibilities. It also seemed likely that the results of large national surveys of women's working patterns and arrangements for caring for dependants would apply equally to social services staff. Similarly, it was possible to draw on national information about the employment patterns of women from black and minority ethnic communities, to supplement the limited information about the ethnicity of women working in social services.

At the time I was writing the report, employers were becoming increasingly concerned that demographic changes would result in fewer school leavers being available to join the workforce. This was seen as a major issue for the 1990s and had received a great deal of media attention. Several reports were published highlighting private and public sector employers who had developed family friendly employment practices. It was also a time when social services agencies were finding it increasingly difficult to recruit staff with professional qualifications, and two national social services employment surveys had been undertaken. [2]

A request for information through a national social services magazine resulted in a number of women contacting me about initiatives being undertaken in their agencies. Others offered me access to unpublished research relating to women's and men's career paths, their attitudes to management and their experiences as managers. Colleagues also helped me to make useful contacts with senior managers and trainers.

By August 1990, I was ready to write the report. It was called *Women in Social Services: A Neglected Resource* (Nottage 1991). The first part was a profile of women in the social services workforce and covered women's employment patterns, occupational groups and women in management. The second part focused on responding to the needs of women staff and considered how to overcome organizational barriers, recognize caring responsibilities and change attitudes and behaviour. The introduction emphasized the reasons why it was important that employers valued their women staff. It gave particular attention to the competitive nature of the labour market and the importance of developing an increasingly skilled and experienced workforce to cope with imminent major legislative changes.

It was agreed that the report would be published through Her Majesty's Stationery Office (which markets government publications). It would have a foreword by Virginia Bottomley, the Minister for Health. It would be 'book size' (rather than A4) to emphasize its readability. It was published in January 1991. Copies were sent to all Directors of Social Services with a letter from the Chief Inspector. A press release was issued and it attracted some media attention. Subsequently an article I had written about it was published in one of the social work journals and a Member of Parliament asked a question in the House of Commons that drew attention to the report.

We decided to promote the report through our regional offices, and an inspector was identified to undertake the work in each region. The report was to be discussed at regional meetings between the Inspectorate and Directors of Social Services. The response was varied. In one instance I was asked to talk at a future meeting. In three others it was decided to organize joint seminars, and representatives of individual departments were nominated to participate in the planning. Through working in this way there was an agreement from the beginning that Directors and other senior male managers would attend the events. It was interesting to find that the Directors who expressed most interest were those from county authorities, where equal opportunities issues had traditionally had a low profile. There was least response from London, where there were most women managers in senior posts, although still very much a minority.

Following the publication of the *Women as Managers* report (Walmsley 1989), NCH (a national voluntary organization) and the Association of Directors of Social Services decided that they would run a series of seminars on women as managers. I was asked to be a keynote speaker and this provided an opportunity to promote both reports. Although the seminars were intended for both men and women, in practice the participants were almost all women. I also contributed to a number of seminars for women managers run by individual local authorities and other organizations.

By this time I had established a wide network of contacts. In addition to those people that I had approached, I received regular phone calls and letters from others who had heard about the work I was doing and were interested in it for a variety of reasons. For some it was a formal part of their work responsibility. Many others were women seeking to achieve greater recognition of the position of women in their agency. These included a Maori woman in New Zealand who had heard about the *Women as Managers* report (Walmsley 1989).

I was concerned by some of the comments of women who contacted me to talk about the position in their departments. Having achieved the significant first step of gaining senior managers' agreement that 'something needs to be done', they were experiencing a range of difficulties in progressing. Some were expected to speak for other women without being allowed to consult them. Others were asked to develop departmental policies or action plans, even though this was not the sort of work they would otherwise have undertaken, and then criticized for the way it was presented or because it was not adequately costed. Women spoke of being expected to attend an unfamiliar, all-male senior management meeting alone, to represent a women's working group or even all the women in their department.

I knew of six or seven women who had been formally designated as responsible for development work relating to women in their department, and I assumed that there must be others. I arranged with Gayle Foster of the National Institute of Social Work to run a joint workshop entitled 'Working for Women' to explore their experiences and develop strategies. Nearly a hundred women responded, representing the majority of the 108 local authorities in England (although interestingly not from Inner London). We therefore decided to run two workshops. In practice the majority of women were from departments where there were no formal initiatives, and were seeking ideas about how to generate them and to network with other women with similar experiences.

By this time, I was part of a group of women from national organizations who were undertaking work relating to women in social services. This provided an opportunity for us to share information about our activities, to coordinate them, to undertake joint initiatives and to provide mutual support. We produced a newsletter entitled *Women's Link* to inform women working in social services across the country about events, publications and issues.

Within the Inspectorate the training aspects of the *Women in Social Services* report (Nottage 1991) were particularly significant. The Inspectorate has lead responsibility in the Department of Health for the national policy on social services training (unlike all other areas of social services policy, where it offers professional advice to the relevant administrative civil servants). At that time there was a special initiative to support management development training. I was given the opportunity of putting forward a proposal for a project to be funded during 1991/2 from a national management development budget. Decisions were taken by a committee including representatives of local authority associations, the Association of Directors of Social Services and training bodies.

I was uncertain about what would be of most interest to them, so I put forward four options. They decided to fund two of them. One was a research study to explore the extent to which the development needs of women managers had been met through the training and other development opportunities that had been available to them, and to identify how management development could be approached in a more gender sensitive way. The second was a video and training pack to highlight how daily experiences in social services agencies can undermine or devalue women and to focus on the action required to achieve change.

The research study was undertaken by Maureen Allan, Reena Bhavnani and Kate French in six social services departments. They interviewed eight women in each department, covering first line and middle managers selected to represent the diversity of occupational groups and to take account of race, age, family care responsibilities and disability.

The study resulted in a report entitled *Promoting Women: Management Development and Training for Women in Social Services Departments* (Allan *et al.* 1992). It highlighted the range of factors that had affected the women's careers, what they considered had aided and hindered them, and the extent to which they had been assisted in developing their management practice. It showed that women's experiences were very haphazard and emphasized the importance of a more systematic approach. The report also covered the ways in which women had accessed management training, and their experience of training courses, including the practical arrangements. Again, there was little systematic planning and women were hampered by inadequate information. Responses to training were generally positive, although in some instances courses failed to recognize the skill and experience of participants.

The women were also asked about the management style of their organization and what would need to change to enable them to develop their full potential. Most of those interviewed saw the culture of the organization as a major barrier to their career development, and could name and describe the factors that discriminated against them. Many perceived a male style of management that they considered both unattractive and ineffective for the future management of change. Good support mechanisms were seen as particularly important to empower women to challenge the cultural assumptions of their organization.

The findings of the study were not new to those of us familiar with women's experiences. However, its value was in providing a vehicle for presenting these messages. The views that women were keen to express in confidential interviews would have been hard, if not impossible, for them to convey directly to their male senior managers. Although the study was small scale, when the same views were repeated by women across the country they gained added weight. It showed that whilst the issues might be complex, there were plenty of women in each social services department who were able to articulate them. In retrospect there would have been advantages in interviewing a sample of men for comparative purposes, and to include the managers of the women interviewed. However, this would have required a much larger, and more expensive, study.

Before I obtained the project funding I had no experience that was relevant to commissioning a video, and the prospect was daunting. Women from other national organizations put me in touch with colleagues who where able to provide invaluable advice about 'dos' and 'don'ts' and costs. I established a project group of male and female managers and trainers to develop the project brief and assist in the selection of the video company. The task was to represent issues about women to a mixed audience in a way that took account of all the nuances of social services agencies.

It was decided that the film would be based on the experiences of four women managers with very different histories and backgrounds. They would describe the opportunities and the barriers that they had faced in their careers as they were filmed going about their daily lives. There would be no commentator, but their views would be juxtaposed with the mixed thoughts and feelings of a senior male manager played by an actor. It was seen as important to have a means of articulating some widely held views that might otherwise be thought and not said, but which needed to be addressed if the video was to achieve its training purpose. It was not considered that any 'real' male manager would wish to be filmed expressing some of the more negative opinions.

We wanted to film outside London, as London experience could be discounted in other parts of the country as 'different'. We also wanted to make sure that we included women from the occupational groups that usually had fewer career opportunities, black and white women, women of different ages and some with childcare responsibilities. A county and a metropolitan authority agreed to cooperate and we identified four women managers from the two departments. They were each filmed for half a day.

Their experience was edited into three sections interspersed with the male senior manager's comments. The sections were entitled:

- 'A Woman's Work' – the issues of combining work and family responsibilities;
- 'Room at the Top' – the ways in which women can be encouraged or deterred from seeking promotion, including the effects of racism on black managers;

- 'Sugar and Spice' – the particular contribution that women bring to the management task and the way that they are viewed within their organization.

Each section ended with graphics that summarized the action required to achieve change. The video was called *Snakes and Ladders*.[3]

I was concerned that, to maximize the use of the video, it should be accompanied by information sheets and training exercises. Maureen Allan, who had led the research study team and co-written the *Promoting Women* report (Allan *et al.* 1992), developed the training material and I prepared the information sheets. I commissioned a design company to do the artwork for the report and the training pack to assist in their joint promotion.

Looking back at the range of women's activities I have undertaken, the video produces the most mixed feelings. The process from first meeting women managers who might be included in the film to receiving the final product took about five weeks. I had been advised to be involved as much as possible. I participated in the selection of women managers and of the actor (although another one had to be substituted). I went with the crew to film the women managers, assisted in the editing of their contributions, helped to script the actor, and suggested titles, subtitles and graphics. The one activity from which I was firmly excluded was the filming of the actor, who I was told would be deterred by my presence. Unlike other activities, such as writing reports or presenting material at seminars, instant and irreversible decisions were required constantly. In various ways I was able to modify what I saw as the film director's excesses. In others I did not realize what was happening until too late; for example, I think that too much film footage was devoted to people driving in cars.

The video could be described as the film of the *Women in Social Services: A Neglected Resource* book (Nottage 1991), as it covers the spectrum of issues relating to women in social services. Between them the four women explore a great variety of experiences in a very concentrated way, and this provides a wealth of material for training purposes. In practice the video focused less on the negative effects of others' attitudes and behaviour than I had originally intended. Not surprisingly, it was far easier for women to talk about these cultural factors as part of the research project than on video.

The use of an actor to represent a senior male manager has produced a range of reactions. Some people, particularly women, feel that he epitomizes managers that they know. Many are amused by him and he serves to lighten the mood. Others see him as an unhelpful and distracting caricature. Nevertheless, his comments frequently provoke discussion on issues which might otherwise not be raised, which is the purpose for which he was intended.

It was decided to publish the *Promoting Women* report (Allan *et al.* 1992) in September 1992, immediately before the joint autumn conference of the Association of Directors of Social Services and local authority associations, during which the video would be launched at a workshop. It was two years after it had first been suggested that we should attend the conference. Copies of the report were sent to all Directors of Social Services, but we did not think it appropriate to distribute the videos in this way. It was therefore agreed to set up a series of regional seminars to promote the video and the report.

In the summer of 1992, when the work on the report and video were coming to fruition, the Inspectorate reorganized into two divisions. This involved separating inspection from policy, development and liaison work. All inspectors had to choose which division they wished to work in and I opted for inspection. Shortly afterwards a promotion opportunity arose and I became the manager of an inspection group. It was no longer considered appropriate for me to combine development work with more formal inspection responsibilities, and I was fully occupied in setting up and managing a new group of staff. As more time was being allocated to inspection work, it also reduced the organization's capacity to undertake such developmental activities.

It was agreed that I should complete the work involved with publishing the *Promoting Women* report (Allan *et al.* 1992) and launching the video. A colleague, Lynda Hoare, then took over responsibility for the regional seminars. Because of the reorganization her first task was to identify a new group of regional inspectors to take the work forward, and to help them to develop ownership of it.

Workshops were run in each region to promote the video and training pack and discuss issues and action plans for social services departments. Again, the response in London was less positive than in other parts of the country. This was interesting at a time when there had been a very dramatic increase in the number of women directors in London to 14 out of 33, a trend which had not occurred elsewhere. It was decided that because of regional variations it was no longer appropriate to take a national approach and that further developments would be negotiated according to the local regional situation. Two regions ran a follow-up day so that social services departments could review progress on their action plans. The Inspectorate also commissioned a Career Development Guide, *Making Positive Choices* by Gayle Foster and Julia Phillipson of the National Institute of Social Work (1994).

Having been so involved in women's work for three years, it was not easy to withdraw and hand over to others. However, there were some advantages. The way that I had become identified with this area of work was not always helpful. It meant that whilst an action plan for the SSI work had been agreed with managers, I was always in the lead and others always referred to me about these issues. As an increasingly large number of people outside the organization became aware of my work, the frequent requests to participate in seminars and conferences grew at a rate that bore no relationship to the time I had available. I also felt that I was getting to the point of exhausting all the ways that I could find to describe issues relating to women in social services, and the channels for doing so. As part of the reorganization, others took over responsibility for defining the nature of the work and the priority it should receive.

I also had many regrets at giving up an area of work from which I had gained great satisfaction and which had offered me so many interesting new experiences. It took considerable self-control to let others take over and not to interfere, and to disengage formally from my links with women in other organizations. When I was approached to participate in seminars, it helped that I could refer people on to the women who had undertaken the *Promoting Women* research and to the video.

My reflections on this work are inevitably subjective. Also, it is difficult to measure the impact of national initiatives on a large number of local authorities and other agencies. I believe that in the approach we took we maximized some of the advantages of working from a central government department. By collecting, collating and publishing information that described the position of women in social services, we identified the issues. We were able to give voice to women's experiences. Because of the position of the Inspectorate, they gained some additional credibility and authority. We also had access to Directors and senior managers and could ensure that these issues were brought to their attention. The use of the Inspectorate's regional structure meant that representatives from almost all departments, and some independent agencies, attended seminars. In some areas Directors made a commitment that their departments would be actively involved in planning such events, which they and their senior manager colleagues attended and in the course of which they were involved in preparing an action plan. Where this occurred, peer group pressure amongst Directors and the wish for their department to be compared favourably with neighbouring authorities had a beneficial effect. Where agencies decided to take action, I believe that our reports facilitated the process of identifying the local issues and deciding how to proceed.

Although we set out to target the material at senior managers, in practice I think it has been of particular value to women staff at other levels. Women have described to me how it has helped to validate their experiences and encouraged and enabled them to raise issues in their own agency. We have also provided a number of networking opportunities, through the 'Working for Women' seminars, through the groups to plan regional events, and by contributing to the *Women's Link* newsletter.

I think that we have also helped to define the training agenda related to gender and produced a range of material to support training activity. The chapter on 'Management Development' in the *Promoting Women* report (Allan *et al.* 1992) has been reprinted by the Open University as part of the Personal and Team Effectiveness Resource file for the Health and Social Services Manager course (B701).

The questions that I had started to raise about whether we had exhausted all the ways of describing the issues and the means of doing so have remained for the team who took over the work. It is arguable that the Inspectorate has covered the issues relating to women in social services as far as it is appropriate to do so on a national basis. To add to this material becomes repetitious. Ultimately it is up to local agencies to take it forward. It would be better for the Inspectorate to move on to other issues, including those relating to gender in service delivery.

The extent to which agencies have been willing to address these issues, and found our approach useful, will inevitably have varied from place to place. However, I believe that we can reasonably claim that the position of women in social services has received significantly more attention as the result of the Inspectorate's work, and that we have accelerated the process of change

NOTES

1 Figures for 1971 are based on published Department of Health and Social Security statistics, which were collected by gender until 1977. Information for 1990 about senior managers in social services departments was collected for Nottage (1991).
   Information about all staff employed in social services departments in England and Wales was collected by Manpower Watch. This was formerly part of the Local Authority Conditions of Service Advisory Board, now incorporated into the Local Government Management Board. Information about part-time staff is based on unpublished Department of Health Statistics.
2 These were the LACSAB/ADSS Social Services Employment Survey 1988 and Social Services Employment Survey 1989.
3 *Snakes and Ladders* Video and Training Pack (Social Services Inspectorate 1992) is available from Concord Video and Film Council Ltd, 201 Felixstowe Road, Ipswich, Suffolk 1P3 9BJ, tel: 01473 726012/715754.

REFERENCES

Allan, M., Bhavnani, R. and French, K. (1992) *Promoting Women: Management Development and Training for Women in Social Services Departments*. London: HMSO.
Foster, G., and Phillipson, J. (1994) *Making Positive Choices: Development for Women in Social Care*. London: National Institute for Social Work.
Nottage, A. (1991) *Women in Social Services: A Neglected Resource*. London: HMSO.
Walmsley, S. (1989) *Women as Managers: Report on a Development Project for Senior Women Managers in London*. London: London Region Social Services Inspectorate.

Chapter 12

Leading in their own ways
Women chief executives in local government

Judy White

This chapter describes and evaluates a research project on leadership based on the work of fifteen women chief executives in local government. While stressing the individuality and diversity of the approaches of these women, the author draws out some common themes and experiences. This work is set in the context of a critique of traditional approaches to theorizing leadership, and a discussion of emerging models.

This chapter sets out to explore some of the concerns about leadership, gender and organizational change which are being raised during the debates about new directions, new functions, and new structures for the public sector. The focus of the chapter is an analysis of the work carried out by Kathryn Riley and the author with the group of women who were in post as chief executives of local authorities in England in 1993 and thereby automatically assumed (by others, if not always themselves) to be leaders, in leadership positions. The project framework grew out of an examination of existing conceptualizations of leadership, which we perceived to be inadequate, and the desire to explore how women's leadership styles and values developed; are used; and have an impact on the leaders and followers in their organizations. We wanted to work participatively with the women chief executives as our research partners, and a part of the chapter charts the processes through which we went to try and reflect their needs as well as our own curiosity and search for new constructs.

We established four distinctive areas which determined this group's attitudes to leadership: personality and values systems; confidence and experience; their preferred ways of working; and the degree to which they work through others for change. We confirmed that not only were they diverse in these different areas, but that they worked at their leadership in diverse ways. They agreed that much of what they *do* as leaders is conditioned by their views of management; their own values and how these accord with the cultures within which they work; and the ways in which they relate to the other leaders and followers in the organization.

The chapter concludes by raising questions about the extent to which such women in leadership positions *are* change agents and *can become so*. There do not appear to be any very clear-cut answers. But there is evidence that the diversity of leadership approaches now developing is helping women to be more positive about their own leadership styles and values. Reconceptualization of leadership by women must take this into account: celebrating difference is a strength, not a weakness.

THE CONTEXT OF LEADERSHIP: WHY IT IS IMPORTANT TO RESEARCH LEADERSHIP AMONGST WOMEN

One of the underlying themes of this chapter is that for change to be really beneficial, women are needed to lead it. But, I argue, it seems very doubtful that the 'old' models of organizational leadership 'fit' in situations of rapid change. These 'old' models assumed situations which were relatively stable and predictable. Environments in which we work and live now are becoming increasingly complex, hostile, and unstable. This tends to make people think that they both want and need firm direction. It is assumed that firm direction comes from, and is part of, firm leadership, from the front, and that firm leaders can reduce the messiness of organizational life and remove instability. Neither of these assumptions is valid. Understanding the increasing complexity of leadership and demystifying it at the same time has occupied considerable space in management development literature. But only a relatively small amount, and in relatively recent times, has seriously examined the gender dimensions of leadership and change. If 'old' models do not fit, how can we reconceptualize leadership? How do we take account of gender specific ways of leading which *seem* to characterise some women? Do we accept that women do lead in significantly different ways from men? Or are we looking at perceptual difference and stereotypical definitions which push differences between genders into rigid, inflexible containers?

The tensions between organizations and leadership, as mediated by gender, have become increasingly fascinating. The context for my interest comes from the recognition of the continuing – and perhaps increasing – turbulence of the public-sector world. Organizations emerging from that turbulence are likely to look very different from existing ones. The people within such organizations will be key players in the change process, as they seek to clarify what the organization's roles are and how they might best be carried out. The development of new expectations and new directions will be a complex task, with a huge range of tensions and difficulties. The pivotal role of leadership is apparent.

A new managerialist order has been ushered into the public sector, based on the 'three Es': economy, efficiency and effectiveness. Managers in local authorities have been confronted by a range of changes which are more far-reaching and comprehensive than in any previous period, and which have impact on internal structures, the raising of revenue, and the delivery of services. The impact of such changes throws up a range of personal, political and organizational challenges for local government chief officers and senior managers. Whilst they have to function within a more structured framework, parts of the organization have much more individual autonomy and operate as separate units. Also they have to work with the consequences of the introduction of market mechanisms manifested not only through the internal and external markets, but also through a greater focus on choice.

These overall changes mean that leaders must try to balance the demands of the 'new managerialism' with the development of interpersonal skills which recognize, appreciate and develop the talents of the staff within the organization. To manage this complexity, it can be argued that there needs to be some fundamental appraisal of the roles of leaders within the organization, and subsequently a rethinking of the nature and characteristics of appropriate leadership for the organization. Questions for those who are defined as being in leadership positions include:

- How do they know when they are leading?
- How can leaders provide stability *and* change?
- How can they manage competing priorities?
- How can they transform an organization and take people with them?
- What can they do most effectively on their own and with others?
- What difference does gender make to the way in which people lead?

For the organizations, there is another set of questions:

- Are there any gender issues in leadership in the organization?
- What is the difference between management and leadership in those organizations?
- Are the leaders they have the ones they need?
- Do different institutions and situations need different *kinds* of leader?
- What makes an effective leader into a special leader?
- Can organizations make effective leaders into special leaders?

We wanted to start to explore some of these questions and dilemmas in a structured way. Our work, through seminars, workshops, individual development, and team development activities with senior managers in local government, confirmed to us the liveliness and importance of the issues around personal and organizational leadership. We had a range of individual and anecdotal evidence to show that there was a well of concern, anxiety and debate about the dimensions of the 'new leadership'; the appropriateness of different approaches to leadership in different circumstances; how individuals could develop skills to be more effective as leaders in teams; and how leaders could develop followers. The concerns of managers who were women also raised issues of 'women as leaders' and 'leaders as women'. It seemed inescapable to many women that they were *always* measured as women, and that there were two measures which were incompatible: measuring them *as women*, how they carried out the leadership role; and measuring them *as leaders*, how they carried out the womanly role.

We needed a way to focus on these gender issues of leadership which would be personally manageable, whilst also providing some more comparative information to feed back into the debates on leadership. By focusing on the small group of women in local government who had reached the top of local authorities, we immediately restricted our population sample. We also centred our work on the top leadership of organizations, thus potentially being unable to consider the ways in which leadership is a collective activity in organizations and occurs (or should occur) throughout it.

Our reasons for focusing 'at the top' were pragmatic, practical and political. The group of women chief executives of local authorities in England had remained very small until 1992. The four who were in post then were the subject of a lot of investigation, discussion and research in the local government world about their background, style and characteristics, much of it in the vein of their 'difference as oddity and tokenism' – they were deviants from the norm! The serious work undertaken by Morphet (1992, 1993) was the exception. She set up a range of debates about strategies for career planning for women to achieve senior management positions; investigated the development and operation of the chief executive's job; and examined the routes which women took to become chief executives, as compared with men in the same position. This work was a key element in providing background evidence and supporting ideas for our work. Another piece of work, by Dixon (1993), was also important in identifying the personal and work-related factors to which four other of the chief executives attributed their success.

At the beginning of our discussions about undertaking some structured research in the autumn of 1992, there was a psychological breakthrough as the numbers of women chief executives reached double figures. Also, by this time it was evident that the variety of individuals being appointed was growing considerably. Coupled with the differences in types of organization taking on women chief executives, in terms of size, location, political control, and culture, it seemed that an excellent ready-made sample population had been created.

Simultaneously, the Local Government Management Board (LGMB) were looking to investigate a whole range of organizational and personal change issues, some emanating from the local government review process, others from the longer term change agendas briefly outlined above. They commissioned us to examine, using 'action research' methods, the changing needs of leadership in local authorities, using the women chief executives in their organization as our research partners, in a pilot project.

The research framework was developed in two complementary and concurrent ways. We worked with the group of women chief executives to discuss what to do and to negotiate how to do it, as we were determined to develop a project which was useful and relevant to them. We also drew on the research which already existed to try and define in what ways it helped and in what ways it was limited, so that we could refine our research questions with the women chief executives.

CONCEPTUALIZING LEADERSHIP: EXISTING RESEARCH

The very word 'leadership' conjures up notions of masculinity and dominance. The whole concept emanated from sets of values steeped in elitism and separatism, in which particular individuals demonstrated unique and spectacular talents which were admired and venerated. Such individuals were always, by inference, male.

Traditional conceptions of leadership were bound up with the classic and scientific approaches to management. Not only did they imply that there was only one 'right' way to lead in an organization, there was also the assumption that 'leadership' was synonymous with the way in which people who are leaders behave. Also, only particular sorts of people were equipped for this leadership. And they had to be men. So pervasive have these approaches become and so ingrained into our consciousness that it is difficult to conceptualize alternative ones. Men with 'charisma', who abuse power and devalue others around them, whilst leading them heroically with their own strong values and drive, epitomize such leaders. Strong values may be neither good nor rational, and if attached to a strong power base they may also be dangerous.

Another characteristic of traditional leadership was that it was interpreted as being based within rigid formal structures, most closely linked with military situations. Indeed, many of the 'everyday' metaphors of leadership are still military and inherently masculine. Highly formalized and hierarchical organizations echoed military hierarchies. They were structured around command and control, around boss and subordinate, around individuals knowing their place, staying in it, and accepting the limits of their responsibility and autonomy.

Theories designed to overcome the military model focused on types of leader who could be effective in organizations, but like other theories these were not backed up by empirical evidence. There was also a continuous focus on the top leadership role, which in some cases denies that leadership can occur at other places in the organization whilst in others implies that top leadership is the only one that needs to be taken account of in assessing the health of the organization. Further, there was little recognition that leaders have followers, and that where there are followers there are leaders. There was no understanding of the relationship between those who lead and those who follow, that 'Leadership is in the eye of the follower.' None of the approaches asked about whether or not we need leaders, or whether we need people who are good at enabling and empowering individuals and organizations. To what extent are the qualities we look for in good workers similar to those of good leaders, and to what extent are they gendered? Some of these limitations were beginning to be explored by writers and organizational consultants in the 1970s, but it was not until the last years of the 1980s that the gender issues began to be taken seriously and researched.

Building on trait and style approaches, the idea of transactional leadership does identify the existence of followers and attempts to define their relationship to their leaders. McGregor Burns (1978:4) argued that 'the relations of most leaders and followers are transactional: leaders approach followers with an eye to exchanging one thing for another.' It may be that this has been the dominant way in which men have learnt to work with subordinates, giving rewards for services undertaken satisfactorily and punishment for inadequate performance. This fits with the model of men 'socialised for domination and conquest' (Eisler 1991:5) in a society where 'masculine' values of toughness and strength are given high social and economic priority. Rosener (1990) found that men described themselves in ways that characterized transactional leadership more frequently than the women in her sample. The men used the power which was available to them as a result of their position in the organization and their formal authority. Rewards and punishments were designed to maintain the existing vertical hierarchies.

The transformational approach is the next stage on the leadership continuum. It attempts to incorporate notions of direction, purpose, leading and following into a coherent model. The model's key elements are vision; culture and values; communication; power and networks; and empowerment. Those who attempt to be transformational leaders try to have 'a relationship of mutual stimulation and elevation that converts followers into leaders' (McGregor Burns 1978:4). Rosener (1990:120) sees transformational leaders as those who get 'subordinates to transform their own self interest, into the interest of the group through concern for a broader goal'.

LEADERSHIP RESEARCH AND WOMEN

Rosener's (1990) work provides us with an extension of concepts beyond the transactional and the transformational. She was intrigued by the differences in the way women and men described themselves as leaders, and interviewed some of those women who described themselves as transformational. As a result, she called their leadership interactive, as they 'actively work to make their interactions with others positive for everyone involved' (p. 120). More specifically she highlighted their characteristics as:

- encouraging participation;
- sharing power and information;
- enhancing other people's self-worth;
- getting others excited about their work and energizing them.

Her discussions led her to argue that this participative style went beyond what was commonly understood as participation, as they were attempting to make their staff feel good about themselves and their work, and to create situations that contributed to that feeling. Further, sharing power and information means recognizing that communication flows in two directions, so creating loyalty between people, setting examples for others, and making it more plain why decisions are taken.

Although the sample used predominantly transformational leadership styles, they were able to switch to using other, transactional ones when and where appropriate, particularly if participation did not work. Most women did this 'naturally' – as a result of their socialization and their career paths. As the average age of the respondent was 51, they were old enough to have had experiences which differed from those of men *because* of their gender. These women were *expected to be* cooperative, supportive, understanding and gentle, to provide service to others, and to derive satisfaction from helping others. Men, meanwhile, had to appear to be competitive, strong, tough, decisive and in control. Further, the women had career paths without long periods of the sorts of organizational position which would have given them *formal* authority over others and control of a wide span of resources, so by default they had to find other ways to get things done. This 'survival tactic' has been developed into an effective leadership style in many organizational settings.

Most of the women in Rosener's sample worked in medium-sized organizations which had experienced rapid change, which created opportunities for women and were hospitable to those who use non-traditional management styles. The degree of change is an important factor: if the organization is in turmoil, tradition is also thrown into question, and established networks are no longer important. The leaders in such environments can use new solutions, new structures and new ways of leading.

Rosener is also clear that it is a mistake to link interactive leadership directly to being a woman:

> We know that women are capable of making their way through corporations by adhering to the traditional corporate model and that they can wield power in ways similar to men. Indeed, some women may prefer that style. We also know from the survey findings that some men use the transformational leadership style.
>
> (Rosener 1990:125)

Finally: 'the fact that women are more likely than men to be interactive leaders raises the risk that these organizations will perceive interactive leadership as "feminine" and automatically resist it' (p. 125).

However, interactive styles are difficult. They require an open and up-front approach, displaying a lack of total expert control and power, and encouraging criticism and conflict, as well as involving the likelihood that decisions will take longer and require more compromise. So women have to learn about and practise as many styles as are appropriate to the contexts in which they work. Good leadership needs a repertoire of leadership styles which will allow the leader to adapt to changing circumstances and the needs of the organization: it is situational. It is a notion of leadership which depends on the capacity of the individual to draw on a repertoire of management styles (Hersey and Blanchard 1976).

As well as research which identified leadership styles which women might use, we felt we needed to consider arguments concerning the significance of the values which women bring to their leadership roles. Helgeson (1990:98) saw women's values, or 'feminine principles', as strong and vital parts of women's leadership, not as management weaknesses. She argued that caring, being involved, and taking responsibility are all part of effective leadership:

> As women's leadership qualities come to play a more dominant role in the public sphere, their particular aptitudes for long-term negotiating, analytic listening, and creating an ambience in which people work with zest and spirit will help

reconcile the split between the ideals of being efficient and being humane. This integration of female values is already producing a more collaborative kind of leadership, and changing the very ideal of what strong leadership actually is.

Nichols (1993) argues that this approach is both too simplistic and sexist. She sees Helgeson's ideas as 'the new maternal metaphor of management': 'elaborate extensions of prevailing sexual stereotypes, the strong beliefs we hold about the way men and women should behave, translated into an organizational context' (Nichols 1993:57). The danger in defining gender roles is that, in so doing, they are perpetuated. Nichols believes that Helgeson's definitions of 'feminine principles' will only reinforce the exclusion of women from senior management: 'The skills which Helgeson claims will make women exemplary managers are the same skills Rosabeth Moss Kanter told us are the emotional characteristics that define the other – the lesser skills that sit beside the rational manager' (p. 57).

But there does seem to be a double bind here. Women *are* judged as women first, not as people. Kanter warned (1977:123) that 'women are measured by two yardsticks – how *as women* they carried out the management role, and how *as managers* they lived up to the images of womanhood'. If one argues that women bring 'special' emotional and communication skills to the workplace, those women who do not do so are likely to be castigated. The double bind is that it appears to be very difficult to bridge the gap between being a woman and being a worker; and even more difficult to move into the top of organizations.

Ely (1992:6) has shown that it will take more than a critical mass of women at middle level to eliminate women's token status in organizations:

> Until women receive adequate representation at the top levels of the organization, sex role stereotypes will persist, largely to the detriment of women, as the basis for women's *own* sense of how they differ from men and as the basis for their *own* sense of their individual and collective value to their organizations.

After studying eight law firms in the United States, Ely found that not only do men view women differently when there is a 'critical mass' of women in top positions in an organization, but women also view themselves differently. Women in firms with few senior women are less serious about their work, less satisfied with their firms, less self-confident and less interested in promotion than women in firms with a significant number of women in senior positions. This may account for the high rate of turnover amongst women which many organizations are facing!

So – double binds, Catch 22s, and Gordian knots: if the only way to get more women to the top of organizations is to have more women at the top, this is a riddle! One possible way forward is to focus on *good leadership*, which is effective at coping with chaotic change. Such leadership incorporates elements of transactional, transformational and interactive styles; it requires an effective blending of repertoires, an ability to play several tunes, and for the women to do the job – in their own way.

THE ACTION RESEARCH PROJECT: THE PROCESS

After an initial dinner in London in the autumn of 1992, we held a workshop in Birmingham in March 1993, inviting all the women chief executives to come. Seven women joined in the debate about the overall direction and detailed problems which the research should address. They were open and honest about what they thought would be *possible* and *useful*, and we refined our research questions together. We also discussed which techniques and processes to use. They also shared 'stories' about their leadership experiences, about how they came to lead as they do, and how they visualized the organization of which they are the leader. This information was very helpful in reconstructing the objectives of the research and the areas we should examine. The areas we finally decided to examine were:

1   their pathways to leadership – the routes and obstacles to their success;
2   the leadership and management styles of the women chief executives;
3   how and to what extent these had been adapted to meet the needs of their organization;
4   how different styles of leadership are manifested in the workplace;
5   how far gender is a factor in the way in which they lead and manage.

To help us to get a better understanding of the diversity of approaches, we wanted to explore what women categorized as effective leadership. The most exciting idea, arising primarily from Rosener (1990), was that the effective and appropriate leadership which generated commitment and understanding between all those working together on common tasks included a range of *styles*, *approaches* or *domains*. The ability to use the appropriate ones for different situations, to develop a portfolio or repertoire, seemed to mark out good women leaders. We wanted to see to what extent we could find out whether the group of women chief executives were working in this way. We were intrigued to know if they recognized this approach as being valid. We also wanted to discover if their preferred styles were interactive, as Rosener postulated, or whether they were transactional or transformational. Also, when they used styles which they found less than comfortable or preferable, we wanted to know why they did so.

Extending Helgeson's work on the importance of women's values in leadership roles, we also felt we should investigate what significance they have in the way in which women conceptualize leadership and carry it out. This was to take care of the common strand we found when reviewing the research literature: that leadership is values based and values driven.

In the summer of 1993 we visited each of the fifteen women chief executives then in post to do four things. First, we taped a semi-structured interview about their education, professional development, personal and professional aspirations, values and visions. Second, we used a prompt exercise designed to elucidate their preferred approaches to leadership and management. Then we discussed how they worked – their perception of their 'daily leadership' – using a repertory grid exercise. Finally, we explained the diary exercise, which required them to keep an account of their activities over a one-week period.

The sessions were a decisive and consistent success, as we set up fascinating dialogues with our partners. They probed us and our preconceptions as much as we probed theirs. We ranged over wide areas and down various culs-de-sac. Everyone was enthusiastic, committed, and energized by the discussions. There were clearly some areas of difference in what each women was willing to discuss, but the key linking factor was the sense of wonder and pride in being able to have legitimate power to change organizations and the people within them.

In November 1993 we held another workshop, attended by another seven of our research partners. We fed back what we had done, what had gone well, and how we could work together in the next phase, when we planned to return to some authorities to interview key groups of staff about how their chief executive's leadership manifested itself in the workplace. The workshop also discussed how they had conceptualized or could conceptualize their leadership; what impact the organization had on their style; and, particularly important, the political dimensions of their leadership in a political environment.

At the beginning of 1994, we revisited three authorities, and used instruments amended from the first phase to hold group discussions about perceptions of leadership styles and cultures in their organization. The perspectives from various groups of staff were designed to act as a counterpoint and to explore how far leadership by their chief executive was effective and appropriate for the various organizational cultures within their organization. We facilitated a variety of groups – chief officers' management teams, chief executive's management teams, and some of the senior women in the authority – as well as the leader of the council. We spent up to two hours with each group, and taped most of the discussions. We kept all the discussions confidential and have fed the various views into our analysis. Some of the views expressed illustrated the complexity involved in trying to engender cultural change. They also reinforced the necessity for explanation, discussion, negotiation and listening in efforts to communicate, over and over again, in all directions, by leaders with their staff. (Cultures of rumour and myth based on misleading or partial evidence are hard to dispel.)

The final part of the research involves feeding back to the chief executives our overall conclusions, and developing some recommendations and implications for organizational change and leadership development for the LGMB.

The parts of the work which went particularly well were the interfaces between the groups of chief executives in the workshops, and the individual discussions with them, especially their pathways to leadership and their leadership styles. We have amassed a lot of material from interviews and diaries, which we have yet to find a way to analyse which will enable it to remain confidential. Some of our group discussions could have been improved with more specific, targeted questions. The bringing together of this group for the action research project also had a political purpose: it was the only forum in which the women met together as women chief executives. So we enabled some useful contacting, support, information exchange and listening to take place, in a natural, friendly atmosphere where the group could share experiences, as well as the more formal and overt debates about their careers and their leadership characteristics and styles.

RESEARCHING LEADERSHIP: KNITTING THE FINDINGS TO THE THEORY

We spent some time developing ideas about leadership attributes, both actual and desired. The discussions illustrated a refreshing self-knowledge and honesty, as well as some dilemmas inherent in owning up to and recognizing particular characteristics. One of the most illuminating activities presented the group with findings from the Gerver and Hart study (1990). This suggested that the women in their study tended to use a mixture of attributes in their work, which they would label, (conventionally but erroneously) as 'feminine' and 'masculine'. They were:

- flexible *and* firm;
- consultative *and* confrontational;
- caring *and* ruthless;
- competitive *and* democratic (p. 6).

Our group added, for their personal attributes:

- considerate *and* intolerant;
- empathetic *and* demanding;
- energizing *and* pushy;
- daring *and* timid;
- confident *and* humble;
- visionary *and* seeing the short term;
- achievement-centred *and* able to let things go;
- setting standards *and* allowing diversity.

For the ways in which they made decisions:

- strategic *and* concerned with appropriate detail;
- fast *and* slow;
- from the front *and* as a team member;
- responsively *and* using guts and experience;
- determined to get things done *and* considerate of others' caution;
- clear about their own expectations *and* letting decisions emerge.

For the ways in which they related to others:

- listeners *and* questioners;
- motivators *and* being able to let others work in their own way;
- taking responsibility *and* giving it to others;
- valuing other people *and* looking for better performance;
- inspiring *and* taking a low profile;

- developing and using networks *and* working alone.

Taking these together – personal attributes, decision-making styles, and ways of working together – gave us a broad definitive picture of what they thought was vital about their leadership behaviours. They incorporated the elements of 'hardness' and systematized (or ritualized?) relationships characteristic of the transactional approach; the 'softer' transformational modes; and the interactive attempts to encourage participation, share power, celebrate the value of other workers, and inspire and energize others. Our discussions highlighted that they all felt each style was necessary *in certain circumstances*, and they recognized the differences inherent in the frameworks. But what excited them and made them feel that they were working effectively was *the ability to gauge and judge* when to use particular styles and approaches. The excitement and difficulty arose when they had to decide *what* to use *when*.

Further exploration led us to look at four key areas which seemed to influence the women in their attitudes to leadership: personality and values systems; confidence and experience; preferred ways of working; and working through others for change. The rest of this section discusses each of these in turn.

Personality and values systems

For some of the women:

> leadership is essentially a *quality* and contains elements such as courage; determination; vision; and tenacity – and probably ambition – and to a large extent is inherent rather than acquired.

They saw themselves as *carriers* of these characteristics, and therefore carrying some responsibility to use them wisely. Most of the group did not articulate this idea in quite the same way, but they did feel that their leadership qualities were connected to their hard work, single-mindedness and determination, which had been evident from their early lives. This confirms the earlier work of Morphet (1992), who found that the four women in her group were 'extremely dedicated to their work' (p. 11). Many of the women now in leadership positions have had, or have made, opportunities to 'practise' in other situations:

> I wasn't born a leader, but I was 'made' one before I got into a position when I was called a 'leader'.

They have built on their desires to be in charge; they want to make things happen; they don't want to set limits for themselves:

> My natural inclination is to take charge, to find a way through problems, to look to the future, and to have a strategy to deal with that future.

They had high achievement needs, some of which were met through leadership roles – inspirer, supporter, motivator, gaining and giving recognition, valuing others, celebrating success. They would agree with Stewart's view that they have 'a divine discontent – things must change' (Stewart 1992:121). They recognized the excitement, fear and pressure which this entailed. Other achievement needs or motivators they identified were concerned with personal self-esteem; with self-belief and success; and with financial reward. Social justice was also uppermost in their minds; there were strong feelings that they had responsibility, both personal and situational, to remotivate people and to be 'evangelical' about the public service – 'to redeem our position in society'. They shared beliefs in the necessity of a responsible and powerful local democracy.

What we have less evidence for from our work is the impact of their psychological make-up on their attitudes to leadership and on the ways they cope with pressure and work. Other research investigating stress and high achievers (Friedman and Rosenman 1974) identified 'Type As' as 'drivers', who were characterized as very competitive; constantly looking for achievement; hasty; impatient; restless; under pressure of time; and challenged by responsibility. They also suggested that such people are often so deeply involved in and committed to their work that other aspects of their lives are relatively neglected. Davidson and Cooper (1980) studied a group of women in various leadership positions, and found that 60 per cent of them overall, and 70 per cent of those aged 41–60, were 'Type As'.

Our group of women are certainly hardy and restless, constantly and impatiently striving to achieve, but having to temper this within the limitations of their organizations. They have a positive belief in commitment. They are likely to remain positive and optimistic in the face of pressure. What is intriguing is the question of how far these attributes are the result of genetic predispositions and how far they are the results of the influence of their lives, socialization, and environment. But not for nothing did we call these women 'the oughters'.

Confidence and experience

The women were positive in looking for challenge and risks, and for ways of fulfilling their ambitions. But there were important generational differences here, which have implications for how and which women might lead the change process. The older, more established group, who had been the 'deviants' who first broke the mould, admitted that they had been 'incapacitated by doubt' as they grew into their leadership positions. They had had little self-confidence and much fear of the challenges. The younger or more newly established group (of eleven) had a deep rooted internal self-confidence in their ability to *do* things and to *succeed* in doing so; they felt able 'to be themselves'; they had a sense of urgency to achieve. But they were aware that their internal self-confidence might spill over into arrogance.

The more newly established group felt that they were still developing; they were still having to learn new competences and new roles which meant sometimes that they had to work through hunch and intuition. At other times they relied on the support of their council leader, members and key individual staff or teams. And at other times again they sought help from fellow chief executives, their mentors or their gatekeepers. The increasing amount of leadership which they had to undertake was sometimes a source of self-doubt: 'I think I'm going to have to grow [as a leader]. There is something about being confident enough to get in front.' But they wanted and needed success to maintain and reaffirm their confidence. They looked for this through personal and organizational change, with the people they worked with and the population they served. In seeking help and support from longer established chief executives, they recognized that this group displayed and used a wider portfolio of leadership styles and approaches than they did. The increase in self-assurance which this brought was also generated through the actual *experiences* of being in a leadership capacity, of having to work as a leader, and having to manage a complex organization from the centre. It was sometimes only in retrospect that they recognized what they had done. But they could analyse what their roles were, how they had a hand in moulding them, and how they were changed by them:

> I regard myself first and foremost as a leader and then as a manager. Management of the delivery of the services, the council's workforce, and the political interface, is my major function. Leadership is about the way I do it to make it work.

> I think I am both leader and manager, both providing organizational direction and making things work effectively.

> I consider myself to be both leader and manager of my organization. The chief executive's job is located in both categories.

They were all careful to differentiate their roles and to emphasize that they had to work constantly to ensure that the most appropriate role was used to reach the outcome they wanted.

Preferred ways of working

The issue of confidence and experience underlies the ways in which the women's careers have developed, or are developing. All of them present a picture of their lives as a tapestry: the younger ones' tend to be rich and colourful, but only beginning to be sketched in. They have developed confidence and expertise in one job or area, and then have transferred these to a new one. The older and more experienced ones have more of their picture filled in, particularly if they have shifted from one chief executive's post to another. This tapestried approach brings with it an ability to be open, to be flexible to change, and it suggests a willingness to transfer skills and knowledge which echoes the findings of Gerver and Hart (1990) in their study of top education managers. But it also raises the interesting question about how different and diverse the younger and newer group of women are from the older and established ones. The diversity is not just from their different tapestries and experiences, but from the ways in which they understand, conceptualize, and articulate their jobs. They *expected* a lot of difference between each other and between them and other leaders. They were very clear that they needed to retain their individual sets of values, and to work within them. They saw it as one of the ingredients they bring to their leadership style. They wanted to work in ways which were effective,so they needed a multiplicity of approaches which they could use *as well as* their own preferred ways.

Work done by Quinn (1988) suggests that effective leaders learn to work in a range of approaches and styles themselves or ensure that the people with whom they work can do so where it is appropriate. The degree and amount of switching, flexibility and shifting will depend on the relationship between the leader and the culture in which she works. It is sometimes a delicate counterpoise, at others a rumbustious one! This group identified with this thesis. They recognized that they *did* have preferences in the way they worked but that they also needed to develop other approaches and enable others to take on leadership roles. They preferred to try and work in transformational ways, but they found it difficult to deal with conflict in an interactive mode, and wanted in some situations to retain control. Transactional approaches were sometimes inescapable. They were more concerned with *building their skills* so that they could learn to read how to act or behave in particular situations.

They also had to believe in and act responsibly toward their influence and power – in changing cultures, creating myths and making things happen. They could enable others to do things:

> The issue is about showing others in the organization that they can be powerful in their positions in the organization.

But this was sometimes a daunting prospect:

> The power is very real. Sometimes it frightens me. Power and responsibility go hand in hand. But if you really sit and think about it, it's awesome at times.

Working through others for change

The women were impatient for change. But they were also politically and organizationally aware. Some of them admitted to finding it difficult and frustrating to work in an environment which outwardly espoused change but inwardly resisted it. They did not know how to overcome this if they had little political support. Others were still unclear how they could, or whether they could, act as change agents. They were not looking to transform their organization but to adapt it, as they believed this was the only possible way forward. And the third group saw their mission, with political support, as being to turn their authority upside down. All were taking risks, in whatever stance or approach they took, that their strategy would fail.

As they work at leadership in their own styles, the impact on their authorities is bound to be diverse and sometimes difficult to analyse critically.

The latest recruits as chief executives have been in either small district authorities or metropolitan boroughs. Those appointed to small authorities often have the task of enabling the authority to survive during and after local government review. They see this as a positive challenge to achieve a change, which will give them experience which they will put to good use when they look to the next step in their careers. Those in metropolitan authorities may be faced immediately with larger tasks of getting to grips with the complexities of the political and internal cultures, and may also feel that the work they can do will take longer as, even though they may learn quickly, there is a lot more change to be undertaken. But we do not have sufficient evidence to do more than speculate whether there are significant differences between those authorities which are appointing women chief executives now and those doing so in the past. Neither can we say whether there is yet a 'new group' of 'newborn' women chief executives.

CONCLUSIONS

This work has been exciting and challenging. It has opened up some of the complexity of the debates around organizational leadership and gender. We had the opportunity to work with a 'live project' and a select group who were very much our active research partners and who acted as a sounding board for our ideas.

Our research framework enabled us to weave in and out of the debates about style, values and approaches to leadership which we had gathered before we started the project. It also meant that, although gender was a constant presence and in the fabric of the research, it did not dominate or obtrude. Rather, it formed the background canvas from which we could draw out threads and patterns.

The gender dimensions of leadership are tantalizing but not altogether clear. Of the group of women working as leaders in their organizations whom we examined, it was evident that what they had in common was not conditional on their gender. They shared needs for achievement; energy; having a belief system; courage; and an ability to stick with what they believed in. They had all worked very hard to get what they wanted. But in these attributes they do not appear to be very different from what drives effective leaders who are men. What does appear to be different is their higher levels of commitment – to their careers, to their organizations, and to their staff.

What this group illustrates clearly is their *diversity*. They have different approaches to life and relationships; they have different perceptions about situations and organizations; they are motivated by different things in contrasting ways; and the directions in which they are heading are distinct. Other differences are a result of their experience, different ages, and varying expectations.

Even having their womanhood in common is not straightforward. The gendering of their womanliness is diverse. They differ in their interpretation and perception of what being a woman means and the part it plays in their life as a leader. They share the belief that it is dangerous to reinforce the 'remedial model' in which women have to be 'brought up to' where men are, or to seen to be similar to them or to the way they work. Neither must *women as leaders* be seen as being exceptional, odd, different, or unusual, *by their very existence*.

Can we talk about 'good leaders' in this group? It is difficult to give a final grand summing up. It is more realistic to admit that the research has opened up complex, unanswered questions. We did not uncover any radical approaches to leadership (although there were some leaders masquerading as having such!). But we did establish, from testing out with our group, that good leadership:

- has a complex relationship to notions of management;
- is values driven;
- is culturally based and situated;
- only works if there are followers who are seen as equal partners and who are given power and responsibility.

We also did not get any definite information on how they might differ from other women in other parts of their organization who were also leaders in their own ways. For example, it would have been useful to have more evidence of their personality types, so that we could have had debates about how this might relate to their common characteristics as leaders. Neither can we discuss with authority the methods they had used to get to the positions they hold; for example, how much collusion was there with the dominant cultures, or how far had they subverted them? Having arrived in positions of power and influence, what do they see as their roles as agents of change for other women who are also aspiring to senior leadership positions?

There seemed to be two distinct groups here. The first group took the position that they were uncomfortable at being seen as role models for anyone, and would certainly not see it as part of their mission to be responsible for the overt development of other women. These women felt their mission to change the organization would include this but that it was not appropriate that women be singled out for positive discrimination. There was a lingering feeling within these organizations that their leader had achieved *despite* the structural and attitudinal blocks and that she felt that other women could do so too. This was compounded by the political sensitivity of this situation for many authorities.

The second group accepted that it was inevitable that they *would* be seen as role models for women and for change, and approached this understanding with varying degrees of pragmatism and cynicism. The pragmatists felt that they had responsibility to initiate (or find ways of making others initiate) programmes designed to open up avenues for women to contribute in as many ways as possible. The cynics also supported this but were concerned that getting more women into positions of influence was much more complex than just developing mechanisms and systems designed to support women. And although they might recognize that they are in pivotal positions to shift attitudes so that women and men begin to question accepted norms and ways of working, they also argued that their own type of leadership may not be replicable or sustainable. What was clear was that organizations are in the throes of major transitions, which are throwing up unexpected problems and challenges. These uncertainties mean that many of these leaders are stretched and working at the boundaries of their own knowledge and understandings. It seems that their best hope of survival is to gather up others with whom they can work through these transitions.

The final picture is unclear. It seems that the present constructs for women as leaders do not give much clarity for enhancing understanding. But work with particular women who are chief executives of their organizations in the public sector has enabled us to present some evidence that the debate about gender and women is far from over. It is difficult to have final views about the extent to which this group are effective or good leaders, or how far they strive to be so. It is more honest to be cautious and to work at developing new constructs which take into account the diversity of leadership meanings for women. It is also necessary to accept that organizational realities make the tasks of change for women immense.

REFERENCES

McGregor Burns, J. (1978) *Leadership*. New York: Harper and Row.

Davidson, M. and Cooper, G. (1980) 'The extra pressure on women executives'. *Personnel Management*, 12(6) 48–51.

Dixon, D.H. (1993) 'Women at the top: a study of women local authority chief executives'. Bournemouth University MA – Human Resource Management, September.

Eisler, R. (1991) 'Women, men and management: redesigning our future'. *Futures*, January/February, 3–17.

Ely, R.J. (1992) *Organizational Demographics and Women's Gender Identity at Work*. Working paper. Cambridge, MA: J.F. Kennedy School of Government, Harvard University.

Friedman, M. and Rosenman, R. (1974). *Type A Behaviour and Your Heart*. London: Wildwood House.

Gerver, E. and Hart, L. (1990) 'Surviving in a cold climate: women and decision-making in Scottish education'. Paper presented to the Conference on Equal Advances in Education Management, Vienna 3–6 December.

Helgeson, S. (1990) *The Female Advantage*. New York: Doubleday.

Hersey, P. and Blanchard, K. (1976) *Situational Leadership*. San Diego: Learning Resources Corporation.

Kanter, R.M. (1977) *Men and Women of the Corporation*. New York: Basic Books.

Morphet, J. (1992) 'Women local authority chief executives: roots and routes'. *Local Government Policy Making*, 19(3) 3–14.

Morphet, J. (1993) *Local Authority Chief Executives*. Harlow: Longman.

Nichols, N.A. (1993) 'Whatever happened to Rosie the Riveter?' *Harvard Business Review*, July/August, 54–62.

Quinn, R. E (1988) *Beyond Rational Management*. San Francisco: Jossey-Bass.

Rosener, J. (1990) 'Ways women lead'. *Harvard Business Review*, November/December, 119–25.

Stewart, V. (1992) *The David Solution*. Aldershot: Gower.

Chapter 13

Redrawing the boundaries
Trade unions, women and 'Europe'

Cynthia Cockburn

Trade unions in Britain have changed their sense of membership in two ways in recent years. They have opened to women, as women themselves have pressed for equality and as male leaders have recognized women as an undeniably significant source of future membership strength. The unions have also begun to prepare for a role in the social dialogue of the European Union. This chapter is based on research which asks whether women are being enabled to use their skills in the new cross-national activities of the unions in Europe and to develop working contacts with their counterparts in other EU member states.

There is a contradiction at the core of trade unionism. It rests on the question: 'Whom do we mean by "we"?' Despite a philosophy of membership and mutuality, trade unions have always included some people only to exclude others, and in some unions at some times the drawing of membership boundaries has been almost as important a function as negotiating with employers. Indeed it has often amounted to the same thing. A craft union such as the London Society of Compositors at the end of the nineteenth century, for instance, devoted a great deal of its energy to ensuring that employers deal only with its members, to the exclusion of a mass of semi and unskilled workers in the industrial vicinity (Cockburn 1983).

Among those who now and then aspired to the jobs controlled by the craft unions, a specially feared and despised group was women. If common labourers were 'other' to the skilled men, that ignoble thing in contrast to which they defined themselves, women were the lower order with which craftsmen often equated the *them*, the unskilled, seeing them as less than real men. Women, besides, were redolent of domesticity and sexuality. Their very presence in the factories and offices, to which they were drawn by the expansion of the capitalist economy, was resented as an intrusion by many men. In particular their attempts to enter skilled occupations were seen as an affront to masculinity and the proper patriarchal order.

When women began to enter unions it was naturally general unions of the unemployed they mainly joined. Within those new kinds of union, however, women remained a particular group of members who enduringly failed to get representation among the elected and paid officers, on delegations, and in the bargaining process. Even the mixed unions were men's unions in effect (Lewenhak 1977; Boston 1980).

To a large extent, due now more to masculine culture than to formal structures, this remains the case in the UK (Cunnison and Stageman 1993), in other European countries (Cook *et al.* 1992) and elsewhere (Briskin and McDermott 1993). Women's insurgency within the trade unions, over the last quarter century in particular, has essentially uncovered one aspect of the core contradiction of exclusion/inclusion. It has asked male leaders and male memberships, in effect, 'Whom do you mean when you say "we"?'.[1]

Another face of the same contradiction is revealed in the scope of the perceived limits of trade unionism and the construction of a set of interests as trade union interests. Although unions have often played a political role at national level, supporting and shaping political parties, campaigning for changes in law and policy, they have usually confined their local representative role to their own membership. As a recent study points out:

> Unions have claimed to be not only bargaining agencies for their members, but also an emancipation movement for all workers ... Their weight in collective bargaining and in the politics of democratic societies includes the responsibility to represent ... the interests of unorganized workers as well as the organized.
>
> (Cook *et al.* 1992: 8)

But the non-employed and unemployed, the aged and young of the population, have seldom been defined as beneficiaries of union support. Home and community have not featured on union agendas except in so far as defence of the worker's wage has been seen as serving them. Housing, education and health care, for instance, have not often been seen as union concerns.[2]. Although increasing numbers of women have come into paid employment, and of those many have joined unions, at heart the labour movement has seemed to see the working class as *having* a wife and children rather than *being* child, woman and man. The extent to which this is changing is considered further below.

In this chapter I want to bring into juxtaposition with the opening to women and the potential opening to 'the social' a somewhat different dynamic of inclusion/exclusion that exists within trade unionism: national versus cross-national interests.[3] Here a similar ambivalence exists. On the one hand, as Cunnison and Stageman remind us, 'the men in the union movement have traditionally claimed a wide agenda, professing concern ... for union and socialist struggles outside the UK as well as within' (Cunnison and Stageman 1993: 242). Trade unionism has always employed a rhetoric of 'Workers of the world, unite!' On the other hand, on concrete issues unions have often looked with suspicion and rivalry on the workers of other countries and have sometimes sided with British capital against foreign competition. While expressing solidarity with liberation movements in the Third World, they have fiercely protected the interests of their own national memberships against competition from Third World labour, whether workers in the sweatshops of formerly colonial countries or those emigrating from such countries to Britain.

Throughout the tensions described above can be detected the crosswise pull of what many would call the fundamental contradiction of trade unionism: the need to wrest from the employer the best possible deal for workers, while not endangering the employer's survival in a competitive world. That is the overall context in which the engagement of unions with a wider world occurs. The involvement of the unions today[4] in the European Union (EU) and the Single European Market involves all these dynamics.

In current research[5] I have been looking at the relationship between the two processes of change in the unions over recent years that respond to the contradictions outlined above, attempting a redrawing of boundaries. The first is positive action for sex equality; the second is engagement in the proceedings of the EU. The context of the research is what is termed the 'Social Dialogue', in which union movements are increasingly involved in the Europe of the Twelve. For unions and their confederations the Social Dialogue gives rise to two kinds and several levels of activity. The first type of meeting (preliminary to true 'social dialogue') is between counterpart unions in member states in order to forge a united 'side'; the second step involves them and their representative bodies in active dialogue with the other 'social partner', the European employer federations and their representative bodies.

As to level (see Figure 13.1), at the 'summit' are occasional meetings, chaired by the Commission, between delegates of the European Trades Union Confederation (ETUC) and the two employers' confederations at European Community (EC) level,[6] the Union of Industrial and Employers' Confederations of Europe (UNICE) and the Centre Européen de l'Entreprise Publique (CEEP). The Commission is also encouraging 'sectoral social dialogue' between the trade union movement's

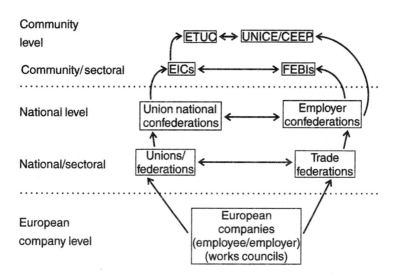

Figure 13.1 The social dialogue and the social partners

European sectoral federations (affiliated as 'industry committees' to the ETUC) and sectoral European employer federations. Third, a draft statute awaiting agreement provides for European multinationals, that is companies with operations in more than one member state, to opt for the status of 'European company'. A further draft directive provides for worker consultation in such enterprises in the shape of 'European works councils', bringing management together with representatives of workers based in different member states.[7] There are an increasing number of instances of company-level 'social dialogue' of this kind occurring in multinationals in anticipation of the new arrangements.

In the research discussed here I have been concerned with the middle level in Figure 13.1: all the processes in the UK trade union movement directed towards or culminating in the Social Dialogue. The questions underlying the research are:

1 What moves are British unions making towards the relaxing of the national boundaries separating European workers?
2 Given recent positive action measures to improve the representation of women and women's interests in British unions, just how active are women unionists being enabled to be in crossing and resignifying such boundaries?

What, in other words, is revealed by a gender analysis of the 'Europeanizing' of industrial relations?

GETTING WOMEN'S VOICE HEARD

In my research I first traced the positive action measures that have been taken in recent years by the UK Trades Union Congress (TUC) and by nine major affiliated unions to enable women to enter representative and authoritative positions and to change the bargaining agenda. The nine unions were selected as being national in scope, affiliated to the TUC, having a membership of at least 100,000 and providing a range of types of membership: public sector/private sector, manual/professional, and manufacturing/service industries.[8]

During the 1970s, influenced by a resurgent women's movement within its ranks and outside, the TUC began to give more recognition to women's disadvantage at work and to put its weight behind equal pay and anti-discrimination measures. In 1975, the year of the Sex Discrimination Act, the TUC published a charter of twelve aims for working women (TUC 1975). A few years later it extended its recognition of discrimination against women at work to acknowledgement of sex discrimination in the unions themselves (TUC 1979). Since that time it has published many papers urging positive action for women in affiliated unions.

The TUC has also attempted to put its own house in order. It has established a Women's Committee on which sit the women elected by an annual Women's Conference, along with any women who are currently members of the General Council. Two women are co-opted to the Committee from the TUC's Race Relations Committee. The Women's Committee is serviced by staff in an Equality and Social Policy Department, headed by a woman, which also services the Race

Relations Committee. (Note the uniting in this department of 'women' and 'the social', two parallel but related extensions of union interests.) A system of 'reserved seats' for women has been introduced on the General and Regional Councils and there is an informal commitment to proportional representation of women on all TUC delegations.

Despite the introduction of this 'women's structure', however, the TUC in practice remains male-dominated. On the officer side, the General Secretary (GS), Deputy General Secretary (DGS) and Assistant General Secretary (AGS) are all male. Of the seven departmental heads, all are male except for the Head of Equality and Social Policy. The TUC has a total of twenty general, sectoral and other committees. The chairs of all these are male, except for the two specifically concerned with women: the Women's Committee and the Equal Rights Committee. On the General Council, though women are present in proportion to their presence (around one-third) in the 7 million membership of affiliated unions, this has been achieved only by the introduction of reserved seats.[9]

Performance on positive action in the nine unions included in the study was patchy. While all had a woman's or equality officer of some kind, they were not in all cases allocated full time to the job of servicing women's interests. Six had a national women's committee, one had divisional women's committees instead, and in two cases an equality or equal rights committee looked after women's interests. Three of these unions had an annual women's conference and two had reserved seats for women on their executives.[10] The new public sector giant, Unison, the result of an amalgamation between NUPE, NALGO and COHSE, came into being in 1993 proclaiming a commitment to proportional representation of the sexes (averaging 70 per cent women across the sectors) on all committees, councils and delegations (Unison 1993).

The inadequacy of the anti-discrimination measures in the unions is manifest in the resulting statistics, shown in Table 13.1.

Of the 44 instances shown, women are proportionately or over-represented in relation to their presence in the membership in only four cases: on the GMB's executive, among MSF's national officers and delegates to TUC 1991; and in the TGWU's delegation to Congress that year. In all other instances it is men who are over-represented, in some instances grossly so. Women are scarce among chairs, presidents and senior paid officers, even of unions with large female memberships. In 1993 there were only two females among the 73 general secretaries of British unions. Since their unions were rather small, the effect was that fewer than one in a hundred trade unionists was led by a woman general secretary (TUC 1993a).

While the women's structures permit women a degree of public activity and a voice, often they fail to connect women to the mainstream. Women remain in reserved seats and fail to get elected to open seats. From top to bottom of the unions, women are absent in particular from 'coal face' positions involving expert knowledge (other than expertise on 'women's issues') or responsibility for dispute resolution or collective bargaining. Consequently, bargaining agendas are resistant to change (Dickens et al. 1988; Colling and Dickens 1989).

Table 13.1 Women as a percentage of union members, committee members, officers and delegates 1991

Union	Members	Executive Comittee	National Officers	Delegates to Annual Conference 1991	TUC
AEU*	15	0	?	11	10
BIFU	57	26	25	36	26
CPSA	72	27	13	36	36
GMB	39	39	12	26	20
GPMU	18	5	11	10	5
MSF	23	18	28	16	26
NUCPS	38	22	24	22	12
TGWU	18	8	6	8	19
COHSE	79	54	?	35	37
NALGO	55	47	10	?	40
NUPE	74	46	50	40	32

* AEU has since amalgamated with EETPU to become AUEW.
** COHSE, NALGO and NUPE have since amalgamated as Unison.
Source: SERTUC (1992).

None the less, we have now seen more than two decades of energetic activism by women for women. This has latterly been accompanied by a dawning recognition on the part of male leadership that they need women: almost all new jobs created in recent years have been 'women's jobs', and, besides, men's union membership 'density' in the UK has been falling at twice the rate of women's (Hastings and Coleman 1992). It is clear that women, particularly part-timers, are the primary source of new union recruits today and that the unions, if they are to survive, must both enrol them into membership and serve them better than in the past. This has mobilized some men as well as women for purposeful steps towards sex equality in the labour movement.

LOOKING TOWARDS THE EUROPEAN UNION

The opening to women has been a significant development in the trade union movement. It has been paralleled by an opening to 'Europe'. The significance of both on the agenda of trade unionism is evident in even a cursory reading of unions' annual reports and motions to Conference in recent years.

Although the Labour Party and the labour movement were originally largely opposed to Britain joining the European Economic Community (EEC), majority feeling in the unions today is that the EU inaugurated by the Maastricht Treaty, and particularly the Social Chapter, notwithstanding the UK government's opt-out, offer advantages to British workers. The Social Dialogue in Brussels, for all its limitations, has a clear attraction for unions that have been frozen out from consultation with employers and government in their own country. The TUC is consequently one of the most committed among TU 'centres' of the EC member states.

We also found those we interviewed in unions unanimous that 'Europe really matters.' Workers in many other EC states have better conditions than in Britain; their unions have more rights; national binding agreements still operate. British trade unionists have become aware that 'We're near the bottom of the pile in Europe today.' They therefore feel they must be active in pushing not only for improved European legislation but also for such European collective agreements as may prove achievable through the revived Social Dialogue.[11]

For the TUC a major priority now is getting Europe onto the bargaining agenda with British employers and getting bargaining going in multinational companies. The commitment is particularly strong among TUC paid officers, many of whom wish to see the Congress 'modernized via Europe'. The Single Market has also begun to colour the concern of the larger British unions from top to bottom. 'I can't ignore Europe and say "that's for someone else to deal with" ', was the gist of what many officers told us. The EC counts, and jumping on a plane to Brussels 'isn't just a nice trip'.

The TUC leads the way on 'Europe', through a range of activities we might categorize as out-country and in-country (TUC 1991a). As far as the former is concerned, first, it participates, along with the national 'centres' of other member states, in the European Trades Union Confederation (ETUC). Through energetic engagement in the ETUC's affairs it tries to influence its strategy in the Social Dialogue and towards the Commission and Council of the EU. Appropriate specialist members of the paid staff play an active part in the ETUC's standing committees.

Second, it seeks to influence the EC's recommendations and directives through consultation among commission secretariats and committees and the lobbying of commissioners and their *cabinets*. A taste of what this involves was given by one participant, who told us: 'You have to know the people ... I keep continually in touch. I'm always having a cup of coffee with this one, a beer with that one, chatting to people. And you have to know the big guns to wheel out as necessary: the Pope or the Dalai Lama.'

Third, the TUC seeks to influence the European Parliament, which controls the EC budget, keeping close contact with the Labour Party Liaison Committee and the Socialist Group of Members of the European Parliament (MEPs). At the time of writing, it plans to open an office in Brussels in 1994.

In-country, the TUC is actively urging member unions into European sectoral and company level Social Dialogue, because 'increased numbers of trade union members work in sectors where European comparisons are used and/or for multinational companies' (TUC 1993b). The TUC seeks to analyse and develop policy on Europe, inform affiliated unions and take soundings of their opinion. It has two vehicles for this. First is the Committee on European Strategy, set up in 1988. This is an important formal committee of *members* – and only three out of a total membership of twenty-three are women. Second is the innovatory and less formal 'Network Europe', formed in 1992. It is attended monthly by *officers* with 'European' responsibilities in affiliated unions: 'These are the bright, involved people.' It channels information both ways and was described variously as 'a sounding board', 'an early-warning system' and a 'rapid response capability' on European matters. The TUC has organized a number of conferences and seminars on the EU and Single Market and has published a series of analyses and guides, including one on *Women and Europe* (TUC 1990).

The major unions too are more and more involved in the EC, not only in response to exhortation by the TUC but also because their own interests increasingly draw them thither. Again we can identify in-country and out-country activity.

In-country, a typical first step in the individual unions has been a branch motion at annual conference to the effect that 'We should know more about Europe.' Some unions have responded to this stimulus by setting up a working party to suggest lines of action. Often the action has involved appointment of an officer, frequently in the research department, to gather information, analyse EC proposals, advise senior officers and issue information to members. More and more unions are developing an educational process for officers and members on such themes as 'What is the EC?', and 'Impacts of the Single Market'. Some have set up a 'Europe' committee or sub-committee. Unison may have gone furthest on in-house activity, with a nominated 'Europe' officer in each union region and sector, attending a quarterly meeting centrally, and with regular meetings of a European Secretariat of key central officers, including the General Secretary. Most unions active on Europe send an officer to the TUC Network Europe monthly meeting, at which information and opinion is exchanged. Some are involved in lateral activity with sister unions to work on particular issues. An example is the TGWU, the GMB and Unison working together on 'acquired rights' – using European provisions to prevent UK employers imposing a deterioration in terms and conditions of work consequent on a privatization.

Union activity is not limited to the UK, however. As with the TUC, it extends out-country, to Brussels and Strasbourg. Unions sometimes 'retain' MEPs at Strasbourg and lobby through them. Some senior officers are active in Brussels – for instance, the general secretary of AUEW is a member of the Economic and Social Committee, the tripartite advisory committee to the European Commission and Council. The TUC 'contracts out' some of its Brussels activity to individual officers of member unions. One union (GMB) maintains its own officer in Brussels.

The most important activity for most unions, however, is engagement in European sections of international trade secretariats, of which sixteen are currently affiliated to the ETUC as 'European industry committees' (EICs). These are considered by the TUC to be 'potentially the most important tool the movement has in Europe'. Some unions have a logical link with only one (for example, BIFU with Euro-FIET) while the interests of more general unions span several (the TGWU is affiliated to no fewer than nine).

A handful of senior officers of British unions serve as officers *of* EICs – for example, the Deputy General Secretary of Unison is President of EPSC (the European grouping of the Public Services International – PSI). Such officers may find themselves representing the EIC (rather than their own union) on the ETUC, or *vis-à-vis* the Commission. They thus also sometimes take part on behalf of the European unions in the sectoral Social Dialogue. For example, the UK members of the insurance committee of Euro-FIET represent that body in meetings with its employer opposite number.

Some unions have been prompted through EIC involvement and by other circumstances to bilateral activity with sister unions in the EC member states. GMB has signed a path-breaking accord with the German *IG Chemie*. The print/media union GPMU has an agreement with its German sister union *IG Media* on a series of two-week exchange visits between groups of members and officers. The aim is 'total immersion' in each other's work and concerns.

EC funding (budget 3:4004) is currently enabling unions from member states involved in the same multinational firms to meet together to prepare the ground for eventual works councils, an activity encouraged and sometimes staged by the EICs (Gold and Hall 1992). A number of British unions are already engaged in such company-specific dialogue. For instance, MSF is involved in talks with other unions (and in some cases with management) in a dozen European companies.

WOMEN'S ENGAGEMENT IN THE OPENING TO 'EUROPE'

Who are the significant actors, then, in these processes leading to the European Social Dialogue? In what capacities do they act, and are they men or women?

The actors appear to fall into three categories.[12] First, there are those who attend European functions *ex officio*, by virtue of having a particular status (delegates to a given meeting, for instance, might be general secretaries or presidents); or by virtue of having specialist knowledge or a sectoral function (a 'low-pay' expert or 'transport-industry' officer, for instance, may be called on to attend relevant meetings). Such *ex officio* activity accounts for the majority of visits to Brussels, both from the TUC and from affiliated unions.

Second, there is a kind of actor that might be called the specialist-on-Europe-as-such. This role involves two activities, both mainly though not exclusively performed in-country. The first is gathering, analysing and disseminating information about EEC business, such as proposals for directives. The second is developing *entrée* to EC processes, institutions and individuals, and fixing up and maintaining contacts for others. We shall see that this has different expression in the TUC and the unions.

The third route to 'Europe' is unavailable to men. Women may be drawn, through participation in the women's structures of the TUC or their own union, into the activity of women's structures at 'European' level.

To consider first the *ex officio* engagement: the leading *ex officio* actor is clearly the current General Secretary of the TUC who, by virtue of his office, is heavily involved in 'Europe'. He takes part in the Social Dialogue at top level, in summit meetings and working groups. His predecessor was President of the ETUC and so had this additional 'top hat' to wear in the Social Dialogue summits.

The other major TUC actors are located in its International Department, which leads on 'European' activity and acts as the General Secretary's secretariat in this regard. Its head, an Assistant Secretary, is secretary of the TUC's internal Committee on European Strategy. A man, he is frequently in Brussels, with or without the GS. Another Assistant Secretary, also male, in the International Department is a member of the Economic and Social Committee, chairing its trade union 'side', and spends a large proportion of his time on Community affairs.

There are, however, few departments of the TUC untouched by Europe today, and in European activity there is 'not the same sense of departmental boundaries'. EEC matters have truly become domestic matters for the TUC and for many unions. Many specialists, for instance in 'health and safety', 'training' or 'company law', regularly attend appropriate European committees. Almost all these are men. The TUC Industry Committees too are increasingly devoting attention to EC matters, and these are strongly male-dominated.

Down among the unions, likewise, since few women fill senior, negotiating or specialist officer roles few are found among *ex officio* actors in 'Europe'. There is, however, a handful of women who have achieved high status in the UK structure either as members or as officers. For instance, of UK delegates to the ETUC executive currently, one 'substitute' (out of the three full and three 'substitute' TUC delegates) is female. The current President of BIFU is a woman, and she attends Euro-FIET functions. One of the six UK union-side delegates to the Economic and Social Committee is a woman. There are notable examples of senior women officers in MSF and TGWU operating in 'Europe'.

It has to be said, however, that the same nine or ten women's names recur on many different bodies, and they participate as a small minority in a male world. The masculinity of this cast of actors is determined partly in the UK and partly in other countries, combining to constitute what Susanne Schunter-Kleemann has called *Herrenhaus Europa* (1992). Men are 'lords of the manor' of Europe. To give but three examples, UK delegates to 'Joint European Bodies' – that is, consultative, advisory and other committees of the EC – are 87 per cent male (TUC 1991b); of our 94 seats on EICs approximately 95 per cent are filled by men (TUC 1991b); and the ETUC executive committee (of international constitution) is 93 per cent male (Braithwaite and Byrne 1993).

What about the 'European specialist' role? In the TUC it is played from within the Economic Department, where one particular senior officer (male) analyses and conveys information about the EC to others in the TUC and to affiliated unons, mainly through the monthly Network Europe meetings that he convenes. The union officers who attend Network Europe are in the main those playing the European specialist role in their own organizations. Frequently they are situated in, or head of, their research departments. Of the current attendance list of the Network, totalling sixty, twelve are women. When the role is played by the *head* of research, the significant actor is likely to be a man. Examples are those of Unison, GPMU and MSF. It is, however, not always the senior person who wears the 'Europe' hat, and it is in this role of 'Europe-person' that there seems to have emerged a significant possibility for women's involvement. Research officers are quite commonly women. We identified several in the contact/fixing role with regard to Brussels. Characteristic are particularly active women officers in Unison (ex-NALGO) and BIFU. The GMB's European specialism is even more strongly woman-led, with one woman European officer in London and a counterpart operating in Brussels.[13]

If information is power, women in this 'European'-specialist role are not entirely powerless. However, despite its apparent responsibility our informants sometimes played their job down, pointing out that officers like themselves are usually relatively low status and low paid because they are not 'negotiating officers', who alone really 'have clout' in unions. One described herself as a glorified travel agent and said 'As soon as it becomes serious or important it's done by a man.'

Finally, there is the 'women's road' to Europe, created through positive action for sex equality. From the TUC Women's Committee, two members and one officer are currently delegated to the ETUC Women's Committee. Thence, of course, some find themselves representing the ETUC on other bodies, such as the Equal Opportunities Advisory Committee of the Commission. Some women go from union women's committees to the gradually increasing number of similar women's committees in the EICs (currently six out of sixteen have such women's structures). As well as the regular committees there are occasional programmes, seminars and conferences for women on women's issues organized by the Equal Opportunities Unit (DGV) of the EC and the ETUC, into which women from the TUC and UK unions are drawn.

The TUC's Women's Committee is, as we saw, serviced by officers of the Equality and Social Policy Department, who have a facilitating, campaigning and lobbying role on women's issues in 'Europe'. Particularly active are the head of the department and a second woman officer within it. There is a significant attempt here to forge an overlap between the women's structure and the mainstream, and these officers frequently brief the GS, DGS, AGS and other (mainly male) leading participants on women's interests, the legitimacy of which are by and large well recognized within the TUC. Issues to which the Equality and Social Policy Department have devoted considerable time have been the EC's draft directives on improved maternity leave and against sexual harassment (for 'dignity at work'), as well as developments on equal pay for work of equal value.

These officers also mobilize a network of informed women in the labour movement and the academic world to help shape EC/ETUC deliberations on social policy. Once identified by one of these bodies as potential contributors, such women, who may be only loosely linked to TU structures, nevertheless become frequent participants for the UK TU side.

There are at the time of writing, in one or two unions, signs that activity is beginning that links 'women' with 'Europe'. For example, NALGO (now part of Unison) organized an orientation visit to Brussels by members of its women's committee. Other unions are gradually beginning to develop educational activity for women on 'Europe'. Half a dozen unions have held women's seminars on 'Europe'. Such an overlap between women's structures and 'Europe'-directed activity is still rather rare, but may be expected to grow.

A recent study carried out by the ETUC, however, shows that the UK is no worse in respect of women's representation, and in some ways better, than most national trade union confederations (Braithwaite and Byrne 1993). It is certainly better than many of the EU and European Commission institutions in Brussels where (as a TUC male participant put it) 'You'd be lucky if one in four of those you're talking to is a woman.'

None the less, it will be evident from the above that it is normally men who represent the women members of UK trade unions in 'Europe', both in unions where women are a minority and in those where they are a majority. While a handful of women are 'fielded' in Brussels by the TUC and some unions, the most consistent woman participants are those from the women's or equality structures. Women are involved only relatively rarely when the matter is of general concern rather than a 'women's matter'. Women are women's main specialism and their main springboard into 'Europe'. One woman told us: 'If a thing's not specifically to do with women's equality, women aren't involved. There's a men's process and a women's process.'

We have to ask, besides, what kind of woman is it that is reflected in the few women actors in Europe? It is by definition a woman in employment. More precisely, it is a woman enrolled in unions – and that implies a certain kind of job. This tends to mean women working full-time for large employers, rather than casual, temporary, seasonal or homeworkers.

It is also a white woman. Just as women are under-represented in the mainstream union structure, so are the black, ethnic minority and migrant members of both sexes of the UK workforce. In most unions that have a women's structure there exists today a similar compensatory 'race' structure: a race relations officer and a race equality committee. The TUC recently created such a committee at national level. There are, however, still very few from such minorities in leading officer or lay roles in the movement. The General Secretary of the TGWU, a black man, is a unique exception.

One reason why black voices are not yet heard in the EC context is that there is as yet no 'race' equality legislation at Community-level, little consciousness in the EC institutions in Europe of the need for anti-racist positive action, and no 'race' structure to pull them through. The TUC is pressing actively, through the ETUC, for Community law combating racial discrimination and harassment, arguing that Article 235 of the Treaty of Rome is sufficient basis for this (TUC 1993c).

Black, ethnic minority and migrant *women* are even more rare than their counterpart men. There is, for instance, no black woman delegated by member unions to the TUC General Council. Very few are engaging on a regular basis in Europe-directed activity.[14] If positive action for women is not altogether successful in getting women into mainstream influential positions, anti-racist action is even less so.

Against that must be set the following. A motion passed at TUC Conference 1993 read 'in view of the staggering under-representation of black women throughout the movement, Conference ... instructs the Women's Committee to consult with black women trade unionists on the best ways of reversing this situation.' And MSF has a Black Women's Network. But the three-way interconnection between action on women/race/Europe is as yet barely existent. A rare instance is NALGO's action in sponsoring for two years a 'black women in Europe' speaking tour for the membership and fringe meetings at Congress and Party annual conferences.

WOMEN'S INTERESTS IN A FUTURE EUROPE

Not all women trade unionists are feminists, and not all women (and not all feminists) are alike in their conception of women's interests. On the other hand, the lives of women in European countries have been shown to differ markedly from men's lives. Women's relationship to the labour market differs over their lifetime from that of men, and women do very different kinds of work, on average for lower pay and on worse terms and conditions. Women remain the ones mainly responsible for unpaid work in the home, and for many social functions including care of the young, ill and elderly (Commission for the European Communities 1992). These differences are differently articulated in different ethnic groups, but gender difference is in no way annulled – indeed it is often increased – by an ethnic analysis.

The completion of a Single European Market signals a growth in production, intensified technological innovation and greater internal mobility of labour. These are developments from which male workers are better placed to profit than females, who lack technological qualifications, are seldom free to move home, and cluster in the vulnerable jobs and sectors more liable to attrition than growth (Hemeldonck 1990; Jackson 1990).

Despite differences in feminist standpoints, a very extensive body of research and analysis since the 1970s in the context of the EC has established at least a minimum set of 'women's interests' on which there would today be little dispute. We could perhaps divide them into three: women's issues as such; 'the social dimension'; and women's interests in wider economic and political issues.

The first category includes equal treatment at work, in society and before the law; equal evaluation of characteristically women's work with work characteristically done by men; compensatory training possibilities; and provision for the convenient reconciliation of paid employment with unpaid domestic and other responsibilities. They are by now taken up and dealt with in a continually enlarging set of directives, resolutions and recommendations shepherded through the decision-making process by the Directorate-General for Employment, Industrial Relations and Social Affairs (DGV) of the Commission for the European Communities. There are Council Directives on equal pay (75/117/EEC), on equal treatment in work and training (76/207/EEC), in matters of social security

(79/7/EEC, 86/378/EEC) and concerning women in agriculture and self-employment (86/613/EEC). In addition to these, proposals for directives awaiting agreement in the Council of the EU deal with parental and family leave; shifting the burden of proof in favour of appellants in equal-pay and equal-treatment cases; and the protection at work of pregnant women and women who have recently given birth. There are recommendations in existence on vocational training for women, and on childcare; and resolutions on combating women's unemployment, on equal opportunities for girls in school education, on the reintegration and late integration of women into working life, and on the dignity of women and men at work (Commission for the European Communities 1991). The inscription of women's right to equal pay in Article 119 of the originating Treaty of Rome, the existence of the Women's Rights Committee of the European Parliament, the Equal Opportunities Unit of the DGV and its action programmes, and the setting up of an Advisory Committee on Equal Opportunities for Women and Men can also be read as direct expressions of women's interests at work in the context of the EC.

The concept of 'a social dimension' to a European Community initially conceived of as 'economic' has, of itself, a special relevance to women. It has been a struggle over the years to ensure that a social dimension of the EC came into existence along with economic and commercial integration. As an EC document puts it, 'the single market programme has done more for business than it has for workers' (Commission for the European Communities 1993a). None the less there have been efforts to strike a balance – pressed by left and social-democratic governments and labour movements in member states.

An early expression of a social concern in the EC was the establishment in 1960 of the European Social Fund to improve job opportunities for the unemployed through retraining and to raise workers' living standards. But social matters have always tended to lag behind economic concerns. The Single Market project was initiated in 1985, but it was not until 1988 that the Commission announced an intention of drawing up a Community Charter of Social Rights, a 'social dimension' to the internal market. The project had the backing of the Social Affairs Committee of the European Parliament, and at a Strasbourg summit in December 1988 eleven member states (the UK opting out) adopted the Social Charter. Two years later an action programme was launched containing forty-five directives and proposals governing such matters as atypical work, working hours, vocational training, provision for pregnant women and handicapped workers, and the right of workers to information, consultation and participation.

The Maastricht Treaty signed in 1993 embodied the spirit of the Social Charter in its Social Chapter (again refused by the UK) and took the important step of opening many matters of social policy to majority voting, to prevent them being impeded by the necessity for unanimity. The Maastricht Treaty also affirmed an important role for the 'social partners' in dialogue. It opened the way to collective agreements at Community level, which can in some circumstances be underpinned by the legislative force of a Council Decision.

There is no way we can say the social dimension in the EU is a women's issue as such. Male interests in the trade unions are quite capable of generating a masculine agenda even within the social: it can be limited to 'workers' rights' and ignore reproduction, unpaid work, everyday life and the community. None the less, the tabling by the EC, continued in the EU, of 'the social' has been a prompt to many unions and confederations in member states to extend their own agendas. And a concern with workers as people does open the way to highlighting the kinds of specifically women's issue listed above. Besides, apparently non-sex-specific social matters such as 'racial discrimination' or 'working time' have, just beneath the surface, a sex-specific reality inviting disclosure. (Race discrimination takes a particular form among women; working time for women includes unpaid as well as paid work.)

More importantly, the social dimension carries the concerns of the EC, to a modest extent, beyond the workplace and into community and everyday life. Thus the Social Charter's principles included the right to improved *living* as well as working conditions; the right to social protection; the protection of children and adolescents; a decent standard of living for older people; and improved *social* (as well as professional) integration for disabled people (Commission for the European Communities 1993a). Given women's greater involvement in care at home and in the community, this shift to a wider social concern has a greater significance for them than for men.

There is a sense in which the Janus-face of the EU, whose two profiles are clear in the current White Paper on *Growth, Competitiveness, Employment* (Commission for the European Communities 1993b) and Green Paper on *European Social Policy* (Commission for the European Communities 1993c), is a gendered dichotomy: the economic masculine, the social feminine. Certainly I found men in the movement putting economic growth and employment forward as 'the main business', while women were more likely to mention the social. But the analogy does not go very far. Women know that women's interests also emerge from a *gendered analysis* of economic and political interests. Unfortunately this analysis is seldom made in mainstream contexts. As Jane Pillinger has written, 'Women were never intended to be the main beneficiaries of greater prosperity in Europe. Nor were women singled out as a group facing particular disadvantages' from economic growth and market integration (Pillinger 1992:43). She points out that the influential Cecchini Report on the benefits of the Single Market (Cecchini Report 1988) made no mention of women. If women are of any concern to the nation states and large enterprises that 'Europe' substantially comprises, it is only in so far as their super-exploitation in the workplace in some countries but not others threatens an 'unlevel playing field' for their game. It has been left to women's own representatives, the Women's Rights Committee of the European Parliament, and women's own bureaucrats, the Equal Opportunities Unit of the Commission's Directorate General V, to commission analysis of the implications for women (Hemeldonck 1990; Jackson 1990). A woman's 'take' on the economy introduces entirely new notions into the analysis, such as unpaid hours of work and unrecognized production of goods and services in the home. A woman's 'take' on the political sphere introduces new concepts of citizenship and rights.

ENABLING WOMEN'S VISION OF A FUTURE EUROPE

Taking the above as a working formula for 'women's interests', we can go on to seek an answer to the question: what steps are needed now to ensure a more cogent representation of women's interests through the Social Dialogue?

We have seen that women are strikingly few in the *ex officio* roles of the mainstream – and that black, ethnic minority and migrant women are entirely absent. Still needed are effective measures of positive action, such as quotas, reserved seats and time limited targets for women (clearly specifying places for women of different minorities) on committees, on delegations and in trade-union officer jobs to bring them up to proportional representation.[15] It is sometimes argued that women as such are not needed for women's interests to be adequately represented: men can do it just as well. It is true that not a few men in the TUC and British unions have been energetically pressing the 'women's' directives and proposals through the EC in recent years. There are also instances of good partnerships between women and men. A striking example is the TUC's current initiative to take a case to Europe against the UK government for the abolition of wages councils on grounds of sex discrimination. But in the course of my research I met more than one man who resented what he saw as too many special measures for equality. One derided the EC as 'fairy godmother' to women.

It can also be argued that not all women see themselves as representing women rather than people in general. The following points, however, are relevant. First, there is a case to be made for women to be present in proportional numbers in the Social Dialogue at all levels to the very top on grounds of democratic rights alone. Whoever and whatever women represent, they should not be excluded from the decision-making process. Second, experience in many countries and many contexts in the last two decades has shown that where women are in a small minority in a male environment it is all but impossible to lodge women's interests firmly on the agenda, even when a woman wishes to do so. Only when a certain numerical threshold has been crossed, when a critical mass of women has been achieved, does this become a possibility. It is not that only women can represent women but, as one trade union woman said in interview, we should ask 'How would men feel if men were normally represented by women?'

Second, we saw that, in small numbers, women are proving their skills and motivation in certain not very senior but none the less valuable 'European specialist' roles. The women filling these roles were in broad agreement on the kinds of qualification and skill the activity calls for and develops. Often the women in question have a highly appropriate qualification in international relations or European studies. They often speak at least one, sometimes more, language other than English. They have an ability for building and maintaining relationships ('psychology'), understanding institutions and their politics ('having an eye for how things can be done'); detecting and exploiting opportunities; learning fast; cultural flexi-bility; and patience. They also needed strength and determination, they said, to be able to operate without discomfiture as a sole women or in a minority among men.

Some of these – languages, communicating, showing patience and under-standing, for instance – are skills often seen as characteristically feminine. They are abilities that should receive better recognition, status and reward. Special training courses for trade union women are needed to help them identify the opportunities in 'Europe' and build on their skills so as to be equipped to seize them.

Finally, we have noted that women's main presence in the Social Dialogue comes through the women's structures, whose impact on the significant decision-making bodies and their agendas is, however, limited. The Women's Committee of the ETUC is arguing today for twin innovations to achieve greater impact. They are 'gender-proofing' and 'mainstreaming'.[16] By 'mainstreaming' is meant ensur-ing that the women's structures, while remaining in place with undiminished authority, are used to enable women and women's issues to find expression *in the main decision-making organs* of the union movement, in general and regional councils, executive and industry committees. It means that those who formally represent women's interests – that is to say, women's committees and women's officers – would have a right to membership of such decision-making bodies, to place items on their agendas and receive documentation in time to intervene in their debates.

'Gender-proofing' means the introduction of a standard and routine procedure whereby all policy documents and papers, on whatever theme, are subjected to a gender analysis. It implies that documents would be drafted or amended to be gender-reflexive, to contain reference to their implications for women specified as a distinct (though inwardly differentiated) interest group. Only through such a conscious device will major social, economic and political questions be understood and acted on in a gender-sensitive way.

Women today are stuck on a curious plateau, reached through the years of positive action. Some gains have been made. But those very successes now make forward movement difficult. The structures have adapted to our pressure, let a few of our representatives in, just to be able, it seems, to carry on as before. Now that women are no longer totally absent and overwhelmingly disadvantaged, the scan-dal-effect has dissipated and it is hard to assert the uncomfortable truth: that *real* equality is still far distant. It now calls for considerable courage on the part of women, and a perceptive awareness on the part of men, to acknowledge the legitimacy of this new cycle of demands. The kinds of measure suggested above will meet with scepticism and resentment.

There is, however, an unused resource in the skills and motivation of trade union women. All the women I met who had some 'European' involvement enjoyed this aspect of their work. They were eager to emphasize that it is not 'glamorous', but actually very hard work. None the less they said, variously, 'There's something attractive about being a European', 'It's a personal, political commitment', 'There's something energizing about it ... the sense that you're part of something wider than just your country.' Women enjoyed the feeling that 'you're making history', 'improving the lot of women Europe-wide'. Some mentioned a discovery of cross-national sisterhood, the surprise and pleasure of finding how much you had in common with women in other countries.

The union women commented on the different way women at international meetings relate to each other. Unlike the men, who often stuck with their countrymen and 'acted as a side', the women seemed keen to reach out to each other and make friendships across national boundaries. Of course, the meetings could be stultifying and boring. But compared with their experience of mixed-sex (that is, male dominated) meetings, the women said they found in women's meetings 'It's a different atmosphere completely, wanting to find out, wanting to listen' and 'there's fun, no fear of losing face, we're not strapped up in all this baggage.'

Women of the EC member states are in a historically salient position. A fast-growing proportion of the paid labour force, they constitute a highly significant collective actor at this moment in time, precipitated into public view by feminist research and activism. Their experiences and their lives furnish the logical standpoint from which to develop a vision of a radically different and more human Europe of the future. For this vision to take shape and find a powerful voice, women need to step across the man-made borders that even now continue to exist inside and between unions, inside and between nation states, and be in touch with each other. There is much at stake for women in the unions' redefinition of 'us'.

ACKNOWLEDGEMENTS

I would like to thank the Equal Opportunities Unit of the Directorate General V of the Commission for the Economic Communities and the Anglo-German Foundation for funding this project, and the City University for accommodating it. I am very indebted to all those in UK trade unions and the Trades Union Congress who contributed in interview. Without them the work would have been impossible and their insights and experience are my main source. My thanks too to Catherine Hoskyns and Jane Pillinger for sharing with me their much greater experience of the institutions of the new 'Europe'.

REFERENCES

Boston, S. (1980) *Women Workers and the Trade Unions*. London: Davis-Poynter.
Braithwaite, M. and Byrne, C. (1993) *Women in Decision-making in Trade Unions*. Brussels: European Trade Union Confederation.
Briskin, L. and McDermott, P. (1993) *Women Challenging Unions: Feminism, Democracy and Militancy*. Toronto and London: University of Toronto Press.
Cecchini Report (1988) *The European Challenge 1992: The Benefits of a Single Market*. Aldershot: Wildwood House.
Cockburn, C. (1983) *Brothers: Male Dominance and Technological Change*. London: Pluto Press.

Colling, T. and Dickens, L. (1989) *Equality Bargaining – Why Not?*. London: HMSO.

Commission for the European Communities (1991) *Equal Opportunities for Women and Men*. Special issue of *Social Europe*, No. 3/91. Brussels: Office for Official Publications of the European Communities.

Commission for the European Communities (1992) 'The position of women on the labour market: trends and developments in the twelve member states of the European Community 1983–1990' (by Margaret Maruani). *Women of Europe, Supplement No. 36*. Brussels: Office for Official Publications of the European Communities.

Commission for the European Communities (1993a) *Building the Social Dimension*. Brussels: Office for Official Publications of the European Communities.

Commission for the European Communities (1993b) *Growth, Competitiveness, Employment: The Challenges and Ways Forward into the 21st Century*. Brussels: Office for Official Publications of the European Communities.

Commission for the European Communities (1993c) *European Social Policy: Options for the Union*. Brussels: Office for Official Publications of the European Communities.

Cook, A., Lorwin, V. R. and Daniels, A. K. (1992) *The Most Difficult Revolution: Women and Trade Unions*. Ithaca, NY, and London: Cornell University Press.

Cunnison, S. and Stageman, J. (1993) *Feminizing the Unions*. Aldershot: Avebury.

Dickens, L., Townley, B. and Winchester, D. (1988) *Tackling Sex Discrimination through Collective Bargaining*. London: HMSO.

Gold, M. and Hall, M. (1992) *Report on European-level Information and Consultation in Multinational Companies – An Evaluation of Practice*. Dublin: European Foundation for the Improvement of Living and Working Conditions.

Hastings, S. and Coleman, M. (1992) *Women Workers and Unions in Europe: An Analysis by Industrial Sector*. IDP Women/WP-4. Geneva: International Labour Organization.

Hemeldonck, M. Van (1990) *Report on the 1992 Single Market and its Implications for Women in the EC*. Document A3–0358/90/Parts A and B. Strasbourg: Committee on Women's Rights of the European Parliament.

Jackson, P. C. (1990) *The Impact of the Completion of the Internal Market on Women in the EC*. V/506/90–EN. Brussels: Commission of the European Communities.

Lewenhak, S. (1977) *Women and Trade Unions: An Outline History of Women in the British Trade Union Movement*. London: Ernest Benn.

Pillinger, J. (1992) *Feminizing the Market: Women's Pay and Employment in the European Community*. London: Macmillan.

Schunter-Kleeman, S. (1992) *Herrenhaus Europa – Geschlechterverhaltnisse im Wohlfahrtsstaat*. Berlin: Ed Sigma.

SERTUC (1992) *A Step Closer to Equality*. Women's Rights Committee of the South East Regional TUC. London: TUC.

TUC (1975) *Charter: Twelve Aims for Working Women*. London: TUC.

TUC (1979) *Charter for Equality for Women within Trade Unions*. London: TUC.

TUC (1990) *Women and Europe: A Trade Union Guide*. London: TUC.

TUC (1991a) 'Building links in Europe'. TUC Information Paper. London: TUC.

TUC (1991b) *Directory of TU Representatives on European Bodies*. London: TUC.

TUC (1993a) *Directory*. London: TUC.

TUC (1993b) 'The next phase in Europe'. Report to Congress, London.

TUC (1993c) *General Council Report*. London: TUC.

Unison (1993) *UNISON News*, March.

Vogler, C. (1985) *The Nation State: The Neglected Dimension of Class*. Aldershot: Gower.

NOTES

1   Current research by Carolyn Vogler examines union journals over time to establish

precisely whom is meant by the 'we' in different contexts in trade union discourse (Department of Sociology, City University, London, work in progress). See also Vogler (1985).

2   A heartening exception, in which a union branch purposefully forged active links with local community struggles, is cited in Cockburn (1991).

3   Here and elsewhere I use the term 'cross-national' in preference to 'international'. The latter appears to imply a relationship between nation states. 'Cross-national' is preferable for leaving open the possibility of links between people and organizations *despite, disregarding or modifying the significance of* nation state structures.

4   This chapter was written in December 1993 and in some cases the latest available data related to 1991 or 1992.

5   The research has two phases. Reported here is a three-month, five-country project on 'Women in the Europeanizing of Industrial Relations', with funding from the Equal Opportunities Unit of Directorate-General V of the Commission for the Economic Communities and the Anglo-German Foundation, which was carried out in the second half of 1993. In 1994 a year's project titled 'The Representation of Women and Women's Issues in the Social Dialogue', looking at a sample of 'European' institutions, was to be funded by the same EC unit and by the Economic and Social Research Council of the UK. The principal investigator in both cases was the author, based in the Department of Sociology, City University, London.

6   The term 'European Union' dates from the Maastricht Treaty of 1993 and relates specifically to the two new 'pillars' of policy to which Community concerns were extended by that treaty: foreign and security policy; and justice and home affairs. The Council of Ministers thereafter became the 'Council of the European Union', but in the case of all other bodies and the activities founded on the original Treaty of Rome the correct term at the time of writing remains 'European Community'.

7   Since this was written, a Directive was passed in December 1994 (No. 94/45) to make employee-consultation procedures mandatory in Community-scale undertakings of a given size and spread. European works councils, as they are termed, are in process of establishment now in many multinationals.

8   The unions in which interviews were carried out were the Amalgamated Engineering and Electrical Union – Engineering Section (AUEW); the Banking, Insurance and Finance Union (BIFU); the Civil and Public Services Association (CPSA); the GMB, Britain's general union; the Graphical, Paper and Media Union (GPMU); Manufacturing Science Finance (MSF); Unison, a recent amalgamation of the National Union of Public Employees (NUPE), the National Association of Local Government Officers (NALGO), and the Confederation of Health Service Employees (COHSE); the National Union of Civil and Public Servants (NUCPS); and the Transport and General Workers' Union (TGWU). In each of these unions either the officer responsible for women or the officer responsible for European affairs (or both) was interviewed. I also draw on written or telephoned replies to my questions from a further nine unions.

9   I draw here on the latest available *Directory* published by the TUC, that for 1993 (TUC 1993a).

10 Data here are for 1991, derived from a survey carried out by the Women's Rights Committee of the South East Regional TUC (SERTUC 1992).

11 The Dialogue, initiated in 1985 by President Jacques Delors, has taken on a renewed momentum since July 1992 in the context of the Maastricht Treaty on European Union. The Treaty affirmed the role of the 'social partners' in the Union and provided for collective agreements between them at European level, which in certain circumstances may be underpinned by the legislative force of a Council decision. Although the UK government opted out of the Social Chapter of the Treaty, UK trade unions and employer federations are not precluded from joining with their counterparts in the Social Dialogue.

12 A fourth type of engagement applies only to affiliated unions, not to the TUC. There is

an incipient tendency for branch secretaries and shop stewards in major firms to be getting involved in company-level consultation in Europe. It was impossible, however, to obtain first-hand information through our interviews on who is involved at this grassroots level of works councils, since our national-level informants themselves did not know. They believed that the general British practice whereby men, rather than women, are the lay representatives engaging in practical collective bargaining prevails also in the special case of 'Europe' – perhaps more so. None the less, the sexual division of labour in employment can have an effect on this, and it may be that in companies in 'female' sectors, such as the food industry, women shop stewards and branch secretaries will increasingly be involved.

13 The research reported here also involved interviews in the Confederation of British Industry and several industry federations. I am reinforced in this perception of a potential affinity among women for this 'European'-specialist role by finding a number of counterpart women on the employer side, with similar qualifications and motivations.

14 The only one, indeed, may be a member of the TUC Race Relations Committee who attends the similar committee of the ETUC.

15 This recommendation is supported by a report by the ETUC on *Women in Decision-making in Trade Unions* (Braithwaite and Byrne 1993).

16 A motion passed at a seminar on 'A Gender Perspective in ETUC Policy' in Milan, 28–9 September 1992, organized by the ETUC Women's Committee, called for these two processes to be instituted in the Confederation. The motion was later adopted at a meeting of the ETUC Executive in December 1992.

Chapter 14

The gender lens

Management development for women in 'developing countries'

Gwendoline Williams and Marion Macalpine

This chapter describes the pioneering international management development programme for women from 'developing countries' created and launched in 1991 in conjunction with the Royal Institute of Public Administration (now RIPA International). It outlines the development and organization of the course, and describes the processes through which the programme has generated a model of management development in which theory and experience are linked together. This model makes visible the gendered relations of power within the Civil Service, and then explores strategies to intervene and change both the institution itself and the gendered outcomes of the service it delivers.

THE RIPA MANAGEMENT DEVELOPMENT FOR WOMEN PROGRAMME

The International Management Development for Women Programme was initiated at RIPA International in 1991, and a pilot course was run for a small group of women managers from India, Kenya, Ghana and Nigeria in that year. In 1992, 11 civil servants from Bangladesh joined a larger international course group of 23, and 15 Bangladeshi managers attended in 1993, as part of a larger group. The 1994 programme involved 20 women managers from Bangladesh, Sri Lanka and Nigeria. Participants have also come from other African and Asian countries, including Tanzania, the Yemen, the Sudan and Nepal. The programme takes place in London over three months of full-time study.

Most of the participants are women with children. All are from the senior and middle ranks of the administrative cadres of the Civil Service, and decisions about who participates are taken by establishment departments of the Civil Service, together with the regional office of the British Council. Participants have included ministerial policy advisers, tax collectors and magistrates, the Deputy Director of a national training department, and other professionals who work in the Civil Service; for example, a Dean from a West African college of technology, a consultant gynaecologist and a dentist, all of whom have managerial responsibilities.

The programme is offered only to women. Most of the participants report that if that were not the case, their male colleagues would be selected instead of them. The absence of men offers a real opportunity for women to analyse their experience in a more open way than on a mixed programme, and to generalize and theorize from those elements of their experience that are shared. There is also an enormous diversity in the group: of ethnic and national origin, age and experience in work, class, marital status and educational background. All have to be graduates to enter the Civil Service in their country.

The work contexts and responsibilities of the participants are varied. Some are responsible for services for users in the local area, with whom they have direct communication. Some of the Sri Lankan delegates have been very senior officers who are responsible for the delivery of all government services within a local area. But the Civil Service is a highly bureaucratic, hierarchical and rule-bound organization: the women may therefore occupy quite senior positions but with little power to influence the direction, practices and outcomes of the organization as a whole. For others, the end users of the service are so remote that it is hard to identify them. The duties of these officers consist of carrying out detailed instructions given daily, and 'the file' appears to be the fulcrum of activity.

Most of the participants have children, and because of this there is an ongoing debate, rooted in the gender and power issues the programme addresses, which is concerned with the advantages of 'in-country' training. Compared with training abroad, this would be far less disruptive for participants with respect to their domestic roles. Training abroad has the advantage of offering the status currently accruing to women and men attending courses in 'the north'. (The terms 'north' and 'south' are used here in the absence of more satisfactory terms: the 'north' for what is termed the 'developed' or 'overdeveloped' or 'first' world, and the 'south' for the 'less developed' or 'underdeveloped' or 'Third' world.) Currently there is an uneasy mix of solutions to the 'childcare problem', with some women performing miracles in organizing, often at very short notice, alternative childcare for children at home during their absence of three to four months. Others bring their children with them, sometimes accompanied by other carers, and continue actively in their multiple gender roles.

Because the delegates are spread around the world, and are often nominated at the last minute, no formal training needs analysis has been possible. But the ideas for the programme content and design have been drawn from a number of sources: from our own past and current political and organizational experience; from an awareness of others' experience through the literature on gender and management and on gender and development; from successive years' experience of running the programme; and from evaluation visits carried out in Bangladesh, India and Sri Lanka after the 1992 and 1993 programmes.

The focus of the programme is on women civil servants as agents of change in the development process. It is concerned with the constraints and opportunities available to women bureaucrats in development administrations. Anne Marie Goetz (1992) points to the importance of paying attention to the gender dimensions of public administration to explain the consistent failure to 'integrate' women in development policy and practice. She also highlights the role of public administration in reflecting and reproducing women's marginality, as well as its importance as a site for opposition and transformation. Naila Kabeer (1992) suggests that gender training include a focus for development planners in bureaucracies on 'how exclusionary structures work within their own institutions, through their hierarchies of authority, rules of recruitment, privileged disciplines and divisions of resources and responsibilities' (p. 23).

Our task in the Management Development for Women Programme has been to bring together analysis, insights and strategies from work both on gender and management and on gender and development in a way that enables the programme participants to intervene in the complex and unequal relations of power within public administration agencies, in the context of unequal north–south relations, to increase women's access to and control over resources Our vehicle for this is a training programme, which aims to use *management development* to assist with *development management*, in a way which contributes to women's immediate practical needs and to their longer-term strategic interests (Moser 1989).

The programme is funded through the British aid programme. This raises all the questions and contradictions of designing a programme which aims at interventions in power relations within a British institution, set within the traditions and influences of the colonial connection, which still powerfully affect all parties. These contradictions deserve a chapter in themselves. Here we only have space to acknowledge them and to present our view of this three-month programme as both an opportunity and a challenge: an opportunity provided by a long and intensive period of sharing and analysis of our experience as women managers internationally; and a challenge to ensure that this opportunity is used to locate our discussions of gendered relations of power within the context of the overarching inequalities of north–south relations.

THE LEARNING ENTERPRISE

The programme has sought to depart from some of the more traditional ways of 'teaching and learning' in management education. It covers many topics to be found in traditional management training: management theories, presentation skills, strategic planning, training needs analysis, staff management, models of leadership, effective meetings, team building, appraisal systems, total quality management, finance management, information technology, and the management of change in organizations. However, the approach to management development used in this programme is very different from a competence-based model of management development, which *separates out* management skills, but usually allows for little in the way of *integration* of those skills within a multilevel gendered approach, or for a value base which puts redistribution of power at its centre. Although the development of managerial skills is an important part of this programme, the complexity of analysis, consciousness and change necessary goes far beyond what can be expressed through 'managerial competencies'. This programme is based on a model of management learning which focuses on empowerment and diversity, weaves together multiple levels of analysis and integrates concrete experience with review and theory building, leading to further action.

The group itself is set up as a 'learning organization', establishing ground rules of collaboration and mutual learning from the differences within the group. Co-consultancy skills (that is, the ability to act as organizational consultants to each other) are developed as a practical example of the learning enterprise in action. Within this learning enterprise, two integrative principles underlie the organization of the learning process. The first is the *integration of theory with practice*; the second is *the integration of multiple levels of analysis* in order to plan for action.

Learning and teaching styles are based on Kolb's learning cycle (Figure 14.1).

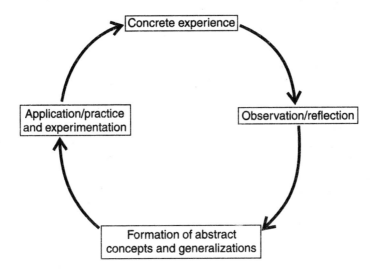

Figure 14.1   Kolb's learning cycle

The starting point for each element in the course and the touchstone used to judge the usefulness of concepts and information from all sources is the personal and professional experience of the women participants. All aspects of management are addressed through delegates' own experience, input from resource persons, and the experience of practising senior women managers from different organizations. Issues are considered both from the point of view of women managers, and from the point of view of the impact of policies on women users and consumers. Differences between women in ethnic origin, class, education background, rural/urban location, sexuality and physical ability/disability are integral to the approach.

We conceptualize the woman civil servant at the centre of a series of concentric circles. Women managers working on development need a gender awareness which encompasses the broadest external level of international negotiations over free trade, human rights, aid and conditionalities; through the societal and the organizational levels, through the intergroup, the intragroup and the household levels, to the personal level. Because of the kind of complex thinking required to understand power relations at all these levels, the programme content requires inputs from many disciplines, while at the same time incorporating experience from the various participants and facilitators. Conceptual frameworks and research come from international development theories, gender studies, strategic management, theories of underdevelopment, and motivation theory, as well as the functional areas of management.

The process of learning is designed as both *integrated*, as we have seen, and *interactive*. Each strand of the programme focuses on one or more levels of analysis, while keeping the rest in view, and the curriculum is conceived as *spiral* rather than modular or linear. This approach offers opportunities for constant reviews and an interconnectedness of themes. The programme rests, then, on the integration and weaving together of a diversity of activities, inputs and processes by and within the group in order to effect integrative learning, mostly around the organizing concept of gender-based power relations.

Topic areas are used to provide an opportunity for skills development and for actual practice of management skills, such as delegation, giving feedback, negotiation, etc. Throughout there is an emphasis on the delegates' consultancy skills, in listening and in providing constructive feedback and support to each other. These are used to provide a model for the kinds of support that women can offer each other for their own development within male-dominated organizations.

In order to maximize the opportunity for self-directed learning, participants work on three projects during the programme. The first is based on a management issue or problem from their own organizations. Each delegate presents a conflict or concern from her own organization early in the programme and provides data for theory-building as well as a number of illustrative vignettes. So for example, Farida, a Bangladeshi civil servant, had prepared all the papers for a particular meeting, and when her daughter got a fever, had arranged for the papers to be delivered to the senior manager who needed them. He, however, insisted that she herself should hand over the papers to him. 'I had no other alternative but to take my sick daughter with her medicine and her milk along to my office by rickshaw and then collect the papers and hand them over.' Her experience contributed to the group's analysis of the multiple roles played by women, as well as the construction and maintenance of gendered power relations within the organization.

The second is an Action Inquiry Project on a particular issue concerning women (such as women and health, sexual harassment at work, women's education), which allows participants to use information and resources available in the group or in London about the international situation. The third is gendered organizational analysis of a department in a local authority in the UK. Participants also apply knowledge and ideas from the programme to produce an action plan for their return to their workplace (Barnes 1992; Macalpine 1993).

Participants' own expectations and career development form another inter-woven strand in the programme. The ideas shared allow the women to consider their individual and collective development within the organization as well as within the community and society. There is a regular weekly 'Where are we now' (WAW) review session, which enables women to review and provide feedback on what they have found to be more or less useful to them, and on how they think the programme is linking to the 'real world' in which they live in their particular country or organization.

LOOKING AT POWER RELATIONS THROUGH THE 'GENDER LENS'

The task of the Management Development for Women Programme is to enable women to intervene in the unequal relations of power within administration agencies and to increase women's control over resources for women's benefit. To do this, the course uses and develops the concept of social relations of power as a framework to apply both to management development and to development man-agement. This framework makes gender relations visible, and views them as materially based, but continually negotiated through language and action. It gives the lie to the idea that women and men interact on the basis of fixed 'attributes' which are deemed to be 'natural'. Since power relations are continually negotiated and renegotiated, this framework allows for change and intervention, even in relatively rigid bureaucratic systems.

The course uses the concept of a '*gender lens*', through which women are invited to look at every aspect of the structure, culture and practices of their organizations. The use of the 'gender lens' makes visible the gendered power relations that are normally taken as natural and therefore invisible, and the multiple roles that women play. The gender lens enables analysis at multiple levels, including the international level of north–south relations; the level of society and community; the social relations of power within the organization and within the household; and the implications of all these for the individual women. In respect of content selection and the focus of discussion, the idea of the 'gender lens' allows us to draw on the work of Massiah (1990). On the basis of her review of development plans for several English-speaking Caribbean countries, Massiah highlights the need for gender visibility for women in terms of mainstream conceptual and statistical visibility and socio-economic, socio-cultural, political, domestic and subjective visibility. We were able to use this notion of visibility in the analyses conducted throughout the programme.

The 'gender lens' and the related issues of visibility reveal the separation of policy making from service delivery. A key insight that the participants quickly seized upon was the tendency to find gender segregation in respect of policy formulation. This was illustrated in the form of the following vignette:

A multi-storey office block in the capital city of a developing country houses the central ministerial offices. Some of its features would be similar to those in the UK. On a floor near the top of the building 'policy making' is going on. The discussions are about the International Monetary Fund, the World Bank, structural adjustment and loan conditionalities, strategic planning, public sector reform, the balance of payments ... and so on. On the lower floor are those persons responsible for the delivery of the services. People in these offices are discussing clinics, the supply of drugs or of textbooks, transport. The people on the top floor are almost all men. Those on the lower floors include many women, who are concentrating on their work, but at the same time are preoccupied with matters of family care and kin ties. They would also be among the users of the services provided. The top floor is served by an express lift: the lower floor by another that stops at each floor.

The views from the respective floors present very different but interlocking scenarios about development goals, service delivery contributors and beneficiaries in public administration in countries of the south (developing countries). This understanding has encouraged a focus on strategies for change in the gendered and other relations of power that have become visible.

Gendered power relations seen through the 'gender lens' can then be used as a template for analysing other relations of power and subordination, recognizing the *diversity* of women through class, ethnic origin, nationality and other identities. It encourages women within the bureaucracy to make changes to meet their practical needs in a way that begins to meet women's strategic as well as practical interests. The concept of viewing social relations of power through a gender lens also encourages women bureaucrats to undertake a task which is even more challenging: to see the clients of their services as agents rather than recipients, who with the help of the 'gender lens' can identify their own needs and interests and in so doing become 'empowered'. Naila Kabeer (1992: 34) describes the process as this:

> Women's strategic gender interests are likely to emerge only through a process of struggling 'against the grain' of commonsense notions about gender inequality. Conscientisation is a first step in the struggle through which women increase their capacity to define and analyse their subordination, and in so doing construct a vision of the kind of world they want and the means by which they may act in pursuit of that vision.

The *gender and development* strand is an essential basis for women's analysis of their environment. For the majority of women, who have been excluded from access to information about global economies, it comes as a shock to learn about 'structural adjustment': that economic and social policies, such as cuts in food subsidies and social services or privatization, are imposed on developing countries by the IMF and the World Bank with the aim of these countries repaying their 'debts' to the north. Using the 'gender lens' then highlights the particular implications of structural adjustment for women in developing countries.

The course therefore explores the role of gender, like 'race', class and other identities, in the creation and distribution of social value. It also challenges the concept of separate domains of societal activities for women and men, with the public service being seen as a 'male preserve' while the home is seen as the private domain where women carry out their reproductive, family care and community roles. Participants examine how this concept contributes to the marginalization of women in the centres of decision making and power; and to the perception of women as the passive beneficiaries of social development services. By contrast, the participants' experiences show that women are *agents* in both the public and the private spheres.

GENDERING THE STRATEGIC MANAGEMENT OF CHANGE

Various strategic management tools are used to assist participants in strategic planning from a gender perspective. For example, a stakeholder analysis is used to identify who has a stake in the organization and to reveal the wide range of interests, from the most senior to the most junior staff, other agencies or government departments, trade unions and service users. Using the 'gender lens' to look at the stakeholders creates a very visible picture of gendered power relations within and without the organization. Often the majority of service users are thus seen to be women, whereas the policy and resources are controlled by men. It is a process of making implicit knowledge explicit.

Another tool is the 'SWOT analysis', which is used to identify strengths, weaknesses, opportunities and threats inside and outside their organizations. Once again the 'gender lens' reveals the location of women and men in this scheme and provides a framework for participants to analyse where they are and what their own power relations are in the organizations. Statements of purpose are linked to outcomes (for service users); goals are costed and linked to budget setting. Like SWOT, 'force-field analysis' is used to plan the management of change by identifying the forces that are going to help them make a change and those that are going to work against it, and then by considering how to reduce the forces against and how to increase the forces in favour. The usefulness of the tool is enhanced by identifying (through the 'gender lens') the gender of the 'helping' and the 'hostile' forces. The 'PEST analysis' is used to identify the purpose, end product, standard and time scale of the task undertaken.

To understand the issues of power, a 'power net' analysis is used to place participants at the centre of the change process and to identify in a diagrammatic way different people in the organization with whom they have a power relation as either a 'superior' or a 'subordinate'. This can make explicit positions of power which they hold and the places where they may be 'powerless'. Having gendered their power relations, they may be better able to see how to enhance their own power and reduce their powerlessness. The 'power net' also reveals where relations of power are reciprocal, and where allies are located across the organization. This enables participants to see how they can build networks inside and outside the organization, and when they are in the middle of a large bureaucracy to create a 'mini-culture' within their sphere of influence, where they can define the terms of reference, the rules and the gender values.

Discussion of *barriers to women's progress* in public administration provides a space for examining women's experiences of gendered power relations (Hollway 1991). The concerns expressed by participants about their work situation are almost overwhelmingly about male power. Like other women managers, the participants on this course have been faced by contradictory demands from men; that they behave *the same* as the male officers, with no recognition of their multiple roles, on which men depend; and that they are treated *differently* from men. For example, an Indian civil servant, on her first night as the only woman in a new station, was told: 'I hope you are aware that our service is for 24 hours, and you have to put up with every problem that you meet.' She was kept sitting until 2 a.m. in the control room, and then sent to a rest house occupied by men she did not know. Some participants considered this acceptable because it was the way that men were treated. A senior Sri Lanka officer in charge of a government district said: 'I do my work ambitiously, bravely, without thinking that I am a woman.' So in some cases there is pressure on women public servants, only recently admitted in some services, to behave *like* men.

At other times, women are treated differently from men in the same position. A senior evaluation officer in Bangladesh found that when she visited projects the senior project personnel:

> always tried to avoid giving me proper attention. They sometimes start gossiping, asking me about my personal affairs such as what does my husband do, how many children do I have. After this type of attitude, I start my questions about their project and they realize that I am not only a woman, I am also an officer who knows every in and out of their project, and then they pay attention to me. To overcome this situation, I always prepare and inform myself about the projects to which I visit.

Only by preparation and determination does she avoid attempts to diminish her role and authority. Another officer was confronted with the higher work standards required from women to achieve recognition: 'Doing my work sincerely from morning to evening, it was very difficult for me to satisfy my boss. It was very difficult for me to get all the work done according to his wish.' Some forms of 'different' treatment are even more blatant, and bring sexuality even more clearly into the practices that men use to control women. A woman appointed to a senior post – the first woman at this level in her area – had to walk up a long stairway on the outside of the place where she was working every day, with all eyes upon her, and had offensive anonymous notes delivered in her post.

Experiences that delegates bring to the programme are used to analyse the structural aspects of women's exclusion from power in hierarchical and role terms, as well as the construction of a masculine culture, where gendered difference is actively constructed and power differentials actively maintained through behaviour, language and symbols. And both of these are set against the apparent neutrality of rules and goals – for example, the absence of formal barriers to women, or promotion by 'merit' – which disguise the gender issues they serve.

Once the 'gender lens' has shown 'enacted' reality to be different from what is 'espoused', strategies are developed both for making this difference visible to others and for bringing about changes at the formal level, and more often at the informal level. All participants use the knowledge they have acquired through the use of strategic management tools to develop action plans, which they will try to implement on their return to work at home in their organizations. Central to all of this work on the course is the 'grounding of theory' in the weekly evaluation sessions: the structured exchange of experience and insights in response to the question 'Where are we now?' This is a vivid and informative exercise. It serves to revise, to review, to work with the connotations of new words, to weave once again the different strands, to feed back to facilitators, and to link input and new concepts to experience.

EVALUATING OUTCOMES

As part of the development of the Management Development for Women Programme, evaluation visits were made following the 1992 and 1993 programmes to the women in their workplace in their home countries:

- to brief the Director of Studies working on the programme in the UK on the local context within which the participants work;
- to evaluate the effectiveness of the course and identify and confirm training needs;
- to keep contact with course participants from previous years, to provide essential follow-up support;
- as a means of increasing the status of participants in their workplace, and in so doing counteracting to a small degree the structural discrimination which women officers face.

Information was gathered from participants and their managers through workplace visits and interviews, workshops, small-groups discussions, and questionnaires (Barnes 1992; Macalpine 1993).

The practical changes women were able to make on their return varied. Some changed the traditional work styles in their own sections towards clearer goals, targets and review of performance. Legal officers in Bangladesh focused on ensuring that women knew their rights and that these rights were applied. In Sri Lanka, the recent decentralization of administration had given far greater responsibilities and therefore opportunities for gendered organizational change to the two delegates. For example, they were involved in a number of women's projects. They participated in new women's programmes at village level; held meetings for women staff; and engaged in the voluntary management of a women's counselling centre attended by about a hundred women each week, the only one of its kind outside

Colombo. They also reported that their personal attitudes had changed and confidence increased, and so they were able to give more opportunities to other women, and be more assertive with male superiors.

A woman tax collector had as a strategic goal in her action plan to increase the access of women users to the service. She had been very much influenced by the use of the 'gender lens' and excited by what it revealed to her about the disparity in access, knowledge and power between women and men. She arranged to spend more time providing advice and information to women on the system of taxation and how it affected them.

Another woman had created an office which was welcoming and friendly, and had developed a very positive relationship with her subordinates, when previously she did not know their names. She was discussing staff development plans with each of her staff. None of this may sound very new, but it was new in the context of the very rigid, hierarchical bureaucracy where she worked and where she had previously operated within established power relations. Most of the women also started noticing gender relations within the household which they had not been explicitly aware of before participating in the programme.

The over-riding benefit reported by all participants was an increase in their confidence, particularly in talking to senior managers.

Never before had I so much confidence in myself: this confidence is being boosted by the use of skills and techniques of communication. Now I am very vocal. I can present very confidently. I met the [Permanent] Secretary, he wanted to know about the course. I presented a seminar about my experience, explained SWOT & PEST – this was new to them. They were surprised and happy to know about it. I put a paper to the Secretary about administrative reform in the UK. He was very pleased. I did a SWOT analysis with my team, my division and the Secretary and his senior colleagues.

Whatever he [the manager] will feel about me, I must express my view. How far he will accept it or not will depend on him, but I must express my view.

Now I am able to say to a man: 'This is my strength, asking for my legal rights. This is your weakness: you are not carrying it out.'

Generally participants reported that their colleagues often commented on their vastly improved confidence as well. However, some of their comments made it clear that applying what they had learned on the course was not always easy or unproblematic:

I am beginning to see the world through the gender lens, and there is turmoil in my heart.

(Bangladeshi delegate)

Women's leadership is often found intolerable to men, the more so when the woman leader is younger in age than the men she is leading.

(Head of a department in a Civil Service
training college in West Africa)

It is clear from the stakeholder analysis that men dominate. Men make the laws, and they make them for the benefit of men.

(Nigerian participant)

I am experiencing something different in my life.

(Sri Lankan delegate)

I have spent eight years working with the Finance Department, just typing their figures. Now I have come to understand.

(Tanzanian delegate)

Participants valued highly their new sense of contextual understanding, on environment and gender issues, on north–south relations, on structural adjustment and aid policies, and on their effects on women and men. Participants commented frequently on their use of analytic models and some also introduced these models to senior colleagues. Many commented that they also used them in their personal lives to solve problems and plan: 'I am now able to analyse and assess my potentialities'; 'We didn't call these strengths, there was no methodical analysis of the situation'; 'I try to find mentors, and also I look for allies whenever I face a problem, and advise my female colleagues to solve the problems in the same way.'

Participants also commented on their much improved presentation skills, which they need for a wide range of meetings with senior colleagues and for meetings with community groups, or donors or politicians in some cases. Many delegates reported a marked increase in the respect that is paid to them by managers, colleagues and by their staff. They commented that in some cases this is due to the status of foreign training; but more commonly their colleagues commented on their increased confidence and decision-making skills, particularly in meetings. 'Their attitude is that this lady is now a changed woman, with new skills and techniques at her disposal. So we should be aware of her.' Several had offered or been asked to undertake new activities since their return. A college lecturer and an assistant professor are now members of examination committees, formerly run only by male college staff. Another wrote a paper for a meeting with the Prime Minister.

However, the response of the women's line managers was mixed. Several were very interested in management, and keen to discuss international trends. Others were unable to identify any management skills required in the course participant's job, and one was only able to evaluate his woman officer in terms of her 'sincerity' and the fact that she is 'god fearing'. He was pleased to 'be surrounded with beautiful ladies'. A senior tax officer was extremely discouraging to the woman officer who was providing additional information to women. She reported that he said: 'Forget about public service, you are a government tax officer and it is not your responsibility to inform the taxpayer.'

Since they returned from the UK participants had been increasingly aware of the discrimination they faced:

What was new was my sense of men's 'disappreciation' for women in the department. I came to realize that it exists.

I never thought that there was any discrimination. After we came back and having the [gender] lenses on, I can always feel that people [that is, men] feel very differently about women colleagues. We are very much depressed about it, there is a great discrimination going on, we feel it very strongly now. I try to deal with it, I am still in the process.

Some have been able to use their new awareness to make changes.

We're still looked down upon as women but we're fighting.

Most colleagues have the same mentality about women that they had before. They have the same feelings and the same thoughts and views about women. But we are not like the women they think can do nothing. We are something different, we can give something. But we really can manage an office. My boss is realizing it – this is the difference.

The course increased our thinking power, made us effective, taught us about working in groups by which we became supportive, sharing and caring. The activities made us reflect and think deeply and explore possibilities, examine and scrutinize and be creative.

(Senior manager from Tanzania)

CONCLUSION

The Management Development for Women Programme continues and goes from strength to strength. Its main objective is to enable programme participants to intervene in the complex and unequal relations of power, and increase women's access to and control over resources. The first stage is for those unequal relations of power to become visible rather than being seen as natural. The '*gender lens*' has provided a powerful concept both to help bring into focus women's ubiquitous experiences of male power, and to make visible the way in which gender structures the differentials of power, not only within the bureaucracy, but also in other contexts.

It has been less easy to focus on other structures of power, such as class, and caste, rural/urban, ethnic differences, physical ability/disability and heterosexuality/lesbianism, for a range of reasons. Belonging to the Civil Service cadre brings with it a strongly developed set of notions of service users as *objects rather than subjects of development*. From a public administration perspective, it is harder to challenge the view of the poor as victims. The concept of *diversity* has been used to make visible some of these power differentials, and the different ways in which they operate in different cultures, using our analysis of gendered power as a template for perceiving differences structured by other factors.

Alongside this has been a focus on *empowerment*, in order for women to see both themselves and the clients of their services as subjects rather than objects of the development process. Leading on from this awareness, interventions by programme participants have varied according to context, but women who have participated in the programme are intervening in the relations of power within their organizations and in service delivery where they can. To do this they now re-engender those relations for women's benefit, a process which requires vision and strength and courage.

ACKNOWLEDGEMENT

The RIPA International Management Development for Women Programme was initiated by Jennifer Barnes. Thanks to her and to Sheena Matthews of RIPA International. The concept of a 'mini-climate' is from Jennifer Barnes. All quotations from participants are with permission: names have been changed.

REFERENCES

Barnes, J. (1992) *RIPA International Evaluation Report on the Management Development for Women Programme 1992*. London: RIPA International.

Goetz, A.M. (1992) 'Gender and administration'. *IDS Bulletin*, 23 (4), 6.

Hollway, W. (1991) 'Advantages and disadvantages for women managers'. *The Journal of Women in Organizations and Management*, 1, Dec.

Kabeer, N. (1992) 'Triple roles, gender roles, social relations: the political subtext of gender training'. IDS Discussion Paper, No. 313, November. Sussex: IDS.

Macalpine, M. (1993) *RIPA International Evaluation Report*. London: RIPA International.

Massiah J. (1990) 'Making the Invisible Visible'. Mimeo. Paris: UNESCO.

Moser, C. (1989) 'Gender planning in the third world: meeting practical and strategic gender needs'. *World Development*, 17 (11), 1799–1825.

Chapter 15

Gender, culture, power and change
A materialist analysis

Catherine Itzin

This chapter looks beyond gender and culture in organizations to consider their relationship to gender and culture in the wider society, and to articulate the implications for change. It develops a materialist analysis of gender and culture and uses what this reveals about the hierarchy of value and power between men and women to consider what change might mean and how it can be achieved.

We have called this book *Gender, Culture and Organizational Change*. Throughout we and our contributors have been concerned with, researched, described, analysed and theorized what has been termed by us and by others organizational 'culture' (Hofstede 1984; Handy 1985; Mills 1992), and throughout we have discussed issues of 'gender' as they are manifest within organizations. The primary – but not the sole – focus has been on what happens in organizations, for in different ways contributors have referred to the relationship between organizations and the wider social context. A number refer to women's domestic responsibilities, to childcare and unpaid work (Harlow, Hearn and Parkin; Itzin; Williams and Macalpine). There are references to racism in the education system and in organizations (Holder), the gender and ethnic composition of people who use services (Thobani; Newman). There is reference to women and the European economy (Cockburn), and to the international economy and the impact of structural adjustment on women in southern nations (Williams and Macalpine). There are references to social welfare, the labour market and the influence of neoliberal political ideology (Newman).

There is a need, however, to look more closely at these 'extra-organizational' dimensions: to explore the relationship between the concept of 'culture' as applied to organizations and what we understand as a/the culture of a society, or the cultures which make up a society, and the cultural products and representations of a society (as in art, literature and music, or pictures and words), and to articulate the implications. Put simply: to what extent is what we mean by 'organizational culture' the same as and different from 'social culture'?

Contributors to this book have a great deal to say about 'gender' as it has been identified within organizations, and reference is frequently made to some of the extra-organizational gender considerations that impact on gender in organizations, such as childbearing/rearing and domestic responsibilities. But we have not made explicit how far gender in organizations is the same as and different from gender in other spheres, and areas and aspects of life, society and experience. Are we talking about organizations as microcosms of the wider society and therefore of its culture(s) and gender relations, or organizations as constituent/component parts of the wider society, or both, or something else? What is the relationship between gender and culture in organizations, and gender and culture outside of organizations?

A central theme of this book is change: wanting it, doing it, making it (or trying to) and wondering whether it is possible. In a sense the book's very existence is premised on the possibility of change and the (explicit) assumptions that:

- organizations can change/be changed;
- organizational cultures can change;
- gender inequality can become equality – of access and status in organizations;
- people can change.

Implicit in these assumptions is another set of assumptions:

- that culture/s can (be) change(d);
- that gender inequality can become equality in society (acknowledging gender differences and using this as a basis for parity rather than differentials and discrimination).

How true is this, and how realistic – and how? Many ideas have been put forward in this book – and initiatives into practice – in pursuit of organizational change, but what evidence do we have that change of this nature can be achieved? If it can, by what processes would/does this occur? What would have to happen for the change which we have proposed in this book to occur, and how would we know that it had? And to what extent is change within organizations dependent or interdependent on change taking place outside of organizations – in the wider society?

The concept of 'social power relations' – which are gendered and also constructed on the basis of class and race and physical ability – is central to this book, and to the approach to gender, culture and organizational change of a number of contributors. Williams and Macalpine teach their management development for women in 'developing countries' from a perspective of social power relations and, using a 'gender lens', show how these are gendered in every area of intra and extra-organizational experience. They also construct a framework of social power relations that includes both race and the structural economic inequality between the north and the south of the globe (which in itself is race-based and currently in the process of being 'structurally adjusted' to increase the inequalities of wealth and resources). Harlow, Hearn and Parkin discuss gendered domination, power relations and the 'silence and din' of oppression within organizations. In my chapters I refer to 'gendered power relations', and Newman and Williams discuss the interrelatedness of different forms of power and oppression and the compounding effects of gender, race and class.

'Gendered power relations' is a term that is used frequently in this book, but what does it mean and what are its implications, with respect, for example, to change? Can power relations change? If so, how? Nationalist, ethnic, territorial, ideological and international economic power relations usually change through revolution and war (and national economic and ethnic power relations through civil war). Does this imply that a balance of power only shifts through threats of violence or use of violence? Does it only shift from one extreme to another – wholly from one 'side' to another? Can power imbalances be balanced? If so, is it through processes of change, as this book implies, or only through upheaval? If we are not simply using the terms metaphorically, these questions are crucial to a consideration of gender, culture and organizational change. It is not possible therefore to conclude this book without considering gender, culture – power – and *social* change, and theorizing the relationships between them. By way of trying to address these issues, I want to develop a materialist analysis of gender and culture as they apply to society in general and organizations in particular, and to use this as a basis from which to consider what change might mean.

GENDER AND CULTURE IN THE WIDER SOCIAL CONTEXT

One of the central tenets of this book is its belief in the value of, and its basis in, 'grounded theory': that is, deriving theory from experience and practice. Frequently the preferred methodology of organizational change has involved the use of 'research', exploring the experience of women and men who work in organizations to evidence, to understand and to theorize gender relations in organizations, and to facilitate change (Itzin; French; Parkin and Maddock; Itzin and Phillipson; Nottage; White). Research methods have often been 'biographical' (work history interviews) and 'experiential' (group interviews/discussions).

Similarly, the starting point for a materialist analysis of gender and culture in the wider society will be a consideration of gender relations as they are lived, experienced and practised, and can be empirically evidenced. Such an analysis must cover work in both the public and the private spheres: the labour market, places of employment and the family. It will include work which is both paid and unpaid. It will cover gender-based violence and abuse as it occurs in all spheres: in the workplace, on the streets and in the family. It will include what is sometimes called the sphere of ideology, ideas, attitudes and beliefs, and how these are acquired through processes of socialization. Last but not least, it will cover the material and the media through which ideas, attitudes and beliefs are communicated: what is sometimes referred to as forms of 'representation'.

In every case it will look to see:

- What is happening?
- Who does what to whom? For whom?
- Who does the work? What is defined as work and what is not?
- Who gets paid?

- Who are the owners? Of property? Of wealth?
- Who controls the money?
- Who is richer than whom?
- Who is hurt, harmed or abused? By whom?
- Who holds the economic, physical, sexual, social and political power?

Sex segregation in the labour market

Women currently constitute 40 per cent of the UK workforce (Kremer and Montgomery 1993). Of women of working age, 72 per cent are in paid employment, contributing approximately one-third of the average weekly household income (Family Expenditure Survey 1991). The majority of women work part-time and the majority of part-time workers are women: of the 4.5 million part-time workers in Britain, 87 per cent are women, and 44 per cent of all women employees work part-time (EOC 1993). There has been an overall increase in the proportion of women working in paid employment over the post-war period. This increase has been almost entirely in part-time work: there has been no increase in women working full-time since 1951 (Joshi 1989; Hakim 1993). The labour market is segregated by sex, both laterally and vertically. Of the 72 per cent of women who are in paid employment, 90 per cent are employed in service occupations. The service sector employs 88 per cent of all part-time workers.

In all sectors of the labour market, women are located in the low grade, low paid, low-status, sex-segregated work. Recent research in banks and building societies found 100 per cent recruitment of women as cashiers and 100 per cent recruitment of men at branch manager level (Ashburner 1991). Recent research has shown that top female managers in the National Health Service work harder than men and are paid less. In addition, male nurses achieve their first management post within 8.4 years on average: female nurses who do not take a 'career break' for children reach the same level on average in 14.5 years (DH 1992). In education, only 3 per cent of professors and principal lecturers are women. In business, only 8 per cent of managers of large companies are women (Byrne 1994). In medicine, only 2 per cent of general surgeons are women, only 12.5 per cent of consultants in obstetrics and gynaecology are female, and only 15 per cent of all consultants are women (Bock and James 1992). In the civil service, only 9 per cent of top posts are held by women (OPSS 1993). In law, male solicitors achieve partnership at twice the rate of women, and three times as many women as men remain assistant solicitors (Hansard Society 1990). In retail, only seven of Sainsbury's 316 stores have women managers (Figes 1994).

Gender-based earning differentials

In Britain the gross monthly earnings of non-manual women workers is, on average, 54 per cent of men's, as compared to 66 per cent in France and nearly 70 per cent in Germany (Rubery 1993). Of the 11 million women in employment in Britain, 3 million earn such low wages they do not appear on national statistical databases (Figes 1994). Low pay is routinely to be found in the low status, sex-segregated occupations: only 4 per cent of secretarial staff, for example, earn over £15,000, and most earn under £10,000 (EOC 1993). But even when women find themselves in the traditionally male-dominated professions, their earnings are less than men's. The earnings of women solicitors working full-time, for example, are only 74 per cent of men's (EOC 1993).

Largely, however, it is part-time work (the majority of which is done by women), which is low paid, without benefits and employment protection, where the gender-based earnings differentials are 'institutionalized' in the labour market. Figes (1994: 134) provides case studies of women working part-time in retail services which illustrate their exploitation as part-time workers. One woman worked four nights a week from 9.30 p.m. to 6 a.m. for Tesco together with 43 other people, 80 per cent of whom were women with children. Only 4 of the 44 staff qualified for full-time status of 36 hours per week: 'her hours on the night shift (34) fall just two hours short of full time status, disqualifying her from a pension contribution paid by her employer and from paid breaks or bank holidays on a pro-rata basis'. At one Co-op branch 90 per cent of staff were employed for less than 30 hours: all women. One store in Leicester only hired people for a maximum of 7 hours per week. A woman 'section manager store instructor' with Sainsbury worked a 40-hour week from 10 a.m. to 6 p.m. five days a week, but because her breaks were not paid for this counted as less than the full-time period of 39 hours per week. She was paid on a part-time hourly rate and earned £100 less per week than she would have on a full-time hourly rate.

Paying part-timers less pro rata than full-time workers and not paying for breaks or holidays is increasingly common in retail industries (Howell and Rubery 1992; Figes 1994). The hourly costs of part-time workers have been calculated at 12 per cent less than their full-time equivalents. The same overall working time can be bought more cheaply from two or more people working part-time than from one working full-time. Employers are not required to pay National Insurance on earnings of less than £54 per week. This 'saving' for employers costs women their entitlement to unemployment benefit, maternity pay and a state pension. Recent legislation (the Employment Protection Act 1993) stipulates that part-timers working less than 16 hours per week fail to qualify for the same protection against dismissal as full-time employees, and the abolition of the Wages Council and the minimum wage (1994) removed the statutory protection preventing women's low pay falling even lower.

Women's poverty

According to government figures (1992), the number of women living in poverty (defined as income below 50 per cent of the mean after deduction of housing costs) had increased from 2.2 million in 1979 to 5.8 million in 1988. Of all adults supported by income support, 63 per cent are women. Women represent the majority of claimants of most of the major benefits, other than contributory ones, paid to people below pension age; and are therefore disproportionately reliant on means-tested benefits and lower value categories of benefits. Although there has been an increase in women's access to independent income through paid employment, labour market trends have been reducing women's opportunity to earn a sufficient income to support themselves and their children because of the predominance of and increase in women in low paid, part-time work (Lister 1992).

Women's poverty in later life

Elderly women are substantially more likely to live in poverty than elderly men (Arber and Ginn 1991). Two and a quarter million women currently earn too little to contribute to a state pension (Figes 1994: 147). In addition, the increase in the divorce rate has increased the number of women who have lost their husband's pension. Low incomes and career breaks mean that personal pensions are of little value to women. Occupational pension schemes favour men because they have higher earnings, have fewer gaps in employment, and are more likely to work for an employer who provides a good pension scheme (Groves 1987; Figes 1994). According to Arber and Ginn (1991: 83), 'women's lower personal income in later life is related to the domestic division of labour and lower earnings during periods of paid employment, reinforced by pension schemes which are based on the assumption of women's dependence on a male breadwinner.' The 'equalizing' of women's retirement age to the age of 65 (where it has always been for men) has further reduced women's retirement income and increased women's poverty in later life.

Paid employment and the burden of children

Children are the main reason women work part-time: 90 per cent of women have at least one child, and most women with children work part-time. The Women's Employment Survey 1980 found that 'most women leave the labour force for several years following childbirth, that the presence of dependent children has a major effect on the economic activity of many women' and 'that the presence of children, and the age of the youngest child, were by far the most important determinants of whether or not women work' (Martin and Roberts 1984: 123). Furthermore, women with children under 16 were more likely to be working part-time than full-time. In 1980, 84 per cent of women without children were working (78 per cent full-time and 6 per cent part-time), compared with 27 per cent of women with children under 5 (7 per cent part-time, 20 per cent full-time) rising to 64 per cent of women with children aged 5–10 (20 per cent full-time and 44 per cent part-time) and 75 per cent of women with children aged 11–15 (30 per cent full-time and 45 per cent part-time) (Martin and Roberts 1984: 13). Martin and Roberts also found that one-third of women who returned to work full-time changed to part-time.

According to Joshi (1990), the earnings of a woman who works full-time from the age of 17, who then takes a 'career break' for eight years to have two children and returns to work part-time while her children are at school, will be 57 per cent lower than the lifetime earnings of someone who works full-time without a break to have children: she will lose about £122,000, almost half of her possible earnings after the age of 15. Women who return to the labour market having left to have children frequently return at a lower level. Over one-quarter of the women in the Women's Employment Survey who returned to work on a part-time basis within a year returned at a lower level, and 44 per cent of those who took a break of 1–5 years (Martin and Roberts 1984).

Britain falls behind most European countries in its statutory maternity provisions. The Employment Protection Act 1993 gives all women an entitlement to 14 weeks' maternity leave regardless of length of employment, but only one in five women currently qualifies for statutory maternity pay. In France women receive 16 weeks' maternity leave at 84 per cent of earnings, and in Italy it is 20 weeks at 80 per cent. In the UK, there are only 12,500 workplace nurseries which provide full-time care for children under the age of 5 (EOR 1992), though there has been a very substantial increase in the market for private nurseries (a 259 per cent increase) and childminders (a 137 per cent increase) in response to the increase in women's employment over the last ten years. In France, where day care provision is generous, 38 per cent of women with children under the age of 5 work full-time and only 14 per cent work part-time (Dale and Joshi 1992). The effects of having children on the career opportunities of women is reflected in an Institute of Management survey which found that one-third of its women members were unmarried, and only half had children, whereas 92 per cent of its men members were married and 86 per cent had children (Coe 1992).

Women's work in the family

More than 80 per cent of people in Western countries at any one time live in households with people to whom they are related by marriage or descent (Delphy and Leonard 1992). In her classic study on housework, Oakley (1974) found that the minimum number of hours women with children spent doing housework in a seven-day week was 40 hours: the majority worked 70–90 hours per week and some did more than 100 hours. Oakley found that the participation of 85 per cent of husbands in housework was low (60 per cent) or medium (25 per cent), and the participation of 75 per cent of the husbands in childcare was low (45 per cent) or medium (30 per cent). Of the men in her sample, 75 per cent did not change their babies' nappies. The Women's Employment Survey of 5588 women and 799 of their partners, carried out in 1980 by the Department of Employment and OPCS, found that 'in most couples the wife is the primary houseworker, doing all or most of the housework. Even when they worked full time, only a minority of wives said they shared housework equally with their husbands' (Martin and Roberts 1984: 186). The Working Women's Lives Survey of 1000 women of working age, carried out by the Northern Ireland Equal Opportunities Commission in 1990, suggested that little had changed in the sexual division of labour in the household over the preceding twenty-five years. Seventy-one per cent of women said that they carried out all or most of the housework themselves: only a quarter said that housework was shared with their partners (and their definition of sharing varied from helping a lot to helping a little). Of the men, 73 per cent never did the washing and 82 per cent never did the ironing. Over a third of husbands never carried out 'the basic household chores of shopping and cleaning and a quarter never cooked a meal' (Montgomery 1993: 30).

Even in dual earner families where both partners worked full-time, all or most of the housework was done by the majority (57 per cent) of women. Oakley captured the 'quantity' of women's domestic work in dual earner families in a qualitative account of 'Mrs Benson, an architect married to an architect (they both work at home) who described the beginning of her workday thus':

07.55   Remind son of time
08.45   Mend daughter's nightdress
09.15   Organize a party and the day's laundry
09.45   Go to shops, laundry, chemist – thread, plant, fish, buns, polish
11.05   Get office coffee, lay out day's laundry
11.40   Work finally started.

'During the same period Mr Benson got up at nine, read his mail, started his office work at ten, and worked through until lunch at one' (Oakley 1974: 119). Overall, the results of the Working Women's Lives Survey 'found that the majority of women continue to carry out the bulk of housework regardless of whether or not they have a paid job', findings confirmed by studies in Britain of 'women working part time receiving little help from their partners despite the fact that the domestic burden will be high for these women, many of whom will be combining paid work with caring for young children' (Montgomery 1993: 29–30).

As with housework, the Northern Ireland survey found that in most cases it was women who carried out the childcare: the majority of women (57 per cent) said they did all or most of the childcare. This was consistent with findings of the Northern Ireland Social Attitudes Survey (Montgomery and Davis 1991), where the majority of men (84 per cent) and women (89 per cent) reported that the responsibility for childcare belonged to the wives. In the Women's Working Lives Survey, it was 'noteworthy that between a quarter and a fifth of fathers had *never* carried out the basic childcare tasks of washing or bathing their children, changing a child's nappy, getting up at night to attend to a child or reading to their children' (Montgomery 1993: 36). Even when women work full-time, they are still largely responsible for housework and childcare (British Social Attitudes Survey 1992).

What these data describe is the unpaid work women do in the family, instead of men and for men. Delphy and Leonard (1992) consider the family as an economic system and explore the economic relationships within the family to show how these are both gendered and hierarchically structured to the advantage and benefit of men.

They define women's work in the family in terms of the 'practical' work quantified by Oakley and the Women's Working Lives Survey: washing, ironing, shopping, cleaning, cooking. They categorize 'childcare' as the bearing and rearing of children. They also include the economic work that women often do to support their husband's employment, especially when he is self-employed. More unusually, they include the 'emotional work' of 'establishing relations of solidarity, maintaining bonds of affection and providing moral support, friendships and love, which gives people a sense of belonging, of ontological strength, of empowerment and thereby making them feel good' (Delphy and Leonard 1992: 21). Controversially, they also include the work of 'sexually servicing men'. They found that the working week of a full-time housewife was 60–80 hours a week and 'has not declined during the course of this century', that 'the proportion of housework done by wives has actually increased this century', and that 'men never do much housework' (pp.75–6). They conclude that domestic work is work that is unpaid and mainly done by women for men.

Gender-based violence and abuse

Women are routinely the objects of physical, emotional and sexual violence and abuse perpetrated by men. It has been estimated that as many as a third of women are survivors of child sexual abuse (Kelly 1987). In the USA the Kinsey surveys in the 1950s found that 28 per cent of women had experienced sexual abuse before the age of 13 (Gagnon 1965). Finkelhor (1979) found a prevalence rate of 19 per cent of child sexual abuse. Russell (1983) found the prevalence of intrafamilial child sexual abuse to be 16 per cent and that of extrafamilial abuse to be 31 per cent. In the UK, 80 per cent of recorded cases of child sexual abuse between 1983 and 1987 took place in the children's own home (Creighton and Noyes 1989). Hall (1985) found that 16 per cent of her sample had been raped or sexually assaulted before the age of 16, and in a study of 3000 readers of *19* magazine, 20 per cent had been abused by adult men in a position of authority or trust. A survey of 4000 women readers of *Cosmopolitan* magazine in 1990 found that 13 per cent of women said they had been sexually abused as children and 34 per cent had been raped (10 per cent) or sexually assaulted (24 per cent) (Itzin and Sweet 1990).

The incidence of reported rape increases annually: by 29 per cent in 1985, 24 per cent in 1986, 8 per cent in 1987, 16 per cent in 1988, 16 per cent in 1989, 21 per cent in 1990, 18 per cent in 1991 and 12.6 per cent in 1993/4 (Home Office Criminal Statistics 1985–94). It is officially acknowledged that rape is massively under-reported: police estimate that only a quarter of such crimes are reported. Hall (1985), in a survey of 1236 women in the UK, recorded a prevalence of 21 per cent for rape and 20 per cent for attempted rape. A survey of 1574 women (largely students) in the UK in 1991 found that 11 per cent said they had been raped, 20 per cent had been victims of rape or attempted rape, and 28 per cent had been victims of unwanted sex (Beattie 1992). That only 2 per cent of the women who had been raped said they had reported it to the police supports the official view that rape is a significantly under-reported crime of sexual violence. In addition, over a third of the women who said they had been raped had been raped more than once. The questions in this survey were taken directly from the survey instruments used by Koss *et al.* (1987) in a national survey of undergraduates in the USA: none of the questions actually used the word 'rape' but they described the activity (for example, 'Have you had sexual intercourse when you didn't want to because a man used or threatened some degree of physical force – eg. twisting your arm or holding you down – to make you?'). The findings were similar in Britain and the USA.

Of the rapes in the Cambridge study, 84 per cent were carried out not by strangers, but by men known to the women. A survey in 1993 of a randomized representative sample of 571 women and 429 men in North London found that just under a quarter (23 per cent) of the women had been raped by their partners, with threats of violence to one in seven of the women and with actual violence to one in ten of the women surveyed (Mooney 1994). Of the women, 6 per cent had been raped in the previous twelve months.

This study defined domestic violence as 'mental cruelty' (including verbal abuse, being deprived of money, clothes or sleep, being prevented from going out), 'threats of violence or force', 'actual physical violence' (being grabbed, pushed, shaken, punched or slapped, kicked or head-butted, suffering attempted strangulation, being hit with a weapon or object), and 'injuries' (bruising or black eye, scratches, cuts, bones broken) as well as 'rape'. Of the women in this sample, 30 per cent had experienced domestic violence so defined in their lifetimes: the prevalence in the previous twelve months was physical violence (12 per cent), threats of violence (8 per cent) and mental cruelty (12 per cent). Only 22 per cent of the women surveyed had reported this violence to the police.

One in five of the men surveyed in this study said they would react violently *every time* they were 'confronted with infidelity, being nagged, their partner always late home without an explanation, a heated row, or when expectations over housework or childcare were not met' (Mooney 1994: 63). The same proportion (19 per cent) admitted to actually using violence against their partners in at least one of these circumstances, and only 37 per cent of the men said they would never use violence against their partners.

Although domestic violence is substantially under-reported (according to British Crime Statistics 1992, only one-fifth of all incidents are reported to the police), nevertheless official statistics provide an indication of the scale of 'violence against women by known – and unknown – men' and some of its effects:

- Around 45 per cent of female homicide victims were killed by present or former partners (Criminal Statistics 1992, Home Office).
- Domestic violence offences comprise around 25 per cent of all assaults recorded by the police (British Crime Statistics 1989; Jones *et al.* 1986; Dobash and Dobash 1980) and around 10–15 per cent of all offences of violence against the person (Violent Crime Survey, Home Office 1989).

- Around a third of all divorces result from violence by husbands against wives (Parker 1985).
- In 1993, 17,000 households were accepted as homeless by local authorities in England by reason of a breakdown in a relationship with a partner due to violence (Department of the Environment 1993).
- Every year the Women's Aid Federation England (WAFE) provides help and refuge for around 30,000 women and children escaping domestic violence; a further 100,000 are given help and support.
- Women entering refuges have been beaten 35 times on average (WAFE).
- Forty per cent of abused women have difficulty sleeping; 46 per cent feel depressed and lose confidence (Mooney 1994).
- Of women abused by partners/husbands, 50–65 per cent seek help from their doctor (Pahl 1985).
- Eighty per cent of abused women seek medical help at least once and 40 per cent seek it on a minimum of 5 separate occasions (Dobash *et al.* 1985).
- One-third of social work cases involve domestic violence (Maynard 1985).

The *Cosmopolitan* survey (Itzin and Sweet 1990) found that 60 per cent of women reported having been sexually harassed, a figure that is frequently reported in surveys. Oftel, the British Telecom Watchdog, reported figures of 10 million obscene phone calls made in 1991 almost exclusively by men and targeted at women. A *Living* Magazine survey (1989) found that more than one in three women had received an obscene phone call in the previous five years; 20 per cent had received more than one; and 74 per cent of women who had received an obscene phone call had not reported it.

GENDERED POWER RELATIONS: A MATERIALIST ANALYSIS

What does all of this have to do with gender, culture and organizational change? The answer is 'everything'. These statistical data and research results provide a picture of gender relations in the culture of the wider society: the context in which organizations – with their cultures and their gender relations – are situated. These are the *material* economic, social, physical, emotional and sexual conditions and circumstances of women's lives in relation to men's: the *material* differences that exist in the relations between women and men in every sphere.

Delphy and Leonard (1992: 13) borrow from Marxism to develop a 'materialist approach' to seeing and understanding 'family households as gendered hierarchies' where women's work is exploited on behalf of and in relation to men: one of the 'diverse forms of... inter-connected and mutually sustaining' divisions of a 'system of male domination'. A materialist approach to the labour market and paid employment which is gendered as I have described it in this brief account shows women's position to be one of systematic exploitation, subordination and relative valuelessness in relation to and by comparison with men. Extending a materialist approach to gender-based violence and abuse and identifying who is doing what harm and injury to whom makes it possible to see the extent to which women are systematically subordinated through physical, emotional and sexual violence. The incidence and prevalence of gender-based violence and abuse is itself evidence of the status and value of women.

The social construction of identity

There is a very substantial literature and body of knowledge on sexual and sex-role socialization and education (Oakley 1972; Chetwynd and Hartnett 1978; Hartnett *et al.* 1979; Archer and Lloyd 1982), on sexism in education (Spender and Sarah 1980; Delamont 1980; Mahony 1985), on the social construction of sexuality (Jackson 1980, 1982; Weeks 1981, 1986; Coveney *et al.* 1984: Lees 1986; Itzin 1986, 1992b), on social learning (Bandura 1971), and on the psychoanalytic processes of gendering (Chodorow, 1971, 1974, 1978; Sayers 1982, 1986; Hollway 1985, 1995). These different but complementary disciplines (psychology, sociology, social psychology and psychoanalysis) are concerned with the complex and various ways in which gender identity and behaviour is learned, internalized and then 'practiced'. Part of what is learned is the hierarchy of gender – male dominance and female subordination – and some of the literature is concerned with the extent to which gender, identity and value are internalized through the routine practice and experience of gendered dominance and subordination in the sphere of representation: the sexual objectification, sexualizing and sex stereotyping of women in all forms of media.

A TUC study (1984) identified certain key sex-role stereotypes: women as the sex symbols of a consumer society (in advertisements and in the emulation of pop and film stars), 'women whose only concerns are the welfare and needs of their immediate families', and a systematic concentration on 'appearance, sexuality and domestic relations' (p. 9). A similar pattern of sex-role stereotyping was documented by the Women's Media Action Group (WMAG) when they monitored the media over the years from 1981 to 1983 and found eleven categories of gratuitous sexualizing and sex-objectification. An Equal Opportunities Commission survey (Hamilton *et al.* 1982) of sexism and advertising concluded that in TV commercials women are 'predominantly portrayed in the traditional roles of housewife and mother, as being essentially dependent on or in need of men's protection or, of course, simply as sexual objects' (p. 38).

In a content analysis of the three best-selling women's magazines (*Woman, Woman's Own* and *Woman's Weekly*), covering the years 1949–74 and 1979–80, Ferguson (1983) found that well over half of the themes were concerned with getting and keeping a man and maintaining a happy family (67 per cent). Just under half (46 per cent) of the roles represented for women were that of wife and mother – or women trying to get married (the would-be wives). Only 3 per cent of themes concerned 'working wives' and only 7 per cent 'women with careers'. Only 12 per cent of the content held out achievement in society as a goal for women (pp. 39–47). Ferguson describes the content of women's magazines as representing the 'cult of femininity', and says 'the fact that women's magazines exist at all makes a statement about the position of women in society.'

Ballaster *et al.* (1991) illustrate the ways that women's magazines 'focus firmly on that which is socially defined as "women's world" – the domestic, the familial or the intimate, sexual and personal' (p. 129), using different 'discourses' with the 'common ground of feminity' (p. 111) and presenting 'a normative model of femininity' (p. 139). Women's magazines present 'women's concerns' as being 'with personal and emotional relationships. primarily with husbands or partners, but also with children, family and friends' (p. 137). They see 'sexuality as central to the cultural constructions of the feminine' (p. 141) – as does Winship (1987) – and find 'paid employment effectively all but ignored' (p. 153). They express concern about the impact of stereotypes and conclude that the 'construction of femininity' they find in magazines is not harmless or innocuous (p. 131).

Women's magazines, according to Ferguson, teach women 'what to think and what to do about themselves' and their relationships: a lesson in passivity and submission to men, who are portrayed as 'dominant, active and authoritative' (p. 5). Ferguson concluded that women's magazines act as 'agents of socialisation ... with implications for how the gender characteristics of females are acquired, and how the position of women in society is determined' (p. 6). Winship (1983) also recognized the influence of women's magazines in moulding women's experiences: 'women's magazines provide what can be described as "mirror images" for women, ie. public images of femininity against which women measure themselves, men judge women, and which are, therefore, formative in actually shaping women's experiences' (p. 6).

Similarly, Goffman (1979: 8) analyses gender advertisements as representing 'male dominance' and 'female subordination ... affirming the place that persons of the female sex-class have in the social structure, in other words, holding them to it... an alignment which does not merely express subordination, but in part constitutes it'. Goffman sees advertisements not as a 'natural expression', but as artifice, a construction communicating stereotyped information about masculinity and femininity: 'Because these stereotypes begin to be applied by and to the individual from the earliest years, the account it affords is rather well implanted' (p. 8). Whatever the media, research has shown that what is represented and communicated is learned. Children, for example, by the age of 5 have internalized beliefs about sex-stereotyped occupations for women and men, even when roles are reversed in their own family (Smithers and Zientek 1991).

Advertisements and women's magazines are examples of media in which women are sexually objectified and their work is sex stereotyped. Pornography is the material which sexualizes violence and abuse against women and women's subordination (Itzin 1992a). In currently available commercial pornography women are reduced to their genitals and anuses, posed open and gaping, inviting sexual access and penetration, and women are presented as constantly sexually available, insatiable and voracious, or passive and servile, servicing men sexually. This is the standard content of most of the seventy-three 'top shelf' titles sold in the UK newsagents. High Street newsagents also sell 'specialist' magazines devoted to the beating and humiliation of school girls and to sexual violence: for example, a woman masked and chained, her genitals exposed, another in dog collar and leather straps, legs trussed up like a chicken ready for stuffing (Itzin 1992c): common to all of this material is the portrayal of women as enjoying being raped, sexually abused and humiliated. This is the material that sells legally in the UK (Itzin and Sweet 1989, 1992).

Illegal material is also easily available. Researchers for a Channel 4 programme on pornography in 1992 purchased titles in Soho sex shops like *Peachfuzz Pussies* and *300 Baby Dolls* promoting child sexual abuse, and sexually violent torture material where women have metal clips on their nipples, are tied in painful and humiliating positions, gagged, with breasts clamped and squeezed and objects inserted in their vaginas. Material in which women are shown having sex with animals is easily available in the UK (Itzin and Wingfield 1992). There is also evidence of the existence of 'snuff films' where women are sexually murdered on camera (Corcoran 1989; Itzin 1992).

All this material is sold as 'sex' for the 'entertainment' of men, part of a multi-million pound international industry (Cohen 1989; Baxter 1990; I Spy Productions 1992; Cowe 1993). Monthly sales of the six most popular of the seventy-plus titles sold in the UK are estimated conservatively to be 2.5 million per month (Baker 1992). In the sexually explicit, sexualized context of pornography, the dehumanization and subordination of women in 'legal' pornography and the violence and torture of women in 'illegal' pornography are not recognized as such (MacKinnon 1984). A materialist analysis of pornography makes visible the harm experienced by women and children through the manufacture and use of pornography. A materialist analysis also makes explicit the gendered power relations that are being practised and promoted, legitimated and 'learned', and considers the function of representation in the construction of ideas, fantasy, imagination and desire, and the influence of representation, through these processes, on action and behaviour (Kappeler 1986; Cameron and Frazer 1987, 1992).

These various forms of representation have implications for the analysis of organizations as symbolic domains, for an understanding of the gendered power relations that operate within organizations, and for change strategies. Although this is an under-researched and under-theorized aspect of organizations, a number of the contributors to this book do illustrate some of the material effects of gender representation and socialization on the culture, structure and practices of organizations. Newman and Williams (Chapter 7) make the link between social divisions and identity. Harlow, Hearn and Parkin (Chapter 6) refer to the construction of gendered subjects by means of language and conscious and unconscious processes. In our research on age and gender, Phillipson and I (Chapter 5) explore the influence of individual attitudes and beliefs on organizational behaviour, and find evidence not only that men's attitudes and beliefs about women, but also women's attitudes and beliefs about themselves conform to the stereotypes of 'oppression', indicating the extent to which gender identity is constructed negatively and the 'oppression internalized.' My chapter on crafting strategy (Chapter 8) identifies ways in which women hinder the progress of other women and fail to recognize (or resist acknowledging) the institutional subordination of women. Parkin and Maddock's gender typology (Chapter 4) illustrates some characteristics of internalized masculinity and the negative effects of this on and for women.

Male and female chronology

It is also possible and instructive to apply a materialist analysis to gender differences in the lifecycle patterns of women and men: to time. Institutional and industrial employment and public policy in Britain are 'based on a model of full time permanent employment stretching from the completion of full time education to the onset of full time retirement and organized around standard working days, weeks and years' (Hewitt 1993: 1). This remains the case in spite of massive changes in the organization of work, some of which have been considered in this book (Newman; Newman and Williams; Cockburn).

This has always been the case, even though it is an organization of work that relates to the male chronology and not to the female chronology (Itzin 1990). The female chronology is defined significantly by marriage, motherhood, domestic labour, and the effects of sexualization. It is characterized by downward social mobility (defined officially by socio-economic status) often on marriage and almost always on motherhood (Itzin 1989), by the movement of women in and out of the labour market during the lifecycle (Delphy and Leonard 1992), and by movement between part-time and full-time employment (Martin and Roberts 1984). It is also characterized by caring: for children, elders, dependants and men, in both paid and unpaid capacities.

The female chronology thus defined fails to take account of the fact that childrearing is a short term 'career': sixteen years from birth to young adulthood for one child, up to twenty or twenty-five years for an overlapping age group of children. Even for women who leave paid employment completely to raise children for this length of time (statistically rare), 'motherhood' occupies only about half of an adult working lifespan from age 20 to age 60 or 65. There are some forty years of life expectancy and twenty to twenty-five years of productive working life for women after childrearing. And the majority of women work throughout their adult years.

Hewitt (1993: 11) describes the 'typical male pattern ... of continuous employment, the typical female pattern ... of discontinuous employment'. There have been significant changes in women's employment ('more employment, less family' and 'less full time, more part time'), but not to the pattern of discontinuity. Hewitt points out that the 'new model of post-industrial working time ... is much closer to female than to male patterns of the past' (p. 6), but that the 'shape of men's working lives has not yet fundamentally altered' (p. 9). Organizations still operate on the model of the male chronology and are resistant and inflexible in accommodating the patterns of the female chronology, as this book has demonstrated. Indeed, many of the 'change' initiatives described in this book are primarily attempts to try to shift the cultures, structures and practices of organizations to accommodate the patterns of the female chronology.

Value

The male and female chronologies are in part about time, as is the organization of work (Hewitt 1993), but they are not just about time. They are also about value. A man's life is largely defined by and takes its meaning and value from work, whether or not he marries or has children. Within the male chronology, the social power and value of males usually only decreases in the absence of paid employment. By contrast, in so far as women's lives are defined and are supposed to take their meaning from marriage and motherhood, they are valued according to sexuality, sexual attractiveness, sexual availability and sexual usefulness (or conversely according to the social control of women's sexuality). This appears to be true across social class and whether or not a woman is in paid employment or has a career. However much women may need to work, want to work and actually do work, they are rarely defined or valued in relation to their employment, and much more likely to be valued in terms of their sexuality or their work as wives and mothers, or in relation to their husband's employment.

Inherently, the work of mothering is work of great value and by any essential standard (reproducing the species/raising the next generation) not less and probably more valuable than any other work. But it is not valued remuneratively and is generally not even referred to as work at all. It is a 'role' or a 'responsibility', and it is called 'childrearing' or 'childcare' or 'raising a family'. 'Keeping house' or 'domestic responsibilities' (meaning shopping, cooking, cleaning) are also work. And in so far as they involve 'looking after' husbands/partners, it is invisible work that is done for men, for domestic responsibilities usually include cooking 'his' meals, washing and ironing 'his' clothes, and 'cleaning' the house that 'he' also lives in, just as 'childcare' means looking after 'his' children. There have been a number of attempts to assess the monetary value of housework (Stephen 1980; Chadeau 1985). The value of the work women do in the family, if it were done for pay outside of the family and sold in the labour market, was estimated at £12,000 in 1987 at a time when men's median earnings were £13,000 (Delphy and Leonard 1992: 103). In 1993 Legal and General Insurance calculated the value of women's work in the home at £18,000 per annum, based on the average housewife's timetable and costing domestic labour by the equivalent hourly wage rates from employment agencies (Oulton 1993).

'Caring' – as in caring for elderly and disabled members of the family – is also work which women have always done in large numbers, and increasingly since the implementation of the NHS and Community Care Act 1990. Care in the community is another form of unpaid work done by women, which has been estimated to save the state between £15 and £24 billion per annum in community care costs (FPSC 1989). None of this work is remunerated, and it does not carry social status or institutional power or influence. It is invisible as work, largely done in isolation, and in a relationship of economic dependency on men.

The 'public sphere' is generally used to denote the domain in which men are dominant and the 'private sphere' as the place in which women exercise power and influence. A materialist analysis of gender and culture, however, shows that women are active participants in the public sphere, in so far as they are permitted to be so, and that the private sphere is also dominated by men, in the forms of male violence and abuse and the appropriation of women's domestic labour for men's benefit and advantage. From a materialist perspective, the language and ideology of 'spheres' (separate but equal) contributes to keeping men and men's work visible and valued and women and women's work invisible and unvalued. It also conceals the incidence and prevalence of violence against women.

Applying a materialist analysis to the public and the private spheres and indeed to the lifecycle in this way shows that, in all spheres *in* time and *over* time (where age and gender intersect and sexuality is a decisive factor), gender relations are defined by a hierarchy of value and power in which men are routinely and normally dominant and women subordinated economically, socially, physically and sexually. It shows that these gendered power relations are systematic and endemic, that in every situation and in every sphere women experience exploitation and subordination and are valued less than men. There is evidence from every aspect of the public and the private spheres that there is a hierarchy of value and power in all relations between women and men which is gendered. Men and what men do are accorded greater value than women and what women do.

This is the wider social – and gender – context in which organizations are situated and operate, so it is not surprising to find these aspects of gendered power relations institutionalized in the culture, structures and practices of organizations: reflecting, replicating, reinforcing, recreating and constructing within themselves the gendered power relations of the wider society. In the simplest terms: what happens in the wider society happens in organizations. The relationship between gendered and other power relations in the wider society and organizations can be illustrated graphically (see Figure 15.1) as a series of concentric circles with organizations at the centre, surrounded by the labour market, the family, gender-based violence and abuse, the processes of education and socialization, and representation. These circles are dissected by the characteristics which are used as the basis for constructing social divisions on grounds of gender, race, class, physical and mental ability, age and sexuality. The effect of social divisions on identity in the context of the wider society can be illustrated graphically (see Figure 15.2) by another set of concentric circles, with the individual now at the centre, influenced by family, education and socialization, representation, organizations and the labour market, and by a combination of factors relating to gender, race, class, age, ability and sexuality.

All of this is what constitutes 'gendered power relations' and what characterizes gender as it is institutionalized in the culture, structures and practices of the wider society: or conversely, this is 'the gender culture' of the wider society. Taken

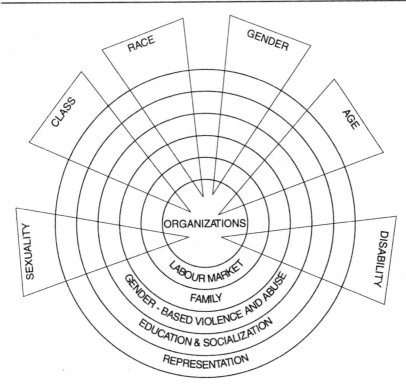

Figure 15.1   The relationship between gendered and other power relations in organizations

together, it provides both evidence of and a measure of the value of women and how women are valued. We can see, clearly I hope, that women's value is low in every aspect of every 'sphere', always lower than men's: there is a system – or systems, interconnected and mutually supportive – in which men are dominant and women are subordinate, in relation to what is valued and how it is valued: always.

IMPLICATIONS FOR CHANGE

Visibility

Contributors to this book have, in Janet Newman's words (Chapter 16), 'surfaced' the many ways in which women are subordinate in organizations. They have also made women visible by researching women's experience (giving women a voice) and theorizing about organizations on the basis of this research. This surfacing and making visible is an important part of the processes of valuing women and women's work. What is invisible and unaccounted cannot be valued: it 'counts for nothing' (Waring 1988, 1989). Making and keeping women's work and its value invisible,

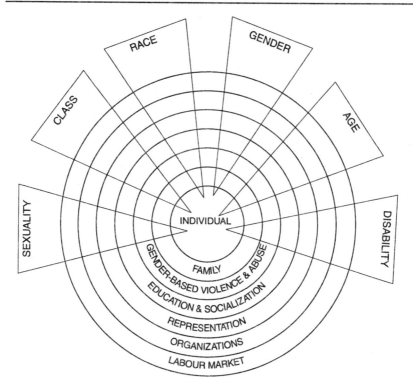

Figure 15.2   The effects of social divisions on identity in the context of the wider society

while at the same time defining women's value, for example, through the exposure and display of women reduced to their genitals in pornography, are key mechanisms in maintaining women's subordination. This invisibility also has a material base and is actively constructed.

This has been illustrated graphically by Waring (1990: 313–14) in the form of 'a short guide' of 'proven ways' for 'governments, departments, planners and others to assist them to keep women invisible' in the management of Third World development projects. Waring's guide (quoted with permission) includes the following advice:

1. Always use non-specific or generic categories such as labour force, pro-ducers, consumers, holder, head of household, reference person, poor, homeless, malnutritive, illiterate, unemployed, without describing gender or age. This helps to conceal the reality of your population and helps to disguise real needs.

2. If forced by policy directives to compile gender profiles, concentrate on the 'condition' of women as opposed to the relative 'position' of women, so

that their practical and strategic gender interests and the need for radical transformation will not be evident.

3. Adopt a sectoral approach to development in general and each project in particular. Do not examine sectoral inter-relationships, especially with the so-called domestic sector.

4. Argue that since women and children are not considered explicitly in the design and implementation of your project, it will not affect their lives. Alternatively argue that since men are central in your project it will, ipso facto, benefit women and children.

5. Use national census data whenever possible (on the grounds that other data collection is too expensive or 'conceptually difficult'). Generally census data renders most women invisible by describing them as 'housewives'. Since 'housework' is nowhere defined, it becomes a convenient residual category to encompass everything that women do in an unpaid capacity:

a) In agriculture this will ensure that the information you have will almost always omit unpaid family workers, seasonal workers, subsistence production, all production other than that of the 'holder', home-based crop processing, preservation, storage, transport to market, all labour by children under 15 and all the labour, production and consumption undertaken by the woman called a housewife.

b) In the business and manufacturing sector, the census data will ensure that informal workers, out-workers, barter, 'under the table' or 'off the books' employees, volunteers and underpaid casual workers will be omitted from statistics.

Women's interests, value and visibility can be diminished by their inclusion within households or families without reference to their subordination without that sphere. To maintain this, Waring advises:

6. Question the head of the household. Presume that what is in the best interests of the head of the household is in the best interests of particular members.

7. Presume, in any scheme plan, that the family is the place where women and children find their material existence guaranteed and their physical safety secured.

8. List who has access to what resources within a household (land, labour, capital, tools, information) but do not describe who has control over them.

9. Do not ask questions of how decisions are made within a household; ignore relative bargaining power; presume equality.

10. Treat most absent husbands as heads of households. View female-headed households as de facto with temporarily absent husbands. Treat polygamous families as one household.

There are also methodological ways of ensuring that women and their work are un-

or under-represented and therefore unrecorded, unaccounted and unvalued. Waring advises:

11. Have a male project officer; insist (for cultural, budget, availability of trained staff or whatever appropriate reason) on male field workers who should ask men what women do. The respondents can be relied on to under-report women's activities.
12. Describe what women do, but do not ask/imply/explain why.
13. Do not record activities including fuel and water collection, food preparation, birthing, education, health care, cleaning, volunteer, neighbourhood or community work, unpaid midwifery/counselling/herbalist or nursing work, laundry etc. as other than 'housework.'
14. Record only that unpaid productive work and reproductive activities are performed; do not clarify which are done simultaneously, consistently or repeatedly. Stick with the unidimensional (and statistically approved) approach of only declaring the 'principal activity' at any one time.
15. Do not specify time allocations in respect of any activity, or whether it is done seasonally or daily. Treat all activities in terms of market, not time value.
16. Do not specify where unpaid activities are being performed (home, field, village, market) or what degree of mobility is necessary to carry them out.
17. Ensure that all development plans are designed for market production or export. View women as the cheapest, most docile and manipulable work force available. Teach them only what is needed for their particular task. Do not teach bookkeeping, marketing, administrative and managerial skills, how to apply for grants, how to repair and maintain machines, how to apply for credit. Perpetuate dependency.

Although this list of some of the ways and means by which women's subordination is constructed and maintained relates to the management of development in 'developing countries' as Williams and Macalpine define it (Chapter 14), the similarities and parallels with (and the material nature of) the ways in which institutions 'retain total control while pretending to do something else' in developed countries is both obvious and instructive, and supports the view that women's subordination, although characterized by its particular historical and cultural context, is as a status both pan-cultural and pan-historical (Rubin 1975).

Beyond postfeminism and postmodernism

The discourses of postfeminism represent women as having achieved equality. A materialist analysis of gender relations such as I have argued and illustrated briefly in this chapter makes it difficult to accept that there is any substance to postfeminist claims. Overall the pay gap between women and men has narrowed slightly since the implementation of sex discrimination legislation in the 1970s, and women's earnings are now (1995) 78 per cent rather than 73 per cent of men's. These changes have been in the professional and managerial grades; in the lower grades the earnings gap has widened, and there has been no change in the gross hourly earnings of women and men. Figes (1994) gives an account of the inherent (and apparently intentional) uselessness of the sex discrimination legislation, and the difficulties there have been in using it to improve the position of women in employment, and argues that 'equality is a myth'.

Postfeminism has been used and/or functioned to obscure (and to maintain) the material basis of gendered power relations and the practices of male dominance and female subordination, and can be regarded as another (material) dimension of the oppression. As such, academic theory and discourse could be added to the series of concentric circles (Figures 15.1 and 15.2) that influence individuals and organizations. Harlow, Hearn and Parkin (Chapter 6), for example, refer to the use of 'poststructuralism and postmodernism to exclude feminism, women, gender, sexuality and violence' and Taylor-Gooby (1994) to 'postmodernism and social policy' as 'a great leap backward'.

This has a bearing on change. Clearly, gender inequality exists not simply as discourse but as material reality: clearly, gender equality has not been achieved either in the liberal sense of equality of access, or in the reformist sense of equality of status, or in the radical sense of equality of outcomes, or, as Cockburn (1991) argues, in the sense of parity which acknowledges difference and diversity rather than sameness. The second wave of feminism never really got much further than documenting inequality and asking for equality in all of these senses: just asking was sufficient to generate a 'postfeminist backlash' (Faludi 1992).

From a materialist perspective, change depends on acknowledging the existence of gendered power relations. It will depend on men deciding to give up their gender-based power and privilege, and also the abuse of their power that takes the form of violence against women. Taking account of the effects of internalized oppression and its function in maintaining inequality, it will depend too on women giving up their internalized passivity, their emotional dependency on men, and their tolerance and acceptance of their subordinate status. For men it will depend on abandoning dominant forms of masculinity and exclusive patterns of male bonding. For both women and men it will require giving up feelings of powerlessness to change themselves and to make change happen around them.

Change will also depend on acknowledging the insufficiency of biological explanations of male dominance and female subordination and ceasing to give them power they do not have. I am reminded of a favourite feminist cartoon of two toddlers, a boy and a girl, side by side, peering down inside the front of their underpants with the caption: 'Oh, that explains the difference in our pay' (Morris 1979). Clearly, genital differences are not the reason for gender-based inequality. But the evidence is everywhere that men are valued and women are not valued: males and females learn in complex and inconsistent, but consistently concurrent and corroborative ways, their 'masculinities' and their 'femininities' – and their value or lack of it. Racial and class value are learned in similar ways. What is learned is relentlessly reinforced by culture and practice, and it includes hierarchies, divisions and competition between women themselves as well as between men and women. This is part of the complexity and can be confusing both to women and to men (the 'women are their own worst enemies' syndrome). The similar hierarchies, divisions and competition that exist within and between racial groups have been discussed in this book (Itzin; Parkin and Maddock; Harlow, Hearn and Parkin).

In theory it is logically possible that what is learned can be unlearned. This book is about putting theory into practice: if we are not to be 'silly' about the possibilities of gender, culture and organizational change, then we must be serious about the possibilities of gender, culture and social change. This means acknowledging the existence of gendered (and other) power relations. It means seeing the disadvantage of inequality and abuse of power; that it is damaging and diminishing in human terms for both those who are dominant and those who are subordinate: that as well as gain in power and privilege and access to resources, it represents deep personal loss and disconnection from self, self-value and inherent humanness. It means deciding that it is possible to move beyond this.

Change can – and arguably should – be driven by legislation and regulation in the wider society and by policy and procedure in organizations, but to effect real and lasting change to the culture of an organization, it is almost certainly necessary to consider how the attitudes, beliefs and behaviour of individual men and women, based on ignorance, prejudice and bigotry, can be unlearned and replaced by egalitarian attitudes, beliefs and behaviour. It is necessary to look for evidence that it can be done, for examples of how to do it, and for proof that it is worth doing. On one level that is what this book is about: using organizational culture as a microcosm of the wider social culture, and creating models of what could be. The other prerequisite to organizational change, to changes in the labour market and in the wider society, is the redistribution of power. The implications of this are beyond the scope of this chapter, but its basis will be the end of the sexual division of labour and women's unpaid work for men in the family.

REFERENCES

Arber, S. and Ginn, J. (1991) *Gender and Later Life: A Sociological Analysis of Resources and Constraints*. London: Sage.

Archer, J. and Lloyd, J. (1982) *Sex and Gender*. London: Penguin.

Ashburner, L. (1991) 'Men managers and women workers: women employees as an under-used resource'. *British Journal of Management*, 2, 3–15.

Baker, P. (1992) 'Maintaining male power: why heterosexual men use pornography'. In Itzin, C. (ed.), *Pornography: Women, Violence and Civil Liberties*. Oxford: Oxford University Press.

Ballaster, R., Beetham, M., Frazer, E., and Hebron, S. (1991) *Women's Worlds: Ideology, Feminity and the Woman's Magazine*. London: Macmillan.

Bandura, A., (1971) *Social Learning Theory*. New York: General Learning Press.

Baxter, M. (1990) 'Flesh & blood: does pornography lead to sexual violence?' *New Scientist*, May, 37–41.

Beattie, V. L. (1992) 'Analysis of the results of a survey on sexual violence in the UK. Cambridge: Cambridge Women's Forum.

Bock, G. and James, S. (1992) *Beyond Equality and Difference*. London: Routledge.

Byrne, A., (1994) 'New horizons for women'. *Public Policy Review*, 94–5.

Cameron, D. and Frazer, E. (1987) *The Lust to Kill*. Cambridge: Polity Press.

Cameron, D. and Frazer, E. (1992) 'On the question of pornography and sexual violence: moving beyond cause and effect'. In Itzin, C. (ed.), *Pornography: Women, Violence and Civil Liberties*. Oxford: Oxford University Press.

Chadeau, A. (1985) 'Measuring household activities: some international comparisons'. *Review of Income and Wealth*, Sept.

Chetwynd, J. and Hartnett, O. (1978) *The Sex Role System: Psychological and Sociological Perspectives*. London: Routledge and Kegan Paul.

Chodorow, N. (1971) 'Being and doing: a cross-cultural examination of the socialization of males and females'. In Gornick, V. and Moran, B. K. (eds), *Woman in Sexist Society*. New York: New American Library.

Chodorow, N. (1974) 'Family structure and feminine personality'. In Rosaldo, M. and Lamphere, L. (eds), *Women, Culture and Society*. Stanford: Stanford University Press.

Chodorow, N. (1978) *The Reproduction of Mothering: Psychonalysis and the Sociology of Gender*. London: University of California Press.

Cockburn, C. (1991) *In the Way of Women: Men's Resistance to Sex Equality in Organisations*. London: Macmillan.

Coe, T. (1992) *The Key to the Men's Clubs: Opening the Doors to Women in Management*. London: BHS/Institute of Management.

Cohen, N. (1989) 'Reaping rich revenue from the profit of pornography'. *Independent*, 18 December.

Corcoran, C. (1989) *Pornography: The New Terrorism*. Dublin: Attic Press.

Coveney, L., Jackson, M., Jeffreys, S., Kaye, L., Mahony, P. (1984) *The Sexuality Papers: Male Sexuality and the Social Control of Women*. London: Hutchinson.

Cowe, R. (1993) 'Paul Raymond still headlines the riches revue.' *Independent*, 15 September.

Creighton, S. and Noyes, P. (1989) *Child Abuse Trends in England & Wales*. London: NSPCC.

Dale, A. and Joshi, H. (1992) 'The economic and social status of British women'. Paper from conference in Berlin.

Delamont, S. (1980) *Sex Roles and the School*. London: Methuen.

Delphy, C. and Leonard, D. (1992) *Familiar Exploitation: A New Analysis of Marriage in Contemporary Western Societies*. Cambridge: Polity Press.

Department of Health (1992) *Business Case and Action for Women in the NHS*. DoH: Women's Unit.

Dobash, R. and Dobash, R. (1980) *Violence Against Wives: A Case Against the Patriarchy*. New York: Open Books.

Dobash. R.E., Dobash, R.P. and Cavanagh, K. (1985) 'The contact between battered women and social and medical agencies'. In Pahl, J. (ed.), *Private Violence and Public Policy*. London: Routledge and Kegan Paul.

EOC (1993) *Women and Men in Britain 1993*. London: HMSO.

EOR (1992) *Equal Opportunities Review*, 42, March/April.

Faludi, S. (1992) *Backlash: The Undeclared War Against Women*. London: Chatto and Windus.

FPSC (1989) *Family Policy Studies Centre Bulletin*, 6, Winter.

Ferguson, M. (1983) *Forever Feminine: Women's Magazines and the Cult of Femininity*. London: Heinemann.

Figes, K. (1994) *Because of Her Sex: The Myth of Equality for Women in Britain*. London: Macmillan.

Finkelhor, D. (1979) *Sexually Victimized Children*. New York: Free Press.

Gagnon, J. (1965) 'Female child victims of sex offences'. *Social Problems*, 13, 176–92.

Goffman, E. (1979) *Gender Advertisements*. London: Macmillan.

Groves, D. (1987) 'Occupational pension provision and women's poverty in old age'. In Glendenning, C. and Miller, J. (eds), *Women and Poverty in Britain*. Brighton: Wheatsheaf.

Hakim, C. (1993) 'The myth of rising female employment'. *Work Employment and Society*, 7, 97–120.

Hall, R. (1985) *Ask Any Woman*. Bristol: Falling Wall Press.

Hamilton, R., Hawworth, B. and Sardar, M. (1982) *Adman and Eve: A Study of the Portrayal of Women in Advertising*. Manchester: Equal Opportunities Commission.

Handy, C. (1985) *Understanding Organisations*. London: Penguin.

Hartnett, O., Boden, G. and Fuller, M. (1979) *Sex-Role Stereotyping*. London: Tavistock.

Hewitt, P. (1993) *About Time: The Revolution in Work and Family Life*. London: IPPR/Rivers Oram Press.

Hofstede, G. (1984) *Culture's Consequences*. London: Sage.

Hollway, W. (1985) 'Gender difference in the production of subjectivity'. In Henriques, J., Hollway, W., Urwin, C., Venn, C. and Walkerdine, V. (eds), *Changing the Subject*. London: Methuen.

Hollway, W. (1995) 'Heterosexual desire: interpretive discourse analysis and the psyche'. In Wilkinson, S. and Kitzinger, C. (eds), *Feminism and Discourse: Psychological Perspectives*. London: Sage.

Howell, S. and Rubery, J. (1992) *Employees Working Time: Policies and Women's Employment*. Manchester: Equal Opportunities Commission Report.

IPM (1992) *Institute of Personnel Management Report*. London: IPM.

I Spy Productions (1992) 'Pornography and capitalism: the pornography industry'. In Itzin, C., *Pornography: Women, Violence and Civil Liberties*. Oxford: Oxford University Press.

Itzin, C. (1986) 'Media images of women: the social construction of ageism and sexism'. In Wilkinson, S. (ed.), *Feminist Social Psychology: Developing Theory and Practice*. Milton Keynes: Open University Press.

Itzin, C. (1989) 'Women and social mobility'. Report to the Economic and Social Research Council on the Families and Social Mobility Study. Colchester: University of Essex.

Itzin, C. (1990) 'Age and sexual divisions: a study of age, identity and opportunity in women'. University of Kent, PhD thesis.

Itzin, C. (ed.) (1992a) *Pornography: Women, Violence and Civil Liberties*. Oxford: Oxford University Press.

Itzin, C. (1992b) 'Pornography and the social construction of sexual inequality'. In Itzin, C. (ed.), *Pornography: Women, Violence and Civil Liberties*. Oxford: Oxford University Press.

Itzin, C. (1992c) 'Entertainment for men: what it is and what it means'. In Itzin, C. (ed.), *Pornography: Women, Violence and Civil Liberties*. Oxford: Oxford University Press.

Itzin, C. and Sweet, C. (1989) 'Tackling the monsters on the top shelf'. *Independent*, 17 April.

Itzin, C. and Sweet, C. (1990) 'What you feel about pornography'. *Cosmopolitan*, March, 8–12.

Itzin, C. and Sweet, C. (1992) 'Women's experience of pornography: UK magazine survey evidence'. In Itzin, C. (ed.), *Pornography: Women, Violence and Civil Liberties*. Oxford: Oxford University Press.

Itzin, C. and Wingfield R. (1992) *Pornography: Visible Harm*. Manchester: Broadcasting Support Services.

Jackson, S. (1980) *The Social Construction of Female Sexuality*. London: WRRCP.

Jackson, S. (1982) *Childhood Sexuality*. Oxford: Blackwell.

Joshi, H. (1989) 'The changing form of women's economic dependency'. In Joshi, H. (ed.), *The Changing Population of Britain*. Oxford: Blackwell.

Joshi, H. (1990) 'The cash opportunity costs of childbearing: an approach to estimation using British data'. *Population Studies*, 44.

Jones, T., Maclean, B. and Young, J. (1986) *The Islington Crime Survey*. Aldershot: Gower.

Kappeler, S. (1986) *The Pornography of Representation*. Cambridge: Polity Pess.

Kelly, L. (1987) *Surviving Sexual Violence*. Cambridge: Polity Press.

Koss, M.P., Gidycz, C.A. and Wisneiwski, N. (1987) 'The scope of rape: incidence and prevalence of sexual aggression and victimization in a national sample of higher education students'. *Journal of Consulting and Clinical Psychology*, 55(2), 162–70.

Kremer, J. and Montgomery, P. (1993) *Women's Working Lives*. Belfast: HMSO.

Lees, S. (1986) *Losing Out*. London: Hutchinson.

Lister, R. (1992) *Women's Economic Dependency and Social Security*. Manchester: Equal Opportunities Commission.

MacKinnon, C.A. (1984) 'Not a moral issue'. *Yale Law and Policy Review*, 2, Spring, 321–45.

Mahony, P. (1985) *Schools for the Boys*. London: Hutchinson.

Martin, J. and Roberts, C. (1984) *Women's Employment: A Lifetime Perspective*. London: HMSO.

Maynard, M. (1985) 'The response of social workers to domestic violence'. In Pahl, J. (ed.), *Private Violence and Public Policy*. London: Routledge.

Mills, A. J. (1992) 'Organization, gender and culture'. In Mills, A. J. and Tancred, P. (eds), *Gendering Organizational Analysis*. London: Sage.

Montgomery, P. (1993) 'Paid and unpaid work'. In Kremer, J. and Montgomery, P., *Women's Working Lives*. Belfast: HMSO.

Montgomery, P. and Davis, C. (1991) 'A woman's place in Northern Ireland'. In Stringer, P. and Robinson, G. (eds), *Social Attitudes in Northern Ireland 1990/91*. Belfast: Blackstaff Press.

Mooney, J. (1994) *The Hidden Figure: Domestic Violence in North London*. London: Middlesex University/Islington Police and Crime Prevention Unit.

Morris, J. (1979) *No More Peanuts*. London: NCCL.

Oakley, A. (1972) *Sex, Gender and Society*. London: Penguin.

Oakley, A. (1974) *The Sociology of Housework*. Oxford: Martin Robertson.

OPSS (1993) *Equal Opportunities for Women in the Civil Service*. London: Cabinet Office.

Oulton, C. (1993) '£18,000 price tag on Working Wife'. *Independent*, 3 February.

Pahl, J. (ed.) (1985) *Private Violence and Public Policy*. London: Routledge.

Parker, S. (1985) 'The legal background'. In Pahl, J. (ed.), *Private Violence and Public Policy* London: Routledge.

Rubery, J. (1993) 'The gender pay gap: some European comparisons'. Paper for conference on 'Women, Minimum Pay and the Wages Councils'.

Rubin, G. (1975) 'The traffic in women: notes on the political economy of sex'. In Reiter, R. (ed.), *Toward an Anthropology of Women*. New York: Monthly Review Press.

Russell, D.E.H. (1983) 'The incidence and prevalence of intrafamilial and extrafamilial sexual abuse of female children'. *Child Abuse and Neglect*, 7, 133–46.

Sayers, J. (1982) *Biological Politics: Feminist and Anti-feminist Perspectives*. London: Tavistock.

Sayers, J. (1986) *Sexual Contradictions*. London: Tavistock.

Smithers, A. and Zientek, P. (1991) *Gender, Primary Schools and the National Curriculum*. London: ASUWT/Engineering Council.

Spender, D. and Sarah, E. (1980) *Learning to Lose*. London: Women's Press.

Stephen, B. (1980) 'What is a wife really worth?' *San Francisco Chronicle*, 25 August, p. 21.

Taylor-Gooby, P. (1994) 'Postmodernism and social policy: a great leap backwards?'. *Journal of Social Policy*, 23(3), 385–404.

TUC (1984) *Images of Inequality: The Portrayal of Women in the Media and Advertising.* London: TUC.

Waring, M. (1988) *Counting for Nothing: What Men Value and What Women are Worth.* London: Allen and Unwin.

Waring, M. (1989) *If Women Counted: A New Feminist Economics.* London: Macmillan.

Waring, M. (1990) 'A woman's reckoning: the majority's perspective on growth'. *Australian Journal of Public Administration,* 49(3), September, 305–14.

Weeks, J. (1981) *Sex Politics and Society: The Regulation of Sexuality since 1800.* London: Longman.

Weeks, J. (1986) *Sexuality.* London: Tavistock.

Winship, J. (1983) *Femininity and Women's Magazines.* Milton Keynes: Open University Press.

Chapter 16

Making connections
Frameworks for change

Janet Newman

This final chapter draws some of the threads of this book together by identifying themes in gendered dynamics of organizations, and exploring some of the tensions and challenges which have emerged in developing strategies for change. It goes on to draw connections between organizations and their environment, setting out some issues in the development of a broader politics of change; and concludes by offering some visions of the future.

WAYS OF SEEING: GENDERING ORGANIZATIONAL ANALYSIS

One of the aims of this book has been to surface the hidden gender structurings and assumptions which underpin organizations; to develop what Williams and Macalpine (Chapter 14) call the 'gender lens', through which it is possible to bring into focus patterns in women's experience of organizational life. We have offered a number of different levels of 'seeing' and understanding organizations as gendered. The first is concerned with gender as a social division within organizations. Several of the case studies highlighted the ways in which work is structured around gender as both a horizontal division (with some kinds of job being seen as 'men's work' and others as 'women's work') and a vertical one (with women systematically occupying lower grades and lower status positions, supporting the whole organizational edifice from below). These divisions are not static, but are constantly being realigned as work is restructured around new kinds of job, with some old occupations losing status, and thus opening up to women, and others becoming harder for women to enter as the jobs move towards the 'strategic core' of an organization. The vertical gendered division of labour is also changing as many low paid and low status 'organizational servicing' jobs, such as cleaning and catering, are contracted out of mainstream public-sector organizations altogether.

The second 'way of seeing' organizations as gendered is concerned with gender as experience, and many of the case studies have outlined methodologies for researching women's experience through surveys, interviews, workshops and equality audits. Researching women's experience brings into focus many of the hidden dimensions of the emotional and sexual regimes of organizations, which are masked by the apparent rationality of organizational structures and by dominant organizational ideologies. This highlights the importance of organizational culture in our analysis. As women we are held in place not just by lack of access to jobs but by the cultural meanings attached to 'gender', which have real consequences for our lived experience. These cultural meanings are not fixed and immutable, and different patterns will occur within and between organizations. But they carry enormous significance for how women and men relate to 'male' and 'female' values, ways of thought and ways of action. They also constitute an important axis through which power and its gendered distribution is reproduced. The chapters in Part I develop the theme of organizational culture as a site of meanings and actions by exploring the symbolic significance of the gendered discourses and practices in which issues of power and identity are enmeshed.

A third way of seeing gender, then, is concerned with culture as a site of gendered meanings and identities. However, the book has also surfaced some of the problems of using 'gender' as a category divorced from other lines of experience and identity. Several authors (Thobani; Holder; Williams and Macalpine) highlight black women's experience of organizations, and Itzin and Phillipson identify the complex dynamics between age and gender. Other chapters (Harlow, Hearn and Parkin; Newman and Williams) explicitly explore the dynamic interrelationships between gender and other social divisions. Any 'gender lens', then, has to be multifaceted, or prismatic, in order to reflect the perceptions and insights of women who experience patterns of oppression around age, disability, 'race' and sexuality as well as gender. It also has to offer us ways of seeing beyond the boundaries of our own experience by opening ourselves up to the perceptions of women in other cultures and nations. White, Western views of gender are by no means universal.

These different levels of analysis suggest that 'gender' can itself be a problematic concept. The term is used sometimes to represent symbolically differences between masculine and feminine modes of thought and action; sometimes to explore the gendered dimensions of culture; and sometimes to explore the dynamic relationship between actual women and men in organizational life. What has emerged from our analysis is the need to move between levels in order to understand how cultures are shaped within and around the structural realities of the low pay, marginalization and disposability which characterize most women's work; and how these realities underpin the symbolic values placed on male and female work.

Given these cautionary comments, how can we develop an effective analysis of gender and organizations? In the period in which this book was written, the climate was in many ways becoming more hostile for such an undertaking. Postfeminist discourse (which states that the battle has largely been won) articulates with new managerial discourse (with its emphasis on consensus and the need for everyone to 'sign up' to the broader project of organizational survival and success) to provide a climate which is hostile to equality issues. The legitimacy of political agendas around equality is declining as public sector organizations struggle to build consensus around new goals and orientations which will enable them to survive in an increasingly hostile climate. Dissent, or even the raising of mildly difficult questions, is seen as diverting energy from what really matters. This is exacerbated by competitive pressures, with compulsory competitive tendering (CCT) in local government, the setting up of provider unit trusts in the health service, and market testing in the Civil Service, each of which tends to be accompanied by a shift towards more authoritarian management styles and practices as well as new pressures on staff. Many of the women working for change have become battle weary; and the ideological climate sometimes makes it more difficult to build allies amongst male colleagues.

At the same time, however, new agendas are opening up. Some of these arise from the changing economic and social context in which organizations pursue their goals. Equality issues can be, and are being, invigorated through a closer link to an organization's strategic goals. Women and other groups are seeking to transcend the constraints of tokenism and the limits of incremental change. Cynthia Cockburn (Chapter 13) comments:

> Women today are stuck on a curious plateau ... Some gains have been made. But those very successes now make forward movement difficult. The structures have adapted to our pressure, let a few of our representatives in, just to be able, it seems, to carry on as before. Now that women are no longer totally absent and overwhelmingly disadvantaged, the scandal effect has dissipated and it is hard to assert the uncomfortable truth: that *real* equality is still far distant. It now calls for considerable courage on the part of women, and a perceptive awareness on the part of men, to acknowledge the legitimacy of this new cycle of demands.

While developments are uneven, this book overall gives a positive picture of the advances won, of the achievements made, and of the continued energy of the women working for change within organizations. Earlier struggles mean that the 'gender lens' is more imaginable now than it was; there are (albeit imperfect) languages for collectively articulating women's experiences, and differences, and for elaborating these into models and strategies for change.

We need to recognize the complex and contradictory nature of change. However, one of the key issues in researching women's experience and developing strategy is that the very ground on which we are standing is itself shifting constantly. The successes and advances which we make change the terrain and alter the conditions of struggle. Progress is never smooth and even; change initiatives may be co-opted, adapted and resisted in different ways across different sites. Progress in some areas may be accompanied by regress in others: for example, as more women enter management, new areas of inequality between them and other women may open up. Change which seems progressive may open up new problems: many of the women appointed to senior levels are having a very tough time, and some decide the struggle is too great. Better maternity and childcare provision may open up a 'mommy track' which runs alongside, but separately from, the mainstream pattern of career progression. Flexibility strategies may be beneficial, but may also lead to greater exploitation because of the low pay and disposability which accompany many forms of flexible working. This suggests that theory building can never be 'finished' but is an emergent process. Developing theory and crafting strategy need to be seen as a twin process which can create knowledge which is both useful (to women in understanding their experience) and usable (by women and others in developing strategy).

BUILDING ALLIANCES: MAKING THE CASE FOR CHANGE

The various contributions to the book have suggested a range of strategies for change. The focuses of these have differed in important ways, but one of the interesting features is how they have tended to draw on a range of approaches in order to develop a multilayered, multifocused strategy, in which the action shifts over time to respond to, and take advantage of, wider contextual changes and new organizational agendas. Several case studies (e.g. French, Chapter 3; Itzin, Chapter 8; Nottage, Chapter 11) illustrate this process, but also raise questions about how far it is possible to build alliances in any particular context. Building alliances is concerned with identifying salient points around which links might be forged with other interests, groups and discourses. This requires an awareness of external pressures and their impact on an organization, together with a realistic assessment of the distribution of power to affect change. But there are considerable dangers attached to pragmatically 'going with the flow' of an organization's shifting agenda, adapting the arguments to suit emerging issues and new external demands or constraints, which require further exploration.

I want to explore these tensions in the context of two examples of discursive terrains on which alliances might be built. The first is concerned with labour market trends and the possibility of 'skill shortages' being used as a means of furthering the recruitment, development and promotion of women. The second is concerned with the process of cultural change within organizations, which creates the conditions in which a 'business case' for equality issues is increasingly being articulated.

The 'demographic time bomb' and labour force changes

In the late 1980s, demographic change and the prospect of future skills shortages opened up a terrain on which the interests of an organization and of women might be aligned; and there was a significant shift in ways in which arguments around improvements in the recruitment, development and promotion of women were presented (see, e.g., Nevill *et al.* 1990). Our case studies show that this discursive alignment created the conditions in which women's employment and development issues were repositioned within an overall concern with developing the 'human resource management' function within organizations. While the recession meant that the much heralded skills shortage was less significant in its impact than anticipated, this repositioning creates a more powerful base from which women's interests might be pursued, and a more strategic concern with employment and development issues for women throughout an organization. At the same time, however, it subordinates equality issues within an overall framework of organizational goals.

There are inevitably dangers in using arguments based on short term changes in labour market conditions to pursue equality agendas. The experience of two world wars has taught us that while economic and demographic shifts have opened up new employment to women and to black minorities, white men have successfully reclaimed their labour market status as soon as conditions have changed. Arguments based on shifting labour market patterns may be of limited value as a major strategy for redressing inequalities in the labour force because they reduce everything to economics; notions of equality may be squeezed out of the debate altogether. However, periods of change in labour force patterns may have a rather different value, in that they can present a major challenge to the orthodoxies of what is 'proper' work for women, and can demonstrate women's skills, capabilities and power in traditional male domains. This was certainly the case where women took on male economic roles in periods of war. In the 1990s, rather different conditions prevail, with industrial decline, the restructuring of the economy around an expanded service sector, and the search for a cheaper, more flexible and 'unorganized' labour force. It remains to be seen what will be the effects of the expansion of women's waged employment in the context of traditional male occupations; but it is already evident that it will not be straightforwardly progressive. Many working women who leave at home an unemployed male 'breadwinner' are having to provide extra emotional labour to sustain both his identity and their relationship, on top of the traditional 'dual roles' of labour in the workplace and domestic labour in the home. At the same time, women employed in organizations where traditional male enclaves are under threat are also finding life difficult; the challenge of dealing with the contradictions which men are facing creates extra stress for women.

Not all of this is bad news; fundamental changes in male roles and identities resulting from labour force restructuring may provide the spaces in which changes in the domestic and employment spheres may be aligned. However, this requires changes in men's relationship to work, to the domestic sphere, and to the balance between them. Evidence so far is not encouraging: French's study of senior men (Chapter 3) suggests that, while they were critical of their work-dedicated lifestyles and of the performance demands they felt they had to meet, they were reluctant to give up even partially what amounted to an 'addiction to the pace, power and prestige' of work.

Economic and labour force changes, then, provide an important element of the context in which struggles for change take place. This context can both create opportunities and present dangers. On the positive side, external change creates new organizational agendas, which may provide opportunities for equality activists to develop new arguments and mobilize new organizational resources. At the same time, however, we may find equality agendas co-opted and distorted in the process of change. This is also the case with the second terrain on which alliance building is taking place: that of a 'cultural change' agenda.

Cultural change and the 'business case' for equality

Public-sector organizations are increasingly concerned to bring about cultural change, in order to become more responsive to customers, to become more efficient and effective, to increase performance and raise skill levels, and to achieve quality improvements. The rhetoric of cultural change agendas usually includes elements such as developing flatter hierarchies and team-based approaches to work, valuing and listening to the 'front line', empowering staff, developing skills, enabling all staff to contribute effectively, responding more effectively to customers and communities, and becoming more 'businesslike' and able to survive in a competitive market place for both services and staff. The equality implications of this agenda run deep, especially if set alongside the results of the research on women's experience cited in this volume, which highlighted wasted talent, wasted energy, poor staff development and training, undervaluation of female labour and inflexible career routes. The cultural change agenda also highlights the links between equality issues and 'good management practice', and enables equality activists to reshape and strengthen their agendas around the broad change pressures which public sector organizations face.

Developing this requires a shift from the traditional inwards and internal focus of equal opportunities towards a wider agenda of service delivery and organizational effectiveness in a changing environment. The new agenda requires a new set of arguments. Drawing on work described in this volume, several themes emerge. The first is that of improving the organization's capacity to deliver quality services by enabling it to respond more effectively to a diversity of needs, requirements and success criteria among its customers. This opens up a range of external equality agendas concerned with service issues. But as Thobani argues in Chapter 9, developing equality plans in service delivery is a much more complex task than developing equality plans in employment, since services vary, and the equality agendas for universal and selective services will offer different challenges. Quality-of-service issues will also be different for different groups of users. In addition, the quality/equality agenda has implications for the make-up and the training of the management tiers that design services and allocate resources, as well as front line service delivery staff. In both cases, it requires the development of a more diverse workforce, and of a culture which places a greater value on diversity. This relates to a second theme in organizational change agendas: that of seeking to become competitive in a changing labour market through flexible employment practices. I have already argued that flexibility can be a double-edged sword in the equalities field. However, in a competitive labour market, if an organization seriously wishes to build a more diverse workforce it is necessary for it to develop employment practices which reflect the requirements and priorities of women staff.

The third cultural change theme is that of recognizing and developing talent in the organization, and preventing such talent from becoming underutilized or 'blocked' by discrimination. This relates to the human resource strategies of an organization. There is some evidence now that effective appraisal and development schemes are vital in providing feedback and in recognizing staff's contribution fairly and equitably. While this is important for all staff, it is particularly significant for those groups whose contribution has traditionally been undervalued. This requires a three-fold strategy: the development of effective training and performance targets for line managers (especially in devolved structures); 'positive action' staff development and training within a corporate framework; and a strong leadership from the top in the direct tackling of discrimination.

The fourth theme I want to highlight is that of building a management culture which can manage change effectively. This means bringing a greater diversity of approaches and styles into management teams. It also means ensuring that change is managed in a way which is perceived as fair and equitable by staff. Each of these is related to the final theme in public sector organizations' 'cultural change' agendas: that of building credibility with stakeholders and communities. This is linked to the 'quality' agenda, but goes beyond it to the overall profile of an organization. It means having more people from groups traditionally under-represented in management in high profile positions, and developing staff effectively for those positions. It also means having a credible and effective equal opportunity agenda; one which says to communities and stakeholders that equality issues are taken seriously.

These cultural change agendas open up new arenas of action and suggest new problems to be addressed as well as new possibilities for change. The challenge is to spot the trends, identify the spaces where change is possible, make the most productive alliances, and mobilize the resources and arguments which can help at any particular moment. In 'crafting strategy', there is a need to understand the shifting political terrain, and to identify how others may be trying to use the same terrain to achieve different objectives.

It is also necessary to identify the potential costs as well as gains to be made in drawing on the managerial agendas to bring about change. 'Organizational effectiveness' or 'business efficiency' is an emerging phase of equal opportunities ideology which, while legitimizing the terrain, robs it of its political inflection. It can be seen as the latest in a series of equality ideologies which began with ideas of social justice (focusing on fair access as equals to the public domain), moved through ideologies of social welfare (focusing on special provision for 'disadvantaged' groups) and social advocacy (focusing on the different agendas emerging from the 'new social movements' of the 1970s), and then on to those of human resource management (drawing on ideas of good management practice, the overcoming of skills shortages and the like). All of these ideologies are still significant in the language of equal opportunities; but there is a subtle shift taking place. Equality is becoming dressed in management garb, and is increasingly being articulated through the language of effectiveness, performance, HRM and competitive success.

However, the possibilities of change within this paradigm will be limited for two important reasons. First, the context of change – whether demographic, economic or political – can shift the managerialist agenda and thereby undermine its effectiveness as a tool for equality activists and others seeking change. There is a need for a coherent framework which can guide us through the shifting sands and changing fashions of organizational agendas, which needs to be built on and energized by a woman-centred agenda. Second, any real change will involve challenges to established sources of power, and so is likely to meet with considerable resistance (Cockburn 1991). For these reasons, change has to be based on a political as well as a managerial activity; it must draw on women as agents of change, not just the recipients of managerially approved amendments to the status quo. This means 'making connections' with other political sites and building affiliations between women engaged in different political struggles.

MAKING CONNECTIONS

Despite my comments on the limits of change, the chapters in Part II of this book show what can be achieved through struggle for change within organizations. The outcomes of change within a single organization are important for several reasons. The first, and most important, is that change may improve the material conditions of women's paid work and their experience of employment. Secondly, while change limited to a single organization will always be piecemeal and partial, it can create a model of the possible by creating an enclave of 'good practice', which can serve as an exemplar for other organizations. Thirdly, it touches all those who have been engaged in change, bringing women together and creating new skills and perceptions. It develops 'organizational wisdom' and political skills, some of which can be transferred across different sites of action: trade unions, voluntary organizations and the wider community. And as well as creating new alliances, networks and friendships, the process of engaging in change can open up dialogue between different groups of women with different perceptions of the 'problem' and different priorities.

In the long run, however, change strategies which consider public sector organizations as sealed worlds, isolated from other domains of social and political activity, will be limited in their effectiveness. Broadening the opportunities for women within organizations requires shifting women's 'private' agendas of childcare, eldercare and health care into the 'public' domain of action within organizations, and at the level of social welfare provision. Change has to involve more than incremental amendments to parental leave provision; it means making the private public, and challenging the assumption that 'women's issues' can be solved or resolved by women alone, with or without the help of 'women friendly' organizational policies. It also means exploring the interconnections between organizational cultures and the changing relations and representations of gender in the wider society. Organizational cultures do not just 'reflect' these, but are an important part of the dynamics through which such relations and representations are both reproduced and changed.

Shifting the boundaries between public and private involves a big challenge for dominant ways of theorizing work organizations. It requires a rigorous analysis of

the influence of wider economic, social, cultural and political domains on organizational practices, and of the gendered division between 'organizational work' and
the non-waged work of women. Making these connections has implications for
academic work in linking different areas of study and different 'disciplines', such
as organizational theory, labour market analysis, social welfare, and public service
management. Each has been more or less influenced by feminist theory, and each
deploys concepts of gender to different degrees and in different ways. One of the
difficulties is perhaps that feminist theory has touched the 'social science' areas of
social welfare and labour market analysis more extensively than it has the 'managerialist' areas of organizational analysis and public service management.

I want to offer ways of beginning to broaden the analysis by exploring some
tentative ideas concerning the role of public sector organizations as both positioned
in, and mediators of, wider sets of social relations in the economy, state and family.
To do this, I want to suggest an image of the public sector organization as having
four distinct points of interface between itself and the outside world, each of which
is gendered and racialized, and each of which invokes a different role of the
organization in its environment. These roles can be briefly characterized as employer (of staff); regulator/rationer (of social welfare provision); provider (of
services); and advocate/representative (of communities and citizens).

The first interface is that between the organization and the labour market. The
role of the organization as employer will be influenced by a number of factors
beyond its control, most notably the national, and increasingly international,
economy, which will influence both the availability of labour and the levels of pay
which are expected. However, as large employers public sector organizations will
also help shape labour markets in several important ways. The first is in the labour
market strategies it pursues: for example, its use of 'flexible' labour as a means of
driving down costs and achieving the 'disposability' of workers in an uncertain
economic environment. This is both gendered and racialized, as Fiona Williams
and I argued in Chapter 7. The second lies in the more subtle distinctions between
paid and unpaid women's work, which organizations help to reproduce in the way
in which they allocate resources. We can see the boundary between paid and unpaid
work shifting with changes such as the expectation (and sometimes requirement)
that mothers provide unpaid labour as classroom assistants in schools, as nurses of
their sick children in hospital, and as carers of the elderly or of people with
disabilities in the 'community'.

Organizations make such decisions about the allocation of resources in the
context of the policy agenda of the government of the day, and so the second
interface between public sector organizations and the wider society is as the vehicle
through which social policy is delivered. In this role, organizations mediate
women's access to welfare benefits and other areas of public provision as regulator
and rationer. In recent years this interface has had to be negotiated in the context
of an increasingly restrictive and punitive approach to social policy, while at the
same time having to become more 'quality oriented' and 'customer centred'. The
always problematic relationship between those who deliver welfare (who are of

course mainly women) and those receiving welfare (also mainly women) is becoming intensified by limited resourcing, means testing, rationing and targeting. And somewhere between the domains of the delivery and receipt of welfare lie the twin demons of the 'poverty trap' and the lack of access to childcare, which condition many women's access to, and disadvantaged position within, the labour market.

The third interface is that of the organization as the deliverer of services to individual 'users'. This includes the areas of social welfare mentioned above, but goes beyond these. If the organization's role as mediator of access to welfare benefits is that of regulator and rationer, the organizational role in respect of service delivery is that of provider in a set of relationships which are increasingly subject to market or quasi-market arrangements. This is occurring in a number of different ways, but each involves the introduction of the discourse of 'customers' to reconceptualize the relationship between organizations and those to whom they provide services. This 'customer language' is ungendered and unracialized, and the rhetoric of 'choice', 'charters', 'redress' and so on which accompanies it serves to mask the patterns of unequal access to services, and the unsuitability of many 'universal' services to the particular needs of different groups of users.

Many organizations have a role which is broader than that of regulator or provider. Health authorities and the social services departments of local authorities, for example, have responsibilities for planning how to meet future health and social care needs, and of commissioning services to respond to those needs. Local authorities have a wide representational role, and increasingly see themselves as concerned with the 'governance' of their communities, representing their interests and meeting the broad needs of an area through partnerships with other agencies. Training and Enterprise Councils, Enterprise Boards and a host of other 'quangos' have responsibilities for developing or coordinating responses to local issues and needs. The interface between an organization and its environment in this case is with whole communities rather than individual customers. 'Community', however, is an amorphous and confusing concept; it is sometimes used spatially to suggest a locality; at other times it is used to suggest ethnicity (as in 'the Bangladeshi community'). Both mask a diversity of interests; and both are ungendered.

Each of these domains – the labour market, social welfare, the provision of services to users and the representation of communities – articulates with the gender dynamics within organizations themselves. Within the labour market, women's work is constituted as peripheral and low paid, despite social trends which demonstrate the increasing significance of women's paid work to the national economy. Social welfare constitutes women primarily as family members, invoking a white, Western and mythic model of the family based on male breadwinner with non-working wife. This corresponds with a structure of welfare benefits, childcare provision and training opportunities which militates against many women's capacity to combine familial and economic roles. This is reinforced by the pattern of public service provision in which education, health and social care are all organized around the assumption that women are available to provide unpaid labour.

Within organizations, then, it is difficult to change the culture to one which values women's work, and which recognizes women's economic role sufficiently to adapt career structures and working practices to enable women to contribute effectively. However, organizational life is not just 'determined' by the wider social and economic environment. It must be recognized that organizations themselves play a significant role in reproducing social values and ideologies, creating real barriers to change. In European countries where social provision exists which is more favourable to women's capacity to combine economic and familial roles, or which encourages men to play a fuller part in caring for children, organizational cultures may continue to act as a barrier. For example in Norway, which has introduced generous parental leave for both women and men, it is still rare for men to take advantage of this because of the strength of the corporate cultures, which disadvantage men who do so in terms of their career prospects. In the US, which has stronger equalities legislation, resulting in more women progressing to senior management positions, there is a serious problem of retaining women in these roles because of the hostility of many of the organizational cultures in which they find themselves (Faludi 1991). In Britain, women's expanding role in the national economy is not fully reflected in their presence and visibility at senior management levels because of the male strategies of resistance taking place within organizations (Cockburn 1991).

The point of exploring these different sets of interfaces between an organization and its environment is to identify the need for political change in a number of different domains. The politics of change takes different forms in each of the domains I have discussed. Action around women's role in the labour market has traditionally been through trade unions. While historically these have prioritized the needs of the male, full-time 'breadwinner', economic and social change has meant a considerable shift, which has led to a greater concern with issues of gender and race, and with part-time and unemployed workers. Increasingly, however, women are looking to Europe for change. While Britain has consistently resisted European intervention in employment issues, legislation on part-time work and on equal value have provided the most promising areas of change in women's pay and conditions in recent years.

Changes in social welfare provision have been mainly informed by the influence of new right views on welfare within the Conservative administrations since 1979. The future depends on the ways in which the Conservative Party's political domination of the 1980s is reconstructed or challenged in the second half of the 1990s and beyond. However, it seems likely that the role of pressure groups and lobbying organizations representing the interests of users, which was marginalized in the shift away from post-war 'consensus' politics through the 1980s, will see a revival. This is already evident in the activities of single-parent lobby groups around the work of the Child Support Agency. At the same time, the development of user movements and groups, for example around disability issues, may also find a point of connection in the reshaping of welfare delivery systems around a focus on 'customers' (though the relative narrowness of the customer focus hardly matches the agendas of user movements and advocacy groups).

Each of these separate domains, then, offers opportunities for women to work for change. However, I want to argue that action within any single domain, while important, will necessarily be limited in its effects. It is the connections between the domains which are significant for the prospect of bringing about any substantial change. I want to outline some key connections which are concerned with the interface between the politics of organizational change and the other domains I have discussed. Each highlights what I regard as a key political issue for the next decade and beyond.

The first is the political issue of the *value of women's work*. This suggests the need to develop organizational practices which take account of women's developing economic role, and which attempt to build connections between women's work as paid workers and as workers in the 'informal economy' of unpaid labour. It has implications for the restructuring of career paths within organizations, and highlights the need for organizations to enable men, as well as women, to play a fuller role in taking responsibility for informal social and health care in both family and community.

The second political issue is that of *inequality and poverty*, and draws attention to the link between women's position in the labour market and the pattern of social welfare provision. The main leverage here is through 'social justice' campaigns on pay and benefits in Britain and in the European Community. However, it also requires organizations to pay due regard to the interface between their employment practices and the economic position of women and other groups of low-paid workers. This is particularly telling for organizations such as local authorities which may be developing 'anti-poverty' strategies for their communities while continuing to pursue local labour market strategies which actually deepen economic inequality.

The third political issue I want to highlight is that of *women's power to shape the pattern and nature of public services*. Organizations are increasingly oriented to issues of quality in service delivery, and in some sectors are becoming more active in seeking user feedback on service delivery, and attempting to take more account of the views of users in designing services. However, 'users' are too often seen as undifferentiated, so issues of race and gender, and the different perceptions of different groups of users, remain unacknowledged. This needs to be redressed through better links between organizations and specific groups of users, and with groups who can express political demands on behalf of disempowered users and non-users. The 1990s has seen the emergence of women's involvement in consumer groups and issue-based campaigns; for example, on services to people with disabilities, on environmental issues, on safety issues, on rural transport, and so on. At the same time, the removal of many areas of public service from accountability through local democratic channels presents serious difficulties to women's role in shaping services. It is evident that women are under-represented on the appointed boards of many of the 'quangos' which have emerged in recent years; and the representation of women's interests (and of *which* women's interests) presents a serious political issue for the future.

The pattern of women's political influence and control in these different domains, then, is complex, and it is shifting as a result of the restructuring of the state, the economy and public service organizations in recent years. As some traditional channels of influence decline, others open up. It may be that the possibility of new linkages and connections between those who work within public sector organizations and those who are working for change as users and in the wider community will provide new ways forward. However, this needs to go beyond the consumerist ethos of individualism and choice in a market-based culture of public services, and to take on some of the wider political agendas I have highlighted.

VISIONS OF THE FUTURE

An important way forward for the future will be to create dialogues between women in different nations by making international links, and by Western women supporting and learning from women in nations engaged in political struggles for change. Making these connections is critically important, in order not only to learn from what is happening elsewhere, but to refresh and revitalize particular struggles. Cynthia Cockburn (Chapter 13) highlights Europe as a crucial domain of women's political activity; while she draws attention to the continued institutional barriers to women gaining an effective voice in Europe, she is extremely optimistic about the skills, resources and energies of trade union women; and both Cockburn and Williams and Macalpine (Chapter 14) illustrate the importance of transnational links between women in shaping future patterns of political change.

Within Britain, there are times when the odds seem stacked against change, when the agenda feels overwhelming, and when the obstacles seem insuperable. However, a great deal of progress has been made, and our case studies show significant areas of achievement. On a personal level, I am continually encouraged by the enthusiasm and energy of the women I meet at seminars and workshops, and within the organizations I work with. At one recent event for women managers in local government, titled 'Managing your future', women outlined their vision of the organizations they wished to build. I can think of no more fitting way to end this book than to share their vision.

These women wanted an organization which was forward thinking, proactive rather than reactive, and self-assured. They wanted it to be strategic, looking towards overall goals, with a focus on issues and outputs rather than problems and barriers, and taking time to think and plan rather than operating through firefighting. They wanted an organization which balanced internal cohesiveness with external competitiveness.

This 'strategic' image was linked to a wider vision of an organization which was value-driven, working towards a stable environment, and retaining the social values of public service, including a commitment to equal opportunities. This organization would be more democratically accountable, engendering a sense of 'community' by demonstrating leadership as well as representing local people. At the same time, the organization would be strongly service oriented, with a client and user focus and an orientation towards 'continuous improvement' of services.

Internally, the organization would be one which gave recognition of different skills and abilities, and recognition and positive acceptance of new ideas. It would be an organization in which all employees were developed to their full potential; with more career progression and means of self-fulfilment; with promotion clearly based on merit; and visionary in its selection and promotion of individuals. It would spend more time developing people and would be proactive in management development. It would have greater flexibility of roles and less demarcation between jobs, with a multiskilled and well-trained workforce. It would enable its staff to have a better balance between home and work. It would be empowering, with more people to take decisions at all levels. As a result of all of this, it would be an organization with high staff morale, with people being proud to work for it. The culture would be one based on trust and communication, teamwork and cooperation. It would be a 'learning' and 'listening' organization. And it would have less game playing and daily conflict.

For themselves, the women wanted recognition of their leadership skills, of their successes and of the good work already being accomplished. They wanted to be able to manage 'without having to prove you can all the time'. They wanted to be respected, and to have the chance to express their views and to be heard. They wanted to do worthwhile, challenging work, with intellectual stimulation and self-esteem. They also wanted more time for themselves outside work. They wanted more power: to be at the centre of things, and to be influential in management. Finally, they wanted to be part of an organization they respected, both in terms of its vision and in terms of its ways of working.

While aware of the barriers, these women were not thinking from the standpoint of 'women' as a static category; and they were not just concerned about equality issues and career success. They presented an image of an effective, forward thinking organization which would benefit all: workers, customers, communities and ultimately, perhaps, the fate of the public sector as a whole. Enabling and empowering women to help shape the future in this mould is important for all our futures.

REFERENCES

Cockburn, C. (1991) *In the Way of Women; Men's Resistance to Sex Equality in Organisations*. London: Macmillan.

Faludi, S. (1991) *Backlash: The Undeclared War Against Women*. London: Chatto and Windus.

Nevill, G., Pennicott, A., Williams, J. and Worrall, A. (1990) *Women in the Workforce: The Effect of Demographic Change in the 1990s*. London: Industrial Society.

Name index

Subject index